# Why Gods Persist

Every human society has engaged in religious practices. In the past religions have provided answers to the basic questions of life: Who am I? Why am I here? What happens when I die? In the modern world, religious answers to these questions are unacceptable to many, yet religions continue to persist.

Religions involve structural beliefs, narratives, rituals, moral codes, religious experience and social aspects. Robert Hinde argues that each of these arises from the nature of humankind. For example, belief in a deity satisfies the human tendency to attribute events to causes, and can reduce anxiety. Or narratives, such as those presented in gospels, appeal in part because we see our own lives as unfolding narratives.

This book is written in such a way that it is easy for anyone to understand. Hinde has chapter summaries, multiple sections within each chapter, and draws examples from a wide range of religions – including Christianity, Judaism, Buddhism, and Hinduism.

Anyone interested in probing the nature of religion, and why religions continue to persist, will be drawn to this extraordinary and unique book.

**Robert A. Hinde** has worked as a biologist, studying animal behaviour, and as a psychologist studying human relationships. He was formerly a Royal Society Research Professor and Master of St John's College, Cambridge. Among his recent books are *Individual, Relationships and Culture* and *Relationships: A Dialectical Perspective*.

# Why Gods Persist

A scientific approach to religion

**Robert A. Hinde**

London and New York

First published 1999
by Routledge
11 New Fetter Lane, London EC4P 4EE

Simultaneously published in the USA and Canada
by Routledge
29 West 35th Street, New York, NY 10001

*Routledge is an imprint of the Taylor & Francis Group*

Typeset in Times by Routledge
Printed and bound in Great Britain by
TJ International, Padstow, Cornwall

*British Library Cataloguing in Publication Data*
A catalogue record for this book is available from the British Library

*Library of Congress Cataloging in Publication Data*
Hinde, Robert A.
Why Gods Persist: a scientific approach to religion/Robert A. Hinde.
p. cm.
Includes bibliographical references and index.
1. Religion. I. Title.
BL48.H475 199998-49646
200–dc21CIP

ISBN 0–415–20825–4 (hbk)
ISBN 0–415–20826–2 (pbk)

# Contents

# Illustrations

**Figures**

# Acknowledgements

It will be apparent from the bibliography that this attempt to draw together insights from different approaches to human nature is heavily dependent on the work of others. In addition, I would like to express my debt to many who have helped me with advice and criticism, though none of them bears any responsibility for the end result. Since some of them hold views different from my own, I am grateful to them for their willingness to enter into free discussion. Joan Stevenson-Hinde read the complete manuscript and her comments led to much improvement. Jessica Rawson and Teresa Morgan also read an earlier manuscript, and made many constructive criticisms and suggestions. Earlier drafts of parts of the manuscript were read by Helena Cronin, Jane Heal, Elisabeth Hsu and Andrew Macintosh: I am very grateful to them for their stimulating and often critical comments. I profited greatly from conversations with a number of other colleagues at St. John's College, Cambridge, especially John Emerton, Patricia Fara, Jack Goody, Gilbert Lewis, Peter Linehan, Manucha Lisboa, Jo McDermott, David McMullen and Malcolm Schofield, and from correspondence with W. Irons and P.J. Richerson, though again they must all be exonerated from the use I have made of their remarks.

# 1   The questions

Throughout human history, religions have played a major role in the lives of individuals and in the integration of societies. This is still true even in the post-Darwinian West, where religious truth and scientific truth have often been seen as opposed. Many of our institutions have religious roots and, in spite of the obvious contradictions between modern science and literal inter-pretations of religious texts, a high proportion of individuals still attend places of worship or claim religious faith. Why should this be so? One possible answer is that religious observance results from pan-cultural human psychological characteristics, characteristics which, in the context of human societies, have shaped religious systems in all their diversity. This is certainly not a new idea, but recent advances in psychology, biology, and the social sciences permit it to be evaluated more precisely. That is the purpose of this book.

This first chapter considers first the prevalence of religious involvement, with special reference to the western world. Then some reasons for regarding the purely destructive approach to religion adopted by some scientists as inadequate are discussed, the present aims are specified, and some aspects of the orientation adopted are described.

## Incidence of religion in the West

### Stability and change

Religions have helped individuals to face injustice, suffering, pain, and death. They have inculcated values of love and respect for others that have been fundamental for the smooth running of societies. In most societies reli-gious and secular systems have been closely interwoven. But religions have also been used to perpetuate inequities, and religious differences have been used to justify torture and horrific religious wars. Religions have provided people with a sense of purpose – though sometimes that sense of purpose has led believers to destroy the ways of life of those who thought differently from themselves. They have provided a medium for much, perhaps most, of the great artistic, musical and literary creations of human history. They have provided answers, satisfying to many, to the fundamental questions of

'Where did we come from?' and 'Where are we going?' – yet those answers have stemmed from systems of beliefs that have always been unverifiable and which, at least if taken literally, can now be seen as wrong in many respects.

The truth value of such beliefs must have been a matter of debate since humans first devised something that could be called religion. In the modern world many, perhaps most, people prefer scientific explanations for natural events to theistic ones, but this certainly does not mean that religious debates have always been shallow, or that science and religion have always been opposed: over the centuries there has been a complex and subtle interchange of ideas between them (Brooke, 1991), though each uses its own models in the search for understanding. But belief in dogma is not necessarily central to religion, and religious dogma is not the only obstacle to the acceptance of a religious system. For one thing, religious belief has nearly always been coupled with a degree of material sacrifice. Whether it is tithes, donations to the priests, burnt offerings, pilgrimages, the building of shrines, erecting monuments to the dead, or even just giving up time, religion can be a costly business. And many other factors have operated in the western world. Society has become fragmented into more specialised units, so that activities formerly seen as religious are now the province of specialist organisations. Thus religious institutions are no longer the main controllers of education, charity, health-care, or indeed of the economic system. Friendly Societies, earlier responsible for much social support and organised locally by individuals who knew each other, have been superseded. Close-knit, small-scale communities have disappeared as a consequence of increased personal mobility and the growth of large-scale industrial institutions. The increased mobility of individuals has involved also the dispersal of the adherents to any particular religious system, and the intermingling of different religious systems in the same locale, rendering each a less effective social influence. And rationality and bureaucracy have led both to a search for more efficient ways of managing our affairs and to scepticism about the possibility of supernatural intervention in the expected course of events (Davies, 1994).

Yet religions have persisted in almost every society in the world – and where they have not they have been replaced by systems of political dogma with at least some features in common with religions (Lane, 1981). This raises the questions with which this book is concerned: why are religions so ubiquitous and persistent, and would we do better without them? These are posed in more detail below.

### The present state

In Europe, the scope of religious beliefs was diminished by the Enlightenment, itself made possible only because some independence of the religious from the everyday world was already accepted (Tambiah, 1990). The debate came to a head in the nineteenth century with the publication of

*The Origin of Species.* Subsequently the Rationalist Press, the Thinker's Library, and other publication ventures recruited some of the best minds of the time to criticise religious doctrine, and religions continued to lose some of their influence up to at least the middle of the twentieth century.

How far this decline in religious observance has continued in recent decades is less clear, in large part because diverse measures of religious involvement have been used. For instance, to many 'being a Christian' means, not church membership or holding Christian beliefs, but attempting to live up to a certain moral code. However, church membership is a convenient measure: its use indicates that religion has declined in the United Kingdom. For instance the data indicate that, between 1900 and 1990, the membership of Episcopalian churches declined from 2.09 million to 1.71 million, Presbyterian from 1.25 to 1.01, Methodist from 0.77 to 0.43, while Catholics increased from 1.22 to 1.67 million. Allowing for an increase in the population of individuals over 15 years of age from 24.68 to 45.11 million, the data suggested a decline in church membership from 25.60 per cent to 13.99 per cent (Bruce, 1995). However this conclusion has been criticised because it neglected the increase in non-Christian religious groups; because of the extent to which children were included; and because so much depends on the precise measure used (Stark and Iannaccone, 1995). A Gallup poll in 1981 indicated that 73 per cent said that they believed in God, and 36 per cent in a personal god (Webb and Wybrow, 1982), though of course a much smaller percentage attended places of worship. In addition, not all Christian denominations have shown a decrease: some, like the Pentecostalists, have shown an increase (Hood *et al.*, 1996). In the 1991 British Social Attitudes Survey only about 10 per cent said they had no religion (Bruce, 1996).

The proportion of people with a religious inclination in the USA has been consistently higher than in the UK: an analysis of the 'General Social Surveys' from 1973 to 1991 indicated that 84 per cent of Protestants, 76 per cent of Catholics, 30 per cent of Jews and 48 per cent of those who claimed no religion said that they believed in life after death. These levels remained virtually constant over the two decades, though that for Jews showed a slight upward trend (Harley and Firebaugh, 1993). Even among scientists, surveys in 1916 and 1996 showed that the proportion who believed in a personal god who heard prayers and could grant immortality remained steady at about 40 per cent (Larson and Witham, 1997). Just what such figures mean is another matter: a 1954 Gallup Poll showed that over three quarters of United States Protestants and Catholics could not name a single Old Testament prophet, and more than two thirds did not know who preached the Sermon on the Mount (Stark and Glock, 1968). It has also been argued that, although Americans seem to be more attached to their churches than Europeans, the churches have changed. 'Radical sects have become denominations. The mainstream denominations have become tolerant and ecumenical. The gospel itself has been rewritten to remove much of the specifically supernatural' (Bruce, 1996: 164). But in any case it is clear that, at least in some areas of the USA, Christian fundamentalism is widespread. For example, while this was being written a report described how the 'Brownsville Assembly of God' was drawing over 3000 people most nights of the week, members of almost every conceivable religious denomination, to hear that Christ is 'coming back with a sword in his hand and vengeance on his mind'. Many devout Christians believe that miracles still happen, and that the faithful can speak with tongues and are able to heal the sick (*USA Today*, 12 June 1997). In addition, with the collapse of Communism the Church has become a potent force in Poland and elsewhere in Eastern Europe.

## Inadequacy of purely destructive approaches

Any number of critics have pointed out that the basic beliefs of Christian doctrine, taken literally, are simply unacceptable to most twentieth-century minds (e.g. Dawkins, 1993, 1995). But churchgoers are still told about the Virgin Birth, the Resurrection and Ascension, miracles, even Heaven and Hell. In Britain, school teachers may still be required to lecture on specific gravity in one lesson and discuss the Gospel story of Jesus walking on water in the next. That it is impossible to accept such doctrines in their literal form has been demonstrated many times, and I have no intention of going over that ground again. In any case, many religious people do not take them literally. But their counter-intuitive nature does raise an important problem: if the basic beliefs and narratives of the Christian or any other religion are not to be taken literally, why are religions so persistent? Given their influence, that question demands detailed consideration. Merely to point out inconsistencies, or to demonstrate that many religious beliefs are incompatible with modern scientific knowledge is, I suggest, unsatisfactory for at least four reasons.

First, such belief systems are important to many people. At the individual level many people gain a great deal of comfort from their religious beliefs. Concentration camp inmates, prisoners and citizens under stress who have religious or religio-political views providing a meaning that points towards a future do better than those without them (e.g. Frankl, 1975; Levi, 1989). A religious approach is claimed sometimes to be valuable in psychotherapy (Anderson and Worthen, 1997). At an everyday level, those who adhere to one faith or another would surely not do so if it did not sustain them or satisfy some need, and there must be some reason for religious revivals. Reviewing the more recent literature, Hood *et al.* (1996: 436–7) conclude that 'In most instances…faith buttresses people's sense of control and self-esteem, offers meanings that oppose anxiety, provides hope, sanctions socially facilitating behavior, enhances personal well-being, and promotes social integration.' Furthermore, in many societies the religious system is intimately intertwined with aspects of the social and group ideology and with the social structure. This is not to deny that religious systems have from time to time been responsible for much suffering: those high in religiosity, except for the most devout, tend to be the more prejudiced; religious beliefs have often been divisive; and religious systems can cater to base emotions. But it is clear that at least some people have found them, and still find them, helpful for at least some of the time (Chapter 17).

In addition, while crime and lawlessness have many causes, the Church used to be the principal purveyor of values in the western world, so it is at least arguable that the decrease in communal responsibility which seems to have occurred in the second half of the twentieth century is not unrelated to a decline in the Church's influence. In the nineteenth century church adherence and attendance served to express and affirm respectability. Even those who did not attend churches were receptive to religion-based social morality (Davies, 1994). Thus the very ubiquity of religious systems strongly suggests that they are, or have been, valuable to many people (Campbell, 1991).

So perhaps it should be incumbent on those who emphasise the shortcomings of religious systems to specify also their positive characteristics, and to indicate how such benefits those systems bestow can be retained if the beliefs are untenable. *Of course* science can do a better job in helping us to understand our origins than can Genesis or any comparable myth. And *of course* science is more help than religion in understanding the relation between cause and consequence in everyday life. Although we must never lose sight of the facts that all knowledge, including scientific knowledge, involves belief, and that even scientists use metaphor, scientific belief is very different from religious belief, and in using metaphors, scientists seek to cash them out in non-metaphorical terms. But are we convinced that science can take over all that religion is about? Before we can attempt to answer that, we need to know much more about how religions relate to life as it is lived, and much more about why it is that the human psyche seems so often to have been satisfied by religious systems over the millennia. That requires input not only from psychology (Hood *et al.*, 1996; Wulff, 1997), but also from other natural and social sciences, from history, and from other humanities.

A second reason why it is unsatisfactory merely to point out the inadequacies of religious beliefs is that the issue is such an old one. Discrepancies between religious belief systems and current knowledge about the world have been a matter for intense discussion at least since the Enlightenment: there is no need to go over all that again. In any case, it is necessary to come to terms with what 'belief' means: many Christians distinguish between 'belief', involving subscribing to a particular set of dogma, and 'faith' involving an attitude of openness to a 'greater' reality (e.g. Armstrong, 1993; see Chapter 3).

Third, although Christians give it primacy, belief is by no means all there is to religion. In Judaism, structural beliefs (see p. 12) are less important than the historical narrative. Hinduism does not necessarily imply any doctrinal agreement except in so far as it influences conduct: the Hindu may pursue work, or meditation and knowledge, or devotion. For Buddhist teachers, values and experience come first, and there is much less emphasis on belief. Many, though not all, Buddhist sects do not rely on reverence for superhuman beings (Orru and Wang, 1992). The early Buddhist teaching emphasised salvation by self-discipline and good works: faith became an issue only in the Lotus Sutra, written centuries after Buddha's death, though purporting to be his last testament (Firth, 1996). Confucius was primarily concerned with how humans could create and maintain an ordered world. Thus, most religious systems involve several interrelated components, of which belief in dogma is only one.

Finally, a purely destructive approach is unsatisfactory because it is unscientific. The near ubiquity of religion poses a fundamental question about human behaviour which cannot be simply dismissed. Dawkins, an avowed and usually constructive Darwinist, has used an evolutionary approach to explain the ubiquity of religion, arguing that human children are shaped by evolution to soak up culture, and using computer viruses as a model for the manner in which religious information spreads (Dawkins, 1993, 1995). But merely to dismiss the literal interpretation of Christian dogma involves a gross simplification of one of the most complex of human activities. While I accept Dawkins's conclusions about religious beliefs, there is more to religion than belief in dogma, and a Darwinian analysis of religious systems needs a more subtle approach than he accords it (e.g. Alexander, 1987; Irons, 1996b, 1998). Indeed, one could say that religion poses the ultimate challenge to Darwinism.

## The questions

My aims here are narrow, and involve three questions. First, how far can the widespread adherence to religious systems be explained by the extent to which they fit certain aspects of the human psyche? As we shall see in the next chapter, religions involve a number of interrelated components, so we must ask how far each can be accounted for in terms of basic human behavioural and psychological propensities that are more or less pancultural. In tackling that issue, it is necessary to refer to aspects of human behaviour outside religious contexts, and to assess how far the principles found there can account for religious behaviour. The view that an understanding of religion requires some understanding of the religious person is an old one: Marx (1847) argued that humans make religion rather than religion making humankind, and Tylor (1913) that religion is the outcome of the human intellect.

The second question is to ask what aspects of religions could explain their widespread distribution across societies and their extraordinary persistence? How far are these due to the nature of religions themselves, to the answers to existential questions that they provide, to their consequences for the believer, to properties of human minds/brains, or to interactions within societies, or to all of these?

And third, if religious beliefs taken literally cannot be sustained, would we do better to dispense with religious systems altogether, or do they still have a constructive influence on people's lives? If they do, even if only in some ways for some people, what precisely is it about religion that has the beneficial effects? Will it be possible to retain the beneficial aspects while discarding current dogma?

It will already be apparent that I am not here repeating the old discussions as to whether God or gods exist. Nor am I concerned with reconciling the presumption of a transcendental reality with scientific habits of thought (e.g. Polkinghorne, 1994). I am aware that many modern theologians equate God with supreme goodness, and hold that most of what the Bible teaches is to be taken as metaphorical. I will not ask here 'Metaphorical for what?' Instead I ask how far the causes and consequences of religious systems can be found in principles of human functioning also in non-religious contexts.

## Orientation

The majority of the world's population hold some form of religious belief or belong to some sort of religious organisation, and many people have experiences which they interpret as religious. Basically, there would seem to be two possible explanations. Either their beliefs, worship, and experiences refer to some transcendental reality beyond the material world, or they can be understood as products of human nature in interaction with society and with the world. The scientific approach which I shall adopt cannot disprove the reality of the transcendental or supernatural experiences of believers: just as the nature of a bat's auditory system enables it to live in an ultra-sonic world that simply does not exist for me except in so far as scientific research has conveyed it to me second-hand, so no scientist can deny the reality of the religious experiences of the believer. It is, however, legitimate and even obligatory for the scientist to seek understanding of the nature of those experiences, and of the interpretations put upon them. To those who do not have religious faith this may seem an unnecessary and perhaps misleading undertaking, but to dismiss the problem would involve neglecting an important part of the lives of many people. My aim, therefore, is to see how far the second type of explanation can take us. In doing so, I am following a course which has been sketched out many times already, but I hope that new developments in the human sciences, together with my attempt to survey both the several facets of religious systems and the inter-relations between them, will prove it worthwhile.

I write as a biologist who has worked also in the social sciences. Perhaps, therefore, I should confess to a hidden agenda. For too long biologists and social scientists have glowered at each other, each asserting that their approaches and models are applicable to problems which the other group sees as its concern. The situation was exacerbated by the extravagant claims of some biologists (e.g. Lorenz, 1935; Wilson, 1975) that they have the keys to the understanding of a wide range of human behaviour, and the defensive blindness of many social scientists on feeling that their patch is being invaded. But the real problem is very obvious, the two groups have been basically interested in different issues. Most biologists (and psychologists) interested in human behaviour have been interested in general properties of the human mind/brain applicable to the behaviour of all humans; whereas most social scientists have focused on differences, differences between cultures or differences within cultures over time, with social class, and so on, attempting to explain the differences in terms of common principles.

I suggest that both sides have been mistaken. In brief, and the theme is developed more fully later, the complexities of human behaviour, and the differences between human groups, must not be underestimated by the biologist, and must be recognised by the social scientist as resulting from the mutual influences of basic human propensities within and between individuals and with the social and physical environment. I am not, of course, claiming that this is a new approach, but merely emphasising that in the long run the focus must be, not on either the biologist's generalities or the social scientist's complexities, but on the mutual influences between them (Hinde, 1991). In general, I hope that such an approach can lead to a *rapprochement* between the natural and social sciences. In the case of religion, the current need is to see how far the complexities and differences can be understood in terms of basic characteristics common to all humans.

Since I have a personal acquaintance with it, I shall focus primarily on Christianity, though using references to other religious systems to expand or validate points which I hope are more generally applicable, or to illustrate the limitations of generalisations. This is, of course, a severe restriction: religion in a post-Enlightenment, mainly Christian, society, that embraces the whole spectrum from fundamentalist believers to equally convinced atheists as well as members of other religions, has a flavour very different from that in societies where the religion pervades the social system, as in many of those studied by anthropologists. Other world religions are, of course, equally diverse: Islam, Buddhism, Hinduism and others, all have their divisions so that generalisations about them are also likely to be misleading. Yet, even if I had the competence, which I have not, an attempt to make detailed distinctions within each of the major world religions would have been irrelevant to an attempt to pin-point the bases of religions in general. In any case, comparisons across contexts can be misleading for a different reason: apparent similarities may conceal real differences and superficial differences may conceal basic similarities. For all these reasons, one cannot be too cautious with cross-cultural generalisations about religion: its associated meanings differ so much between societies.

In trying to draw together material from different disciplines, I have inevitably touched on issues controversial within those disciplines. While I have tried to avoid such matters as far as possible, and to take an overview, there will be specialists who disagree with the line I have taken. I can only ask them to consider how far any disagreement would affect the main points I am making.

Focusing primarily on Christianity but including references to other religions has also posed some curious stylistic problems, such as the necessity for the umbrella term 'religious specialists' to cover priests, diviners, shamans, and so on. Perhaps because of my upbringing or respect for some of my friends, I find it awkward not to capitalise the deities of Christianity and other world religions, which may leave the unintended impression that other gods are regarded as necessarily inferior. And, on a different issue, I hope that it will be understood that where I have used masculine pronouns, they are usually intended to refer to either sex except where the context specifically indicates otherwise.

## Plan of the book

Chapter 2 is concerned with some basic issues from various other disciplines which pertain to virtually all subsequent chapters. In it the several interacting and mutually supportive aspects that together constitute religion are listed. Consideration is given next to the way in which human behaviour in all its diversity depends on progressive interactions between a number of pan-cultural human psychological characteristics, with cumulative consequences. Of special importance for the understanding of religious systems is the nature of the self-system, and how that interacts with human relationships and with the socio-cultural structure of beliefs, values, myths, and so on.

Chapters 3 to 16 take each aspect of religious systems in turn, exploring the extent to which they depend on basic human propensities. Special attention is paid to structural beliefs in Chapters 3 to 7, to narratives and ritual in Chapters 8 to 11, and to moral codes in Chapters 12 to 14. Chapters 15 and 16 concern religious experience and the social aspects of religion. Chapter 17 focuses on the bases of the persistence of religious systems, bringing together material from earlier discussions. The final chapter considers the benefits and costs of religious systems at this time.

## Summary

Although the influence of religions might seem to be declining in parts of the West, the data are difficult to interpret. Certainly it is still strong in many areas, and even stronger in many other parts of the world. In view of the contradictions between scientific findings about the origin of the earth and the nature of humankind on the one hand, and literal interpretations of religious texts on the other, this poses a problem.

The purely destructive approach to religion adopted by some scientists appears to be inadequate because it aims to remove something that appears to be of value to at least some people, it assumes that religions consist only of belief in dogma, and it neglects the challenging Darwinian problem posed by the persistence of religions.

This book is concerned with three questions. How far do the several aspects of religious systems depend on pan-cultural human psychological characteristics? How can we account for the persistence of religions? And if religious systems have some beneficial consequences, how can these be retained while literal interpretations of their basic beliefs become unacceptable?

# 2 Some background issues

This chapter prepares the ground. The first section lists the aspects of religious systems that, for the sake of convenience, are discussed separately in later chapters: this in no way denies their interdependence, which will be apparent throughout and is emphasised later. The following sections, though they may initially seem remote from religion, consider two issues essential to later chapters – the existence of basic human characteristics and how they interact to produce complex behaviour; and the nature of the self-system. Discussions of some other theoretical issues are postponed to where they are most relevant.

## The components of religions

Religion involves feeling, thinking, acting, and relating, and there are tremendous individual differences in their relative importance. Religion has been institutionalised in the form of churches, denominations, sects, and cults, though some religious people prefer to practise their religion in solitude. Nowadays many seek 'spirituality', a connectedness with a transcendent force, taking such elements as suit their needs from several religious institutions (Pargament, 1997). But most, perhaps all, religion involves belief in some form of transcendence or in beings or entities which are outside normal experience.

That does not mean that belief is necessarily a central issue, or indeed that a religious orientation should necessarily be regarded as a unitary disposition: many people abide by religious principles but lack religious belief, and many do the reverse. When westerners' responses to questionnaires containing both religious and secular items are analysed, religion usually emerges as a single factor, indicating that an individual accepting some aspects of a religious system tends also to accept others. However, if the questionnaire involves only religious items, a number of separate religious orientations can be identified (see Chapter 3). For present purposes it is convenient to treat religion as involving a number of more-or-less distinct yet interrelated components, of which belief is but one, and which are differentially emphasised in different cases (cf. Malinowski, 1954). Thus most religions involve at least some of the following elements:

1    Structural beliefs. These usually involve an entity or entities which are related to but are in some sense outside the world in which we live, have at least some improbable and counter-intuitive characteristics, and are usually independent of time. For Christians, this includes beliefs associated with the doctrine of the Trinity, the Creed, life after death, and so on. The beliefs may concern complex concepts which give rise to controversy.
2    Narratives, such as the story of Jesus's life set out in the Gospels. These also usually concern, directly or indirectly, the entities with improbable characteristics. They may also include the teachings and experiences of lesser religious figures.
3    Rituals, prayer, sacrifice, and other aspects of religious practice. These may involve the recitation of creeds and the use of texts concerned with the structural beliefs and narratives, and may be conducted by religious specialists.
4    A code of personal and group conduct, associated with an implied or explicit system of values. To an extent which differs between societies, this may be related to the conventions, norms of behaviour, and ideology of the society or of its components.
5    Religious experience.
6    Social aspects.

Some systems that we refer to as religious may lack or under-play some of these, but all are present to some degree in most.

In possessing these several aspects, religion resembles other aspects of the socio-cultural system. For example, in societies in which racism is institutionalised, there are likely to be beliefs about the characteristics of the out-group and their inferiority as compared with the in-group; narratives about relations with them; rituals, such as those of the Ku Klux Klan; a code of conduct governing encounters with the out-group; experiences associated with interactions with them, and, of course, a social aspect.

I shall treat these six categories as contributory elements: no one is to be seen as central for they are interrelated, and I shall refer to their interdependence as involving a 'religious system' which forms part of the culture of the society. The structural beliefs influence the form of the narratives and are explicated by them. The narratives not only supplement the structural beliefs but also convey values. The rituals are informed by and support the beliefs and values, and may involve religious experience. They may or may not be socially performed. And the religious experience is influenced by the beliefs, narratives, values and rituals of the religion in question. Some aspects of religion can be seen as combinations of two or more of the above categories – for instance prayer may depend on the narratives and involve both ritual actions and religious experience. In later chapters these aspects of religious systems are discussed in turn, their interrelations being considered in Chapter 17.[1]

This approach may seem unduly analytical and reductionist. To some, it may appear to neglect the spiritual. However, a number of studies have shown that search for the spiritual is correlated with that for more secular goals, self-esteem, comfort, intimacy, meaning, and so on, and many religious people see the spiritual as residing in humankind (Pargament, 1997). To others, seeking for the psychological bases of religion may seem like simple reductionism. Here there are two issues. First, the whole is more than the sum of its parts, and good science does not stop at analysis, but re-synthesises the products of analysis in order to understand how they function in the whole (Tinbergen, 1951). In this volume I attempt only to discuss how the components reinforce each other: for the emergent consequences of their interaction a more holistic psychodynamic or object-relations approach may be more applicable. Second, and more importantly, just as Newton's demonstration that white light could be decomposed into the colours of the spectrum has not undermined the beauty of the rainbow, so the suggestion that the elaboration and acceptance of a religious system may depend on basic psychological characteristics need not diminish the importance of the whole to individuals.

## Human propensities

### *Possible objections to a scientific approach*

Religions are almost infinitely diverse – almost, but not quite. They all involve, albeit to varying degrees, at least some of the above mentioned aspects. The question thus arises, can they be understood in terms of basic human characteristics – characteristics likely to have been shaped by natural selection? This, of course, is no new idea: Malinowski (1944) linked social institutions to human needs. But such a possibility has been anathema to many. Most of those concerned with the nature of religions, theologians and anthropologists, have eschewed any contribution of human universals – the former tending to see religious systems as externally inspired, the latter naturally focusing on their diversity.

Rather than deploying counter arguments, it seems preferable to let the approach adopted here be judged in its own right. However, I cannot resist taking issue with one sally aimed directly at the approach that I am taking.

Kolakowski (1982: 153) has argued that those who attempt to find the hand of natural selection in the genesis of culture

> must be suspected of constructing from our biological equipment a frame of reference by means of which to understand culture, and thus of implying that the entire cultural creativity of man – language, art,

religion, science, technology and philosophy – may be sufficiently explained in terms of its instrumental function in serving the allegedly basic and unalterable needs we have in common with other species.

This statement contains three errors of fact, and misses the point with a non sequitur. The first inaccuracy lies in the reference to 'our biological equipment'. Human morphological and psychological characteristics cannot be divided into those that are 'biologically' and those that are experientially or culturally determined. All characteristics depend on both, and those that are pan-cultural must depend on an interplay between biological factors that are universal and aspects of the environment that are experienced by all humans (Oyama, 1985).

The second inaccuracy lies in the implication that the biological factors in human development are concerned solely with needs that we have in common with other species. That 'need' is a tricky concept is obvious enough, and discussion of the semantic issue is unnecessary in the present context: it is sufficient to say that humans have motivations not present (at any rate to anything like the same extent) in other animals – for instance a predisposition to understand the world by attributing events to causes.

Third, biologists do not allege that most human 'needs' are unalterable. Of course, we must eat and drink to live; but it is an obviously false assumption that the common characteristics of any species, including our own, are fixed and unalterable. No two people (even identical twins) are exactly alike, and every human characteristic is subject to variation through differences in genes or environment. Some individuals have an imperative need to assert themselves, or to find sexual release, others do not. Of course the nature of human beings sets limits to the variability, but limited variability is always present.

The non sequitur lies in the implication that, if our biological equipment provides a frame of reference to understand culture, then the diverse manifestations of culture must themselves be explicable in terms of their effects on survival and reproduction. But neither that nor the now-dated social scientist view that culture is somehow *sui generis*, added onto what is biologically given, is adequate. The human propensities and activities that create culture (in general, and religion in particular) may themselves have been shaped in evolution, yet this does not necessarily imply that the cultural characteristics that result from those propensities and activities or from their interaction are themselves adaptive in a biological sense. The diverse aspects of a cultural system are common to many individuals, but are not 'out there': they lie in people's heads or in their creations, and are a consequence of human activity. Part of the aim of this book is to explore the extent to which religious systems, whether or not they are adaptive for the individuals concerned, can be understood in terms of basic and pan-cultural human psychological characteristics.

### The bases of the current approach

This book is not an attempt to assess whether religious systems as wholes are or are not adaptive in a biological sense – that is, whether or not the practice of religion favours the reproductive success of individuals in the context of the society in question. Some have proposed that to be the case (e.g. Wilson, 1975), and there is evidence that around half of the variance between individuals in religious attitudes and values is due to genetic factors (Waller *et al.*, 1990). At least one attempt to find hard evidence for the view that religion is adaptive has been made. As the result of a broad survey, Reynolds and Tanner claimed that cultures in which the relevant codes of conduct favoured a high reproductive rate tend to be those in which the environment is unpredictable. They conclude that the ' "instructions" religions give to individuals are "adaptive" ' (1983: 293–4). The implication behind this is roughly that in unpredictable environments it is better to reproduce as fast as you can when you can, so that at least some young will survive, whereas in predictable environments it is a better policy to produce a few high quality young who will do well in intra-specific competition. Although these authors scan a great range of material, much of it is insufficiently analysed: the result is an interesting overview, backed up by few measures of reproductive success, but scarcely meriting a hard conclusion.

The approach adopted here leaves open the question of whether religion as a whole is or has been adaptive, but is instead concerned with whether it can be understood in terms of human characteristics that are themselves ubiquitous and were probably themselves the product of natural selection. While it will be stressed that religious systems may have consequences for societies as wholes, and may be manipulated by elements within a society for their own benefit or that of the society, the consequences are not seen as directly determining the nature of the religious system, and the approach is not functionalist in the traditional sense. Rather the religious system is seen as the effect of concatenating basic human psychological characteristics, and as influencing reciprocally the behaviour of individuals, their relationships, and through them society itself (cf. Cancian, 1968). This is far from the first time that this approach has been adopted (see e.g. Irons, 1996a, 1996b), but previous work has concentrated on one or other of the facets of religious systems. The argument can thus be seen as involving two steps.

(a) The identification of pan-cultural human psychological characteristics of relevance to religious practices. There are two points here. First, it is rarely possible to prove that a given characteristic is completely pan-cultural, for data on every characteristic in every culture in the world are simply not available. In practice, therefore, it might be better to claim that they are 'widespread'. However the characteristics that I shall mention seem so much a part of being human that I believe that reservation to be unnecessary.

Second, it is not essential that all the psychological propensities to which I shall refer are or have been adaptive in a biological sense – that is, that they foster or have fostered the survival or reproductive interests of individuals. I do in fact believe them all to be a product of natural selection, but to prove their adaptedness it would be necessary to show that, other things being equal, individuals with them are (or have been in the past) on average more biologically successful than those without: for the most part individual variation is insufficient to do this, and anyway other things never are equal. But the nature of such psychological characteristics is such as to further individual survival and reproduction, and it is reasonable to suppose that most were crafted by natural selection to solve the problems posed to our ancestors in the environments that they encountered (Barkow *et al.*, 1992). The argument in this book, concerned with the ubiquitous (though individually variable) human psychological characteristics that make religious ideas and practices acceptable and permit their passage across the generations, is therefore by implication Darwinian. The discussion, however, will necessarily involve also the social processes through which these psychological characteristics affect the practice of religion.

(b) The second step involves assessment of the manner in which such characteristics contribute to the various aspects of religion. Here again, it is as well to note the precise nature of the claim being made. A given psychological characteristic may contribute to a given religious practice yet not be essential for it: indeed it may be possible to compare two phenomenologically similar practices, one of which does and the other does not depend on the characteristic in question. For instance, religious belief may be facilitated by fear of death in one context or in one person, by loneliness in another; religious ritual may be made more meaningful by bright lights and music for some, by simplicity for others; religious experience may be facilitated by the presence of co-worshippers in some contexts, but comparable experience can result from solitary prayer. Nor is it possible to prove that a given aspect of religion depends solely on such ubiquitous aspects of human psychology: it is always possible for a religious person to make claims beyond the realm of psychology. Just as it is impossible in statistics to prove a null hypothesis, so a psychological approach cannot disprove such claims. It can, however, make them seem unnecessary.

Since the issue of pan-cultural psychological characteristics is fundamental for what follows, it is best to address it directly, though it requires a considerable digression. (Those who are familiar with the application of biological principles to human behaviour should move onto p. 26.) Here we will consider first what is meant by pan-cultural characteristics; second their development; and third the ways in which they contribute to and interact with the socio-cultural structure. This will provide occasion for raising the questions of how they are transmitted across the generations and how pan-cultural characteristics can give rise to cultural differences; and finally how, even if they have arisen as adaptive characteristics in the course of evolution, they may give rise to maladaptive or adaptively neutral behaviour.[2]

### *Relatively stable human behavioural characteristics*

The search for pan-cultural human characteristics of behaviour and psychological functioning which might serve as building blocks for more complex activities has had a long but not necessarily respectable history (Atran, 1993; Count, 1973). A major problem has been that the search has focused on the wrong level of complexity (Hinde, 1987, 1991). It may be that all societies have religious practices, and all societies use fire, but these are pretty sophisticated patterns of behaviour: not only would a human individual brought up without contact with other naive individuals be unlikely to invent such practices, but they are unlikely to serve as basic building blocks for the great diversity of human behaviour. However, if we concentrate not on complex patterns of behaviour, but on more basic psychological propensities, a different picture emerges.

It is a commonplace that we all have noses, though no two noses are identical. It is equally apparent that we all have patterns of ridges and furrows on our fingers, though the patterns are almost infinitely diverse. However, we tend to overlook the fact that, in exactly the same way, we all have certain characteristics of perception, responsiveness to stimuli, motor patterns, motivations, emotions, cognitive processes, and so on, though there is always individual variation. We all distinguish figure from ground, have certain facial expressions, are (sometimes) willing to work for food, and so on. More importantly, and especially easily overlooked as a commonplace, we all have basically similar sets of goals, and the ability to use variable means to attain them. I refer here not only to the more obvious goals of food, security, and sex, but also to issues like making sense of the world by attributing events to causes, feeling in control of one's life, or attempting to achieve status, all propensities which, I shall argue later, contribute to religious observance. These and other basic human propensities (or 'Relatively Stable Characteristics', Hinde, 1991) can reasonably be assumed to be present, to varying degrees, in all individuals (or at least in all those of a particular age/sex/class) and in all populations, and to provide the material from which human behaviour in all its diversity develops.

Although my emphasis is on their ubiquity, it is reasonable to assume that such aspects of human behaviour were or are adaptive and evolved under the influence of natural selection. Thus we would not be here if our ancestors had not been reasonably proficient at finding adequate food, keeping themselves safe from predation, and reproducing. Survival and reproduction must be facilitated in individuals who understand the relation of events to causes, and who can monitor their ability to do so: experimental evidence shows that even animals kept in unpredictable environments develop neuroses (Seligman, 1975). Considerable evidence indicates that, in polygynous societies with limited contraception, it has been biologically adaptive to identify the markers of status in the society and to strive to achieve them, and that such conditions held for much of human evolution (Betzig *et al.*, 1988; Irons, 1998). Similar arguments apply to other psychological characteristics mentioned later in the book. I am not making any claim that such characteristics are independent of experience, either in development or contemporaneously. Thus I am not reverting to the now out-moded distinction between behaviour that is innate, instinctive or biological and behaviour that is experientially determined (see Oyama, 1985). Nor am I claiming that such apparently basic propensities are unanalysable (Hinde, 1997a): this is a matter on which further light will be cast as we gain more understanding of the processes involved in human development. But I trust that the near-universality of such propensities will not be controversial. Because of their ubiquity they may seem to be of little interest in explaining the complexity and diversity of human behaviour, but it is from their individual variability and from the *interplay* between such basic characteristics, and between them and the social and physical environment, that complexity and diversity must arise.

## *Development*

This brings us to the second issue, the development of these relatively stable characteristics. While it is perhaps a truism to say that even the most complex aspects of human behaviour must ultimately depend on human propensities that are more or less pan-cultural, the operative word is *ultimately*. As noted above, the basic propensities must first themselves develop. They are, of course, not present in the genes, but result from a complex interplay between the organism as it is at each stage in development and its environment. And since individuals differ to some extent in both their genetic constitution and in the environments they encounter, these basic propensities will differ slightly between individuals. But at the same time, there are common features in the environments that individuals encounter. No humans escape the force of gravity; virtually all suck from the mother's nipple or from a nipple feel-alike; most are told by their caregivers 'If you do this, then that will happen', or learn the same lesson from observation. Characteristics that are ubiquitous depend on commonalities in genetic constitution and in relevant environmental factors. Then in turn these *relatively* stable characteristics interact, perhaps in many stages, to produce the complexities of human social life, and in particular the complex religious systems in which we are interested. These interactions do not lead to the mere summation of basic characteristics, but to new emergent features. The road of development is a long one and as yet far from understood, but in later chapters we shall see that such pan-cultural psychological characteristics are basic to most and perhaps all the components of religious systems.

## Levels of complexity

But, to come to the third issue, the environment to which every developing individual is exposed involves both physical and social elements, and the latter includes interactions and relationships with others and participation in groups and societies. In practice it is convenient, in seeking to understand human behaviour, to distinguish between several levels of complexity. The psychological processes within an individual, the behaviour and propensities of that individual when alone, short-term interactions, behaviour in relationships (involving a succession of interactions over time), and groups or societies, all represent increasing levels of complexity, each involving both objective behaviour and subjective phenomena. Each level requires a somewhat different approach, in part because each has properties that are not relevant to the level below. For instance, the behaviour of two individuals in interaction may or may not mesh each with that of the other – but meshing is a property simply irrelevant to the behaviour of an individual in isolation. Again, we use different explanatory concepts at each level: we may explain the behaviour of two brothers fighting over a toy (i.e. interaction level) by saying that they both want the toy, but we explain why they are always fighting (a property of the relationship) by invoking 'sibling rivalry'.

But more important in the present context is the fact that each level is affected by other levels: the nature of a personal relationship is affected not only by its constituent interactions, but also by the group in which it is embedded, for each partner's relationship with the other is affected by relationships with third parties. The individual's development is influenced by his social environment, but at the same time he is influencing that environment. The parent–child relationship depends on characteristics of both child and parent, and both are changed as a consequence of their interaction (Figure 2.1).

Furthermore, each of the levels of complexity affects, and is affected by, the socio-cultural structure[3] of the ideology, beliefs, values, norms, institutions and so on more or less shared by the individuals in the group or society. These abstract categories of 'norms', 'values', 'beliefs' and so on, refer to what is more or less common to all individuals in the society or group. They include, often as an important element, the religious system. Indeed the boundary between the code of conduct insisted upon by the religious specialists and the conventions and norms governing everyday behaviour may be very shady. Since the psychological worlds which we construct tend to have some coherence, the various aspects of the socio-cultural structure tend to be reasonably compatible with each other, but they are not necessarily completely so. Thus there may be discrepancies between the religious moral code and the ideology of the society: a religiously based

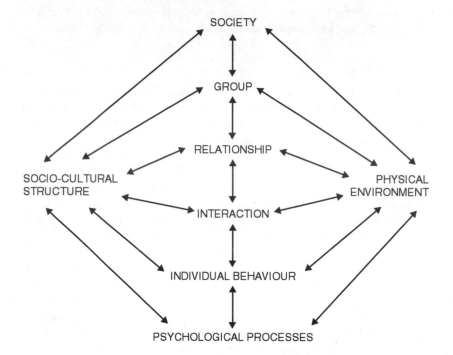

*Figure 2.1* A simplified view of the levels of social complexity. Each level influences, and is influenced by, other levels, by the physical environment, and by the socio-cultural structure (which includes the religious system). The influences involve behavioural, affective, and cognitive processes in the individuals concerned, mediated by the meanings attributed to events and situations. Though not illustrated in the Figure, the scheme is to be seen in diachronic perspective. Each level must thus be treated not as an entity but as involving processes of continuous creation, change or degradation through the dialectical influences within and between levels.
*Source*: Modified from Hinde, 1991.

moral precept that people should be treated equally may conflict with a societal norm implying that blue-eyed blonde people are superior to brown-eyed ones or to individuals of another ethnic group.

Though the socio-cultural structure may be codified in literate societies, what matters is what is, or what becomes, internalised in the head of each individual. Parent (and child) are influenced by the norms, beliefs, myths, and institutions (including the religious system) of the society in which they live – in other words by the traditions inherent in the socio-cultural structure. But how parents behave to their children, and indeed how all members of a society behave, affects that socio-cultural structure. In this century we have seen not only how social norms influence the way in which women and men behave to each other, but also how the way in which women and men behave has influenced the social norms. Again, the frequency of divorce depends on societal conventions about marriage, and reciprocally those conventions within the socio-cultural structure are affected by the frequency of divorce. These mutual influences can be called dialectical in the sense that they result in the continuous emergence of new 'truth' – though a truth that may be in continual flux. For that reason each of the levels, including both the individual and the socio-cultural structure, can best be seen as consisting not of entities but of processes, in continuous creation, maintenance, or degradation through the agency of these dialectical processes between levels (Hinde, 1987, 1997a).

In case all that sounds abstract, let me summarise the points in terms specifically relevant to the current issue. The proposal, to be explored in more detail later, is that the several components of religious systems – beliefs, rituals, and so on – are to be seen as depending on basic human propensities, such as the propensities to attempt to understand events, to learn from others, and to seek a sense of self-efficacy. These propensities themselves have a developmental history, and the various aspects of religious activities develop in each individual as a consequence of interaction between the propensities and the environment, especially the environment provided by parents, peers, mentors and authority figures, who themselves are influenced by the beliefs, values, and so on, that characterise the society (see Figure 2.1). A religious system (as part of the socio-cultural structure) is not a static entity, but is continually influencing and being influenced by the behaviour of those who embrace or criticise it. Belief in a relationship with a supernatural being both depends on, and affects, the norms and values of the individuals concerned and of the group to which they belong. Of course, as we shall see, there are powerful forces conducive to stability, especially in codified religions, but it remains the case that stability is not a necessary, or even a usual, property of a religious system. One consequence of this approach is that arguments about whether religion 'serves society as a whole, rather than the individuals who compose it' (Towler, 1974: 45) are rendered superfluous.

### Initiation and transmission across the generations

These two-way causal relations between the socio-cultural structure and the behaviour of individuals in relationships or groups operate both immediately and over time. The beliefs and practices of the socio-cultural structure not only originate in the psychological propensities of individuals, but also influence those characteristics and tend to persist because they fit those characteristics. Thus practices seen as traditional may have originated in the psychological propensities of individuals, but be used now as part of a cultural ritual. Consider, for example, the fact that virtually every social system incorporates elements of hierarchy. In most situations, greater height or elevation gives a measure of physical and psychological advantage, an effect perhaps stemming from the very nature of the human body. In each generation it is used in speech (superior-inferior) and in space (higher-lower) to represent and reinforce status and power differentials. Thus the Fellows of a Cambridge College sit at a 'High Table', raised slightly above those at which the undergraduates sit. Bishops and Kings sit on thrones, and Christian churches are usually arranged so that the congregation's attention is focused upon the priest and the 'holiest' part of the church – the altar in the sanctuary. The altar is usually elevated somewhat above the level of the floor of the church, brightly lit, and so on (Rawson, 1995, 1998a; Winter, 1997). In addition to height, the distinctions are accentuated by devices that utilise other human propensities. On formal occasions the Master of one Cambridge College sits in the centre of the 'High Table', with large silver platters displayed on the wall behind him and serving to focus attention towards that end of the hall. Kings wear crowns that are attention-getting, made of bright and valuable material, often sparkling with jewels, and increasing their apparent height. Their coronations involve ritual objects, such as a mace, which is derived over the centuries from a weapon and symbolises their power. Such cases indicate how practices arising from human nature can be transmitted down the generations and influence the behaviour of later individuals.

There are two points to note here. First, that the high/low symbolism exploits an aspect of human psychological functioning that appears to be acquired by the majority of people early in life (see Toren, 1993, for an example), and is probably universal. Second, that this is exploited in turn to affirm the position of those in power – Master, King, or Bishop. This may not be the result of personal intent by the individuals in question: rather it may have become encapsulated in traditional custom which nevertheless has the same consequence.

The symbolism of the mace raises another point. Every cultural practice has a history in which its form, causation and consequences may have changed in many ways, but the factors leading to those changes, as well as those that lead to its initiation at any time, must ultimately depend on basic human propensities. For instance, a change in societal values, involving attempts to make the congregation more equal participants in the service, has led to the altar being moved to the same level as the congregation in some Christian churches.

Consider another example. In the recent past, it was considered polite for a man to raise his hat when meeting an acquaintance, and especially a woman, in the street. It is claimed that this custom originated in a knight's removing his helmet, a gesture which left him vulnerable and thus indicated non-aggressive intent. Saluting is similarly claimed to have arisen from raising the visor (Eibl Eibesfeldt, 1975). The removal of the helmet or raising of the visor thus depended on aggressive and submissive propensities of individuals, and full understanding of hat-raising (or its absence) involves understanding its history and the propensities on which that history is based, including the hierarchical nature of the societies concerned. Today, the origin of the gesture has become quite forgotten. Indeed in some circles where greater emphasis is placed on equality between men and women, such a gesture may be seen as not merely quaint, but impolite: whereas formerly women were happy to accept the greeting, now a change in cultural values has led to its being seen as reminiscent of the former subordinate status of women. There is always a continuing interchange between what people do and the values and other aspects of the socio-cultural structure.

This brings us to a critical point, implicit in what has been said but insufficiently emphasised. Human cultural traditions, including those that contribute to religious systems, are passed down the generations. If we are to understand them fully, we must therefore understand also the mechanisms of transmission. For instance, in any particular society, to what extent are values and customs passed down from parent to child, to what extent are they acquired from other authority figures, and to what extent are they acquired from the peer group? Are they acquired by the individuals in each generation because they are in some way attractive to those individuals? If so, what makes them attractive? Are their attractive properties linked to beneficial properties? Or are they merely soaked up but without any significant consequences? Are there penalties for not acquiring them? Does the process involve simply following instructions, or emulating behaviour seen to be effective, or copying what the majority are doing? Or do some individuals, acting in their own interests, impose them on others? These are all processes which we can see happening in our own society: it will seldom be possible to prove that particular ones are important in the transmission of aspects of religious systems, but in some cases the evidence will be strong. These are issues to which we shall return in future chapters.

### Basic human propensities and cultural differences

The suggestion made in the preceding sections boils down to this. Apparently complex sequences and institutions depend on pan-cultural goal-orientations such as seeking for power or influence, and exploit common human attributes such as the tendency to respond to bright colours and to be impressed by height. This, perhaps it should be said, is in no way incompatible with the diversity of cultures: behavioural propensities are expressed in diverse ways as a consequence of the two-way influences between the individual, others, and society. Consider the case of colour perception. Light involves a continuum of wavelengths, but we perceive it categorically as a series of proto-typical colours. Although wavelength changes continuously, discrimination of wavelengths is sharper across the boundaries between these perceived colours than within them, and the categories are at least very similar in different cultures. Similar instances of categorical perception are well known in other species, so it would seem likely that the categories are not simply consequences of the linguistic labels that we use. However, cultures differ in the number of colour labels that they use. Red is a salient colour in all societies, and it is claimed that, in societies with a limited number of colour names, red is the most likely to have a label after white and black (Berlin and Kay, 1969). But the significance of red differs between cultures: in China it is auspicious, and greeting cards and celebratory banners are usually red, while in the West its primary signifi-cance is as a sign of danger, though it can also signify warmth, high status,[4] and so on. Interestingly, for the Ndembu, who have colour terms only for white, black, and red, white has a primarily positive symbolic significance, black a generally negative one, and red is ambiguous, signifying both good and ill (Turner, 1967). Thus, although there are universal propensities to perceive colours categorically, and for some to be more salient than others, the colours have different meanings in different societies. Understanding of the differences would require an historical perspective (Morris, 1987).

### Maladaptive behaviour

So now we turn to the final issue, namely the manner in which behaviour and psychological characteristics, adapted in evolution, may come to be used in inappropriate and even deleterious ways. This is important to the present discussion because the incorporation of propensities, originally adaptive in one context, into another quite different one could provide a mechanism whereby religious practices have arisen. In the anatomical sphere it is well established that a characteristic originally selected in evolution in one context may come to have a quite different function later. For instance the hyomandibular bone, originally part of the articulation of the lower jaw, is now one of the tiny bones in the mammalian inner ear; and legs adapted for locomotion on land can be used for swimming, or kicking footballs. The same is true for psychological characteristics: the abilities (such as they are) that I deploy in using a word-processor were certainly not originally evolved to that end. Thus it often happens that psychological characteristics that were originally adaptive in one context come to be used in ways that are not beneficial and even maladaptive in another. There are at least four ways in which this may happen.

First, a psychological propensity may be expressed in an inappropriate or excessive way. Thus normal eating is adaptive, but excessive eating (gluttony) can be detrimental to health. The sources of gluttony then pose further prob-lems, which may also be understood in terms of basic human propensities. If the over-eating is not explicable in physiological terms, does it have anything to do with large people being seen as more powerful, either because they can afford to eat more or because large people seem to gain power more easily? Or is it secondary to a cultural value concerned with the merits of good fellow-ship displayed by eating together? Or is over-eating a way to show off, people indulging themselves to demonstrate that they can afford to do so?

Again, the tendency to behave positively towards individuals perceived as kin (see pp. 151–2) is adaptive in a biological sense in many contexts, because it results in enhancing the chances of survival and reproduction of an individual who has a complement of genes very similar to one's own, including especially the tendency to behave positively to others (see pp. 150–63). But if it involves sacrificing one's interests for others who are perceived as kin but are actually unrelated, it may not be so. In time of war propaganda phrases such as 'brothers in arms' may be used to facilitate such sacrifices.

The second possibility is that the behaviour in question was adaptive given particular features of the environments in which humans evolved, but is no longer in our present physical and social circumstances. For instance, some of the so-called 'irrational fears of childhood' (e.g. of falling, of darkness, of wide open spaces) are no longer important for most humans.

The third source of maladaptive behaviour concerns constraints placed on the individual by others, or by the values, norms, and rules of the socio-cultural structure, which cause the individual to behave in ways that do not favour their biological interests. The behaviour of members of celibate communities, when joining brings no reproductive advantage to themselves or their kin, would seem to be an obvious example. Traditions may favour some classes or individuals, but not necessarily everyone. All human societies tend to be hierarchical in some degree, and those with power can enforce their values and conventions on others and thereby influence their behaviour. While the imposed behaviour may lead to less successful reproduction by the subordinates, its adoption may yet be the best strategy in the circumstances prevailing.

Usually, however, behaviour that is now neutral or maladaptive is the result of interaction or conflict between propensities each of which is itself adaptive, and could in other circumstances lead to an outcome which is in the individual's biological interests. Cigarette-smoking, a partly social activity, certainly did not favour survival. Yet it depended not only on the sensory consequences of holding the cigarette between the lips, which seems to have been akin to sucking, and on the physiological consequences of inhaling, but also on the emulation of peers: each of these can be presumed to have had a biological basis. Again, collecting stamps involves amassing resources and usually a degree of competition with other philatelists, acquisitiveness and assertiveness both presumably being adaptive in other contexts, but it is highly improbable that stamp-collectors would be found to leave more offspring than others, and if they did it would be unlikely to be due to philately *per se*. It is important to note that in each of these cases influences from the socio-cultural structure operate – for instance stamp dealers used to appeal to assertive, status-seeking propensities by advertising philately as 'The king of hobbies and the hobby of kings'. In the case of cigarette smoking, the effectiveness of advertisements depended on other characteristics of our species: the advertisements were initiated by the assertiveness of the executives in cigarette companies, and appealed to both the macho and social motivations of the consumer. And this of course only skims the surface of the complex processes that must be involved in such cases.

To make the relevance of this to the present discussion quite clear, let us consider a particular argument sometimes used to counter the view that religions could be based in the products of natural selection. This argument suggests that the Christian demand that one should love one's enemies, and the Buddhist's renunciation of worldliness and even contempt for a life that can be nothing but misery, must be incompatible with natural selection acting to promote survival. Now natural selection was shaping human psychological potentialities long before Buddha or Christ walked the earth. The questions that one might ask, therefore, concern whether it made sense for these particular potentialities to be brought to the fore at the times in question. Could a human propensity to behave prosocially to others, even to enemies, have been the best strategy for Christians in the social conditions of persecution pertaining when Christianity developed? Could contempt for this life have been a way to maintain self-respect and personal integrity for the homeless wanderer in the Ganges basin who renounced the world, and is not the maintenance of self-respect and integrity a human characteristic likely to have been favoured by natural selection? And, over the generations, is not the tendency to learn from elders who were themselves successful, itself biologically advantageous? In any case, might it not be advantageous to high status individuals to perpetuate this view that people should learn from them? And might it not augment their authority even more to inculcate the view that they are purveyors of truths coming from a still higher authority? We shall return to these issues later.

## The self-system

A profoundly religious person perceives himself as different from those who do not share his faith. If asked to describe him*self*, he is likely to give a very different sort of description from one who does not share his faith. The devout Christian may speak of 'Giving him*self* to God', but what is this *self* that he is giving? Discussion of the bases of religion must therefore be underpinned by understanding of the self-system. Here we move not only from biology to psychology, but into one of the most difficult and controversial areas within the latter. Again, we must be concerned with background material which will temporarily take us away from religion: those who are familiar with the psychological literature on the self should turn to p. 33.

For at least some of the time, one passes through the day without consciously thinking about what one is doing or feeling. One leaves work to return home and arrives safely without once considering which turn to take. But if one stumbles, or meets a friend, one may be angry with oneself for being so clumsy, or experience pleasure at the reunion. One may even wonder why one was so angry with oneself, or why one felt so glad to see the friend. It thus sometimes seems convenient to distinguish between a 'subjective self', aspects of the brain/body that guide our behaviour without our being aware of what is going on, and an 'objective self', which is aware of at least some of our own psychological processes, and may allow us to reflect on what we are doing, thinking and feeling, and to plan future courses of behaviour (Lewis, 1992). But the concept of an objective self implies a dichotomy between what it is that does the knowing and what is known or is unavailable to knowledge, between what William James (1890) called the 'I' or self-as-subject and the 'Me' or self-as-object.[5] We say, for instance, 'I remember what I (Me) did yesterday'.

In interpreting people's behaviour, including our own, we find it convenient to use such a concept of 'self'. Although our behaviour is liable to change according to whom we are with, we account for the continuity in our lives by postulating a 'self', and we assume that other people have 'selves' too. For present purposes we need not worry what it means to say that someone *has* a 'self', or to ask where the 'self' is, or even that 'having a self' may be a reflection of modern understanding (Taylor, 1989), we can simply see the 'self' as a useful concept for explaining the perceived continuity in our lives, and as a convenient abstraction which helps us to integrate aspects of the social world and to assess how our relationships with others will affect the course of our lives. As a concept, it is more related to processes than to things.

The usefulness of a concept of self must have emerged gradually in the course of human biological evolution, and indeed there are differences of opinion about its relative importance in different historical periods and in different cultures (McAdams, 1996; Ouellette, 1996). There are also differences between cultures: people from individualistic cultures, such as those in the western world, are likely to see themselves in terms of what they do, accomplish, or possess, while those from collectivist cultures see themselves more in terms of the groups to which they belong. We shall see later that, in the West, the concept of self has become closely related to that of the soul – an issue which makes many cross-cultural comparisons tricky. In any case the western concept of the 'rational, indivisible, morally autonomous individual who is sovereign of his or her own consciousness and has the right to communicate directly with God' is very different from the concept in some eastern religions where the phenomena that define the self are seen as burdening the soul, which longs to get rid of the self-defining *karmas* (Humphrey and Laidlaw, 1994).

Study of the self may sound like a scientifically risky undertaking, since the data involve what individuals think about themselves. But what an individual thinks about himself is something that can be assessed with at least some degree of precision, and for many purposes it is what people think about themselves that matters. Providing that one can be sure that respondents are not deliberately dissembling, such data can be treated as just as hard as any other. Thus we can find out about the self by asking people to describe themselves. (Of course problems arise. We say 'He is not himself today' when no doubt he would say that he was: we shall refer to how individuals defend their self-images against contrary evidence later.)

Most of the information that people use in describing themselves comes from observing how others behave to them: we evaluate ourselves from seeing how others respond to us (e.g. Mead, 1934). The important issue here is how we *perceive and remember* others to respond to us, not how they actually do. And how we interpret the behaviour of others to us is affected by how we perceive ourselves, and by how we perceive others to perceive us, so there is plenty of room for complexity. Most important, of course, are our perceptions of the behaviour to us of those close to us, and especially our perceptions of interactions with the primary caregiver in infancy: it is now clear that, in infants raised by multiple caregivers in institutions, personality development takes a course different from that in infants reared consistently by their own parents (Bowlby, 1969/1982).[6]

But although it is the individual's perceptions of the opinions of others that is basic, this is augmented throughout life by introspection. We evaluate ourselves by describing ourselves to ourselves and making comparisons with our perceptions of others. Similarly we evaluate our situations, plans, and so on by re-presenting them to ourselves. Language is a usual, and perhaps essential, intermediary. And we see ourselves in relation to a background – a background of physical environments but also, and more importantly, a background of the ideas and values in which we live and have lived, taken in part from life and in part from literature and the media.

Now while some people behave in a more consistent fashion across situations than others, everyone tends to tailor their behaviour according to whom they are with. If it were not so, social life would be impossible. We present a different persona to family, to friends, to colleagues at work. Thus, although one feels the same 'self' all the time, it is not surprising that people tend to describe themselves somewhat differently according to the situation. It has been put in this way: 'A woman psychologist in the company of a dozen who work at other occupations sees herself as a psychologist; when with a dozen male psychologists, she thinks of herself as a woman' (McGuire and McGuire, 1988: 102). There are also age and sex differences: for instance adolescent boys are more likely to describe themselves in terms of achievement and autonomy, girls in terms of friendship, dating and popularity (Acitelli and Young, 1996).

For the most part people see their behaviour as changing only within limits, and their 'self' as persisting across situations. But some people do see themselves as having a number of selves, for instance a work-self and a home-self, or a good-self and a bad-self. A sense of unity may yet prevail because of resemblances between the selves and the sense of continuity over time. However there are occasions when individuals present a persona which appears to be quite different from their 'normal self', and indeed some cultures recognise a multiplicity of selves, seeing each self as defined by roles which change with the context. Buddha described the self more as a process than as an entity, and early Buddhist scriptures have diverse views of the self, some holding that each individual has several increasingly refined selves (Carrithers, 1983). In extreme cases, where an individual appears to have no sense of his own continuity, he may be labelled as having 'Multiple Personality Disorder', a state in which the person's behaviour appears to involve two or more personality states, each involving its own pattern of thoughts, emotions, and relationships to others, which periodically takes control of his or her behaviour (DSM IV, 1994) (see e.g. Humphrey and Dennett, 1989).

Thus each person must have a store of knowledge not only about the sort of person he (or she) perceives himself to be, but also about how he behaves in different situations. But since one sees oneself slightly differently in different situations, it must contain also knowledge of those other situations in association with the several ways in which one sees oneself. And how one sees oneself is influenced also by comparison with others, and with information from books, myths, and so on, information which must also be stored in, or in association with, that about the self. An individual's religious orientation forms an important element of this complex. We may call the whole the 'self-system'.

Especially important here is the formation of close relationships in which we 'identify' with the partner. This has been described as incorporating the other into the self (Aron and Aron, 1996), a metaphor for describing how the self becomes modified as a consequence of relationship formation. Such a metaphor can also embrace many other facts about close relationships. For instance, errors made in naming other individuals often involve substituting for the name intended the name of someone with a similar relationship to the speaker, as when a father calls one child by the name of another (Fiske *et al.*, 1991). Again, individuals who have a close relationship with each other are more likely to attribute a given event to similar causes than are individuals who are strangers (Aron and Aron, 1996).

One sees one's past and future largely in the form of narratives which are incorporated into the self-system. Though usually based on real experiences, the narratives are reconstructed in an attempt to make sense of events, and do so in a way that imposes 'meaning' on life – such as seeing a purpose in life, or events as steps towards (usually desirable) outcomes. Thus the data indicate that people construct the narratives so that, if possible, they can see their lives as leading towards either tangible goals (e.g. graduation, wealth) or fulfilment (happiness, salvation). Some of the most devastating experiences are those which we cannot fit into a narrative, which elicit the feeling 'I can't make any sense of it'. The narratives also involve criteria that can be used for making moral choices and assessing one's own actions, for perceiving oneself as in control of one's life, and for evaluating one's self-worth (Baumeister and Wilson, 1996). It has been suggested that one's identity rests on the capacity to keep a coherent narrative going (Giddens, 1991).

The self-system can thus be seen as involving also the scripts, scenes, internal working models, narratives and so on; but it is important to emphasise that it is not only a matter of memory. There may also be knowledge of what one might be like, ought to be like, or could be like (Markus and Nurius, 1986). And it is not only knowledge that is stored: there may also be emotion scripts, concerned with the course of emotions in specific situations (Fitness, 1996). The many ways in which we use a concept of self, and the important role that it plays in our lives, strongly suggests that the propensity to hold such a concept is a necessary part of human nature as we understand it, and that it is a product of biological evolution.

A number of different models of the self have been proposed, but in practice they have a great deal in common (Hinde, 1997a). In so far as the self is a concept that we construct to help to make sense of our lives, it makes no difference whether we see the knowledge of values, conventions, situations, relationships and so on as part of the self or as available to the self or as influencing the self. But it is important to note that, in so far as the knowledge structures involve cognitions and affect relating to the self, others, and situations, they must be seen as forming an interdependent system.

Although it changes to some extent with age and situation, the self-system has considerable resistance to modification. In the course of interactions and relationships, individuals may encounter information which runs counter to their views about themselves, and a variety of defence mechanisms may operate (Bretherton *et al.*, 1990). While some have emphasised that people try to maintain a positive image of themselves (Rogers, 1959), others point out that they try to maintain their own self-image (Swann *et al.*, 1992): probably both processes operate. The processes involved are diverse. Backman (1988) has suggested that individuals try to maintain 'congruency' between how they see themselves, how they see themselves behaving, and their perceptions of how others see them. Thus a person who believes himself to be intelligent, sees himself as behaving intelligently, and perceives others to behave to him as if he were intelligent, experiences congruency. If an individual does not experience congruency, he may adjust his actual or his perceived world in a number of ways:

1   By cognitive restructuring. For instance one may misperceive the evidence, or attend selectively to aspects that do confirm the self-concept. One may be especially sensitive to remarks that enhance one's self-esteem, or interpret ambiguous evidence so that it does so.
2   By selective evaluation – for instance altering the importance of items to increase congruency. One may accept the views of those who provide praise, but discredit information that seems to contradict it, regarding those who point to one's weaknesses as unreliable.
3   By selective interaction, choosing to interact with others who provide congruency and avoiding those who do not.

4   By response evocation, presenting oneself in a way that calls for a congruent response. Thus individuals who see themselves as likeable behave in a way that promotes liking, making more confidences, speaking more positively, and disagreeing less.

5   By selective comparison. For instance one may associate with someone of lesser intelligence, thereby confirming one's own.

Such attempts are mostly unconscious, but they may have important influences on behaviour. For instance such mechanisms may enable individuals to deceive themselves that they have behaved more honestly than has been the case, and this may in turn make it easier for them to present to others a more convincing picture of themselves as honest citizens than would be possible if they recognised their own shortcomings.

What, you may ask, is the relevance of all this to the nature of religion? At the very least a strongly held set of beliefs of some sort, associated with precepts about how one should behave and perhaps with special forms of experience, must form part of the way in which one thinks about oneself, part of the self-system. An early 1960s study of individuals' self-concepts in the USA found the 24 per cent of men and 35 per cent of women offered either a denomination or other religious identity as one of twenty separate answers to the question 'Who am I?' Only answers concerning the respondent's occupation and marital status were given more frequently (Mulford and Salisbury, 1964). Another study found the salience of religious references to be greater in self-descriptions in members of minority than in those of majority or conventional religious groups (Kuhn and McPartland, 1954). Thus religion can become part of an individual's social identity: self-perception as a Protestant or Catholic may be more important than the specific beliefs involved (cf. Beit-Hallahmi, 1989), and often endures after the beliefs have been discarded.

Furthermore, religious belief and observance are perhaps especially suitable for integrating the diverse aspects of one's life. They can become part of the self, providing objectives, a role in life, a perspective on relationships with others, a moral code. The religious system provides guidance as to where the individual stands on a whole range of moral and practical issues. Experiences like Saint Paul's on the way to Damascus, or the loss of firmly held beliefs, are devastating just because they involve a radical change in the nature of the self, and that means a reorientation to events in the world. We have seen later that attributions are woven into narratives such that a more or less coherent picture of one's life emerges, and that narrative forms part of the image one has of oneself, that is, of the self system (see also pp. 101–2).

In addition, an important difference between religious systems lies in the extent to which the participant feels himself to be in a personal relationship with the deity. Gods may live in the far away mountains, interfering rarely or not at all in human life, or the believer may 'take God into his heart' and feel part of a close relationship. An impersonal god who merely rewards and punishes will change the believer's perspective on the world, but a relationship with a personal god can change the core of his being.

Finally, since religious beliefs are taken into the self-system, the maintenance of congruency may be a critical issue. If religious beliefs seem to be incompatible with the evidence, the evidence may be misperceived or discredited, or attention may be focused selectively on aspects that are compatible with the evidence. Behaviour which falls below the standards required by the religious code may be seen as unimportant, and attention focused on that which meets it. Believers may choose to associate with those who share their beliefs, thereby receiving confirmation that their beliefs are valid. They may strive to behave in ways that will be seen by others as meeting their religious ideals. As implied above, such strategies are part of human frailty, and by no means limited to those who are religious, but it is important to bear them in mind when considering religious practices.

In brief, a firmly held religious belief system can become integrated with every part of the self-system, and serve to validate its goals and the values elicited in the pursuit of those goals.

## Summary

This chapter has been concerned with three background issues basic for the understanding of religious systems. First, religions are seen as involving a number of interdependent elements, emphasised to different extents in different religions. These are: structural beliefs; narratives; rituals; codes of conduct; religious experience; and social aspects.

Second, this book's primary concern is with the extent to which these components of religious systems, along with other aspects of socio-cultural systems, depend on more basic pan-cultural psychological characteristics. The nature and development of the latter, and the manner in which their interactions lead to the complexity of human culture, are reviewed. That the psychological characteristics in question are or have been adaptive in a biological sense is probable, but definite evidence is usually lacking. What is important for the present argument is not their (perhaps erstwhile) adaptedness, but their universality with (limited) individual variability. This chapter also introduces the question of how cultural practices are transmitted down the generations, and reviews ways in which psychological propensities can give rise to maladaptive behaviour.

Third, the nature of the self-system is discussed. We account for the continuity in our lives by postulating a self, based primarily on our perceptions of how others perceive us, and we use this concept to assess and direct the course of our lives. Incorporated in or closely related to the self is information on relationships with others and the beliefs, values, etc., of the socio-cultural structure. For the firm believer, the religious system becomes part of the self.

# 3 Structural beliefs

## The nature of religious belief

Structural beliefs have played a vital role in the history of Christianity, and at least some role in all other religions. Martyrs have died for their religious beliefs, wars have been fought over cultural beliefs expressed in religious terms. Beliefs also pervade, to a greater or lesser extent, all other aspects of religious systems. It is thus convenient to consider them first, though this does not carry the implication that beliefs are necessarily the most 'important' (in any sense) aspect of all religious systems.

The phrase 'I believe' means different things to different people, and even to one person at different times or in different contexts. This chapter, therefore, discusses the nature of religious belief, its relation to scientific belief, and how it can vary in intensity and quality.

All societies have structural beliefs embracing such issues as the origin of the world and what happens after death, and usually involving supernatural agencies seen in animistic or anthropomorphic form. In many societies, these beliefs are part of, and indistinguishable from, the socio-cultural structure as a whole: the distinction between sacred and secular is much less clear than it is in the West today. Nowadays we tend to distinguish between such *beliefs* and what we *know* about the world but, in societies in which the religious system is pervasive, such a distinction is far less clear-cut.

For many Christians, belief has been primary: 'Believe, and ye shall be saved'. At the present time those churches or denominations which are most successful in recruiting and maintaining numbers are those which demand most from their congregations in the way of belief – in the Catholic case, traditional dogma, in the Protestant case, sometimes the literal truth of the whole Bible. Muslims believe that the Koran is the word of God dictated by the Angel Gabriel to Mohammed, and must therefore be taken literally. But insistence on dogmatic belief is much less characteristic of many other religions. Judaism has less precise dogma – perhaps because the Jews were bound together by a culture and relied on common practices rather than beliefs to maintain their integrity (Steinberg, 1947). And, as we have seen, Buddhism and Hinduism are much less dogmatic and belief plays a more secondary role with emphasis given more to experience and good deeds.

Religious beliefs usually involve beings, entities or experiences that are outside normal experience. They include counter-intuitive claims; complex concepts which are never fully explained or understood and may indeed be the subject of much controversy, such as the Holy Trinity and Holy Spirit of Christianity; and apparent inconsistencies, such as the need to pray to a god who is held to be omniscient anyway. Inevitably, therefore, societies usually contain both believers and sceptics. Furthermore different religious traditions may become merged, or at least exist happily together. In China popular religions, involving festivals, funerals, and often shamans, have existed alongside Confucianism, Buddhism, and Taoism, with no apparent perceived contradiction (Teiser, 1996). While this may seem strange to western eyes habituated to seek for one 'truth', eastern world-views make greater allowance for diversity (Rawson, 1998a).

## What is religious belief?

A critical but extremely difficult question, which must be faced head-on, is what it means to say 'I believe'. Of course belief is not characteristic only of religious issues – it permeates every aspect of our lives. As one meaning for 'belief', *The Shorter Oxford Dictionary* gives 'Mental assent to or acceptance of a proposition, statement, or fact, as true, on the ground of authority or evidence'. This would seem to cover everyday usage, but at the same time it papers over differences of degree in the nature of the 'authority or evidence' between the religious use of 'belief', the everyday use of belief, and scientific belief.

Even science has developed on the basis of belief in hypothetical forces or entities perceivable only through their effects, such as magnetism and gravity. Religious belief is like science, and like much of the knowledge we gain from experience in the world or with other people, in that it involves postulating hidden forces whose source is not immediately apparent. Thus we observe human action, and postulate desires, beliefs, and intentions that motivate and guide the action. Newton postulated forces of attraction between bodies to account for their movements and, until recently, genes were postulated entities known only by their effects (Harris, 1997). Now we see Newton as a founder of modern science, but feel apologetic about his fascination with alchemy, which we see as part of a tradition from which he was not yet wholly weaned. In actuality Newton's alchemical beliefs contributed to his postulating forces of attraction between bodies, though his critics accused him of introducing occult forces under another name (Fara, in preparation).

But in other ways religious beliefs tend to differ, at least in degree, from science and from the knowledge we acquire from our own experience in the world. They rely more on authority, tradition, argument and consensus within a group, reinforced by their relations to basic human propensities and by the subjective experiences they engender (or from which they stem), than does what we see as scientific knowledge. Religious beliefs are not subject to empirical verification: supposedly empirical evidence may be adduced to support the beliefs, but such evidence usually concerns single non-repeatable instances. Of course religious beliefs are not totally peculiar in this respect: our knowledge about many cultural norms, values, and myths derived from societal traditions are acquired in the same way.[1] But discussion within a society about differing views on such issues usually occurs with respect to agreed criteria, be those criteria concerned with authenticity or with the consequences of moral precepts for the society. By contrast, discussion of religious beliefs between a believer and a non-believer can seem superficial to the former and frustrating to the latter, whose self-system is set to receive knowledge of a different kind in a different way. In a manner not easily comprehensible to an outsider, the believer does not need empirical evidence, perhaps because he or she experiences a different sort of verification. He may see his faith as producing a coherent image of the world, and may pity those who lack it. Everyone is prone to hold mutually contradictory beliefs about the various aspects of life, but it is because of this difference in the nature of verification that religious persons seem to find it especially easy to do so.

In this respect discussion between believer and non-believer may resemble interaction between individuals from very different cultures. For instance Lewis (1995), attempting medical treatment among the Gnau of Papua New Guinea, found that his search for clinical signs and symptoms were seen as beside the point. While he was concerned with the *process* and *mechanism* of the disease, they were interested in the *agent* who was responsible for the disease, and his or her *intent* in causing it. While the literal content of many religious beliefs can easily be ridiculed by the sceptical, the subjective reality of those beliefs cannot be denied, although those who hold them may seem not susceptible to rational discussion about them. Religious beliefs may be meaningful to those who hold them, even though they appear to be empirically empty to outsiders. And it can be argued that what matters about religious belief is the difference it makes to the believer's life.

As stated already, the question of the literal truth of religious beliefs will not be pursued here. For one thing, it is old ground which has been gone over too often: in the West, the boundary to where religious explanations apply has been steadily eroded since the Enlightenment. But, more importantly, even where science provides more plausible explanations, the religious person can claim that the literal truth of his beliefs is irrelevant, and that their meaning is metaphorical, or subjective and personal. In the West (and not only in the West) there has been a continuing dynamic between traditionalist believers and modern innovators or sceptics. For that reason many religious persons are reticent about their beliefs, finding discussion threatening, distasteful, or irrelevant. While the sceptic can regard this as a cop-out, the attraction of the beliefs to the believer still needs explanation.

Of much greater interest than their empirical validity is this question of why people hold beliefs that are counter-intuitive and often empirically invalid. This question involves both their causes, that is the manner in which they were acquired, and their consequences for the believer and the society. We shall return to these issues in later chapters. First, it is necessary to pursue a little further the nature of religious belief.

## Varieties of believing

### Material or immaterial deities

Both within and between groups the nature and intensity of religious beliefs show enormous variation. An extreme view is that religion itself does not involve acceptance of a doctrine, but commitment to an inherently absurd position. On this view it is necessary to believe in order to exist, but believing something that is obvious or even plausible is inadequate (Kierkegaard, 1944, cited Gellner, 1992). In psychological terms, this comes near to saying that commitment to the unprovable is a necessary part of the self-system. That could be the case, but is unproven and fails to specify which commitments are and are not valuable.

Moving to something a little more specific, there are some for whom religious belief does not concern a supernatural being but an abstract entity described by a phrase like 'the essence of absolute goodness'. Some physicists, for instance, are struck by the elegance of the laws of nature: forgetting that beauty lies in the eye of the beholder, they see them as embodying an absolute goodness which lies 'out there', in (or beyond) the world. Such a view provides material for modern intellectualist theologians who argue that beauty is goodness, and that God is the essence of supreme and unimaginable goodness. Such a god is seen as non-interventionist in the world in which we live, anthropomorphic images being written off as metaphors.[2] While such views may be satisfying for those who seek a god to believe in but find conventional religious dogma unacceptable, it is far removed from the deity worshipped by most of those who attend Christian churches or participate in most other religious systems.

Of course, portraying a being that is supposed to be all-powerful has always posed a problem: Isaiah wrote 'To whom then will ye liken God? or what likeness will ye compare unto him?' (Chapter 40, v. 18), and St. Anselm saw God as that which nothing greater can be conceived. But even Isaiah was compelled to write of him as though he were a person – 'He shall feed his flock like a shepherd' – and it is that sort of supernatural entity that is envisaged by most Christians and by members of most other religions. It is with the everyday believer that we must be concerned if we are to understand the persistence of religious systems.

### Degrees of believing

A firm believer can be described as incorporating the religious system into the self-system. Such a person may feel God to be always present, inside him or her everywhere. Some even profess to be a 'bride of Christ', implying a relationship comparable with that between human lovers, who have been described as 'including the other in the self' (Aron and Aron, 1996). Such absolute belief is sometimes referred to as 'believing in', as contrasted with 'believing that': the former requires an act of commitment and involves 'faith', while the latter is a matter involving a degree of speculation (Donovan, 1979).

For most people, however, the religious self fades into the background for much of the time, or is taken out for an airing on Saturdays or Sundays. Religion may be worn as a cloak, put on for special occasions or used as a protection when conditions are inclement, but usually kept in a cupboard. During the week it may operate only in certain contexts, for instance when moral issues are at stake. We tend to resist any implication that we are inconsistent, but the fact is that we often are: the believer's religious self may not be to the fore all the time.[3]

In any case, the world cannot be divided into believers and non-believers: belief is not all or none, total commitment or none at all (Lewis, 1987), although it can sometimes seem like that. In an oft-cited study, Thouless (1935) asked students and those attending Workers' Educational Association classes to rate, on a 7-point scale, their certainty about various propositions, some of which were religious. Certainty about the non-religious items showed a wide scatter, but replies to religious ones tended to indicate either absolute certainty or absolute rejection. Thus of the responses to the statement 'Jesus Christ was God the Son', 49 per cent indicated completely certain acceptance and 27 per cent complete rejection, leaving only a quarter of the respondents who had doubts one way or the other. But one must be careful in the interpretation of such data: certainty is a tricky concept, and an individual may be certain at one level of analysis and much less so at another. Over religious issues, self-rated certainty is almost certain to be misleading: because it was supposedly meritorious to believe, those who were nearly certain would be likely to over-estimate their certainty, and unbelievers to emphasise their disbelief in reaction against the convention (Altemeyer, 1988; Hood *et al.*, 1996).

There are several reasons why belief is seldom absolute. First, by the nature of things, belief in the unprovable is unlikely to be absolute: most people must be scattered along the spectrum from belief to scepticism, even though they profess one or the other. While the ardency of the evangelical fundamentalist may stem from joy in conviction, one cannot help wondering if he would need to be so ardent if he were quite sure. Second, as forcibly argued by Goody (1997), many aspects of religious involvement inevitably provoke ambivalence – the internal contradictions in the structural beliefs, the use of material images of immaterial beings, the ambiguity of ritual. And even the churches themselves often seem to be confused about what is appropriate to believe: the Anglican Church still prints the Thirty-nine Articles, agreed by a Convocation in 1562, at the end of the Prayer Book, but few Church members would subscribe to them. Third, even in animals causal factors for more than one type of behaviour are nearly always present, and humans spend much of their lives deciding between, or dithering between, alternative courses of action. The actions required by adherence to a religious system may be incompatible with everyday concerns, and it is therefore tempting for the believer to disregard the system of beliefs for at least some of the time. We shall return to all these issues later.

Thus, 'belief' includes a broad spectrum of meanings. For the fundamentalist, its meaning is absolute, the dogma should be accepted as divinely given and is not to be questioned. Internal contradictions and incompatibility with modern scientific knowledge are seen as irrelevant, for the world of religious truth is not to be confused with the world of logic and scientific truth: it is claimed that different languages are involved.[4] Such a believer takes, consciously or unconsciously, a 'step of faith' such that the contradictions do not matter. While to the non-believer this seems like a tactic to evade issues and avoid the truth, to the believer it does not seem like that at all.

But for many religious people 'believing' is not the same as 'certainty', but merely means 'I will accept it as true' or 'I will act as if it were true'. In secular as well as religious contexts, much early socialisation involves just that – more or less uncritical acceptance of what parents or other authority figures say, and incorporation of it into the self-system without appraisal: social life would be impossible if we never abandoned scepticism. Some mature individuals may accept some aspects of the religious system, including the moral code, but pay only lip-service to the structural beliefs, in which case they may experience conflict between the intellectual and the emotional or moral aspects of the self or, being less analytically minded, are less motivated to examine them. For many, belief is basically emotional, but intellectually supported as part of the process of integration of the self-system. But conflict between religious and secular aspects of the self must be seen as usual, and various devices are used to ameliorate it. Individuals may accept that religious assertions cannot be literally true, but may be true in some other, perhaps allegorical or 'deeper', sense. For instance the Creation story and much of the Old Testament may be taken as conveying the idea that God reveals himself gradually, in a manner suited to the human capacity to understand in successive eras. Religious assertions may be held to require another method of apprehension which is not deductive or inductive, and the difference between the believer and the non-believer lies in the ways they apprehend the same data (Wisdom, 1953). Even church authorities have argued that religious statements, even if not literally true, may have value as expressions of 'spiritual truths' (Report of Church of England's commission on Doctrine, 1938, cited Bambrough, 1969). But in such cases there is a danger that the religious beliefs become vague and unintelligible, with no links to the rest of knowledge.

Others may be selective in their beliefs, accepting some aspects but not others. They may, for instance, accept the doctrine of the Trinity but reject some issues seen as more peripheral, such as the reality of Purgatory or the existence of angels, and explain away Christ's miracles. Yet other Christians will say that they do not *really* believe in the Virgin Birth or the Resurrection of the Body, but profess belief for the sake of others – seeing this as a beneficent gesture to those less clear-headed than themselves, or as a means for maintaining church unity.

But perhaps the majority do not really think about what they mean by 'I believe' at all, though they find the form of words useful. Bambrough (1969) illustrates this by supposing that one is walking along the seashore with Homer on a stormy day. Homer looks at the waves and says 'Poseidon is angry today', and one might well answer in the same terms, 'Certainly, Poseidon is very angry today'. But whereas Homer thought he was explaining the lashing of the waves, for the sea could be seen as the body of Poseidon (Smart, 1996), with modern knowledge one would be merely describing it – though in terms that have some accuracy in that there is something in the lashing of a stormy sea that is correctly described by saying that it is angry. However Bambrough points out that people who use religious terminology in a purely descriptive sense are in no position to regard one system of religious beliefs as more true than another, and so can no longer be said to be believers.

## Belief and the religious system

As indicated in Chapter 2, structural beliefs form but one component of a religious system, a system with complex influences between its several parts. At the individual level, belief does not in itself necessarily presuppose a great deal of knowledge of the details of religious doctrine, or much involvement with the rest of the religious system. People claiming to hold religious beliefs may nevertheless seldom attend religious rituals and be almost ignorant of the basic doctrines of the religious system to which they claim to belong. As we have seen, a survey of individuals describing themselves as Protestants or Catholics in the USA showed that many could not name a single Old Testament prophet (Stark and Glock, 1968). For such people religion may have primarily social or political implications.

Although it is possible for an individual to claim religious belief without further religious involvement, it is less clear how far, at the cultural level, a religious system can hold together without at least some common structural beliefs. While beliefs are less important for some systems than for others, some are always present. And religions have sustained qualities that societies value, most obviously in the moral codes that they purvey. If structural beliefs become less acceptable to individuals, can other desirable qualities of religious systems be retained? This is a question that lies between the lines in nearly every chapter of this book, and is addressed in the final one.

### Religious orientation

Surveys using questionnaires touching on a variety of aspects of religion (e.g. beliefs, church attendance, private prayer, religious values) can yield a measure of 'religiosity' which conveys the strength of an individual's overall orientation to religion. However everyday believers differ markedly not only in the strength but also in the nature of their involvement, and it has sometimes been seen as useful to distinguish two general orientations. Where an individual appears to 'live' his or her religion, the orientation is described as 'intrinsic', whereas religion used primarily to satisfy needs is described as 'extrinsic' (Allport and Ross, 1967). An individual with an extrinsic orientation would be likely to endorse such questionnaire items as 'I go to church because it helps me to make friends' or 'I pray for protection', while one with an intrinsic orientation would favour such items as 'I often feel God's presence', or 'It is important for me to spend time in prayer'. It is suggested that extrinsic religiousness tends to be associated with prejudice, authoritarianism, rigidity, intolerance of ambiguity and authoritarian control, and low self-control and social responsibility, and that extrinsic believers tend to treat religion as merely one of many influences on their lives. By contrast the answers of the intrinsically religious are seen as indicating that they are committed to their beliefs and way of life, and high on internal control. They feel responsible for their actions, having a sense of purpose and being prone to feel guilty. Individuals scoring high on internal religiosity tend to score highly on other measures of religious involvement, such as church attendance. External and internal religiousness have been compared to two stages of moral development described by Kohlberg (1976) – the conventional stage of adherence to values because of authority or convention, and the post-conventional stage when actions are performed because they are good in their own right.

Although this distinction has proved useful in some contexts, it is clearly simplistic, and the two orientations may be more complex than they seem. It has been argued that the intrinsic scale measures merely religious commitment, and the extrinsic is a reflection of more general cognitive or personality characteristics (Batson and Ventis, 1982; Kirkpatrick and Hood 1990). A number of variants and refinements have therefore been proposed. For instance those showing external orientation are sometimes divided into those in which the religion is directed towards personal benefits and those in which the rewards are social. But, more importantly, the apparent good/bad simplicity of the intrinsic/extrinsic distinction may be deceptive. For one thing, it may have different meanings for different denominations

(Strickland and Wedell, 1972). Of greater interest, studies have shown that individuals who score highly on intrinsic orientation tend also to be high on self-deception and on managing the impression that they make on others. An 'experimental' study, involving simulation of the parable of the Good Samaritan with college students, indicated that students on their way to give a talk on the parable were no more likely to give help to a groaning man than others who were in a hurry for another reason. However, among those who did stop, those high on intrinsic religiosity tended to give more help, but in a rigid, partly inappropriate, manner (Darley and Batson, 1973). While a number of studies have shown that intrinsically religious individuals claim to be more helpful than others, and see themselves as altruistic, others show them to be more authoritarian and ethnocentric and less concerned with justice for racial minorities (Batson and Flory, 1990). One sample was not rated by judges as higher on compassion. In their own study of psychology students with religious backgrounds these authors found that self-reported helpfulness was correlated with intrinsic religiousness, but studies using behavioural measures were less supportive of such a correlation, and indicated that any support given was not related to the recipient's needs. Batson therefore suggested that such individuals might give help in order to obtain the personal and social rewards for living up to the high moral standards associated with intrinsic religion, or to avoid guilt from not doing so. In an experimental task it was shown that intrinsic religion was associated with helping behaviour that was motivated by the need to be seen by self and others as helpful.

Thus the motivation associated with intrinsic religiosity may be 'really' extrinsic, though the individuals concerned are not aware of it, the needs that their religion satisfies being below the level of consciousness. Such individuals may believe that they live up to their own standards, but are basically very concerned with appearances (Leak and Fish, 1989; Gorsuch, 1994). These studies undermine Allport's claim that intrinsic religiousness is associated with transcending self-centred needs, but it must be noted that not all the data point in the same direction, and the matter certainly cannot be regarded as closed.

A third dimension of 'quest' is said to involve honestly facing existential questions in all their complexity, while at the same time resisting clear-cut pat answers. An individual scoring high on this dimension would recognise that he or she would never know the final truth, and tend to be low on fundamentalism, indicating a general 'don't discriminate' attitude (McFarland, 1989). High scores tend to be associated with social sensitivity and with helping others in a sensitive way (Batson and Ventis, 1982). The significance of this dimension of quest is controversial, but it is claimed to be unrelated to measures of internal and external orientation, and not to be a matter of mere agnosticism (Batson and Schoenrade, 1991).

In summary, it is clear that much depends not on religiousness *per se*, but on the nature of the religious orientation, some forms of religiousness having negative associations with prosocial behaviour. Given the many problems associated with the collection of such data and especially the differences that may accrue from the nature of the samples chosen for study, generalisations are elusive.

## *Belief and personality*

Everyday believers differ markedly in the nature of their beliefs, and the variation probably has some relation to their psychological characteristics. Considerable research effort has been devoted to establishing links between the psychological characteristics of individuals and the nature and extent of their religious beliefs. Although some of this work is referred to elsewhere in this book (e.g. p. 227), it is not considered in any detail because of the intrinsic difficulty of separating individual, experiential and social issues; differences according to the index of religiosity used; the possible curvilinear nature of the relations between variables; and the critical influence of the nature of the sample chosen for study. Detailed reviews are available (Beit-Hallahmi and Argyle, 1997; Brown, 1987). But, as a broad generalisation, individuals who make coherent responses to questionnaires about religion (irrespective of their content and whether they are for or against it) tend also to display conservativism and authoritarianism (Brown, 1987).

Three issues, arising from the preceding discussion, must now be underlined.

## *Belief and the self-system*

First, the acquisition of deeply-held beliefs may involve a major change in the self-system, with widespread repercussions. This, of course, is true of all beliefs, but perhaps especially so of religious ones: for a firm believer, faith may change his whole outlook on life. Incorporation of religion into the self-system can provide a more coherent world outlook, reconciling contradictions (for instance between what is comforting and what is rationally perceived); provide clear guidelines between what is good and what is evil; and give a sense of belonging to a community (see Chapters 5 and 16–17). Conversion to a new faith, or loss of an old one, may involve a major change in the personality. There is, inevitably, great resistance to change, and elements of the old faith may be retained. Thus in recent years most of the inhabitants of Tikopia have converted to Christianity, perhaps in part because this was the religion of white men whose command of resources and political power was attractive. Although the change appeared to be sincere, the old gods were still regarded as existing in their spirit abodes, to which they had been despatched with placatory words explaining why they could not be asked to return (Firth, 1996).

We have seen that, for many individuals for whom belief is not absolutely central, the religious self may become prominent in some contexts but is subdued or concealed in others. Nevertheless, even in such lukewarm believers the belief system may have an unconscious influence on everyday life. This can be illustrated by a study in which between 52 and 120 students (with the sexes balanced) in each of twenty-five countries were given a list of three hundred adjectives and asked to indicate whether each adjective was more applicable to men or to women. The adjectives were also rated for favourability, activity, and strength. The relevance of this study lies in some differences that emerged between countries according to their predominant religious faith. Comparing seven predominantly Catholic countries (Bolivia, Brazil, France, Ireland, Italy, Peru, and Venezuela) with seven predominantly Protestant ones (Australia, England, Finland, New Zealand, Norway, Scotland, and the USA), the authors found that men and women were seen as more similar in Catholic countries than in Protestant ones, and that the extent to which the female stereotype was more favourable and less weak was greater in the Catholic ones. They ascribed this to the roles of the Virgin Mary and of female saints in Catholic Christianity. A similar comparison between India (predominantly Hindu, with a pantheon containing goddesses as well as gods) and Pakistan (Muslim, with the significant religious figures all male) indicated that the sexes were seen as more similar in India than in Pakistan. Furthermore, while in Pakistan the male stereotype was more favourable than the female, in India the reverse was the case. Although some data from an Indian group living in the officially Protestant South Africa were anomalous, the data indicate that the presence of female figures in the religious pantheon is related to a more favourable stereotype of women in everyday life (Williams and Best, 1982).

As another example of the unconscious influence of religious orientation, consider the following. In the south of the USA people who hunt are more likely to be Protestants than not. That may be the reason why Protestants are more likely to own firearms. But while the proportion of hunters who own guns is similar between Protestants and non-Protestants, among those who do not hunt, Protestants are the more likely to have guns. Among these non-hunters, ownership is related to a complex of influences including the American frontier spirit, being reared in a rural area, and Fundamentalism. Thus here religion is part of a system of mutually supportive orientations which is associated with gun ownership (Young, 1989). (The relation between Protestantism and masculinity will be noted later.)[5]

It is perhaps important here to emphasise again the ubiquity of individual differences. Some individuals adhere to the culturally accepted religious beliefs, others do not. Among those who do, some are conscious of their influence on every aspect of their lives, while for others the influence is less and often unconscious. And even those who do not profess adherence to the religious system accepted by others in their society may nevertheless be influenced by it.

## Emotional aspects of belief

The second issue to be emphasised is that the common implication that religious belief is solely a cognitive, intellectual issue is, in fact, far from the case. The very existence of diversity in 'believing' indicates that, except perhaps in societies where the religious system and the social system are very closely linked or indistinguishable, believing is not simply imposed by the culture but involves personal adjustment, a change in the self-system to which some are more amenable than others. Furthermore, as we have seen, religious faith does not depend on rational arguments: conviction comes in other forms. Related to this, religious belief may have a strong emotional component – the believer feels a need to believe, a dependence on believing. Belief may involve a feeling of relationship with the deity. Finally, religious belief usually involves some commitment to action: religious belief that had as little to do with everyday life as doing crossword puzzles would hardly count as such.

## Interpretations of belief systems

The third issue to be mentioned here is that the structural beliefs, and the religious narratives or myths that go with them, have been interpreted in a variety of ways. This issue will come up again later, but it is important to note it here. Some interpretations focus on the motivation for believing. Thus religious belief can be seen as pseudo-science, answering questions about the world, or conveying a view of tribal or family history. Some see religions as related to emotional rather than intellectual issues (in so far as that is a useful distinction), countering the fear of death or providing security that suffering will be alleviated. Other interpretations focus on their social consequences – for instance their role in integrating society and supporting social life. Yet others see them as having a hidden structure which, though not necessarily perceived consciously by the members of the society, provides them with means for classifying and thereby understanding both social relationships and relations in the natural world. The latter approach implies that, when reciting a myth, the individual is really speaking about something of which he is entirely unaware. This seems improbable, and convincing evidence in favour of this hypothesis is not obviously to hand. In this book I shall take the view that on the whole people mean what they say in speaking of religious matters, unless they are consciously using a language which has emotional or metaphorical meaning to them without necessarily accepting its literal content. This, of course, in no way denies that what people say may contain much more information than they intend.

## Summary

Belief, used in a religious sense, often seems to mean something differing at least in degree from its everyday sense, and from what belief means to a scientist: in attempting to understand religious systems one must be aware of that difference, whatever one's views of what is correct.

Religious belief varies greatly in the nature of the object or entity believed in. It may be 'absolute', partial, or intermittent, partially or wholly integrated with the rest of the self-system.

Independently of the strength, the psychological bases of belief are diverse: intrinsic, extrinsic, and quest orientations have been recognised, though the precise status of these categories is controversial.

The nature of belief may differ with the personality of the believer, and in its relation with other aspects of the religious system. Religious beliefs are likely to have widespread repercussions on attitudes and other aspects of the self-system. Belief must not be thought of as a purely cognitive or intellectual matter, for it may have a strong emotional component.

# 4 Structural beliefs

## Dynamics, codification, and relation to the social system

In the last chapter we saw that the nature of religious belief differs greatly between individuals: this one discusses the dynamic nature of religious beliefs and religious systems, and some dimensions of difference between them. Any one religion is liable to change over time, and religions differ in the extent to which they are codified, according to whether they depend on revelation, and in the extent to which they are specific to a particular social group. Furthermore, the relations between religious and social systems has given rise to much controversy. Discussion of differences between the deities that are the objects of belief is postponed to Chapter 6.

### Historical changes

Religious beliefs tend to change with time: within Christianity neither the potency nor the nature of belief has remained constant. In Europe in the Middle Ages many people took the Bible literally: some mediaeval priests even felt obligated to eat the vomit of a dying man who had just received the Sacrament, on the grounds that it had actually been transformed into the body of Christ (Rubin, 1991): now the bread and the wine are more usually seen as symbolic (see p. 125). According to Febvre (1982), in sixteenth-century France all private and public life was permeated by Christianity, and there was no question of choosing to be a Christian or not. *Rites de passage*, food prohibitions, the healing of diseases, even the granting of academic degrees, were orchestrated by religion. The words 'rationalism' and 'determinism' were simply not yet in use, and 'scepticism', if used, referred to the unreliability of evidence from the senses. The 'witch-crazes' of the sixteenth and seventeenth centuries were an integral part of the whole cosmology of the time. Tambiah (1990: 89–90) writes 'Unless there occurred a social transformation, the social basis of the belief would remain, and unless there was a critical change in the whole cosmology, the beliefs would continue'. Only at the end of the seventeenth century, with the advent of modern rationalism, was biblical fundamentalism put on the defensive, and even then only among the educated. The symbolic, poetic aspects of religion remained powerful at the popular level through into the eighteenth century, and indeed still do (Thompson, 1978). But with the Enlightenment the cognitive, intellectual, doctrinal and dogmatic aspects of Christianity came to predominate, and the Protestant rationalism which saw religion primarily as a series of beliefs was passed on to the twentieth century by the Victorians (Tambiah, 1990).

However, the veracity of many of the beliefs came to be challenged yet further both by developments in biological science and also by some more rational Christians.[1] As the tenets of the Christian church became more distant from modern thought, and with the concomitant social changes, two apparently discrepant modes of adaptation have been pursued (Firth, 1996). One involves emphasis on the human aspects of religion, stressing its importance for social justice and the development of individual personality, with more liberal attitudes to divorce, birth control, and so on. The other involves stressing the other-worldly character of religion, with stress on Christian teaching as revelation and on the transcendence of God.

## The dynamic nature of religious systems

Such changes over time suggest that no religion is static. At any one time the current religious system may promote conservative acceptance, but there will always be differences between individuals in their adherence and interpretation. It is in the very nature of a religious system, and especially of one in which faith is seen to be crucial, that individuals should insist that their view is the right one. Those whose beliefs or practices diverge are likely to endeavour to convert the views of others to their own, in part because they can obtain validation of their otherwise unverifiable beliefs only by perceiving others to agree (see p. 200). The resulting dynamic may be augmented by pressures from religious and/or political leaders who wish to promote the *status quo*, and from dedicated or charismatic individuals motivated by considerations of social justice or personal ambition to change it. Pressures for change may be especially potent if they challenge the structural beliefs of the system, as we have seen the growth of science challenged many of the previous fundamentals of Christian belief, relegating concepts like that of a Heaven above the clouds and a Hell populated by devils to the sidelines. In the longer term the process set in train is perhaps best seen as one in which fairly concrete beliefs, held with minimal ambivalence, came to be perceived more and more as metaphors, until finally they were discarded even by many of the religious members of society. But such processes are always two-way. Religious beliefs colour the views that people have of the world, and world views affect religious beliefs: the process is dialectical, with new views and new 'truths' constantly in the process of creation – though the rate of change varies with time, and was, of course, accelerated by the Enlightenment.

A similar dynamic is operating in the Muslim world, though its bases are somewhat different from those in Christendom. Reformers are convinced that western influences have diluted and polluted Islamic ideals, to which they attempt to return. Confronted by the real world, some have been content with adherence to ritual and statements of belief, permitting a degree of compromise, while others have had recourse to violence and oppression to achieve their goals (Firth, 1996).

Thus there must always be a continuing dynamic resulting from individual differences in interpretation of the existing system, the influence of the prevailing system on individuals, other aspects of the socio-cultural structure, conservative pressures and pressures for change.

## Some differences between the structures of the world religions

We may note here some characteristics of and differences between the main world religions that are relevant to the questions posed in this book. First, there are a number of potential differences in the nature of belief between literate cultures with codified religious systems and non-literate cultures where they are transmitted orally. Non-literate peoples can keep folk-tales and legends distinct from, but in harmony with, the doctrinal aspects of the religious tradition through adjustments in the reciter's tones and attitudes to his audience. But once they are written down they can be read in private by the literate, and the need to distinguish between what is and what is not 'true' becomes more acute (Goody, 1968; Smart, 1996). This is not to imply that non-literate peoples are less concerned about the truth-values of statements that are made, indeed the opposite may be the case. But where the distinction between folk-tale and dogma is conveyed ephemerally by tone of voice there is less basis for questioning than if both folk-tale and dogma are similarly carved in stone – or typescript.

Codification may lead to an emphasis on the physical representation itself. In Islam the Koran in Arabic is regarded as divinely revealed in form as well as in content, and translations are seen as lacking its essential essence. Christians see the Bible as 'Holy', and the book itself may be treated with reverence, even though many now do not think of it as the word of God in the way Muslims think of the Koran.

A further consequence of codification is that it leaves open the door for the dynamic between conservative and progressive forces to lead to schism. The Church of England's Articles of Religion, drawn up in 1592 'for the avoiding of Diversities of Opinions', include (as Article XVIII) 'They also are to be had accursed that presume to say, that every man shall be saved by the Law or Sect which he professeth…', but they may have exacerbated that which they sought to constrain. In practice the Christian Churches have oscillated between intolerance of discordant viewpoints, as when heresy was punishable by burning at the stake, and the current ecumenicalism with its attempts to reconcile the several branches of Christendom. Within the major divisions of the Christian church, the supposed descent of authority from the apostle Peter to the current Pope has constrained divisiveness within the Catholic branch, but Protestantism has been characterised by sectarianism. Practically every sizeable town in the USA has half a dozen or more different and to a large extent rival churches.

Yet another difference between codified and non-codified systems lies in the interpretation of counter-intuitive events. In the former, an unusual happening, if genuine, must be interpreted either in rational or 'scientific' terms or in terms of the codified religious system. If we see a man levitating in the street, we can appeal to one of two experts – the scientist or the priest. In an oral society there is more flexibility, and interpretation may be initially a matter of speculation. Thus Boyer (1995) suggests that an event or situation, such as an individual having a fit, may initially be merely conjecturally identified as an instance of a particular category (e.g. spirit possession). Further conjectures are then made about a supposed cause (e.g. a spell cast by someone in the next village). There may be an unspoken presumption that the cause–event relation would be valid only under certain circumstances, but these may also be unspecified. In such a case the relation takes the form of an hypothesis rather than a belief, though it may become hardened into a belief by discussion, or by further circumstances.

A second dimension of difference is that between revealed and non-revealed religions. The main world religions, unlike most folk religions and religions of non-literate cultures, trace their sources to originators who claimed new insights, revelations, or special relationships with the deity. This is clearly the case for Christianity, Islam, and Buddhism, but is also the case for Judaism. Buddhism, Hinduism and Taoism have all had a succession of visionaries and teachers. But in all these cases the religious system was initially propagated in opposition to, or was grafted onto, an existing religious system, either a non-codified local religion (or religions) or an existing revealed religion, taking over some of the previous ways of thinking. That similar amalgams form even in the modern world is shown, for instance, by the manner in which Catholicism has become grafted onto local religions in parts of South America. Revelation tends to be associated with insistence on a single religious system, transmitted texts, and a hierarchy of religious specialists. Buddhism and Hinduism are again intermediate, permitting a greater flexibility of belief. By contrast, the majority of the world's religions do not depend on a supposed revelation, but on traditional beliefs and practices diffused down the generations, often from 'the ancestors'. Such religions are specific to a relatively small group of people, and perhaps appropriate to their local situation. As a crude generalisation, they may be as or more rigid in their practices as compared with revealed religions, but less so in their beliefs.

This distinction roughly corresponds with that between codified and non-codified religious systems, for all the major world religions are codified and non-revealed religions have been held largely in non-literate societies, where the religious system is transmitted orally. The latter, not unexpectedly, are more prone to depend on narratives of events rather than abstract principles.

A third and very important issue, mentioned briefly already, is the extent to which the religious system is seen as specific to the social group. In small-scale, non-literate societies the supernatural entities are seen as belonging to the group, their 'own' gods, so that believing is part of group membership. Adherents to the major world religions, whose spread has been facilitated by that of literacy, tend to believe that their truths are universally applicable, and thus not intrinsic to any particular group or society. With the exception, perhaps, of Hinduism and present-day Judaism, they can therefore be seen as 'missionary religions'.

## The religious and social systems

The relation between the structure of the religious beliefs and that of the social system has given rise to much discussion. In the first place, the several aspects of a religious system must be to some extent compatible with each other: for instance some coherence between beliefs and moral precepts is necessary. Thus the Buddhist prohibition on killing humans and other creatures is in harmony with the doctrine of re-birth and with the goal of achieving serenity; their ban on drugs goes with the ideal of mindfulness as part of the training involved in the Path; and Buddhist compassion is linked with appreciation of the ubiquity of suffering, and the latter with the attainment of peace and liberation and the tolerance of a very wide range of beliefs (or their absence).

Beyond that, while in some western societies the relations between religious and social systems are much attenuated, in many non-literate societies the religious system is integrated with the rest of the socio-cultural structure, with its conceptual ideas unified into an all-embracing cosmology. Thus ancestor cults, as practised for instance in pre-industrial China, can be seen as a continuation of the proper respect shown by children to parents, and the family is seen as involving many generations, past, present, and future (Teiser, 1996). In an hierarchical society, supernatural entities are likely also to be seen as arranged in a hierarchical manner. In theory, for Islamic fundamentalists there is no distinction between divine law, natural law and human law (Firth, 1996). By contrast, people in western societies are seen as operating in many different fields of symbolic action (Douglas, 1970a). But even where the relation of principal religious belief and ritual to the political and social structure has been close, spirit medium cults for contacting the gods or the dead could exist alongside the official system, as in China (Lopez, 1996; Rawson, 1995) and Tikopia (Firth, 1996).

Some have claimed that the religious system may support the social order by expressing that order in symbolic form (Morris, 1987). Thus Durkheim (1964) argued that the world was divisible into the sacred and the profane. The sacred referred to things 'set apart', whether holy or unclean, and was associated with religion, while the profane was associated with society, the society perhaps being represented by a totem or other symbol. In totemic societies, on this view, the totem is a symbol of both god and the society. Individuals do not necessarily understand the symbolism, nor may they fully realise the nature of the society, but (it is suggested) their respect for or worship of the totem can be seen as society worshipping itself. In practice the distinction is far from clear, sacred and profane being better seen as opposite ends of a continuum, or as representing different aspects of particular actions (Leach, 1954).[2]

While a shared religious system, and perhaps especially shared religious ritual (see pp. 201–4), is likely to favour the cohesiveness of a group, how far the nature of the religious beliefs is related to, affects, or is affected by, the social structure is controversial. The fact that in many non-literate societies the religious and social systems are difficult to distinguish is not the same as saying that the religious beliefs (or rituals) symbolise or reinforce the social structure. Even where it is possible to draw parallels between social structure, or an aspect of an idealised social structure, and religious practice, causal connections between the two are likely to be complex and difficult to substantiate. That there should be parallels in many societies is hardly surprising, and can be seen as a consequence of a tendency to align different areas of experience, or to avoid dissonance. But where parallels can be drawn, they are likely to result from bidirectional causality, the social structure influencing the religious system and vice versa. Any causal relations are likely to be mediated by the behaviour of individuals, and must be seen in the context of the dialectical relations between the several levels of social complexity and the socio-cultural structure, as discussed in Chapter 2.

In any case, in modern societies the suggestion that religion has such a role seems unnecessary or inappropriate. Most societies are bound by cohesive forces other than religious ones, and many modern societies embrace diverse religions. While the religious beliefs of individuals may affirm the social structure – for instance by making a sub-group feel that it is rightly privileged, or that it is a virtue to accept that state of life unto which one is called – such effects are usually best seen both as consequences of the religious orientation of individuals, and as (perhaps unconscious) causes of their behaviour.

## Summary

Religious systems must be seen as in a dynamic flux, with believers and sceptics, adherents to the traditional order and innovators, rulers and ruled, asserting their disparate points of view. This is not to deny that many religions remain in a more or less stable state for long periods, but the stability is dynamic, the constancy maintained by those in whose interests it is to do so.

Three dimensions along which religions differ have consequences for their nature – the role of codification, revealed versus non-revealed religions, and the extent to which the religious system is seen as specific to a particular group or society.

There has been much discussion about the relation between religious and social systems within societies. In pre-literate societies the two are usually closely integrated. In all societies the causal relations between the religious and social systems are likely to be two-way.

# 5 Structural beliefs

## Why do individuals hold religious beliefs?

The issue of why individuals adopt religious beliefs or a religious way of life must be taken in three stages – why religious beliefs are acceptable or satisfying to individuals, the nature of those beliefs and how this contributes to their appeal, and the processes by which individuals come to acquire them. This chapter focuses on the first of these questions, suggesting that religious beliefs are associated with a number of basic human propensities. Discussion of the other two issues is postponed to the following chapters.

## Belief and basic human propensities

Many have seen religion as a source of comfort. Marx (1847) described religion as 'the sign of the oppressed nature', and Weber (1965) argued that the need for salvation is an expression of distress, so that religions involving redemption appeal most strongly to the under-privileged. Nietzsche (1968) saw Christianity as a sickness, an expression of envy by the poorly endowed who invented an ideology glorifying weakness and intellectual poverty. Others have seen it as a way of coming to terms with death (e.g. Malinowski, 1954). Yet others have stressed that religious belief systems interpret the world and give meaning to the experiences of life (Geertz, 1975). Thus one thing seems certain: the rewards that people may obtain from their religious beliefs are diverse, and it is folly to seek a single explanation for religious involvement. Systematic proof that any issue is an important causal factor for religious belief would be difficult if not impossible to obtain, but this chapter reviews evidence strongly suggesting that religious beliefs are associated with a number of basic human propensities that are of biological importance in other contexts.

### Attribution

We all seek to understand what is going on around us, and 'understanding' in this context implies attributing events to causes: it is reasonable to suppose that such attempts at explanation aided survival in the environments in which humans evolved. In our everyday life we use principles which we already possess to make attributions: thus if we see a tree fall over we attribute the event to an exceptionally strong wind or to rot in the trunk. If we are explaining the behaviour of another person, we may invoke an internal state ('He is running away because he is frightened'); and if two people are involved we may make double use of a 'theory of mind' ('He is running away because he knows that X intends to get him'). But if the event is inexplicable, we may invent an agent to account for it ('She won the lottery because luck was on her side'). From there it is only a short step to ascribing organic or human properties to the agent ('She won the lottery because Lady Luck was on her side'), and from there only another to ascribing states of mind to the agent ('She won the lottery because the gods were pleased with her').

Far from involving weighty causal analysis, the attributions we make in everyday life are often immediate and automatic, the very act of perceiving involving both attribution and understanding. However they are likely to be influenced by past experience and cultural conventions stored in the individual's memory, by self-interest, and by emotional responses triggered by the event (Forgas, 1996). For example, there is evidence that the sort of attributions made differ between 'individualist' (e.g. western) and 'collectivist' (e.g. Chinese) societies. When American and Chinese attributions were compared, the former tended to attribute behaviour to internal, personal dispositions, while the Chinese showed a bias towards external, situational factors (Morris and Peng 1994; Morris *et al.*, 1995). This is perhaps related to the way in which the self is organised about relationships: westerners tend to see themselves more as a bundle of internal traits and abilities, while many non-westerners have a stronger sense of relationships and tend to see the self-in-relation-to-other (Markus and Kitayama, 1991).[1]

Everyday attributions often involve more than simply postulating cause for effect. In seeking to understand an event, one may be concerned also with discerning its meaning for oneself or others, or with maintaining one's own self-image and self-esteem (Rusbult *et al*, 1996). Attributions may involve the elaboration of complex causal accounts involving not only the immediate cause(s), but a ramifying series of causes of those causes, facilitating events, and so on, taking a narrative form which, when appropriate, is likely to be linked to the self-system (e.g. Howe, 1987). Under certain conditions, attribution leads to the construction of 'alternative realities' which 'violate the intuitive constraints of our ordinary understanding' (Johnson, 1997: 1025). Such models may serve a variety of purposes in addition to accounting for events: they may be aesthetic, they may carry a moral (as in some science fiction), they may be just fun. In making attributions, the conditions that seem most conducive to the construction of 'alternative realities' involve a lack of information, uncertainty and an inability to explain phenomena, coupled with a feeling of lack of control (Woolley, 1997).

The nature of the attribution or of the 'alternative reality' may depend on the initial orientation of the individual involved. In a study of psychology students in the USA, religious attributions were more common when the individual was a conservative Christian. Not unexpectedly, attributions to God were more common when the event to be explained was positive and when it was of life-altering importance, and the somewhat rare attributions to Satan occurred when the outcome was negative (Lupfer *et al.*, 1996).

The tendency to attribute inexplicable events to pseudo-human causes is common in everyday life: references to 'Lady Luck' are still frequent. Such references are made even in the absence of belief in the entity to which reference is made. As an example, Royal Air Force air crews in World War II were prone to ascribe aircraft malfunction (and even their own errors) to 'gremlins', mischievous sprites who took a delight in causing problems. (Good gremlins were more rare, but sometimes took the place of Lady Luck.) A considerable mythology about gremlins grew up although, of course, they were not really believed in. By providing causes for events, gremlins appear to have fulfilled several functions. First, they provided a route for making a half-joke about issues that could spell disaster. There may be a relation here to the cross-cultural finding that the presence of capricious gods in the pantheon is associated with an element of fear in the human–god relationship (Lambert, 1992). Second, they were a means for deflecting blame from aircrew or maintenance staff when things went wrong. This had the additional advantage that a repair could be requested without a suggestion that the malfunction should not have occurred in the first place, and thus without impairing the aircrew–maintenance staff relationship ('There is a gremlin making the artificial horizon go haywire: please see if you can get it out'). And third, as a common point of reference they promoted solidarity among those involved. Such an example suggests that it is not surprising that postulated deities can be used as explanations for events in the everyday world even though belief in them is not wholehearted. Two processes must be involved: first the postulation of a (usually animate, see Chapter 6) cause for the event, and then the ascription of properties to the causal agent – gremlin, spirit, deity, or what have you – on the basis of tradition or authority.

Deities which could be seen as causing events that one could not understand would have considerable appeal (see also Hood *et al.*, 1996). Even a god who was merely responsible for natural phenomena which one could not otherwise understand, like volcanoes and rainbows, would satisfy a basic need, providing an illusion that one understood the world. In so far as the causes of noxious events are attributed to gods, those gods may come to be feared, yet they can still relieve the impression that the world is unpredictable, and still offer the possibility that things will improve if the gods are placated. In practice, attributions are often made both to a god and to a naturalistic cause, as if they were two aspects of one process, or at any rate not incompatible with each other. As we have seen (p. 245), the Trobrianders performed religious practices alongside, rather than instead of, their agricultural practices; and a gremlin in the airspeed indicator was no bar to reporting the matter to the instrument maintenance staff.

There is no suggestion here that a religious system will necessarily ascribe all inexplicable events to one source. Rather in many societies religious entities may be postulated *ad hoc*, and linked together only loosely, often with contradictions.

In any case, there are considerable cultural differences not only in the explanations given for natural events, but in the events that are seen to need explaining. For instance, explanations for the origin of the world have considerable importance for Christians, but always face the problem of who created the Creator, for how can the created represent the Creator? (Goody, 1997). Eastern religions appear to have been less interested in this issue than western ones perhaps because, if existence is seen as cyclical and involving a series of stages endlessly repeated, the problem of the origin becomes less important. For many Hindus the world has been seen not as created once and for all, but as continually re-creating itself and dissolving back into its unformed condition (Zaehner, 1962). In China Taoist beliefs indicated that the meaningful past was the period preceding the legendary sages, and postulated that an original whole, having infinite possibilities, was progressively subdivided into parts of lesser potential (Teiser, 1996).

### Control, self-efficacy

Of course, with the growth of scientific understanding we no longer need to find causal explanations for most natural phenomena, and for many people the need to postulate supernatural forces has been pushed back to events preceding the Big Bang. But while understanding the causes of events is an important contributor to the individual's peace of mind, it only takes one part of the way: the need to understand is closely related to a second issue, namely the need to feel in control of the events that influence one's life. Both an individual's well-being and the success achieved depend on confidence that he or she is able to cope with the world. The importance of 'self-efficacy', that is of belief in one's ability to organise and execute the actions necessary to reach one's goals, has been documented by Bandura (1997), who cites numerous experiments showing that perceived self-efficacy contributes independently to both motivation and performance on a wide variety of tasks. Feelings of lack of competence, of an inability to cope, may result from real needs or deprivations, or from perceptions of one's own position relative to that of others. Individuals who do not feel in control lack a sense of autonomy, and may show the symptoms of 'learned helplessness', such as apathy (Seligman, 1975), or be especially susceptible to cardiac and other diseases (Wilkinson, 1996). Or they may display a susceptibility to magical thinking – a point well illustrated both by the persistence of fortune tellers and astrologers, and by the extraordinary rationalisations of those who attend them. The need to feel in control contributes to some forms of superstitious behaviour: nearly half the adults surveyed in the USA were prone to take such actions as touching wood, avoiding walking under ladders, crossing fingers, and so on (Woolley, 1997), practices perhaps originally based in the belief that doing these things somehow holds dark forces at bay, though now assimilated almost as a cultural norm.

Thus while a deity who could be seen as causing events that you could not understand would have a certain appeal, one who could help you to achieve your goals would have very much more. In Humphrey's (1995: 17) words, 'The art of religions and quasi-religions...has been to offer a way of looking at the world in which explanation and assurance are part of a single integrated package'. In many religions, including Christianity, power to intervene in the world is ascribed not only to the principal supernatural beings, but also to figures of intermediate status, godlings, saints, and the like. The Christian saints have been supposed to act as intermediaries with the higher powers in order to ensure the fertility of humans or animals; to provide protection against diverse forms of adversity including sickness, pests, storms, and enemies; to ward off devils; and a wide variety of other matters (Wilson, 1983b).

Deities who control events could help also in related ways: they might point the way for decisions between alternative courses of action, know whether the time was auspicious for particular undertakings, and so on. Deities have in fact been used to reduce uncertainty in many different ways: an appeal can be made to oracle bones, or a messenger sent to Delphi (see Chapters 11 and 17). And if one has to accept inevitable unpleasantness, it may give some relief to know that it was inevitable, decreed from above, or by 'fate'.

However, not all supernatural beings are seen as willing or able to intervene in the world. The Jewish Jahweh created the world but remained at a distance from it: he demanded certain standards of behaviour and might inflict punishment if they were not observed, but for the most part could not be prevailed upon to interfere helpfully in human affairs (Steinberg, 1947). The highest god in the Yoruba religious tradition apparently never did anything in the world of ordinary affairs. He gave instructions for the creation of human beings, delegated powers to other deities, could be praised, but suffered no ritual approach (Lawson and McCauley, 1990). The Kikuyu god Ngai was similarly little interested in ordinary life, and could be approached only by family units, not by individuals (Firth, 1996). Many Buddhists believe that they have no direct access to Buddha, but that his influence can be felt through his teaching, his physical remains and shrines. Presumably such religious beings have had an appeal other than the provision of a sense of understanding or controlling current events, or else delegate immediately causal functions to lesser deities.

Furthermore, not all supernatural beings are seen as helpful. We need to understand adverse events, as well as needing help to overcome or avoid them: hence the postulation of devils, witches, and evil spirits – and, as noted before, gremlins. Many religions include a belief in evil spirits, which perhaps provide an explanation of inauspicious events. Once part of the culture, they provide an opportunity for others to rise in status as specialists in nullifying their effects. 'Spellbinding', a Chinese account of how to deal with demons written in about 217 BCE, lists appropriate procedures. Some of these imply that the demons were seen as real entities who could be shot with an arrow, struck, or frightened (Harper, 1996). Zoroastrians recognise two beings, a force for light and goodness and another for darkness and evil, eternally opposed to each other. The casting out of devils is still sometimes practised in Christian countries, though priests seem to regard it as catering to the superstitions of the unsophisticated: in the past it has been seen both as the province of the clergy and of necromancers and conjurors (Christian, 1981).

*Adversity*

Closely related to the need to feel a sense of control, individuals need a means to cope with persecution, suffering and illness. Religion can help in such situations in several ways. It can assist the sufferer to accept the situation as inevitable, as God's will, and thus release him from the pain of kicking against the pricks. Alternatively, it can remove the devastating feeling that there is nothing that one can do, for at least one can pray and transfer the responsibility elsewhere. It can even suggest that there is a merit in suffering, or that it is God's will that one should accept one's station in life: such a panacea would perhaps have been especially acceptable in periods of persecution such as that to which the early Christians were exposed. It might also be fostered by high status individuals in order to maintain harmony in society. Or religious belief can provide hope for deliverance or for better times in this world or for a better world to come: where control seems beyond the bounds of possibility, relief may be found by belief in succour from 'the everlasting arms' of an ultimately benevolent deity. And religion offers a way of justifying one's own way of coping with adversity, by seeing it as acceptable to, or guided by, a higher power. In harmony with these possibilities is the fact that lack of power, illness or adversity may increase religious belief.

Pargament (1997) points out that coping with adversity is an active process: people do not merely cope *with* stressful events, they cope *in order to* obtain significance. To this they bring their own resources, and religion often offers a more compelling route to significance than non-religious alternatives. In Pargament's view, religion's effectiveness comes from the fact that it is not merely a form of tension-reduction or denial, but can affect the significance that is sought, and how events are constructed: religion itself may be affected by the coping process. And it is not merely religious belief that is involved:

Through ritual, the individual may be encouraged to 'let go' of old objects of significance. Through prayer, the disorientation that accompanies threat and loss may be replaced with new purpose. Through relationships with others in the religious community or through mystical experience, new visions may be generated in the place of shattered dreams. Through religious models and methods, anger and resentment may give way to peace and goodwill.

(1997: 270)

*Mortality*

Yet another major source for the attractiveness of deities lies in the desire for life after death. All organisms are adapted to strive for survival as necessary for reproduction. While intrinsically religious and committed individuals may claim a positive attitude to death (Spilka *et al.*, 1977), and most people profess to accept the prospect of death, indirect methods (for instance reaction time studies showing that responses to death words are delayed compared with responses to neutral ones) indicate that unconscious fear is widespread (Beit-Hallahmi and Argyle, 1997; Hood *et al.*, 1996). Even for a believer there may be uncertainty either about the fact of survival or about the nature of future existence, and uncertainty is likely to breed fear. Belief in a benevolent deity and a happy after-life can allay such preoccupations.

Loss of a loved one also brings intense psychological disturbance and a need to reconstruct the self-system. In the short term, and of special significance in the current context, are efforts to maintain the relationship. These may take the form of seeking out places of special significance, using objects of concrete or symbolic significance to the deceased, seeking out clothes, perfumes, and so on, looking at photographs of the deceased, talking or having an inner dialogue with the deceased, and having the illusion that he or she is present (Parkes and Weiss, 1983). Belief that there will be a reunion can greatly ameliorate such anxieties.

Just under 80 per cent of Americans believe in an after-life, and most believe that it will be happy and peaceful: between 50 and 70 per cent believe in Hell (Hood *et al.*, 1996). Evidence for an association between religion and preoccupation with death comes from North American survey data showing that religiosity increases from the age of sixty. Some, but not all, studies indicate that old people are more likely to be religious and to believe in an after-life than younger ones: while this could be in part a generational effect, older individuals being more likely to have been brought up religiously, it has also been found not only that fear of death tends to be less in more religious individuals, but also that old people who are religious are happier and better adjusted than those who are not (Brown, 1987). Furthermore, soldiers in combat report that they have been helped by prayer (Stouffer *et al.*, 1949), and belief in God is often augmented by war experience: spiritualism flourished during and after

World War I (Winter, 1995), and again in World War II. People who believe in an after-life see it as equally or more pleasant than this one.[2]

Patriotism can overcome fear of death, but only religion can offer another life hereafter, and it is hardly surprising that most religions include beliefs about an after-life. As always, there seem to be some exceptions. Individual survival seems less important for many Jews, and some hunter-gatherers show grief when a relative dies but no clear evidence of belief in an after-life. It has been suggested that the latter is related to the facts that their everyday lives are focused on the present, food being consumed when or soon after it is obtained, and that they have little investment in artefacts or commitment to others (Woodburn, 1982). But the vast majority of religions do show concern about survival after death. Although belief in an after-life does not follow from everyday experience, it may come easily, for one meets the dead in dreams. Furthermore, it is difficult to imagine non-existence, because one is imagining oneself as unable to imagine, although one's image of the world after one has left it inevitably involves oneself behind the eye that perceives the image.

Our curious reverence for the past may also be due in part to a desire to perceive continuity over time, thereby diminishing the impact of one's demise through belief in an after-life. Most societies hold ancestors in special regard, but perhaps this is seen most clearly in China. Throughout history the Chinese have performed rites for their ancestors, though how many generations of ancestors are respected has differed according to the individual's rank, and over time: in some periods ancestor worship was practised to the limits of human memory – that is, over a span of five generations. During the last centuries BCE the Chinese developed a formal notion of the underworld structured with a bureaucracy like that of the Chinese state: such beliefs persisted alongside the official religion (Rawson, 1988a). The funerary practices in the Han dynasty were directed towards facilitating survival after death or placation of the spirit – prolonging life on earth, preservation of the body from corruption, provision for existence in another world, assistance and support for the spirits of the dead, appeasement, and so on (Loewe, 1994; Rawson, 1998a). It was supposed that the spirits could influence events on earth: some performed miracles and were worshipped as gods, some were malevolent and could bring misfortune to the living (Hansen, 1996). Taoist beliefs indicated that life could be extended by proper living, ultimately into immortality, and at all periods in China respect to the dead was offered in a variety of contexts – at family altars, in homes or temples, and also at the tomb.

Belief in an after-life is associated with many practices whose performance tends to affirm that belief. For example, at least in past centuries, money was often left in wills to pay for services and for prayers for the soul of the departed, and some institutions still pray for the souls of past benefactors.

Also facilitating belief in an after-life are the not infrequent reports of 'near-death' experiences. For example, an individual who believes himself to be at death's door may report a feeling of occupying a mind that has become external to and is even looking down on the body it has left. These and other comparable phenomena have been reported in many cultures (see for instance Evans-Wentz, 1957), and provide a basis for the International Association of Near-Death Studies. In western societies such experiences may be in part induced by partial oxygen deprivation or by drugs used in medical procedures, but the point being made is that their interpretation is in harmony with an association between fear of death and belief in the supernatural.

It seems likely that the way we use the self-concept can also contribute to beliefs about life after death. We have seen that the self is used to account for the continuity which we perceive in our lives. The self is seen as having desires, thoughts, and so on – in other words mind-like properties. It is also part of you but at the same time outside you: it is *your* self, and you describe it 'objectively', so in a sense it must be separable from you. It can thus be seen as independent of the body, and as no longer present in the body after death. However, dead people appear in dreams (Tylor, 1913), and the soul is seen as surviving death. It is thus not unreasonable to suggest that the concepts of self and soul are closely related – though there are considerable cultural differences in the concepts of both (Smart, 1996). As we shall see, spirits and souls usually have all the properties of a mind but not all those of a body (see also Humphrey, 1995).

Of course, there are other ways of coping with the inevitability of death. Lifton (1979) has differentiated five means which people use to overcome their perception of mortality – religious, through believing in a continued existence or a relationship with God; mystical, through emphasising the experience of oneness with all things; creative, involving doing something in life for which one will be remembered; biosocial, living on through one's descendants; and nature, perceiving that we are all part of nature. Whereas the mystical mode is primarily experiential, though subsequently expressed through cognitive concepts, the others are primarily cognitive. Individuals identify with memories that others will hold of them, with the evaluation of their work by others, with being part of the processes of nature, and/or with beliefs that indicate personal survival. Of these, the religious mode has been found to be most strongly related to fear of death (Hood and Morris, 1983; see also Vandecreek and Nye, 1993).[3]

While western individualistic religions stress individual survival, many religions in non-literate cultures stress the continuation of the lineage line, of life, or of the whole cosmic order (Bloch and Parry, 1982). The main aim of most Jain, Buddhist, and Hindu sects has been to escape from this world to something that is beyond the passage of time (Zaehner, 1962). The view of existence as a series of stages endlessly repeated may have provided a way of coming to terms with mortality, individuals being enclosed in a pattern that outlasted everything (cf. Loewe, 1994). It is claimed that Judaism can provide hope that death will be transcended not only in these ways but also, and perhaps even more importantly, by survival of the race (Steinberg, 1947).

More difficult to explain is why a considerable proportion of individuals have believed in Hell (Hood *et al.*, 1996) – a belief which would surely augment fear of death in all but those with the purest consciences. Did Heaven have to have a counterpart? Or perhaps those who were religious believed that Hell was not for them? Or, since bad events need causes as well as good ones, perhaps the Devil must live somewhere. Or is Hell a construction facilitated by religious specialists or secular powers in order to coerce the general population to behave in ways that they consider appropriate?

Thus, a variety of data support the view that religious beliefs can depend in part on preoccupation with or fear of death. Since the deceased must have somewhere to go, this inevitably leads to belief in spirits of some sort – spirits which may continue to inhabit our world or live in some sort of spiritual abode.

### Relationship factors

Humans seek social contact, and loneliness can be an important cause of distress. Indeed the sharing of experience is an important facet of all close relationships. A study of biological and anthropological field workers returning to civilisation showed that many experienced a need to share their experiences with someone who would understand them, and some became disoriented when they were unable to do so (Hinde, 1978). The dissolution of a close relationship or bereavement involves a loss of part of the self-system. We continue to need attachment figures throughout life (Parkes *et al.*, 1991).

Communication with a deity can ameliorate the effects of loneliness, and many religious people find it deeply satisfying to mull over recent happenings in supposed communion with an all-understanding being. In harmony with this view is an experimental study in which questionnaires assessing internal, external and quest religious orientations (see pp. 40–2) were given to students. A week later they were set a writing task that made vulnerability to loneliness salient, and then given the questionnaires again. Subjects high on loneliness-salience scored more highly on the intrinsic scale than previously, those low on loneliness did not. The external and quest scales were not affected. This suggests that intrinsic religiousness is used as a buffer to loneliness (Burris *et al.*, 1994).

Individuals may thus gain satisfaction from communication with a supernatural entity, each according to his or her own nature. There may be a feeling of trust and reliance, someone with whom to talk over and share the day's events, someone who can be relied on in time of trouble. Of course not all deities lend themselves to that sort of relationship, but the feeling of being in a close relationship can be a potent force for many Christians (and perhaps especially members of the Pentecostal church) and for some Hindu sects, for example. Trust, or faith, is a critical component of such a relationship with the deity, for belief must remain in the face of current adversity, and there must be trust in his loving forgiveness for human error.

### Social factors

Religious belief is not just an individual matter. Beliefs are more or less shared with others, and there are powerful social forces that ensure that it should be so (Chapter 16). There is often a gain to the individual from the sense of community, and a gain to the community from the effect of the shared beliefs on the loyalty of individuals: positive feedback is obtained from the consensual validation by others (p. 200) of the otherwise unverifiable beliefs. Indeed for some individuals social cohesion itself may be a goal. Religion can give a sense of power through group membership: some religions describe their followers as being 'chosen'.

In addition, religious beliefs are held not just in a society of equals, but in one that is hierarchically organised. There may be political reasons why those of high status should wish to reinforce the religious system – to maintain the position of the priests, or the divine right of kings, or to make those at the bottom feel content with their lot. Authority is often critical in the acceptance of belief systems.

### The meaning of life

Perhaps for many the apparent potency of religion can be encapsulated by saying that it gives a coherent meaning to life (Geertz, 1975), though whether the need for meaning is primary, or depends on some of the issues previously mentioned, is an issue that need not detain us. Some argue that 'the search for significance is the overarching, guiding force in life' (Pargament, 1997: 95). Analysis of 4000 letters to the Bishop of Woolwich after the publication of his *Honest to God*, a book which most Christians found highly controversial, indicated both a need for certainty and a desire for meaning in life (Towler, 1985). Religion can provide orientation within a meaningful world which, without it, appears chaotic and meaningless. This issue is considered further on pp. 216–25.

It is often suggested that the tangible world is inadequate to provide material for the construction of credible compensation for non-available resources of the types mentioned above, that belief in a meaningful universe requires a designing agency, and that religions would lose their appeal if they lost contact with the supernatural. However, an interesting study of a Lutheran 'Free Congregation' on the island of Mors, near Denmark, throws doubt on this last point. In this community religious practices have changed little this century, but it is said that belief in the supernatural has all but disappeared with the view that science can or will be able to explain the world. The religious rituals and ideology still provide meaning and a frame-work for individual experiences and emotions (Buckser, 1995).

### The diversity of the bases of belief

In the preceding paragraphs it has been argued that a number of basic propensities, which are probably ubiquitous in humans though differing somewhat between individuals and cultures, are basic to religious beliefs. Proof that religious beliefs are absolutely dependent on such propensities would be hard to obtain, though some studies cited in Chapter 17 are relevant. To the extent that such is the case, religious beliefs can be seen as basically Darwinian. There is of course nothing new in this view: others have made similar suggestions. I should perhaps add that there is no implication that these issues are all there is to belief systems. We shall see later that they, and the myths and narratives associated with them, may have diverse consequences in a society (see also Chapters 16 and 17).

What is not yet clear are the interrelations between the several propensities associated with religious involvement. Intuitively, seeking to understand the causes of events and to feel in control of one's life seem to be closely related to each other and to the structure of the self-system. Thus the postulated elaboration of working models of relationships (see note, p. 28) can be seen as related to achieving self-efficacy in relationships; and seeking for congruency (see pp. 30–1) as related to understanding the world and one's position in it: the use of consensual validation to confirm beliefs is a means to that end. Attempts to feel in control of one's life are related also to the sometimes contradictory tendencies to see oneself as one really is and to maintain a high view of oneself, as well as to seeing relationships as stable, believing in survival after death, desiring for equitable or advantageous exchange (see Chapter 13), seeking for status, and many other aspects of our lives (Hinde, 1997a). We must look to further research for light on these issues.

Furthermore, it is not claimed that the issues discussed are the only ones that support religious belief. Clearly, attempts to make overall generalisations about why people hold religious beliefs are likely to be simplistic. Different beliefs may be appropriate to different individuals in different social systems for different reasons, and any one individual may be impelled in diverse ways, emotional and intellectual. The same religion may offer different benefits to different congregations or communities, to the different individuals within a community, and to a given individual at different times. As one example, a distinction can (or could formerly) be made between High Islam, carried by urban scholars and emphasising order, rule observance, sobriety and learning, and Folk Islam, which may involve magic, ecstasy, and saint cults. Gellner (1992) stresses that each may have its own appeal. The former appeals to the trading bourgeoisie, reflecting the tastes of the urban middle classes, and provides the society with its constitution. Folk Islam is entrenched in the tribal and semi-tribal countryside, where the saint cults involve ecstatic rituals providing an escape from the austere conditions of life. It provides also a route for mediation between groups and a symbolism by which illiterate believers can identify with a scriptural religion.

## Belief and emotion

As mentioned already, in discussing beliefs it is difficult not to give the impression that belief is a solely intellectual matter. Nothing could be farther from the truth. We now know that the cognitive and emotional aspects of human psychological functioning are much more closely interwoven than was formerly thought to be the case (e.g. Damasio, 1994), and this is especially important for religiosity. The very fact that religious beliefs involve counter-intuitive phenomena, and that people continue to adhere to beliefs which are contradicted by empirical evidence, suggests that intellectual conviction is not the sole issue. For most people, belief is not initially acquired as the result of an intellectual decision: as we shall see, it is usually the consequence of a variety of processes during socialisation, with parents and others with whom the child has an emotional bond playing an important part (Chapter 7). Indeed, an 'intellectual orientation', involving enjoyment of intellectual discussion, was found to be a potent predictor of relapse from religious participation in a group of Australian students (though not in previously studied Canadian students) (Hunsberger and Brown, 1984); and one study has found that those who lose their faith tend to be more highly educated than those who do not (Wadsworth and Freeman, 1983).

## Belief in what?

We shall see some other ways in which religiousness has consequences beneficial for the individual later, but here an important issue must be underlined. For the beneficial consequences of religious belief which have been mentioned, belief in *something* is essential but, though there are some differences in health and other concomitants of religious involvement even between Christian denominations, within wide limits it is an open question how much the nature of that *something* matters. There must be some sort of fit with the social system, but beyond that the very diversity of belief systems to be found in the world suggests that belief systems with a wide range of contents can bring satisfaction to individuals. We return to this issue on pp. 216–25, where it is suggested that a critical issue is that religious involvement can induce a state that could be referred to as 'peace of mind' or an 'integrated self-system'.

It is worth noting that there are many points of contact between the major religious systems. Smart's (1960) imaginary discourse between representatives of different world religions demonstrates limited concordance as well as divergence. There are points of contact between modern Christian theologians who emphasise an impersonal Being rather than a personal God, the Buddhist view of the Absolute, and the Hindu's non-anthropomorphised conception of higher reality whose only attributes involve Being, Consciousness, and Bliss. The Christian and Islamic views of a personal God are both associated with the view that natural life is limited but there is a subsequent existence in Heaven or Paradise, while the Buddhist and Hindu views of re-birth in a succession of lives see Heavens and Hells as part of the cosmos. In the cycle of re-birth you can be re-born in Heaven, and ultimate liberation can take you beyond that heavenly condition. Attaining Nirvana (meaning liberation, in the sense that the extinction of desire or craving brings about liberation from the endless round of re-birth) has many characteristics with the Christian view of experiencing God. Nirvana is a 'deathless place', out of time, and permanent, corresponding with the Christian God's immortality. It is seen as a haven of peace, just as the Christian God is seen as a refuge. Those who attain Nirvana are seen as acquiring strength and purity, as God grants grace and strength. This is not to deny the many differences – Nirvana is not a substantive Being, not a Creator, is not worshipped, is not prayed to, and so on: the point being made is that people could find satisfaction equally from both. For some Buddhists Paradise is 'far to the West' – perhaps almost far enough away to correspond to the Christian Heaven. In so far as the Christian view of immortality involves dwelling with God beyond the grave, it is not so far from the Eastern descriptions of 'release'. As we shall see later, there are resemblances between the Christian Trinity and the beliefs of other world religions.

Yet again, the Christian doctrine of original sin is not so unlike the transference of bad *karma* on re-birth. The idea of sacrifice for the good of all mankind applies not only to Christ, but also to the Bodhisattva who makes a personal sacrifice by delaying his own Nirvana in order to work for the salvation of mankind. And although Christians have much less respect for animals than Buddhists, there is a similar feeling behind the Christian view that humans were the result of a special act of creation, and the Buddhist view that the human state is superior to that of animals.

Such considerations should not be taken as supporting the view that any religious system could bring the same benefits as any other to everyone: rather the juxtaposition of differences and similarities suggests that other people's religions may be better for them in the circumstances in which they live than the system operating in one's own culture would be. In other words, tolerance is essential. We shall return to the question of the limits to be put on that tolerance.

## Summary

Belief in a deity is related to a number of human propensities, especially understanding the causes of events, feeling in control of one's life, seeking for security in adversity, coping with fear of death, the desire for relationships and other aspects of social life, and the search for a coherent meaning in life.

The relations between these several issues are little understood. It is again emphasised that belief is not solely an intellectual matter. Resemblances between the belief systems of the world religions are compatible with the view that they have similar beneficial consequences.

# 6 Structural beliefs

## Religious representations

Religious systems display great diversity over whether deities are seen as anthropomorphic, the extent to which their properties are counter-intuitive, in how many deities are recognised, in whether they are materially represented, and in the psychological characteristics attributed to them. In this chapter we discuss how these diverse characteristics of deities are related to various individual propensities and mesh with a variety of cultures, and how individuals maintain a degree of cognitive consistency between their secular and religious representations.

## The nature of deities

### Essence or entity?

Some religious systems apparently postulate causes for otherwise incomprehensible events, without speculating further about the nature of those causes. The Dinka, pastoralists of southern Sudan, are said to attribute responsibility for natural events, such as lightning, to formless 'Powers', without ascribing any further properties to them (Lienhardt, 1961). The Nuer sometimes felt their god to be present, and sometimes far away in the sky: animistic ideas are almost entirely absent from their concept of spirits (Evans-Pritchard, 1951).

More often there appears to be a tension between whether the gods are perceived as all-pervading essences or as concrete beings with well-defined physical and moral characteristics. Taoists conceived of the Tao as a unifying organising principle underlying existence, but thought of it sometimes as both nowhere and yet as immanent in everything, and sometimes anthropomorphically. Similar ambiguity is present in their conception of the spirit world, which many Taoists see as both infinitely remote and immediately present – with, for instance, a spirit-administrator in every part of the human body (Bokenkamp, 1996). The Chinese emperor was seen as carrying the 'mandate of Heaven', where Heaven was seen as a divine, semi-natural, semi-personal force. If all went well, Heaven was seen as approving, but if there were famine, drought or political upheaval, Heaven was seen (retrospectively) as disapproving, and a change in dynasty might be portended (Loewe, 1994). Many Buddhists and Jains, although acknowledging lesser gods, have not accepted an impersonal Absolute or a personal God, but recognise an extra-temporal essence that pervades the universe and inheres in all human souls (Crook, 1990; Küng and Kuschel, 1993). Most forms of Buddhism refer to an 'Ultimate Reality', and see humans as capable of enlightenment and thus of uniting with that Reality, while any supernatural beings that are recognised and worshipped are seen as ultimately impermanent. Some of the earliest Hindu writings recognise many gods, but after a while the first principle came to be seen as a single divine Absolute that transcended and pervaded all. That is not seen as incompatible with the worship of different gods by different sects – each with his or her own characteristics and existing in different incarnations: while the whole world is seen as sustained by the mysterious impersonal power of Brahman, lesser gods are also worshipped (Armstrong, 1993; Zaehner, 1962). For many Hindus, all gods and the whole universe are present in each human body, and there is an homology between the body and the cosmos: 'the spiritual essence at the core of the individual self, is the same as the Brahman, the absolute, universal and impersonal self within all living beings' (Porterfield, 1998: 61). Some hold that all category distinctions belong to a superficial world of appearances, so that the divine and the human are ultimately the same. To Gandhi, God was truth, love, ethics, and morality. Today many Hindus see the worship of particular gods as a matter of convenience, such gods representing lower aspects of the ultimate deity whose higher aspects lack anthropomorphic attributes: the power that sustains the cosmos is seen as residing within the individual, but each individual's self is part of one great Self. (This, it will be noted, involves a concept of self different from that discussed earlier, and perhaps closer to some Christians' concept of soul.)

In the Judaeo-Christian tradition there has been continuing tension between a conception of the deity as an anthropomorphic being, or more accurately as a Being perceived as having created man in his own image, and the concept of an all-pervading cosmic essence which could be seen as the basis of reality. The Hebrews saw Jahweh as abstract, and made no images of him, yet then and now most Jews individualise the deity (Steinberg, 1947). Modern academic Christian theologians are inclined to dispense with the concept of a personal god, though to some extent this may be a matter of sophistication, with the more educated Christians tending to see God in more abstract terms. On that view, God may be sought in the self rather than in the outside world – a view shared by St. Augustine and by the non-theistic Buddhists and Hindus (Armstrong, 1993). However, such a view can come into conflict with the view of some Christian authorities that it is blasphemous to claim too close a relationship with God. And in the individual tension is often still present: Barrett and Keil (1996) showed that people who profess to hold a theological view that rejects any anthropological constraints on God may yet use anthropomorphic concepts of God in order to understand stories. As we shall see later, this conflict between an immaterial entity and an anthropomorphic being is partially solved by the concept of the Trinity.

At the other extreme, some cultures have seen their deities as little different from ordinary mortals. The Greek gods could be ranked in a rough order of power and precedence; they drank, ate, enjoyed sex and played around just like mortals, and the Epicureans saw them as little interested in the affairs of mortals.[1] The Chinese around the time of the Han dynasty seem to have seen the universe as unitary, with no clear distinction between gods, other creatures of heaven and earth, and humans (Loewe, 1994). The Chinese pantheon aped the secular bureaucracy: the Jade Emperor was seen as in charge of a number of bureaux, with bureaucrat gods in charge of the subdivisions. In general, cultures that recognise a number of gods are likely to see them as hierarchically organised and specialised: often lesser gods are used for everyday purposes and the Supreme One not bothered unnecessarily.[2]

It may be suggested that the tension between regarding the deity as an all-pervading essence or as a material entity can be understood in terms of the various functions deities perform. If a deity is to be available to every individual, if (s)he is to be experienced in natural beauty and in goodness, (s)he must be everywhere at once, an all-pervading essence. If a deity is to function as a causal agent, then (s)he must be animistic. If (s)he is to be someone with whom a relationship can be formed, (s)he must be anthropomorphic. Such an hypothesis is supported only in that it seems to fit the facts, but the data showing that many Christians vacillate between an immaterial and a personified Deity according to the context (see above) is certainly supportive.

### The counter-intuitive properties of deities

Most religious belief systems concern beings with some intuitively impossible abilities, as well as some human characteristics as experienced in everyday life. For instance, in our own folk-lore ghosts are a kind of supernatural being with particular improbable properties: they are semi-transparent and can pass through walls. At the same time ghosts are seen as having certain human-like properties: they may wail, have beliefs and desires, and talk aloud. Boyer (1994, 1995) has given an account of religious representations which indicates that this ambiguity plays an important role in their acceptance. He suggests that the counter-intuitive properties are reported and discussed because they are salient, but they are coupled with properties implicit in everyday experience which facilitate assimilation and understanding.

The counter-intuitive properties of deities must be learned one by one, but this is not the case with their everyday characteristics. We shall see in the next chapter that biological kinds are seen as though each had an 'essence' which allows inferences about its properties. Thus, if an animal is identified as a tiger, we know that it will eat meat and may be fierce, and it will still be a tiger if it loses its stripes. Similarly, in so far as deities are seen as anthropomorphic, inferences about them can go beyond the information that is immediately offered. For instance, in some cultures spirits, like biological species, exist in kinds each with its own essential 'essence', so that identifying the kind to which a spirit belongs permits expectations about many of its characteristics, such as what it will do. If spirits can talk, they are likely to have beliefs and desires, they may be angry or unhappy, and so on. While their counter-intuitive properties are transmitted explicitly, such everyday properties are natural and self-evident. In the same way, people in western societies have both a concept of God that includes counter-intuitive powers (God can attend to everything at once; God can see everything) and a concept more in keeping with intuitive expectations (God can get angry if people do not do what He wants).

The mixture of human and counter-intuitive properties is well illustrated in Chinese fiction. Given the Chinese concern for their ancestors, it is not surprising that visitors from the after-world have figured prominently in Chinese literature since the beginning of Chinese history. The boundary between fiction and non-fiction is often shady, and belief in ghosts has been neither well-defined nor universal: many of the stories about them seem designed to prove their existence and potency as integral phenomena of the natural world. Like ghosts in western legends, they have counter-intuitive properties: they are immaterial, weightless, and liable to sudden appearance and disappearance. Yet at the same time they can suffer just as if they had bodies; they can be vengeful and vindictive, or wise; they can eat, drink, form relationships, and make love – a common theme is that of the ghostly temptress. Many of the stories display paradoxical similarities and differences between this world and that beyond the grave (Dudbridge, 1995).

In Buddhism, the counter-intuitive properties are seen not as pre-existing characteristics of a deity, but rather as acquired by those who achieve 'enlightenment', involving permanent deliverance from the sufferings of the world. The Buddha was born into a royal family, but renounced his royal status and spent his life instructing disciples throughout the Indian subcontinent, thereby achieving enlightenment. Buddhists recognise that other buddhas have achieved enlightenment both before and after his time. Some Buddhists see these buddhas as approachable, but even more approachable are the Bodhisattvas who, advanced on the path to enlightenment, choose not to attain Nirvana while other beings suffer (Sangharakshita, 1993).

A combination of supernormal (though not supernatural) characteristics can produce adulation even in the secular world. Shortly before this book was written, Princess Diana was killed in a car accident. Public reaction was unexpected and unprecedented. Hundreds of thousands of people lined the funeral route in utter silence, flowers showering onto the hearse so that the driver had to stop to clear his windscreen. Millions watched on television in countries all over the world. People queued for many hours to sign the books of condolence. The mountains of flowers left outside places associated with her were uncountable. Was this extraordinary response due to her special combination of qualities? Was it that she provided something beyond ordinary people's reach, something they could both look up to and admire, and yet at the same time she was someone with whom they could identify? She was in some ways out of the ordinary world – regal, rich, remote, beautiful. Yet at the same time she was intensely human, a sufferer from bulimia, and displaying immense humanity – a humanity perhaps especially salient after the self-centred competitiveness of the Thatcher era. A few months after her death newspaper reports indicated that she had been included with the Virgin Mary in many Christmas cribs in Naples (*Sunday Telegraph*, 7 December 1997).

Boyer's suggestion, then, is that religious concepts involve a balance between explicit, counter-intuitive, and therefore attention-getting properties, and implicit properties in harmony with assumptions made about the everyday world. Gods may be non-physical, ageless, omniscient, but at the same time they conform in other respects to the properties of animate beings. The assumptions about their properties that are counter-intuitive are explicit but do not lead to further inferences: you cannot infer anything from the knowledge that a ghost can walk through walls other than that it can walk through walls. By contrast everyday properties permit further inferences: if a god has desires, one can make inferences about how he will act. A balance between the everyday and the counter-intuitive properties is necessary because, if all an entity's properties were counter-intuitive we should not be able to relate to it or to remember them; while if none of its properties were, it would not be sufficiently interesting. Of the religious entities created and communicated in a culture, 'Only some…have the potential to support both imaginative scenarios and intuitive inferences. These are the ones that combine a rich intuitive base, with all its inferential potential, and a limited series of violations of intuitive theories, which are attention-demanding' (Boyer, 1994: 122). Amorphous religious entities are much harder to come to terms with.

The combination of counter-intuitive properties and implicit assumptions is seen by Boyer also in the causal powers of religious entities. These involve explicit, counter-intuitive claims constrained by, but made plausible by, everyday principles. Although in non-literate societies knowledge of the powers of spirits is largely transmitted by specific instances, it is assumed (in accordance with general principles that apply to living kinds) that other spirits of the same kind have similar causal powers: their counter-intuitive, attention-getting powers are seen against a background of intuitive ontologies projected into the religious domain. But the powers may be ascribed to the spirit *post hoc*, to explain an event: the conclusion that a spirit caused a man's illness may initially be a tentative attribution that brings the illness into an accepted causal framework, rather than being deduced from a general principle that illnesses are caused by spirits.

### Lesser deities and related figures

Most religions differentiate between one or more major deities and lesser figures who may act as mouthpieces or intermediaries, and usually themselves possess miraculous powers. The Christian Saints are a case in point, similarly combining human and counter-intuitive characteristics, though the Christian church usually makes a distinction between worshipping God and venerating the saints. Many of them are portrayed as marked by piety, often achieved after overcoming sore temptations of types to which all humans are susceptible, as a result of which God either bestowed supernatural power upon them or was willing to listen to their intercessions. Thus they could serve as a reproach to the lay people as well as helping to satisfy some of their needs (Weinstein and Bell, 1982). Their ability to bring about miraculous happenings was the essential sign of their power, and drew worshippers and pilgrims to the monasteries which contained their shrines, while their humanity made possible a relationship more personal than that with a deity. While Christian saints are necessarily dead, the saints of Low Islam (see p. 64) may be living persons (Gellner, 1992), and in eastern religions holiness may be ascribed to spiritual teachers (Smart, 1996).

The principal function of the saints, like that of the Old Testament prophets, has been to act as intermediaries with higher powers. In sixteenth-century Spain, illness, threatened disasters, or narrow escapes were liable to precipitate an appeal to a saint, usually accompanied by a vow. Often the matter was seen as a conflict with an evil spirit or devil, and it is claimed that treatment by exorcism was derived from the classical treatment by evacuation, the demon being expelled by defaecation or vomiting. Some saints were supposedly specialists: for instance in the case of pestilence the peasants of New Castile turned to St. Sebastian, whereas for insects attacking the vines they turned to St. Gregory of Nazianzus, St. Gregory the Pope and St. Pantaleon. In other cases choice of advocate fell on the saint whose day had witnessed a disaster, and in some cases the appropriate saint was chosen by lottery: a number of candles were lighted and the saint whose candle burned the longest was chosen. If an appeal was unsuccessful, the saint might be temporarily abandoned and another advocate chosen. Some saints, particularly the Virgin Mary, were generalists, seen as able to help in any adverse circumstance. Visions led to the building of chapels and shrines, most frequently to the Virgin Mary and St. Sebastian. The powers of patron saints were not infrequently used for political ends by both religious and secular authorities – for instance their supposed powers were used to deter enemies. Accounts of the relations of lay people to these Christian saints are no less bizarre to twentieth-century minds than are those of many African religions (Christian, 1981; Wilson, 1983b). Indeed, for much of the Middle

Ages church leaders themselves were ambivalent about many of the superstitious beliefs of the laity, not wishing to discourage them if they fostered popular devotion.

It is worth emphasising that the Christian view of religious entities as sacrosanct is not shared by all religions. Gellner (1992: 12), writing about Folk Islam, states 'Rustics use saints, revere them, and joke about them'; and Firth (1967) has described how the Tikopia apologised to their tribal gods as they put them away when Christianity took over. In many parts of India the household gods of Hinduism are often only half believed in: attention is given to them when the occasion is appropriate, much as many westerners might produce a rabbit's foot, a four-leaved clover, or a medal of St. Christopher.

In so far as deities have anthropomorphic characteristics, it is hardly surprising that deities and sub-deities should be seen as forming an hierarchical system, comparable to those in the secular world. Such an hierarchy also helps to meet the tension between the deity as an all-pervading essence and an anthropomorphic being, with those lower down being more human-like, more approachable, and with more limited (yet sometimes specialised) powers.

## Material representations of deities

In some religious systems, the deity is not materially represented. Thus the Jews were prohibited from making an image of Jahweh: even though for some purposes they spoke of Jahweh as though he were a person, they were not allowed to pronounce his name. It has been suggested that this prohibition resulted from a belief that possession of the image of a being gave one power over that being (see p. 124): individuals could not be allowed to have power over their god. A similar prohibition was held by the early Buddhists, and still holds in Islam. In the modern period Calvinists destroyed all religious images.

With most religious systems, however, the opposite is the case. Images of Christ, and of the Virgin Mary, have played a prominent part in most Christian sects. The dissemination of Buddhist images was encouraged in China by references to the miraculous re-births that awaited those who produced them. The completion of an icon was accompanied by an 'eye-opening ceremony' intended to transform the inanimate image into a living deity (Sharf, 1996b). And idols and icons have often been worshipped as if they were the deity itself: indeed belief in a universal impersonal Brahman makes it possible for Hindus not only to see their many gods as facets of ultimate reality, but also to equate god and image. More generally, they can be seen as having functions similar to those of texts, and therefore as being especially important in non-literate societies: they attract attention and facilitate a focus on the deity.

In considering this diversity, it must not be forgotten that most religions, other than the few 'world religions,' are specific to a particular social group. In a sense the group 'owns' the deity, and it may be important to its members that their deity is different from that of their neighbours. The Hebrews were surrounded by idol worshippers, so that their own rejection of images marked their distinctiveness.

Goody (1997) has given a different, but by no means necessarily incompatible, explanation for this patchy distribution of representations of the deity, namely that it is due to an inevitable ambivalence about making material that which is immaterial. On the one hand, especially among non-literate cultures, there is a need for a material deity. People need a focus for their supplications and for their worship. Goody records that the early Christians started to use abstract signs as symbols for divinity, then moved to image signs, and then to figurative representations. On the other hand, if god is everywhere, it does not make sense to create an image of him. He (or she) can perhaps be worshipped through his creations, as in pantheism, but not in a material object.

Furthermore, images can be identified too closely with everyday reality on the one hand and with the deity on the other: an image may involve contradictions between sacred and profane, natural and spiritual. And making an image gives rise to inevitable contradictions as it involves the creation of the Creator, the act appearing to duplicate the act of Creation itself: for created man to make images might be seen as a threat to the uniqueness of the Creator. Another source for ambivalence is provided by the possibility of imperfection in the image: if the image were imperfect or damaged in any way, it could no longer be worshipped. In any case, an image may be mistrusted because it is a deceitful representation of supposed reality.

Just as a relic or possession of an ancestor can serve to focus attention on the deceased, so an image can serve to focus attention on the deity. It is thus not difficult to see how, among the adherents of many religions, the deity is seen to be both there and not there in the image. Perhaps because of this ambivalence, representations of gods are sometimes stylised, so that the image becomes clearly a symbol rather than a representation of the deity. In Hinduism, representations of an erect penis stand for the god Siva. Christians may use a crucifix with startlingly realistic representations of Christ's wounds, as seen in many Mediterranean and South American churches, or a simple cross. However, there still remains an ambiguity as to whether it is the object itself which is to be worshipped, or whether it 'stands for' something else. It seems that there is an inevitable tension between the need for gods who satisfy certain human needs and the need for cognitive consistency.

These issues apply less strongly to lesser gods. Indeed, polytheism requires that the several gods be differentiated, and that inevitably means personified. In Africa the 'High God' is not represented in any way, as he is all-pervasive, but lesser gods may be (Goody, 1997). A similar trend is present in Christianity: with notable exceptions, God the Father is seldom represented, and the Holy Spirit can, of course, be represented only symbolically, but images of Christ, the Virgin Mary, and the saints are commonplace. There is a tendency, however, to regard the images as primarily for the less sophisticated.

## Multi-faceted deities: the Trinity

In so far as deities appeal to different people in different ways, and to the same individual in more than one way, their personalities must be, like those of humans, multi-faceted. Supposedly strictly monotheistic religions appear to be rare, only Judaism and Islam among the world religions seems to qualify with certainty, and even within Islam Shi'a involves reverence for divine martyrs. (The case of Christianity is discussed below.) Yet there is some tendency to assume that monotheistic religions are preferable. Hindu scriptures suggest that the Supreme Reality pervades everything, and the more sophisticated Hindus see local gods as representing parts of Reality. Japanese Buddhists, although praying to many Bothisattvas and Buddhas, see all Buddhas as in essence one 'Ultimate Reality'.

Several reasons may be suggested for this. One is simply a matter of economy: belief in one god is simpler than belief in many. More importantly, experience of transcendence is more naturally interpreted as experience of one Supreme (and usually immaterial) Being than as experience of many: it is not so easy to envisage a deity who is one of many as transcendent. And multiple deities often seem to have conflicting personalities, and thus to fall short of what people want to worship as the ultimate deity. Finally, religions which claim to purvey universal truth cannot involve worship of gods that have only local or limited significance (Smart, 1960).

However, at the same time it is necessary for gods to have multiple characteristics, and even personalities. A central issue is the extent to which gods have either masculine or feminine characteristics or both. Eastern religions have long recognised that yin and yang must be present in a whole person in a balanced way, and western psychologists have recognised that men may have feminine characteristics, and women masculine ones. The same seems often to be true of deities. Polytheistic religions usually have gods of both sexes, while in supposedly monotheistic religions the god often has both male and female qualities. Many African gods are genderless (Firth, 1996); and some modern Christians, in response to feminism, have come to regard their God as bi-gendered or feminine.

The gender attributes of the gods may reflect the interests of the dominant class: since this has usually consisted of males, it is not surprising that supernatural entities are more usually seen as masculine. However, a distinction has been made between male-oriented ritual-centred priestly religions with strict rules, in which women are often excluded from the rituals, and moral-centred prophetic religions which are more charismatic and involve not only knowledge but also the feminine characteristics of wisdom and insight. Mysticism, related to the sensual aesthetic world of painting, music, and drama, also leans towards the feminine.

It has been suggested that the gender attributes of the deity are related to the functional needs of the society, and differ according to the socio-economic conditions. Judaism required a primarily masculine deity. Early Christianity was militant and father-centred, but the cult of Mary, proclaimed in the fourth century, enabled Catholicism to provide both a masculine God and a feminine Mary. Later most Protestant sects rejected Mary and reverted to a masculine orientation embracing rationality and enterprise, and emphasising the masculine traits of both God the Father and of a militant Jesus, who must do battle with Satan (Schoenfeld and Mestrovic, 1991). Jesus, however, also has the feminine characteristics of compassion, tenderness, and perception.

Of course, gender is not the only issue. The religions of many non-literate societies postulate diverse deities with diverse functions, sometimes one for every object. Others, as we have seen, have subscribed to one main deity with other more subordinate ones. If the ultimate reality is seen as impersonal, the gods that are worshipped every day can present diverse characteristics. While the ultimate Hindu deity is seen as beyond good and evil, the person-alised gods that are actually worshipped have their own characteristics, and yet must be reconciled with each other. The Hindu Siva is seen as the recon-ciliation of opposites – creator and destroyer, male and female, good and evil. His consort is seen as part of himself, but may be worshipped sepa-rately, sometimes as the mild Parvati but more usually as the blood-swilling Kali. Some cults in Southern India worship a loving God who is:

> 'effortlessly active though ever at peace' His activity is his Śakti, his eternal consort, through whom he creates and loves what he has created...just as Śiva and his Śakti are eternally one and united in substantial love, yet eternally distinct in that without distinction love is impossible, so is the liberated soul oned with and fused in Śiva-Śakti, but still distinct in that it knows and loves what it can never altogether become.
>
> (Zaehner, 1962: 89)

To the Hebrews monotheism involved a repudiation of idol worship and a statement of the unity of reality and of the deity (Steinberg, 1947). While the nature of the Christian Trinity has given rise to much controversy over the centuries, from the present point of view it can be seen both as necessary to reconcile Christ's teaching with the monotheism of Judaism, and as bringing together the immaterial and the anthropomorphic. God is held to exist in three persons and one substance, Father, Son, and Holy Spirit. Possibly foreshadowed in the Old Testament, and implicit in a few places in the New, the doctrine developed in the centuries after Jesus became divinised, but there was continuing discussion as to the precise nature of and relations between the three Persons (Armstrong, 1993).[3]

In general, the Father is seen as ungenerated, and thus responsible for the Origin: He is the Creator. The term Father does not imply simply the human concept of father, but rather is used to imply characteristics involving both human and divine attributes. The Son, co-equal with but generated by the Father, combines many human attributes with miraculous powers. Langer (1953: 190) describes Him as 'the God who has a personal appearance even to the cut of his beard, a personal history of birth, death, and glorification, a symbolic cult, a poetic and musical liturgy'. No doubt the humanity of the Son contributes to His acceptance, the Gospels being full of assumptions intuitively derived from His humanity. The Holy Spirit embraces many of the counter-intuitive assumptions, being seen in the Old Testament as the intermittently active but impersonal power of God, present at the Creation and inspiring valour, strength, wisdom and understanding in many Old Testament figures. In the New Testament the Holy Spirit is seen as empowering or as driving Jesus into the wilderness and enabling many of His acts: to a large extent it can be seen as the divine aspect of Jesus. After His death and Resurrection the Holy Spirit became more generally available. It was personified only to the very limited extent that it performed or empowered works similar to those of Jesus and was active in Christianity, uniting believers with Christ or with the Lord.

Thus the doctrine of Three Persons combines the Father, who is given that title primarily in association with His role as Creator; and a Son with primarily human properties whose counter-intuitive abilities are partly ascribed to a non-intuitive Holy Spirit which lacks human characteristics. The problem of the creation and the combination of intuitive and counter-intuitive properties in a divine being are solved by the notion of three 'Persons' in One. A rigidly monotheistic religion could not tolerate the idea of incarnation, because it would be blasphemous to identify God with a human being: the doctrine of the Trinity circumvents this problem by emphasising Christ's full humanity (necessary because only if fully human could He bear the full weight of human sin), but at the same time recognising His divinity.

Within Christianity the several churches place the emphasis differently, some seeing Christ as so God-like as to be scarcely man, others so human as to be hardly a god. At the same time the intimate relation between the three Persons is taken to represent purest love. Historically the issue has given rise to considerable controversy, in part because it gave rise to disputes about the relative status and divinity of the Three Persons, and in part because of the fine balance that had to be maintained between the unity of Substance and the Trinity of Persons. If the unity is stressed too much, the distinction between the Three Persons is blurred, and the distinction is critical because only the Son assumed human form and God the Father must not be seen to have suffered in the flesh. On the other hand, if the distinction between the three Persons is emphasised, Christianity ceases to be monotheistic (Robb, undated).

Interestingly, early Hinduism involved a triad of gods, which is said to have originated from solar cults, the 'three-bodied sun' creating with his fertilising warmth, preserving with his light, and destroying with his burning rays. The membership of the triad (Varuna, Mitra, and Aryaman) changed over the ages: they were sometimes thought of as three separate gods, and sometimes as components of a single one (Ions, 1967).

## Authority and popular demand: the Virgin Mary

So far, the characteristics of deities have been discussed as though they were simply responsive to the basic human needs, as discussed in Chapter 5. That, however, is only part of the picture. The characteristics of deities may reflect the current social scene, be heavily influenced by both tradition and popular demand, and be used by secular and ecclesiastical authorities to further their own ends. This is exemplified in Christianity by the changes in the nature of the Virgin Mary (Warner, 1976).

Mary, the mother of Jesus, receives scant mention in the New Testament, and did not become an important figure until the fourth century. The legend of her virginity, derived largely from Apocryphal books, is interwoven with Christian ideas about the dangers of the flesh and their connection with women. After the preceding centuries of persecution, Christians saw suffering, and the denial of earthly desires, as meritorious, and this was coupled with veneration for virginity. Many Christian myths involve women who became martyrs in order to defend their virginity – an issue exploited by Shakespeare in *Measure for Measure*. The Assumption in corporeal form was seen as resulting from the conquest of sin and sex, and thus consequent upon Mary's immaculate conception and virginity. And her virginity is a symbol of Christ's divinity and purity.

Over the centuries, various aspects of the Virgin Mary have been emphasised. Images of Maria Regina have served to affirm the divine right of rulers from the sixth century. After the iconoclasm originating in eastern Christendom in the eighth and ninth centuries, images of the Virgin in triumph both reinforced the status of the images themselves and indicated the secular and spiritual powers of the Pope in Rome. Later kings and emperors used the Virgin to assert their authority with icons showing themselves being crowned by her. In the twelfth century images of Christ crowning his mother appeared, and at this time she was also shown as young and beautiful, embraced by Christ. But, in another strand, she was transformed from a distant queen into a gentle merciful mother, and later, in response to the Franciscan emphasis on humility, her image lost its regal trappings. Her acceptance of the Incarnation, and images of her kneeling before her child, further emphasised her humility. And more recent images show her as sympathetic, as sharing the sorrow of the bereaved, as conveying fertility, and as an Intercessor. Contrasts with Mary Magdalene, seen as a whore, have emphasised the Virgin's purity, and in 1854 the Pope proclaimed her Immaculate Conception so that, like Christ, she was seen as born without sin.

But problems have arisen with respect to her status relative to that of Christ. Her Assumption immediately after death can seem to give her a higher status than her son, who spent three days in the grave. The Vatican statement in 1964 indicated that she had cooperated with her son in overcoming evil. At the time of writing, the Pope is considering an appeal to have her declared as Co-redeemer, Mediator, and Advocate, an appeal which has attracted millions of signatures including those of 500 bishops. However, the idea is opposed by the Pontifical Mariological Academy on a number of grounds. It would be an affront to Christ's unique standing as the sole Redeemer and Mediator; Mary cannot be seen as the Mediator of all graces, even those before she existed; and the Holy Spirit is seen as the sole Advocate, the title having been given by Christ (John, 14,16). Moreover, such a move would shock Protestants, and be contrary to the ecumenical goal (Laurentin, 1998). By including the Virgin, Catholicism would either become effectively polytheistic at the popular level, or it would be necessary to recognise a Holy Quartet (*Independent*, 24 August 1997).[4]

There is, of course, also the problem of weighing the popular importance that she has for many Catholics against the image she presents to modern women – the incompatible goals of virginity and motherhood, and the virtues of female passivity and abnegation. A book by a Sri Lankan Catholic, Fr. Balasuriya, which stripped off some of the mythology surrounding the Mother of Christ, questioned the importance of the virgin birth, and attacked the anti-sexual bias in Catholic spirituality, offering instead an image of Mary as a mature woman and a partner in Christ's mission, was regarded as heretical and led to the author's excommunication, but was favourably reviewed in a Catholic journal (Rayan, 1997). The excommunication was subsequently lifted when the author signed a declaration of reconciliation.

The ascription of diverse and changing characteristics to an individual in order to support political or cultural goals can operate in a similar manner to create a 'secular saint'. Patricia Fara (in preparation) is documenting how Isaac Newton, at one stage a retiring seventeenth-century mathematician, was converted into an international cultural hero. Initially held up as a model of patience and sociability, in the nineteenth century he was often seen as a solitary eccentric verging on insanity. He is now portrayed not only as a dedicated scientist emotionlessly investigating a mechanistic world, but also as a neoplatonic alchemical experimenter, and a biblical exegete seeking to know more about God.

## Why do religious beliefs take the form that they do?

We have seen that most deities have at least some human characteristics. It is worth considering why this should be so.

The extent to which the movements of objects appear to be self-initiated helps infants to distinguish between animate and inanimate objects. Though this may not be the only criterion that is used, it is an important one. Thus when a mountain which has always seemed to be solid rock erupts and suddenly gives forth fire and lava, or when a smoothly flowing river breaks its banks and becomes a torrent, we are inclined to look for an animate cause. Even today we speak of volcanoes as 'belching' fire and lava, and the torrent as 'raging': animistic clichés, even if not explanatory, come naturally. Indeed a tendency to attribute movement to animate causes may have been conducive to survival for our ancestors, for movement might reveal the presence of a predator. Most animals are alerted by, and may show fear responses to, movement in the environment: for instance young vervet monkeys respond to a falling leaf as though it were an eagle (Cheney and Seyfarth, 1990).

For most humans, the first animate object to be encountered is another human, so it is not surprising that we tend to see the causes of otherwise inexplicable events as not only animate but as human. There may even be more to it than that, for there is considerable evidence that the evolution of human cognitive abilities was due to selection for competence in interacting with other individuals, and that requires understanding of the causes of their behaviour (Humphrey, 1976). Ascribing an event to human causation may therefore be an indirect result of the way we are constructed. Guthrie (1993), who has given a well-documented review of the use of anthropomorphic and anthropocentric attributions in everyday perception, in the arts, in philosophy, and in science, as well as in religion, comes to a related conclusion. On his (somewhat extreme) view, novel or ambiguous stimuli are likely to be interpreted as anthropomorphic unless there is evidence to the contrary. Certainly, some of the artefacts left by early *Homo sapiens* indicate that anthropomorphic thinking has a very long history in our species (Mithen, 1996), and it has been suggested that the perception of similarities between the categories used for the natural and social worlds would have been of practical value in predicting how animals would behave (Douglas, 1990).

Yet another issue may contribute to the tendency to postulate anthropomorphic beings. All humans dream, and dreams concern beings with human properties though, like religious beings, they may have counter-intuitive properties as well. Dreams have been seen as real in many pre-literate societies (Lévy-Bruhl, 1923). The Australian aborigines see the origin of the world in a 'Dream time', and dreams play an important part in many religious systems. Traditional Chinese tales of the Tang dynasty suggest that dreams were treated as real (Dudbridge, 1995). This also may contribute to the anthropomorphic nature of divine beings.

Thus looking for human or pseudo-human causes for inexplicable events is a common and almost certainly a pan-cultural feature of human behaviour. As usual, one must not be too hasty in ruling out the role of experience: Lewis (1995) has suggested that the very concept of causality is acquired as a result of the subjective experience of making something happen, and that could be a step on the way to seeing anthropomorphic beings as agents of inexplicable events. And it is not necessary that a religious entity with some human psychological characteristics should be seen as human-like in every respect. For instance Lewis (1995) notes that the Gnau do not blame spirits for the actions attributed to them as they would a human agent. And the Christian God, though having some human attributes, is seen as absolutely Other than humans, so that claims to have contact with Him have been seen as blasphemous (Smart, 1971).

There is, as we have seen, a problem with anthropomorphic deities. While an impersonal force or a superhuman essence can pervade the whole universe including humans, an anthropomorphic god has human properties as well as being all-powerful, and it is necessary that his humanity should not detract from his super-human properties. A god cannot be worshipped if god and man are similar. Thus, while supernatural beings are usually seen as having some human properties, precisely how human they are can be a problem: for Muslims Allah certainly has some human characteristics, but to worship and avoid blasphemy it is necessary not to think of him as a super-man.

Finally, one can ask why the gods have the particular psychological characteristics that they have. Studies of the concept of the Christian God have revealed qualities including a wrathful, avenging and damning God; an omnipotent and omniscient God; and a God expressing unconditional love and acceptance (review Brown, 1987). While most Christians' conceptions of God probably involve a range of properties, it is clear that any attempt to equate God with a father-figure or a mother-figure is simplistic.

Some studies have claimed relations between the benevolent/malevolent nature of the gods and socio-cultural practices. An analysis of sixty-two (apparently preliterate) cultures indicated that the more kind and supportive the parents, the more the gods tended to be benevolent and to be highly regarded. Such benevolent gods received more frequent and valuable sacrifices. Where children were more harshly treated, the gods tended to be more malevolent, received fewer sacrifices, and were less important in ceremonial and daily life. While the direction of causation here is far from clear and is probably bidirectional, the correlation suggests that:

> Malevolent gods lead parents to prepare their children for a malevolent actual world, with emphasis on self-reliance, mundane verbal aggression, and achievement orientations. Kind gods, however, lead parents to

reward nurturance in children under the assumption that reciprocal helping of others will continue to be the rule that has governed life in the family of the child who is being benevolently socialized.

(Lambert, 1992: 226)

The data further suggest that sacrifice is related less to ameliorating the anger of the gods than to a relationship of reciprocity with them, payment for help received or expected.

## Summary

The gods which figure in the various religions are extremely diverse, ranging from immaterial entities to anthropomorphic beings. Deities have a combination of everyday properties which depend on a characteristic 'essence', and counter-intuitive properties. Given some everyday property, the presence of others can be deduced as resulting from the 'essence', but the counter-intuitive properties must be acquired one-by-one.

This combination is seen also in lesser deities and saints, and may evoke admiration even in mortals. This diversity may be due to the diverse human needs that deities serve.

Material representations of deities provide a focus for worship in some cultures, but are rejected in others.

Most religions are based around gods with diverse characteristics. In some cases this involves polytheism, in others recognition that the god has more than one 'personality'. The Christian Trinity was concordant with the monotheistic Hebrew tradition, but met the conceptual needs of the new doctrines.

The characteristics of holy figures may be the result of a continuing dialectic between tradition and authorities on the one hand, and popular demand on the other.

That deities are usually animistic and even more often anthropomorphic, is in keeping with their roles in satisfying human needs to attribute events to causes, etc., as discussed in Chapter 5, and with the appearance of dead people in dreams.

# 7   Structural beliefs

## The development of beliefs

In this chapter the focus is on how religious beliefs, and also other aspects of religious systems, are acquired by individuals. Religious beliefs are seldom acquired as the result of logical discussion. Most controversy about their validity involves those who are already believers and seek to justify their belief, and sceptics who have never experienced firm religious belief or have come to doubt it. Such discussions rarely lead to a resolution. For most people religious beliefs, or susceptibility to their acquisition, are a consequence of experience during socialisation, and this involves accepting norms, values, and counterfactual beliefs solely on the example and authority of others. In this, the acquisition of religious beliefs differs only in degree from other aspects of socialisation.

Recent studies of early learning have shown that children 'know more than they can have learned', in the sense that early learning is guided by pre-existing constraints and predispositions with some specificity to particular domains of knowledge. This work greatly facilitates our understanding of how religious beliefs are acquired, and some aspects are reviewed in the first part of this chapter. However religious beliefs concern entities with properties that seem to contradict experience in the everyday world: gods can be in more than one place at a time, perform miracles, and so on. This poses special problems for the acquisition of religious beliefs.

With these issues as background, some factors affecting the development and maintenance of religious beliefs are discussed.

## Domain-specific knowledge

In order to understand how people assimilate the notion of deities, a sketch of some recent work on how we acquire our knowledge of the world may be helpful. This will involve a brief excursion into a fast-growing area of psychology where the concern is with how the acquisition of knowledge differs between domains (e.g. the physical and biological domains), with language subsequently playing an important role in their integration. The relevance of this work to the development of religious beliefs will become apparent later.

## Constraints on what is learned

Until the mid-twentieth century it was assumed that, leaving aside issues of overall capacity, what organisms learned was determined solely by their experience. However research on animals clearly demonstrated that members of a given species were predisposed to learn some things more easily than others, and to learn more readily in some contexts than others (Hinde and Stevenson-Hinde, 1973; Lorenz, 1935; Seligman and Hager, 1972; Tinbergen, 1951). For instance, the chaffinch has to hear chaffinch song in order to produce the species-characteristic pattern of notes, but can learn only chaffinch song, and not that of other species (Thorpe, 1963).

## Domain-specific learning

Independently, cognitive psychologists and linguists have concluded that human learning is similarly subject to constraints and predispositions. First, there is much evidence to indicate that development proceeds more or less independently in a number of distinct domains, such as language, the physical world, the animate world, the human social world.[1] For instance, some deficits in behaviour seem to be specific to a particular domain: autistic children lack an ability to reason about the mental states of others, but may perform at a high level on mathematical tasks. On the other hand some individuals show exceptional brilliance in one domain, such as mental arithmetic, but are ordinary in other respects (e.g. Damasio, 1994). And many instances of damage to the brain are associated with highly specific psychological deficits – such as an inability to deal with numbers, or to recognise individuals. How far the distinctions between the principal domains are independent of experience is controversial and a matter irrelevant to the present context: the important issues are that such distinctions appear early and seem to be a general human characteristic.

Beyond that, within each domain a growing body of research indicates that children often know more than they can have learned. Mental development depends on basic predispositions or constraints, likely to be pan-cultural, influencing the way in which knowledge is acquired in interaction with particular aspects of the animate and inanimate environment. These predispositions and constraints may be influenced by earlier experience but, if so, for many of them such experience must be effectively common to all individuals.[2] Not only are they relevant to the acquisition of religious concepts, but also they illustrate more generally how pan-cultural psychological predispositions pave the way for the acquisition of complex concepts, and how knowledge acquisition is channelled. We may consider how they operate in four domains.

### Language acquisition

Chomsky's (1965) earlier suggestion that this depends on predispositions to acquire some grammatical structures rather than others has led to detailed studies of how language develops. In the first place there are certain attentional predispositions. Soon after birth infants attend to language in preference to other sounds, and learn to distinguish their native tongue (i.e. the language that is spoken around them) from others by the time that they are four days old. At a few months they attend preferentially to features that will have syntactic value, such as the cues that correlate with clause boundaries in their language. This is not saying that these and other predispositions are genetically determined: experience plays a critical role. Other studies show that infants soon become sensitive to a variety of other characteristics of spoken language, such as the difference between relative pitch, which is linguistically relevant, and absolute pitch, which is socially but not linguistically important. In general it seems that infants have predispositions and attentional biases that facilitate learning of any language, and then select particular ways of representing and processing language as a consequence of exposure to their own (Karmiloff-Smith, 1992).

The linguistic input to which children are exposed is insufficient in itself for language to be acquired. For instance, if an adult points to a cat and says 'Look, a cat', how can children know whether the object referred to is the whole cat, its whiskers, its tail, or the mat on which it is sitting? One route to understanding appears to lie in their use of three probabilistic rules: they assume first that it is the whole object that is referred to; they assume that the reference is to a basic category level (i.e. cats in general, not Abyssinians or Persians in particular); and they assume that any new label refers to an object for which they have not already got a label. This last rule enables those who already know the word 'cat' to interpret 'Look at its tail' to mean something other than the whole object or cats in general (Gleitman, 1990; Markman and Wachtel, 1988).

In addition, quite early on children show sensitivity to quite complex aspects of syntax. By presenting children with simultaneously verbal commentaries of the type 'X is doing something to Y' or 'Y is doing something to X', with a videotape of one of such events, it has been shown that even 17-month-olds look longer when the verbal input is appropriate to the visual display. Further, at an early age they make ontological distinctions, for instance between artefacts and living things, and recognise which predicates apply to which. For instance, it makes sense to say 'The lion runs' or 'The lion eats', but not to say 'The hammer runs' or 'The hammer eats'. A child hearing a story that mentions briefly entities which they had not previously encountered, such as a hyrax, will make domain-appropriate inferences. For instance he might infer from the statement 'The hyrax is sometimes sleepy' that a hyrax might be hungry, but would deny that it was made of metal (Keil, 1986). Children use semantics to work out syntax, and syntax to predict semantics (Gleitman, 1990), and by the age of three or four are able to speak and understand fluently. Beyond that, it has been suggested that the linguistic representations are re-represented and become available for reflection and manipulation. This last stage, which is of critical importance for more complex processes and for using language knowledge in other domains, may be preceded by a temporary phase of increased linguistic errors as re-representation occurs (Karmiloff-Smith, 1992).

### The physical domain

Infants soon come to display assumptions about the nature and motion of physical objects. For instance, 4-month-olds display surprise if one object appears to pass through another, and 6-month-olds if a falling object stops in mid-air. Here Spelke (1990) has identified a number of principles which guide infants' perceptions of objects and understanding of their nature. For instance, objects move as wholes in continuous paths, do not pass through each other, and cannot act on each other unless they come into contact.

Karmiloff-Smith (1992) suggests that such basic knowledge, which allows the infant to respond appropriately to external stimuli and thereby gain knowledge by interacting with the environment, is internally re-represented in such a way that the acquired knowledge can both be used to build theories about the physical properties of objects and also be deployed in other domains. Thus while 4-year-olds could balance a symmetrically shaped but asymmetrically weighted bar by moving it back and forth until they felt proprioceptively that it balanced, 6-year-olds continually attempted to balance the bar about its geometric centre, apparently using a theory, which had served well earlier but was not yet explicable verbally, that objects balance about their middles. Eight or 9-year-olds balance such a block readily, apparently using a further re-representation providing explicit knowledge of the geometric centre and a naive theory of moments.

### The biological domain

Of special importance in the current context is that quite early on infants distinguish animate from inanimate objects on the basis that the former are capable of self-propelled motion. It is not just that animate objects move, but that their movement changes without outside mechanical influence. This criterion is soon augmented by others, such as the ability to cope with irregularities in the terrain, the possession of locomotor organs, and the material of which they are composed (Gelman et al., 1995).

Children readily learn the names of living organisms and classify them into kinds initially corresponding very approximately with biological species or genera (e.g. dog, cat, kangaroo), and later in subordinate (e.g. terrier) and superordinate categories (e.g. mammal). One issue, of considerable importance for understanding the way in which deities are envisaged (see pp.

70–3), is that individuals assume that all exemplars of each living kind have similar properties and that those properties are due to an underlying nature or essence. They are aware that an exemplar of one living kind cannot be changed into an exemplar of another, but that this is not necessarily true of physical objects and artefacts. Categories of artefacts are defined by function and, unlike living kinds, do not presume an underlying nature. Shape and size are important to young children for categorising artefacts, colour and pattern for non-living natural kinds. At least some of these findings seem to be valid cross-culturally (for recent surveys of this work, see Atran, 1990; Baillargeon *et al.*, 1995; Carey, 1995; Gelman *et al.*, 1995; Karmiloff-Smith, 1992; Keil, 1995; Leslie, 1988; Spelke *et al.*, 1995; and other contributions in Sperber *et al.*, 1995).

### *Theory of mind*

In addition to distinguishing between animate and inanimate objects, children progressively acquire a 'theory of mind' – that is, an understanding of mental states in other individuals. Basic here is the distinction between statements involving 'propositional content', that is a description of the world (e.g. 'There is a fly in my soup'), and those involving 'propositional attitudes' or states of mind ('I believe that there is a fly in my soup'). Statements involving propositional attitudes express the mental state of the speaker with respect to the world. Having a 'theory of mind' implies imputing such states to others. That is, the behaviour of other individuals is understood in terms of beliefs, desires, and so on (Baron-Cohen *et al.*, 1985; Karmiloff-Smith, 1992; Leslie, 1987).

'Theory of mind' is not a unitary faculty, and emerges gradually in development. Soon after birth infants respond preferentially to face-like patterns and to human (especially their principal caregiver's) auditory input. Over the following months they pay special attention to how humans (again, especially their principal caregiver) move and behave. From birth, they process information about the animate, and especially the human, environment differently from the way in which they process information about the physical environment (see above). Pointing and mutual attention are used as means for requesting or calling attention to objects in the environment. By about eighteen months, children's pretend play reveals the beginnings of a theory of mind by the manner in which properties are ascribed to objects which clearly do not possess them, as the child is well aware: a block of wood is treated as though it were a car and had wheels, but furry toys are treated as though they had intentions. This occurs before the child uses mental state verbs his/herself, and before the idea of pretending is fully available to conscious reflection. However pretending may be 'marked' by a change in tone of voice, exaggeration of movement, and so on, keeping it salient in the child's mind. Such 'markers' indicate to the child and others how the action is to be represented and processed. There is some evidence that these phenomena are not limited to western children (Avis and Harris, 1991).

The precise way in which a fully-fledged theory of mind develops is a matter of some controversy and need not detain us here. It involves biological predispositions interacting with pan-cultural aspects of the socio-cultural environment in a number of stages, with language playing a role in the later ones. As soon as language involves the ability to refer to objects that are not present, this in itself implies 'belief'. But while the behaviour of a pre-verbal infant might indicate varying degrees of certainty about the location or qualities of an object, it is far from clear that they could know about their degree of uncertainty/belief, or how to convey that to another, or whether they could use knowledge about belief to explain the behaviour of another.

The general principle that the acquisition of knowledge proceeds in basically similar ways in different domains, but that domain-specific predispositions and constraints operate, is likely to be pan-cultural.[3] This, of course, does not mean that the distinctions between domains are 'hard-wired' or 'pre-programmed', or that experience is unimportant in their development – only that any relevant aspects of experience are likely to be common to all environments in which children develop. Finally, it must be emphasised that this is a fast-growing area of research and much work remains to be done. Some of this must involve both the linking of emotional and cognitive experience, and new attacks on the nature of subjective experience.

## Knowledge storage

A further issue relevant to the nature of religious systems concerns the manner in which knowledge is stored once acquired. In the first place, acquiring a concept implies the storage of a series of assumptions about the 'object' (which may be tangible or intangible), the assumptions being related to each other. The stored information about a concept is referred to as a 'schema'. For instance a pen can be held in the hand, has a nib, uses ink, which is not inexhaustible, and so on. Instances can be identified as belonging to a concept to the extent that they possess a number of characteristics (e.g. Rosch and Lloyd, 1978), though not all characteristics are necessarily essential. Thus birds have feathers and wings, they fly, they have two legs and lay eggs: however ostriches are birds although they do not fly, and bats are not birds although they do. Some instances may be more central, in the sense of being more easily recognised, than others: a robin is more readily recognised as a bird than an ostrich. In the case of artefacts, especially, assumptions about which characteristics are essential may have a logical basis in a theory about causation or function: a car must have wheels because it must move about, but is still a car if it does not have headlights (Atran, 1993; Boyer, 1994).

Knowledge that can readily be linked to existing representations is more readily acquired than knowledge that is entirely novel, without previous potential associations. Items of the latter type may require more or less prolonged learning, but the human capacity to form representations of representations may be used to embed notions which would otherwise be assimilated only with difficulty. This ability allows people to work over information that they only partially understand, playing with the idea of an idea, and is important in gaining understanding and in the acquisition of counter-intuitive ideas (Atran, 1993; see also Sperber, 1994).

Additional complexities arise in the representation of interactions and relationships between individuals. As we have seen, Bowlby (1969/1982), a psychoanalyst, postulated that children form 'internal working models' of the self, others, and relationships which form a guide for social behaviour. Such working models, formed initially in the course of a close relationship with a caregiver, form the basis for future relationships. The early model(s) are somewhat resistant to modification, fulfilment of expectations and defence processes playing a role (Bretherton *et al.*, 1990). Mental models of a somewhat more sophisticated but more limited kind proposed by Johnson-Laird (1980) involve analogue models with a structural similarity to the situations that they represent.

Thus work in this area involves the postulation of concepts that account for the way in which information and emotion is acquired and processed. Although we are dealing with something far less tangible than modes of behaviour, here too we have to do with psychological propensities that are likely to be pan-cultural.[4]

## The acquisition and maintenance of religious beliefs

With that as background, we may now consider the ways in which individuals acquire religious systems. It is unusual for people to come to believe as the result of sudden conversion, and for the majority of individuals the role of religious instruction is secondary. Rather the religious system is usually acquired during the ordinary processes of socialisation as the child is exposed to the 'things people do and think' in the society. For that reason, it makes little sense to consider the acquisition of the belief system separately from that of the rituals of praying or going to church, or from the learning of the code of conduct, or the first acquaintance with religious experience.

### Early religious involvement

In our own culture, the children of practising Christians are taken to church long before they have any real comprehension of what it all means. Some are even taken before they are four, so cannot have any understanding of what belief means, as they would have at most an incomplete 'theory of mind'. They go because they are taken there, because it is what people (and especially people with whom they have a close relationship) do, or do on Saturdays or Sundays. If the religious building has a special atmosphere, if the religious specialists and others present speak in an unusual tone of voice, if the adults they are with behave in a special way, the situation will be marked as special, and the procedures and behavioural sequences will be linked to the self-system as part of life. The meaning and validity of the procedures will be simply accepted. And such occasions may be coloured by special feelings – there may be a strong emotional component to what is stored. The acquisition of the religious system involves the assimilation not so much, or not only, of specific beliefs or of a coherent system, but of a jumble of fragments roughly integrated to provide an orientation to life, the religious outlook becoming part of the self-system. But in the acquisition process the principles discussed in the preceding section will come into oper-ation. Thus gods, spirits, and so on will carry with them the assumptions appropriate to animate beings – that all instances of a particular type have similar properties (e.g. all angels have wings) and share an underlying essence, so that all entities with some human properties are likely to have at least some others, and so on.

## The modes of action of parental influences

Individuals who accept religious beliefs are likely to have been exposed to religion in childhood (Brown, 1987), and positive attitudes to religion incul-cated in the family are resistant to change (Hunsperger and Brown, 1984). The acquisition is built on the everyday experiences of love and conflict, joy and frustration, of the child's life, with parental authority as a major issue. The religious system is thus re-constructed into the self-system as part of life, with religious stories and rituals stored in the same way as secular scripts (see Chapter 8) and the moral code seen as part of how people are ordinarily expected to behave. A recent review is given by Hood *et al.* (1996).

Parental influences may operate in diverse ways. Of course deliberate reli-gious instruction may play some part, perhaps especially in those societies where religious system and social system are somewhat tenuously related. But the instruction comes from a (hopefully) respected adult, and at first critical appraisal may play little part in its assimilation. We shall see later that the tendency to acquire knowledge from particular categories of others is probably a pan-cultural human characteristic (Chapter 13). Soon, however, the child starts to question adult accounts, and the child's religious conceptions are co-constructed as a result of the discourse between them (Josephs, 1996).

While teaching may be important, example is probably even more so. An important factor is probably the tendency, present in at least many non-human primates as well as in humans, for the child to do what the mother (or another adult with whom there is a close relationship) is doing and to adopt her attitudes to events and situations. When a human adult is cooking, a child may play happily with saucepans on the floor nearby. When a chimpanzee mother is 'fishing' for termites, her infant may do likewise, persisting when its efforts are entirely unsuccessful and probably never have been successful. Emde (1984) stresses the importance of such 'social referencing' in situations of emotional uncertainty: confronted by a strange situation, a toddler will look at a parent to see how she or he is responding to it, so that fear of a stranger can be ameliorated by the presence of a sensitive and confident mother (Emde, 1984; Stevenson-Hinde, 1989). In the awe-provoking atmosphere of church, temple, synagogue or mosque, where people will be seen as behaving in strange ways, social referencing must be particularly potent.

In some cases, the image of God may be built on that of the parents. Much of the research on this matter has been descriptive (Hood *et al.*, 1966), but some representative studies may be cited. In traditional families the mother may play the greater part in religious education, but some studies claim that the deity is usually modelled more on the father than on the mother. One study found evidence to support the view that parental images of God constituted ideals which the parent tries to emulate in parenting, and that children hold images of God that are shaped by and similar to their assessment of the parenting they receive (Hertel and Donahue, 1995). If children aged four to eleven perceived their parents as nurturing, they perceived the deity as nurturing; and if they perceived them as powerful, they perceived the deity as powerful. Cross-culturally, punitive parents tend to be associated with punitive gods, and more sensitive parents with loving gods (Lambert, 1992; Lambert *et al.*, 1959; see also Spiro and D'Andrade, 1958).[5] For some children, as they separate from their parents with age, God can become the perfect 'attachment figure', providing both a companion and an authority figure – perhaps an authority figure who can be constructed to be more flexible than the parents were (Dickie *et al.*, 1997).

Another study indicates that the relationship with the parent may affect subsequent susceptibility to religious influences. Among those whose mothers had not been religious, respondents who perceived their mothers as having been rejecting and thus as not providing them with a 'secure base' in childhood (i.e. were 'avoidantly attached') were most religious. They were also more likely to have experienced sudden religious conversions during adolescence and adulthood (Kirkpatrick and Shaver, 1990).

The so-called 'influence of tradition' thus means simply that the individual assimilates 'What we do here', 'What we believe here' and 'What we value here' from these social origins and reconstructs them as his or her own. Not only is the nature of the deity re-constructed by each individual, but also it tends to develop with age and to differ between individuals. Stages have been described ranging from a pre-conceptual trust in a magical and pre-anthropomorphic god, through a stage when the god is seen as a kingly but fair law-giver, to more adult and sophisticated conceptions (Fowler, 1981). In all such matters, influence from the socio-cultural structure, with its legends and stories and pictures, impinge on the developing mind of the child or adult.

Subsequently the ideas that have been assimilated are passed to other individuals. We shall see later that ideas may tend to pass preferentially along some paths rather than others – for instance from parent to child, or from the majority of adults to the individual. However, it must be remembered that, in human communication, the meaning of a message received is not always the same as the message transmitted (Smith, 1977): on occasion communication may achieve little more than a resemblance between the thoughts of communicator and audience.

## The counter-intuitive properties of deities

The acquisition of religious systems raises special issues because the entities involved do not figure in ordinary life and, as we have seen, they may combine everyday and counter-intuitive characteristics. This requires another brief digression. In general, concepts are devices which bring together exemplars that share some properties. Each concept must include assumptions about which characteristics are relevant and which are not. Now some of the properties of a concept are causally linked and thus conceptually cohesive. Thus 'cars' must have an engine, transmission, wheels, a body, and so on. They also have certain other characteristics which are less closely linked to the central ones, such as being expensive. Boyer (1994) calls the former the 'causal schema' of the concept and the latter 'non-schematic assumptions'[6]. In the previous chapter we used the phrase 'counter-intuitive characteristics' to refer to the non-schematic assumptions about deities.

Now we have seen that children use different reasoning systems for physical, biological and psychological domains. We have also seen that all exemplars of one living kind are seen as sharing certain properties which are due to some underlying nature or essence. Now the fact that ghosts have certain human-like properties suggests that they have a human 'essence' which may also form the basis of other human-like properties: it is not surprising that they have desires and talk aloud, for instance. And it can reasonably be assumed that they have minds which can form beliefs on the basis of perceptions, and intentions on the basis of their beliefs. Whereas the counter-intuitive properties of transparency and the ability to pass through solid objects are arbitrary and are talked about and communicated to children one-by-one in the course of socialisation, their other properties are assumed as characteristic of human-like beings: because they have some human properties it is assumed that they have others.

But why are the improbable characteristics accepted? We have seen that young children interpret events in the light of principles which are appropriate to physical, biological or psychological spheres. They recognise that solid objects cannot pass through each other, that they fall downwards, and that animals may grow larger but do not become smaller. If an event violates such principles they not only express surprise, but they re-examine the situation in an attempt to find a possible explanation. Since many aspects of the religious system are counter-intuitive in such ways, we must consider how children come to reconcile such ideas with the everyday world.

No doubt parental (or teacher's) authority is a major issue, the immediate mechanisms by which authority operates resembling those that lead us to accept the reality of atoms, genes, electricity, or gravity. In a religious family the child is immersed in a culture of belief, and experimental data show that children are more likely to accept the possibility of an event that violates physical principles if others (claim to) have experienced it (Subbotsky, 1994). Of course, cultures differ, and some are more conducive to the acceptance of religious beliefs than others: whereas, when children talk to imaginary companions that adults cannot see, many Indian parents treat the companion as real but invisible, most western parents treat it as imaginary (A. Mills, cited Woolley, 1997). Nevertheless, if the child deifies the imaginary companion, western parents may do likewise.

In addition, in most cultures children will have been exposed to innumerable myths that involve magical happenings, witches who fly on broomsticks, frogs which turn into princesses, and such like; and they may have been encouraged to induce magical events by hanging up a stocking for Father Christmas to fill, or putting a tooth under their pillow. They will thus have become acquainted with a category of events that violate the normal causal principles by which they have seen the world to operate. More importantly, they may have been encouraged by parents, whom they regarded as utterly reliable, to believe that such magical events can happen. That is not to say that the way that parents behave prevents children from seeing God as in a different category from Santa Claus, but only to suggest that counter-intuitive secular entities may pave the way for the acceptance of counter-intuitive properties in deities. Even if the parents indicate that the magical events belong to a 'let's pretend' world, that world may be accepted as half-believed in, just as we have seen adults can use gremlins without really believing in their existence (see p. 55). Therefore, if attempts to find an explanation of a surprising event in terms of ordinary principles fail, children may label the event as magical. This does not imply that they think a supernatural power is at work – they are simply categorising the event as one that conflicts with the principles with which they are familiar.

Indeed, it seems that children can show a positive emotional reaction to fairy-tales and the like just because they already have a stable set of causal principles that operate in the real world but not in the fairy-tale world (Harris, 1994). They see the world of magic as separate and distinct from the real world, and the former as exciting just because anything may happen. Religious or pseudo-religious concepts, like those of Father Christmas and St. Nicholas, may be especially attractive to young children just because they have a magical, counter-intuitive, quality. In both secular and religious spheres, people enjoy stories of the miraculous, but the extent to which they accept them is context-dependent (Humphrey, 1995). In secular contexts veracity may be qualified by the phrase 'Once upon a time' or by prosodic or paralinguistic elements in the communication. In religious life acceptance may be facilitated by a phrase like 'Dearly beloved brethren' or by the physical or temporal context of the occasion. Such 'markers' can be critical in indicating how a communication is to be stored and interpreted.

But under the influence of an authority figure – a parent or a conjuror, for instance – the two worlds may come together and the children may behave as though magic had happened or could happen in the real world. Some recent experiments on this issue are of considerable interest in the present context. Three and 4-year-old children generally understand very well the difference between the real world and the make-believe world, distinguishing clearly between real objects and objects that they have imagined. Yet some pre-school children, when asked to imagine that an object is present in a box which they know to be empty, subsequently act as though their imagination corresponded with reality. When subsequently asked for the object they may look inside the box 'just to see', or report that they had some doubts as to whether or not the object was there. One possible explanation is that children see some situations as permitting magical thinking, while others do not. Thus they may feel free to act as though their imagination referred to a real object if there are no ill consequences for doing so, but not if they perceive the situation to call for a practical, utilitarian response (Johnson and Harris, 1994; Woolley and Phelps, 1994). In religious contexts, other issues may be potent. As we have seen, statements about deities come from authority figures who make no distinction between the truth values of statements about deities and statements about the everyday world: it is thus understandable that the child should see them as one (see also Woolley, 1997).[7]

Another approach to understanding the assimilation of improbable concepts, not necessarily incompatible with this, focuses on differences in the ease with which new concepts can be assimilated by becoming linked to representations that are already established (Sperber, 1985). Acquisition of new concepts normally involves assimilation to existing representations. Thus if one is given a new pen, one can relate any properties it has to the category of pens, and assume that it has other properties generally known to be characteristic of pens without necessarily investigating the matter. But acquisition depends on the nature of the concept. Some abstract representations, such as those concerned with fashion, and rumours, spread rapidly through a society but are easily distorted in the process so that they may soon disappear: others, like notions of honesty and equality, may be stable and long-lasting in a particular society because they can be linked to other concepts. For instance the concept of social equality can be linked to notions of physical or numerical equality, which can be diluted to 'sameness' and is thus readily assimilable (cf. Dawkins, cited below). Similarly, it has been suggested that animal and plant species are often used as totemic symbols because human minds readily apprehend them, and they can conveniently serve to anchor more fluid symbolic thoughts.

But it is still the case that the non-schematic properties of supernatural beings contradict assumptions about the physical world and fit no pre-existing category: assimilating such concepts requires something other than the usual processes involved in the acquisition of knowledge. As implied earlier, it has therefore been suggested that such concepts are subjected to another form of processing, 'symbolic processing', whereby half-baked notions can be embedded in ideas one already has, perhaps at a higher order of representation, and the memory searched until the concept or property can be assimilated through associations that are only partially relevant. The search is presumably directed preferentially in particular directions by pre-existing memory structures. How far the distinction between the rational and symbolic modes of cognitive processing is really one of mechanism, and how much the distinction is inferred from the end result, is an issue that need not detain us here. The point is that, whereas in the primary mode ideas can be tested against other ideas and against empirical data, and can readily be played with until they are fully understood, 'symbolic processing' allows counter-intuitive concepts to be taken in even though they cannot readily be assimilated to existing representations. Such treatment, it is suggested, can allow diverse phenomena to be linked even though contradicting everyday experience: unlike scientific truth, symbolic truth permits re-interpretation to fit new circumstances (Atran, 1993; Boyer, 1995; Sperber, 1985). According to Atran (1993: 62), the elaboration of higher order cognitions differs between scientific and mystico-religious ways of thinking. While, in the acquisition of ordinary knowledge and of science, this playing with the idea of an idea can lead to more complete understanding, in the case of mythico-religious thinking it may 'draw people ever deeper into unfathomable mysteries by pointedly outraging everyday experience' in a manner that nevertheless links together diverse phenomena.

There are thus a number of mechanisms which may facilitate the assimilation of religious beliefs. As we have seen, they usually come initially from authority figures in whom the child has complete trust. In addition, the counter-intuitive nature of religious entities may make them the focus of attention, and certain cognitive mechanisms may contribute to their acquisition. We also saw, in Chapter 5, how deities may facilitate the realisation of certain psychological propensities: the extent to which they do so no doubt contributes to their stability through life. In addition, the beliefs about improbable entities form part of a religious system – an issue to be discussed later.

### Transmission across generations

The preceding paragraphs concern the assimilation of ideas by individual minds. But a further problem concerns how they spread through the population and are transmitted across successive generations. One descriptive approach, which by-passes the question of the psychological mechanisms involved, depends on the characterisation of items of information as 'memes' which can be passed on from one mind to another. For instance, Dawkins (1976, 1982, 1993) has suggested that human minds have properties which make them susceptible to 'memes' of particular sorts, for two reasons. First, minds can replicate input readily and with reasonable accuracy: the stability of local accents is cited as one example, and 'crazes' may sweep through a population. Second, they can obey coded instructions – for instance children told to kneel in prayer are likely to kneel in prayer. Religious memes, Dawkins suggests, are like viruses and are good at spreading from one mind to another: here the mechanisms discussed in the preceding paragraphs are clearly relevant. Dawkins further suggests that religious memes also readily gang up in groups that flourish in each other's presence.

A number of other authors have discussed the mechanism of the cultural transmission of ideas, basing their approach on the analogy of genetic transmission, and discussing possible mutual influences between the transmission of cultural characteristics and genetic ones (e.g. Boyd and Richerson, 1985; Durham, 1991; Irons, 1996b). This, and the question of the route of transmission (i.e. parent to child, peer to peer, majority to child), will be discussed briefly in Chapter 13.

### Later experience

Of course, the impact of early experiences is not the whole issue. A study of adolescents from six Christian denominations in the USA found that parents, peers, and later religious education were all related to religious behaviour, but the direct influence of parents was not particularly strong. However, they did have a partially indirect influence operating through religious practices at home, through the religious education to which the children were exposed, and, interestingly, also through their influence on the general world view of their children (Erickson, 1992).

As might be expected, the relative importance of early experience declines with age. In the West, at least, the cultural broadening in school and college, which can produce more liberal attitudes and cosmopolitanism, as well as religious scepticism and relativity, has conflicting effects which can more or less cancel each other: very religious students tend to become more religious, those only moderately religious become less so (Ozorak, 1989). Social experience in childhood and adolescence was found to be relatively unimportant for religious commitment in 33- to 42-year-olds who had grown up in

Presbyterian churches in Pennsylvania; but adult experiences, including current religious observance (influenced of course by earlier experience) and recent life events (number of children having a positive effect and inter-faith marriage, divorce and moving house the opposite), were related to church involvement (Hoge *et al.*, 1993).

While religious beliefs are usually acquired early in life, religious conversions at more mature ages do occur, especially around the time of puberty (Hall, 1904). Often, though not necessarily invariably, the individuals involved tend to be low in self-esteem, insecure, and lacking in social support. Conversion experiences, both into and away from religious involvement, are especially likely to occur in adolescence and old age (Beit-Hallahmi and Argyle, 1997).

### Commitment to a relationship and commitment to a religious system

Once acquired, religious beliefs may or may not be maintained. As we have seen, realisation of certain basic propensities may play an important part in their maintenance. However, it is of special interest here that some of the factors that influence commitment in close personal relationships (Hinde, 1997a; Rusbult and Buunk, 1993) have parallels in commitment to a religious belief system, with the role of priests or other religious specialists and processes of positive feedback playing an important role:

1   Commitment to the partner in a close relationship depends in part on satisfaction with that relationship, and that in turn on preceding expectations about rewards stemming from the relationship. The rewards obtained from the relationship are matched against expectations, but if the rewards fall short, defence mechanisms may minimise the deficit. The same principle applied to commitment to a deity or to a religious system suggests that belief could be self-reinforcing: the greater the belief, the greater the perceived reward, and thus the greater the commitment. It is important to note that it is the *perceived* rewards that matter, not those that are actually received, and a believer re-defines the perceived world to re-align it with the belief system. A comparison between Catholics who remained in and moved out of the church indicated that the difference was apparently not due to the empirical evidence, which had been similar for both groups. The two groups agreed about some of the deficiencies in the religious institution, but those who retained their religion perceived and interpreted them in a different way (Kotre, 1971).

2   Commitment to a personal relationship is greater, the greater the dependence on that relationship, as determined by the availability of alternatives. On this principle, it is not surprising that religious specialists should insist that other gods are inferior, or that it is a sin to

worship them. Nor is it surprising that people should be drawn to religion especially in times of adversity, danger, and so on.

3    Commitment to a personal relationship is enhanced if one makes sacrifices for it. The effect of doing so induces a cognitive shift so that expectations about the future of the relationship are strengthened. Thus a study of a student sample showed that the more individuals put into their relationships, the more committed they were to them and the longer they lasted (Lund, 1985; see also Lin and Rusbult, 1995). When communes were springing up in the 1960s and 1970s, those that were most durable tended to be those that demanded most from their members. In part this is an aspect of a common human fallacy (which has become known as the Concorde fallacy) – the more you have put into an enterprise, the more there is to lose if you pull out, and thus the more committed you tend to become. For that reason those who give time and alms to the religious system are more likely to be committed to it and, reciprocally, the more committed they are, the more they will give time and alms. Furthermore, for this reason it is in the interests of the religious specialists to encourage worship.

4    Commitment to a personal relationship is greater, the more central it is – that is, the more it brings meaning to life and is linked to personal identity: once again there is plenty of scope for positive feedback in the religious case.

5    Finally, in a personal relationship, the more that one individual sees the other putting into the relationship, the more convinced he or she is of the other's commitment. In a similar way, the more faith an individual has in the deity, the more he or she will see the deity as a committed relationship partner, and the more faith he or she will have in him/her. And the more the individual sees a religious group to be well organised and its members to be dedicated, the more likely is he or she to become committed to it.

## Some conclusions

At this point it may be helpful to summarise briefly the main conclusions of the preceding chapters on religious beliefs.

Not only do religious systems differ in the content of their beliefs, but within any one system there are great differences between individuals in the degree of certainty with which the beliefs are held, in the extent to which they permeate the self-system, and in their quality. They may also differ in relation to the personality of the individual and the nature of the society.

Religious beliefs are not static, but are subject to dynamic influences for stability and change. Religious systems differ in the extent to which the beliefs are codified, in whether they are seen as having been 'revealed', and whether they are specific to a particular social group.

In spite of this variability, the religious entities believed in are such as to satisfy a number of basic human needs, including that to understand the causes of events, the need to feel in control of one's life, the need for security, the need to cope with the fear of death, the need for personal relationships, and the need for a coherent meaning in life.

The religious entities in which belief is placed are extremely diverse, and tension between whether the deity should be perceived as an all-pervading essence or as an anthropomorphic entity is common. Religious entities usually have both everyday and counter-intuitive properties. This diversity reflects both the diverse needs that they can satisfy and the need for some degree of cognitive consistency in the believer.

The acquisition of religious beliefs seldom involves a cool appraisal of evidence, but is usually a gradual matter occurring during the course of socialisation. It depends on domain-specific principles common to cognitive development in other spheres. Even the assimilation of deities with counter-intuitive properties does not involve new principles. Parents and other authority figures play an important role.

In general, therefore, the evidence is consistent with the view that religious beliefs depend on cognitive and emotional processes that operate in the secular world, and that they are associated with certain basic psychological propensities. They are thus compatible with Darwinian principles.

## Summary

Principles derived from the study of children's cognitive development are relevant to understanding the acquisition of religious beliefs. In particular, early cognitive development involves constraints and predispositions which differ between cognitive domains: for instance, animate objects are distinguished in part by their capacity for self-initiated motion, and are seen as having an essential 'essence' responsible for their properties. Children only slowly acquire the ability to interpret other's actions in terms of intentions (theory of mind).

Storage of knowledge in the brain involves the formation of concepts by linking new information to existing concepts.

Religious beliefs are normally initially acquired in the course of socialisation, with authority figures playing an important role. Acquisition of the counter-intuitive properties of deities may be facilitated by previous experience of the world of magic in folk-tales, etc. Experience with the parents is, of course, of special importance, but other influences become important later.

Processes involved in the maintenance of commitment to a deity resemble in many ways those involved in commitment to a personal relationship.

# 8 Narratives

The structural beliefs of a religious system are outside time, but in other respects are barely separable from the narratives that explicate them and integrate them with other aspects of the religious system. In this chapter we shall see that the use of the narrative mode is a fundamental and ubiquitous characteristic of human social life.

## Narratives in everyday life

As discussed in Chapter 2, we see ourselves, our pasts and our futures, largely in narrative form. Much of our thinking about our lives is in narrative form, most usually loosely linked vignettes of incidents, real or imaginary, such that experience is organised into comprehensible episodes. Such accounts make sense of events, and tend to do so with emotional power in a way that gives meaning to life. Allowing insight into the complexities of thought, emotion, and behaviour involved in human interaction, the use of the narrative mode has been contrasted with the paradigmatic, the way of logic, mathematics, and the physical sciences (Bruner, 1986). The narrative form allows the individual to grasp a longer past and to conceive the future and the social environment in a more intricate and variegated fashion than would otherwise be possible. It is not merely a matter of the sequential story form: narrative thought permits understanding of the complex webs of information provided by the interactions between particular individuals. It captures the attention of the listener or reader, focusing it on particular situations yet allowing the imagination full play, and permits the drawing of general conclusions more effectively than could either representation of a succession of isolated events or a paradigmatic exposition of principles.

Parents use narratives in socialising and educating their children, and children love to hear stories. Interestingly, parents are more prone to encourage beliefs in imaginary beings associated with particular events, like Santa Claus and the Easter Bunny, than in witches, fairies and monsters which are associated with a range of occasions; and children are more prone to believe in entities of the former type (Rosengren and Hickling, 1994).

Most importantly, we use narratives which include characterisations of the self and others as part of the self-system to bind together different aspects of the real or perceived past, present, and future. They influence how the present is construed, and how the present is construed may affect memories of the past. The accounts may be private, or elaborated in dialogue with others. Sometimes they are contradictory, presenting accounts suitable for different audiences, accounts that represent different aspects of the self (e.g. Bruner, 1990; Carrithers, 1992; Fletcher and Fitness, 1996; Harvey *et al.*, 1989; McAdams, 1996).

Such narratives have some degree of consistency, but they may also be changed to suit circumstances or to maintain coherence with current views. As an example of this flexibility, in one study couples were asked to describe the early stages of their relationships soon after marriage and again two years later. On the second occasion the couples were divided into those who had experienced a fall in marital well-being over the two years, and those who had not. Soon after their weddings, the descriptions given by the two groups did not differ in positivity/negativity. But, at the end of the two years, the less happy couples, unlike the more stable ones, described their early relationship in much more negative terms than they had used earlier (Holmberg and Veroff, 1996).

We also use narratives to manipulate the behaviour of others. Rumours, propaganda, advertising, all employ narrative to influence others. Rivalry between Greek and Turkish Cypriot societies has been exacerbated by conflicting narratives of the history of the island (Papadakis, 1995), and the history of Pearl Harbor has been re-told as a moral narrative (White, 1997; see also Wertsch, 1997). Many narratives can thus be seen as a transaction between story-teller and listener, the former attempting to foster his or her own interests, the latter gaining information.

While it is undeniable that use of the narrative form is a ubiquitous human characteristic, it has also been suggested that the propagation of narratives can be a powerful way of influencing the reproductive success of successive generations, and that the propensity for story-telling is a result of natural selection (Steadman and Palmer, 1997; Sugiyama, 1996): this is a reasonable suggestion, but satisfactory proof would be very difficult to obtain.

## Religious narratives

### Role of religious narratives

In view of the ubiquity of the use of narrative in everyday life, its use within religious systems is hardly surprising. In nearly every religious system, the structural beliefs are supported by narratives which help to define the nature of the deities and near-deities and to relate them to the everyday world.[1] Metaphors which relate religious experience to the everyday world are commonplace – God the Father, soldiers of Christ, the bread of life, holy mountains, and so on. Narratives are located in time, but exemplify the timeless structural beliefs, enriching and extending them. The imagery involved makes the structural beliefs vivid and acceptable. In monotheistic systems the narratives are usually interrelated, but in cultures where a number of gods are recognised, the stories about them may have considerable independence.

There is much greater latitude in the required acceptance of the narratives than there is of the structural beliefs. This latitude tends to be less where the narratives are codified, as with the Christian Gospels and accompanying books of the New Testament, when it can lead both to discussion about their historical truth, and to attempts to distinguish between their historical accuracy and their religious message. But even when the narratives are codified, there may be great differences in the status accorded to them. Some are accepted, others are seen as apocryphal, and the former may be seen as literally true or as metaphorical.

Religious narratives do not serve only to support the structural beliefs. They may purvey values, either explicitly or by presenting models of behaviour. Furthermore the narratives central to a religious system may be accompanied by others which provide exemplars for people to follow, such as the *Lives of the Saints* and Bunyan's *Pilgrim's Progress*. These may be acknowledged to be fictional, yet serve to convey models of behaviour. Here the nature of 'truth' becomes tricky: narratives may be seen as 'psychologically true' – that is, true for the individual if they have a positive influence on his attitude to the world and if they help him to behave according to the established code.

In other cases narratives may contribute to the interpretation of religious experience: religious visions often refer to the narratives of the religious system (Chapter 15). They may also purport to explain the past or to foretell the future, for instance the coming of a Messiah, or help to preserve a collective memory of the past, and thus the identity of the group or society.

Of course there may or may not be an element of historical truth in the narratives. Beyond that their precise form will depend on many factors including the local geography (gods are likely to inhabit inaccessible places where their presence cannot be verified) and the values of the culture. But in oral cultures narratives must change with re-telling and as memories waver, just as the stories of Christ's life changed in the years before they were written down; and in literate cultures narratives may be revised or re-written to suit current needs.

Which stories are to be included in the religious canon may be a matter of dispute, and the interpretation of a given story may change with time. A clear example is the Old Testament Song of Songs, which has been regarded sometimes as predicting the mutual love between Christ and his Church, and at others as a secular love song.

*Religious narratives and the social system*

The narratives are influenced by the social system in that they are usually based around issues of individual or social concern – the relations between ruler and ruled, the mysteries of birth and death, sex, and so on. In any case, everyday matters are interwoven with the supernatural in a manner that is appropriate to the society in question. Thus most societies, and most belief systems, involve some sort of hierarchy – Jesus and the disciples, Allah and Mahomet, the supreme god Nzambi and the ancestral spirits and the antisocial witches of the Ndembu (Turner, 1957). The setting in which the supernatural beings are portrayed is also culturally appropriate. The Christian God is usually portrayed (especially in post-biblical literature and art) as sitting on a throne in a situation resembling a mediaeval court. The abstract qualities of that court are explained in terms of the concrete, secular Middle Eastern preoccupations with gold, precious stones, and light. Thus descriptions of Heaven in the Book of Revelations resound with references to gold (e.g. 'crowns of gold', 'golden vials', 'golden altars', 'streets of pure gold'), precious stones (the new Jerusalem had walls garnished with jasper, sapphire, chalcedony, emerald, sardonyx, sardius, chrysolite, beryl, topaz, chrysoprasus, jacinth and amethyst in successive layers), and above all with colour and light – a rainbow surrounded the throne, and there was no need of sun or moon because the glory of the Lord lightened it.

In China jade took the place of gold, the worlds of the Chinese immortals shimmering in the 'white moonlight glow of luminous jade' (Rawson, 1995). The Christian view of Heaven is simple compared with the rich pantheon of gods, ghosts, local deities and spirits seen over many centuries in China as populating the other world. Of special interest in this context is the free interchange that was seen to go on between this world and the underworld, as recorded in Dai Fu's eighth-century collection of stories (Dudbridge, 1995). Although the underworld was regarded as alien and unseen, its surroundings, customs and institutions were similar to those of Tang China. Tombs were seen as the houses of the dead, with figurines of guards, attendants and servants who performed the functions appropriate to them in life (and sometimes caused problems by quarrelling among themselves) and with material objects for use in the after-life. The underworld had its own bureaucracy, and people were believed sometimes to go from one world to the other. Occasionally humans were summoned to the underworld in error, and sometimes they managed to come back. Money was transferred symbolically in both directions.

Thus the nature of deities, or of the other world, is usually communicated in the form of stories. Our picture of the life of Jesus is derived from the narratives of the Gospels, and the Book of Revelation provides a vision of Heaven in the form of a narrative. As we have just seen, the Chinese picture of the underworld is portrayed in stories. Such narratives may explain, and thus make acceptable, the structural beliefs, and to that end may be propagated by the religious specialists. They may explain aspects of the world, as in origin myths. Their spread and the tenacity with which they are held will follow the same principles as those outlined for the structural beliefs.

## Summary

The use of the narrative form for conveying aspects of the religious system is in keeping with what is known about human cognitive functioning. Religious narratives portray the nature of the deities, convey the moral code, form the basis for ritual, are based on the current social scene, and may have diverse social consequences. The content of the narratives reflects the local scene.

# 9 Ritual

## Background considerations

It is difficult to imagine a religious system that did not involve ritual of some sort. Ritual therefore forms the subject matter of this and the next two chapters.

The term 'ritual' can include a wide spectrum of behaviour from primarily social, public occasions to private worship and meditation. There are differences between religions, between denominations, and between individuals in the importance attached to ritual.

To many, public rituals are seen as unnecessary and superficial, for others they play a central role. The focus of religious rituals may be on the performance itself, on a specific more or less tangible goal such as the curing of a sick person, or on the subjective state induced in the participants. And that subjective state may seem to be primarily cognitive, as in meditation, or emotional, as in ecstatic performances, though of course the two overlap and are interrelated.

This chapter begins with a digression concerning the relations between cause and consequence, as a lack of clarity on that issue can lead to misunderstandings of the 'meaning' of ritual. That is followed by a brief discussion of the nature of ritual, intended as background to the material in the next two chapters.

### Cause and consequence

Why do rituals play such an important part in many religious systems? That question is central to the following three chapters. But 'Why' questions about behaviour can be answered in a number of ways. Biologists classify these into four categories, which can best be presented by an example. Suppose you were asked 'Why does your thumb move in a different way from the other fingers?' You might give an answer in terms of the differences in skeletal structure and muscle attachments between the thumb and the other fingers – an answer referring to the immediate causation of thumb movement. You might give a developmental answer, describing how, as the finger rudiments developed, one came to have a different structure from the others. As a third possibility, you might say that an opposable thumb makes it easier to pick things up, or to climb trees – a functional answer. Finally, you might give an evolutionary answer, saying that we are descended from monkey-like creatures who had opposable thumbs. Biologists interested in behaviour have found that these four questions – immediate causation, development, function, and evolution – though independent and logically distinct, are often inter-fertile (Tinbergen, 1963).

Now let us ask how these four types of answer apply to complex behaviour, like that involved in religion. Developmental issues have been mentioned in several contexts already: in this context they present no particular conceptual problem. If the thesis of this book is correct, the evolutionary origins of religious systems lie in their genesis from more basic pan-cultural psychological predispositions, which may themselves have been adapted by natural selection in other contexts. About the further evolutionary history of religious systems we know little and are unlikely to know much more in the foreseeable future (but see e.g. Mithen, 1996).

So that leaves us with questions about the causes and functions of the religious activities themselves. To the biologist, function is a sub-category of the consequences of behaviour, and refers to consequences enhancing survival and reproduction through which natural selection has acted to maintain them in the species' repertoire. But the effects on survival and reproduction may be very indirect, acting through long causal chains. And every behavioural act has many consequences, some of which may give plea sure or pain to the individual concerned and many of which are quite irrelevant to survival and reproduction. Furthermore, in intentional behaviour consequence is linked to cause – the cause of the act is the intention to bring about the consequence. Thus the cause of behaviour may or may not have anything to do with its several consequences, and the (anticipated) consequences of behaviour may or may not be causal to it. It is especially important to be clear-headed about this issue when considering religious ritual, as discussions of the 'meaning' of ritual are sometimes bogged down by it. For instance, discussion as to whether ritual is functional or expressive can involve confusion on this matter, for behaviour leading to beneficial consequences may or may not be intended, and expressive behaviour (i.e. performed for its own sake) may (though it need not) lead to beneficial consequences.

Both the causes and the consequences of behaviour may be diverse. This is sometimes overlooked. Consider first the causes of behaviour. If we ask 'Why did A go to church?', the reply might refer to A's earlier history (a developmental answer) – for instance it might be said that he came from a religious family: this implies that he acquired a feeling of rightness and security in church attendance, and that the anticipation of such feelings acts as a cause of behaviour. The expected security may come from enhanced self-esteem consequent upon doing what is proper, or from an enhanced sense of community with like-minded individuals, or from a belief that he is pleasing God, or that church attendance will lead him to rewards in an after-life. Or the reply might refer to one of two types of contemporaneous cause –

currently acting, predisposing factors, or immediately acting, eliciting factors. Predisposing factors might involve a recent bereavement, or a vague feeling of gratitude for benefits he had recently received. And, immediately, church-going may be elicited by his wife's insistence, or by the realisation that he will feel better if he does (i.e. anticipated consequences) and/or by the sound of the church bell. In practice, several such causal factors would act together.

The point, then, is that religious observance has many causes, developmental, predisposing, and eliciting, social and individual, and their potency will differ between individuals. And these causes will have other causes – in the societal norms, or in the activities of the religious specialists (whose actions also have many causes), or in the individual's own experience. If ritual performances are to be understood, it is essential to bear in mind that what the participants are supposed to believe themselves to be doing may differ from what they actually think is going on; that their subjective experiences (cognitive and emotional) may be idiosyncratic and tenuously related to the supposed nature of the ritual; and that what the ritual specialists say is going on may differ from what they think is going on. On the last point, the ritual specialist may tell the participants that it is an occasion for worship, but himself see the ritual as educational, or as having a disciplinary function whose regularity sharpens the will or provides opportunity for reflection.

Now let us consider the consequences of going to church. First, the individual may obtain a sense of comfort, feel blessed, or have an enhanced sense of belonging, and thereby achieve his goal in going to church. There may be a second group of consequences that are incidental and irrelevant: he may frighten a spider as he sits down in his pew. And a third group may be equally unintended yet affect his future desire to go to church: he may feel too hot in his Sunday suit, or as he leaves he may unexpectedly get into conversation with a nice young woman whom he had always wanted to meet. Furthermore the consequences of his going to church do not reside solely in him. Perhaps others, seeing him there, will feel a greater sense of community – or possibly that they will never go to church again if he is going to be there. Perhaps the young woman will see him as a more desirable partner if he goes to church. Perhaps his singing the hymns will inspire others to do likewise.

Thus the consequences, like the causes, of going to church are diverse. Some are intended, and will affect the probability of future church attendance. Some, like the spider, will be irrelevant. Some will affect the likelihood of church attendance in the future even though not intended. And some are relevant only to others. These issues will be familiar to sociologists, for it was central to Weber's (1976) thesis that actions could have unintended consequences.

It will therefore be apparent that many of the consequences of ritual performance as seen by an outside observer may be unrelated to the motivations of those involved. For example, when Turner (1957) suggested that a particular Ndembu ritual performed for a woman suffering from leprosy, had a number of 'social effects', his list included: reducing the hostility of the villagers to the woman, whom many had seen as a witch, by making her an object of sympathy; closing a breach between different factions in the village; giving prestige to the host village; re-establishing friendly relations with other villages; exemplifying Ndembu beliefs and values; offering an alternative source of prestige to those with limited authority; and affording certain ambitious persons opportunity to enhance their prestige. With the exception of the last two, these are mostly consequences which may have had little relation to the motivation of those taking part.

The diversity of causes and consequences operating make generalisations about ritual hazardous. If individuals within one culture differ in their (conscious or unconscious) reasons for religious observance, the differences are likely to be even greater between cultures. Thus a generalisation of the type 'Hope that a god will intervene in time of trouble is a cause of religious observance' is not invalidated for all societies by the observation that in some societies gods are not perceived as interfering in human affairs.

## The category of religious ritual

### The nature of ritual

Ritual, like religion itself, has proved extremely hard to define, and is often seen as involving a number of features no one of which is essential (Needham, 1985). Usually, however, it involves a series of actions which are repeated from time to time in a (usually) fairly rigid sequence, and which are seen as distinct from everyday normal actions. Two issues seem to be of special importance. First, the sequence of the actions is in large measure predetermined, and does not depend on the actor's intentions or on the intellectual and emotional experiences that they undergo (Humphrey and Laidlaw, 1994; Lewis, 1980). Indeed tradition usually plays a major role, the antiquity of a ritual being perceived to contribute to its value (see also McMullen, 1987). The behaviour proper to a ritual is usually acquired from example, as part of the acquisition of the religious system, so that there is nearly always a 'right' way to perform a religious rite. According to Hindu Vedic belief, a ritual correctly performed inevitably produces its appropriate result, but one incorrectly performed may bring about catastrophe.

The second issue is that the ritual involves more than the actions that constitute it. In performing a ritual the participant is doing more than is immediately apparent, and it is that which gives the ritual its significance. Ritual behaviour is sometimes said to differ from everyday behaviour because it 'stands for' something over and above the actual actions involved. This, however, is a slightly dangerous way of putting it, because what the ritual 'stands for' may depend on the attitude that the participant brings to it: individuals may attribute their own meanings to the rites they act out. The meaning they reach will have been partly constructed in development under the influence of social forces, it will be affected by their preconceptions of the ritual, and it will be immediately influenced by their current state of mind (Humphrey and Laidlaw, 1994).[1]

In addition, it is important to note that ritual may involve a specific goal (e.g. healing a sick person, marrying a couple), and induce experiences among the individuals involved. In some rituals the former predominates, in others the latter; but in all cases participation can result in a new state of consciousness and in the longer term a new orientation and a new self-image, and thus help to establish, confirm, or change the individual's religious beliefs and attitudes. The emotional aspects of a ritual may be more important than the intellectual messages that it is purported to convey: whereas ordinary language is usually used only to talk about emotions, ritual can transmit them so that, while some rituals permit or encourage idiosyncratic experience, others can co-ordinate the feelings of individuals.

### Religious and secular ritual

Any attempt to distinguish religious from secular rituals soon becomes problematic. For example, the so-called 'popular religions' of China were focused round various types of ritual – funerals, New Year festivals, consultations with mediums, and the like. These were shared by most people regardless of their affiliations with one or other of the main religions of Taoism or Buddhism, and were independent of them (Teiser, 1996). In the West the procedure and actions that mark the family Christmas dinner, or even the family evening meal, have characteristics in common with religious rituals. The rituals involved in politeness help to keep a society together, though they lack the deeper significance which is said to characterise religious ritual. Religious and secular rituals are often interwoven, as in remembrance gatherings for those killed in war, and many rituals that seem primarily secular today have historical religious origins. The procedure for the admission of a new Fellow by the Master at some Cambridge Colleges bears a close resemblance to the ritual between a lord and his liege at Charlemagne's court, and presumably came down through the monasteries (cf. Ganshof, 1961). Indeed some secular occasions have many characteristics in common with religious rituals: spectators at football matches show deference and adoration towards the star players; they may become in some degree ecstatic; and the game may be preceded and followed by rule governed actions. Nor is it easy to make a distinction between religious rituals and those used in magic, or even everyday superstitions (see pp. 122–5).

## Development

As we have already seen (pp. 91–2), young children attending church simply see it as what people do on Sundays. They may (or may not) enjoy it as a social activity, but only gradually do they become aware that the acts involved (kneeling, praying, singing, and so on) have special significance for adults, and even later, perhaps, discover special significances of their own.

## Religious specialists

Where religious specialists are recognised, they may play a part in every aspect of the religion, but their role is perhaps especially conspicuous in the rituals. Where communication with the deity is the issue, it may be direct, or it may be facilitated or mediated by religious specialists. In some religious rituals, like the Jain puja (Humphrey and Laidlaw, 1994), there may be no intermediary, individuals attributing their own meanings to the rites they act out. In Islam clergy are theoretically absent: there is no sacramental distinction between preachers or ritual leaders and laity, though the former are expected to be more competent, and especially more learned (Gellner, 1992). There were no priests in the early Christian church (Armstrong, 1993), though they have an essential role in many Christian procedures today.

Religious specialists are expected to have special properties. If they are to intercede with the deity, this is hardly surprising. In some societies, it is merely a question of holding a certain rank (e.g. chief), but in others special personal properties may be required. The prophets and some priests are recognised by their ability to speak for the deity, mystics by their ability to have experiences beyond most people's reach and by their self-control, sages by their wisdom, gurus by their character and authority – in each case, therefore by a certain charisma. Among the Hebrews only Levites without any physical deformity could become a priest, and they had to maintain their purity by marrying a virgin, not touching dead flesh, and so on. Modern rabbis, however, though expected to be genuine and dedicated, are not thought to possess special powers other than those due to their training (Steinberg, 1947). In Christian cultures priests are inducted in a special ceremony (ordination), selection and training for which is taken to ensure certain properties, including certain moral characteristics perhaps facilitating communication with the deity. Ordinands may try to reinforce their position by assuming a certain charisma: an Australian study cited by Brown (1987) indicated that clergy who stressed their role in this world rather than in other-worldly terms were more likely to encounter difficulties with parishioners.[2] A recent Vatican instruction is designed to limit the role of the laity in the Catholic Church, and emphasises the unique position of ordained ministry based on apostolic succession.[3]

Boyer (1994) regards the assumption that ordinands have certain special properties as an extension of the use of categories for the natural world: as we have seen, categories such as species always involve the assumption of an underlying trait or essence to be found in all exemplars. He suggests that we have or acquire a 'charismatic proclivity' – a tendency to interpret social positions in terms of personal attributes. For example, discussing the four basic castes in Buddhism, Carrithers (1992: 120–1) writes:

> To call someone a Khattiya, for example, was not just to designate him as a bearer of arms or a ruler, but also to attribute to him qualities as a person: generosity, heroism, nobility. A Brahman was not just a priest by vocation but inherently endowed with wisdom, virtue, learning, personal purity, and purity of birth.

In our own culture we tend to see priests as having certain personal qualities, or expect them to have them, even though such qualities are not officially necessary qualifications for being an incumbent of that role: they are expected to behave more impeccably than the laity, and their transgressions are seen as more culpable. Indeed the formal criteria are often seen as a consequence of the personal qualities, just as children, in discussing natural kinds, often see the external identificatory features as consequences of underlying traits. This 'essentialist' characteristic of religious offices makes it easier to understand the powers that the incumbents are seen as having, and how it comes about that individuals who undertake tasks for the sake of their souls or the good of the community, like pilgrims, come to have an aura of holiness. The use of an initiating ceremony, and the wearing of special clothes, can be seen as external markers of the underlying trait.

Where the religious specialists form a cohesive social body, further steps may be taken to mark their position. In the Christian church of the Middle Ages the priesthood and the way the priests lived were designed to support their role in justifying the church's claim to exclusive and universal mediation of grace and supernatural power. The clergy were increasingly set aside in life-style, duties, clothing, training, and language from the community (Rubin, 1991). The balancing act between the role of a mediator with the Almighty and being an accessible fellow human being is a real problem for the priesthood in the modern world, especially for those who work in the armed forces and educational institutions.

## Background conditions

The meaning of words in a conversation depend on background assumptions about the context, the intentions of the speaker, and so on. In practice, the specification of all the background conditions necessary for the full interpretation of an utterance is likely to be an open-ended task that can never be completed, because it is never possible to foresee all the contexts in which the utterance might be interpreted (Austin, 1975; Good, 1995).

In the same way, certain background conditions are necessary for the performance of a ritual to be seen as valid. To be seen as authentic, the ritual may have to take place in a special place perceived as 'holy', be conducted by persons perceived to have special powers, or involve special words and actions. In literate societies, these conditions may be fairly clearly defined. Thus a Mass is not a Mass unless conducted by an ordained priest. Other background conditions may be expected but not required, their absence making the performance less effective: thus a marriage in the Church of England may be seen as less 'well-performed' if there is no organ music. Furthermore the significance of a marker or signal intended to indicate the special quality of a ritual or other religious occasion may depend on the context in which it is given and on background assumptions made by the participants. However in preliterate societies the background conditions for successful performance may not be fully specified: as we shall see later, this provides a route for explaining away failure (Boyer, 1994).

## Summary

In discussing the nature of religious ritual, it is especially necessary to be clear about the relations between cause and consequence. For any particular act or act sequence, both may be diverse, and they may or may not be related.

Religious ritual is difficult to define, but rituals usually involve a prescribed series of actions which are held to 'stand for' a meaning which may not be immediately apparent and may be shared or idiosyncratic to the performer.

There are many similarities between religious and secular rituals, and the two may be intertwined. Ritual performances are often the responsibility of religious specialists, who are held to have special properties. Background conditions, often not fully specified, may be necessary for authentic performance.

# 10 Ritual

## Form and sequence; magic

A conspicuous feature of many rituals lies in the form and sequence of the activities involved. In this chapter, therefore, we ask how far the form of ritual procedures can be seen as reflecting pan-cultural human characteristics. As we have seen, some ritual performances are private or individual matters, but here we shall be concerned primarily with public occasions. Two interrelated issues are of special importance, namely the extent to which the procedures are attention-getting and memorable, and their symbolic value.

It is convenient to start with the elementary actions. The symbolism of the actions and of the artefacts employed can then be discussed, and finally the organisation of the sequences in which the actions are performed.

## Characteristics of ritual

### Ritual actions

There are some parallels between ritual actions and those performed in everyday life. Children enjoy counting and rhyming songs and games, often played repetitively. Many go through a stage of minor superstitious rituals, like avoiding the cracks between paving stones, which seem to stave off imagined terrors: comparable practices occur not infrequently in adults. Whether these have any relation to the obsessive/compulsive rituals of some adults, and whether either have any relation to religious rituals, is uncertain, but some similarities are worth noting. Both young children and sufferers from obsessive/compulsive disorders may exhibit the 'just right' syndrome: this includes strictly circumscribed ways of arranging objects, doing things in precisely the 'right' way, preferences for symmetry, wholeness, and so on (Evans *et al.*, 1997). Obsessive/compulsive rituals are often repetitive in the same way as repetitive chanting or the manipulation of a rosary. (The latter has been compared to the use of worry-beads in some Mediterranean countries to overcome anxiety, though the successive beads of a rosary may be associated with a specific series of meanings or meditations.) Obsessive/compulsive rituals, especially those used by women, often involve repetitive washing or cleansing, and this seems to be related to indiscriminate fears.

Often such rituals are accompanied by magical or superstitious beliefs that have become fixed and are carried to extremes. They may involve checking that tasks have been done or possible dangers monitored, and their performance is believed to avert harm. The sufferers are more likely to ritualise when they feel tense, and usually feel better afterwards. They suppose their behaviour to be normal (Marks, 1987). All of these characteristics have echoes in at least some religious rituals, though the similarities may be superficial.

Many of the actions used in public rituals differ from everyday actions in their attention-getting or signalling properties. In considering such differences, it is useful to think in terms of the evolutionary changes by which the movements of animals have become more effective as signals: these include the development of conspicuous structures to enhance the movement (which in the human case would include the use of artefacts); changes in the form and speed of movement; and an increase in the stereotypy of the movement so that it becomes more easily recognisable (Tinbergen, 1952). Many of the actions used in religious ritual exploit similar principles. It is, of course, unnecessary to emphasise that that does not imply that religious rituals are reducible to anything resembling animal signalling.

Some of the finer details of ritual performances do play on human psychological characteristics to make the actions more conspicuous and memorable. The gestures used, the exaggerated forms of movement, the special tones of voice, play on human perceptual mechanisms to make the ceremonial more impressive. The stereotyped form of the actions and the ordered nature of the ceremony may convey an aura of specialness which in turn may facilitate the acceptance of counter-intuitive ideas. The atmosphere engendered is suited to the occasion: it may be fear-provoking, as in the initiation ceremonies of some pre-literate societies and those used by Freemasons (Piatigorsky, 1997); or comforting, as in some rituals for the relief of sickness; or stirring, as on religio-bellicose occasions. Rhythmic stimulation can induce an ecstatic state, and may be involved in many shamanistic performances and regenerative experiences. In addition, as we shall see, the movements may have symbolic significance.

In the same way, ritual performance may involve artefacts which, by virtue of their visual characteristics, workmanship, and associations, are likely to engage the attention of those present (Wulff, 1997). Light and radiance and valuable materials draw the gaze – and perhaps also symbolise purity and power. Often everyday objects made in elaborate forms, with considerable expenditure on precious materials, are used. Thus Zjou court rituals used jade axes, clearly reminiscent of real ones, and elaborate bronzes of superb workmanship (Rawson, 1995). Eye-like shapes are conspicuous in many artefacts: eyes are inherently salient even to young infants, and their attention-getting properties are employed in some rituals. The Mesopotamian votive statues and painted votaries had enlarged staring eyes, often emphasised with lapis lazuli or bitumen for the iris and shell for the surround: the eyes were focused on the deity in whose sanctuary the royal image was placed. The wide eyes reflect a response of admiration to the awe-inspiring deity (Winter, 1997). The foods or animals offered in sacrificial rituals are often those deemed to be most precious in the society (see also Lewis, 1980).

Rituals are usually performed in a particular place, such as a church or temple. Such sites or buildings constitute a 'marked-off space', in which ordinary things become special and sacred simply by virtue of their location (Smith, 1987).

But here, as so often, one must be careful of generalisations. In some cultures the use of artefacts is seen as a barrier to true worship, and simplicity and austerity are cherished as providing a clearer path towards contact with the deity. Perhaps in such cases the simplicity is itself provoking because of the contrast with the complexity of life in the everyday world.

### Symbolism in ritual

Not only are the perceptual aspects of the ritual likely to be such as to make the performance salient, but the particular actions and artefacts may have a symbolic significance. The artefacts and gestures used in ritual carry meanings, some of which will be general to all present and others different for the different participants. Tradition nearly always plays a role: many ritual performances are seen to be authentic only if they are carried out in the way that they have always been carried out.

Often the significance of the symbolism is easily comprehensible. Water is used for purification, red wine for blood, and so on. Again, the equation between above/below and superior/inferior seems intuitively to be a conse-quence of the ubiquitous relation between height and value, perhaps depending in turn simply on the way that the human body works (see pp. 21–2) (Leach, 1972). It is presumably because height is associated with value that gods are usually thought to reside either in mountains or above the world. Indeed, height is intrinsic to the literal meaning of 'transcendence' ('climbing beyond'), though transcendence as used in religious contexts also carries an implication that space is irrelevant. The spires of Christian churches and cathedrals point to the sky, and the clerestory gives a sense of space above. Conveniently, the sun is in the sky, and life-giving rain also comes from the sky, and the fire used in sacrifice has associations with the sun and sends smoke upwards to the higher regions (Smart, 1996). Conversely, bending down, kneeling or prostration are indicative of accepted inferiority or humility. Sometimes the specific symbols used are easily linked to more complex concepts, or to both an existential problem and its solution. For instance the Christian Cross evokes thoughts both of suffering and of deliverance from suffering; and the bishop's crook thoughts of the Good Shepherd who saves lost sheep (cf. Batson and Ventis, 1982).

Rituals in early China used the reality of this world to create notions about the after-life. Tombs were based on aspects of dwellings in this life, and conveyed the supposition that the after-life would be basically similar. The bronze vessels placed in tombs were elaborations of everyday cooking pots (Rawson, 1998b).

In other cases the symbolism may be apparent to some but must be explained to the young and the uninitiated. The Jewish Seder is a case in point, for elaborate symbolism is employed: a sprig of parsley represents the renewal of life each Spring, salt water represents the tears shed by the Jews in captivity, horseradish the bitterness of slavery, and so on (Porterfield, 1998). Depending on the religiosity of the family, the significance of the procedures may or may not be apparent to the participants.

Sometimes, however, the symbolism is even more abstruse. Some rituals are difficult for the participating laity to understand, and involve concepts that are intrinsically unverifiable, but come from, or rather through, religious specialists who are perceived to have authority (see Morris, 1987). Since ordinary verification procedures are impossible, the stage is set for the hearer to construct an explanation of the type 'God is speaking through the priest who is speaking of God's intentions'. When spirit messages are conveyed by mediums, diviners or shamans, such a construction may be facilitated by the fact that the religious specialists are believed to be ( and perhaps are) neither conscious nor responsible for what they are saying – so where else could the message come from?

The symbolism in some mortuary rituals provides an example of symbolism somewhat less obvious to westerners. Death involves both the individuality of the deceased and the continuity of the social order in his or her absence. Accordingly, in non-western societies mortuary rituals often represent death as part of a cyclical process of renewal, with symbols of sexuality and fertility prominent. In some societies symbolic death may precede physical death, the individual subsequently being treated as one who has no place in the world of the living, or after physical death, when some symbolic act is performed on the corpse. However, anthropologists do not always agree in their interpretations, which often seem difficult to verify and may not coincide with the interpretations of those present (see e.g. Bloch and Parry, 1982).

The symbolism of Mass supposedly represents the Last Supper of Christ and the disciples, at which He gave them bread and wine which He had blessed, saying 'Take, eat; this is my body' and 'Drink ye all of it; For this is my blood of the new testament' (Matthew, 26, 26–8). However, the precise nature of the ceremony has been a matter of controversy throughout the history of the Christian church – did the bread and wine merely symbolise Christ's body and blood or, as proclaimed in the thirteenth century, were they actually converted into them? The latter possibility led to elaborate procedures to cope with eventualities such as the priest spilling the wine, or the recipient vomiting after he had taken the bread into his mouth: in the latter case the priest might be obligated to consume the vomit himself (Rubin, 1991).

The artefacts often have an historical significance. Thus the Christian Mass uses a chalice, made of valuable material and often decorated with precious stones, but also of a traditional shape with associations with the past (Rawson, 1995). The ceremony reminds participants of the Last Supper and of the promise of redemption made by Christ to his apostles. 'The concrete presence of the chalice and the physical enactment of the ritual bring to mind directly and indirectly associations, complex ideas about life and death and redemption' (Rawson, 1998a: 24). The gesture of elevating the chalice, marking the moment of consecration, became important in the twelfth century, and has been retained to this day. Lights, bells, and incense may be used to mark the occasion (Rubin, 1991), and the pageantry may excite the senses and accentuate the experience of the worshipper. Traditional music plays an important role in most Christian churches.

In other cases there is evidence for a quite specific biological connection elaborated by cultural forces. That snakes play a role in many religions is a matter of particular interest, since responsiveness to snakes is a consequence of dialectical relations between a basic tendency to respond to snakes, social referencing, and the myths of the society. Snakes are especially salient stimuli to young children, the response given depending in large measure on that given by their caregiver. If the mother responds with marked fear, the child is likely to acquire a long-lasting fear of snakes. Similar phenomena have been demonstrated in rhesus monkeys (Mineka, 1987).[1] A whole range of properties of snakes may augment their fear-eliciting potency. Thus the snake's venom, its crypticity, its mode of locomotion and its ability to disappear into holes may link it with danger and the underworld in a manner which is irresistible to humans (Lawrence, 1964). But the very fact that snakes have come to portray evil in the mythology of many cultures also contributes to their potency in eliciting fear or related responses. The Rubens paintings of lost souls going down into Hell with snakes gnawing at their genitals convey a feeling that must have made people believe that it was very undesirable to go to Hell (Hinde, 1991; Hinde and Rawson, 1995; Mundkur, 1983). The importance of cultural influences is shown also by the way in which snakes have taken on other meanings in other cultures. Thus in southern India, although snakes are generally regarded with aversion as in other parts of the world, they are seen also as a source of power. The primal snake, the so-called 'snake without end', acts as the bed-rest of Vishnu, and is seen as the source of universal energy and cohesion. One may speculate that their use as symbols of power or protection may have an ultimate basis in their fear-eliciting nature. Their association with immortality in the legend of Gilgamesh and in the biblical story of the Creation probably derives from their ability to shed their skins and be 'born again', and the same property has led snakes to be associated with the moon, and thus with menstruation: part of the penalty for acquiring Knowledge of Good and Evil was the curse of menstruation (Warner, 1976).[2]

In yet other cases principles of sympathetic magic, such as the principle of contagion (see below), can account for the potency of artefacts or symbols: the use of relics is an obvious example. Relics have been believed to take on miraculous powers in both Buddhism and Christianity, and played an important role in the mediaeval Christian church. The early cult of the martyrs had been centred on their tombs, but spread through the use of substances or objects which had been in or near the tomb. It became a requirement that every consecrated church should have a relic placed in its altar. The bones of saints were seen as especially holy, and a trade in relics developed which sometimes led to competition between churches or monasteries. But, as Goody (1997) has pointed out, people tend both to revere the bones of the dead and to distance themselves from them, perhaps out of fear of negative contagion: furthermore the use of relics to address immortals through their mortal remains is inevitably paradoxical.

In eastern Europe, icons came to take the place of bodily relics (Wilson, 1983b). However representations of the deity are prohibited in Islam and have given rise to dissent among Christians. This arises from several sources – from the use of manifestly bogus items, from the failure of relics or icons to produce the effects that they were supposed to produce, and from biblical prohibitions (Goody, 1997). In the West, Protestantism led to the rejection of relics and the destruction of shrines.

Differences between the artefacts used in rituals within a culture may also be related to the occasion: thus Leach (1976: 27) suggests that the Christian practice of dressing a bride in white and a widow in black conveys the information that one is entering a marriage and the other leaving one.

### Sequence and form

While some rituals have a degree of flexibility most, like the Catholic Mass, involve a recognised 'correct' procedure. Although rituals are sometimes regarded as poor vehicles for communicating information because of their stereotyped nature (Bloch, 1989; Boyer, 1994), it is often in part just because of their invariance that they are so effective and memorable. It may be that insistence on correct performance of the Catholic Mass has been conducive to the maintenance on the centrality of that ceremony in the life of the Roman Catholic Church (Porterfield, 1998).

The sequence and form of many religious rituals are often related to the occasion and to the beliefs and narratives of the religious system. Their performance can then be seen as symbolic action re-enacting (and confirming) those beliefs and narratives (Leach, 1954). For example *rites de passage* can be divided into preparatory, transitional and concluding phases, each marking a stage in the transition from one socially marked status to another (Van Gennep, 1965). In the transitional phase of some initiation rituals the individuals concerned may be seen as sexless or bisexual, or they become uncategorised, being treated as newborn or dead, and they may be naked. There may be role reversals, and there is often a period of seclusion when the initiate is removed from everyday life, and the authority of the religious specialists is absolute (Turner, 1967).

In Church of England *rites de passage* traces of three phases are still to be found. According to the 'Book of Common Prayer', infants are seen as born in sin. At baptism the priest requests remission of the child's sins, and the godparents undertake, in the name of the child, to renounce the devil and all his works, to believe in the Trinity, and to obey God's will. The child is then baptised. In the last phase the priest tells the congregation that the 'child is regenerated, and grafted into the body of Christ's Church'. Similarly Confirmation is preceded by instruction in the Catechism. At the service the child is asked to renew the promises made on his/her behalf at Baptism, and the service is concluded with prayers that God's favour and protection be bestowed on the new full member of the Church. In a longer time frame, the years between baptism and confirmation can be seen as a transitional period during which responsibility for the child's spiritual wellbeing is taken over by the godparents.

Again, in the marriage service it is still considered by many to be 'unlucky' for bride and groom to see each other on the morning of the wedding, and the bride enters the church with whoever will 'give her away', usually the father. In the Church of England service the priest is in charge, asking the couple whether they can lawfully be married with the words 'I require and charge you both, as ye will answer at the dreadful day of judgement…', and mediating the transference of the woman from her family to her husband-to-be. The priest, by his presence and words, validates the marriage, but the presence of the congregation is important in making the union a publicly recognised one. Subsequently husband and wife leave together.

Of course, one must not make too much of this. The fact that three phases can be distinguished in most *rites de passage* is hardly surprising: the point being made is that the form of the ritual is associated with its function in society. In literate societies the links between the beliefs and the ritual may be explicit, as in the Mass. In such a case the order of the ritual has a certain logic: the consecration of the bread and wine must come before its symbolic use. But Boyer (1994) argues that in preliterate societies the ritual assumptions and beliefs supposedly associated with a ritual are not essential for its performance. This is also somewhat the case in the Jain *puja* ritual (see below). Such assumptions may provide conjectures that enrich the representation of the performance and explain it, but it is still possible for the participants to have idiosyncratic interpretations. Rituals of this sort are thus to be seen as contexts in which religious representations may be expressed, but it is the individual's representations that give meaning (perhaps idiosyncratic) to the actions. Thus the sequence of ritual actions (its 'syntax') may have considerable independence from the religious assumptions associated with it (its 'semantics').

Indeed it is likely, in view of the young age at which children are first introduced to many rituals, that the sequence may be learned intuitively from observation of and/or participation in its performance, stored in just the same way as secular sequences (though with an important difference to be mentioned below), and the religious representations added to it subsequently.

Lawson and McCauley (1990) have proposed that assumptions about action common to other spheres of life constrain religious ritual. Using the analogy of linguistic competence, they suggest that the successive actions in a ritual are generated by a set of recursive rules such that the participants have intuitions as to whether or not a ritual has been performed correctly. Even if the religion involves apparently bizarre beliefs about supernatural entities, Lawson and McCauley hold that the representations of the sequences of ritual action will respect the general logical distinctions which inform an everyday view of action sequences. Thus drinking the wine from a chalice held by a priest in the Mass differs from drinking wine from a glass only in that the agents, actions and objects are special. It is the conceptual scheme that supplies the semantic information which makes the ritual special, not the sequence of actions itself.

There is, however, a difference between everyday action sequences and some religious rituals in the nature of the links between the sub-sequences. Most everyday activities can be analysed into a succession of goal-directed actions. Even a mechanical task like hammering a nail can be divided into actions like 'raise the hammer', 'strike the nail', 'see whether the head of the nail is flush with the surface. If not, raise the hammer again', and so on (Miller *et al.*, 1960). Each stage in this sequence is necessary for the next. We encounter a similar phenomenon in the scripts, postulated as part of or related to the self-system, which detail a sequence of goal-directed sub-sequences of actions, each leading to the next, in such activities as 'making a date' or 'going to a restaurant'. While religious rituals, like the Mass, do have a logical sequence, Boyer (1994) has argued that in many cases of ritual performance, at least in pre-literate societies, the sub-sequences are not describable in terms of goal-direction or intentionality. Taking Firth's (1967) description of the long series of Tikopia rituals known as the 'work of the gods', Boyer points out that the successive sequences and sub-actions (e.g. building a fire in a particular location; sitting in particular places; laying the firestick on leaves, etc.) can be explained only by saying that they are perceived as necessary for the whole sequence of 'throwing the firestick'. The ritual as a whole has the goal of putting the land in a special state, but the sequences within the ritual do not have successive sub-goals. The rigidity of such sequences may be related to this lack of sub-goals. Because the intentional structure of the links is unspecified, and because the background conditions necessary to make the ritual a success are not fully specified, the validity of the ritual depends on its being performed in a set sequence. This is true also of many pathological obsessional rituals.[3]

## Pan-cultural propensities and ritual

In several contexts in these chapters on religious ritual, attention is called to the extent to which the causes and consequences of ritual serve a number of human propensities, and to how the form and sequence of ritual performance utilises devices which engage with pan-cultural psychological characteristics in ways likely to make it more effective to the participants. At this point it is perhaps as well to emphasise that there is no suggestion that the occurrence or content of ritual is *determined* solely by such factors. Rather in every society there is an ongoing dialectic between the religious system with its ritual and the characteristics of the individuals involved, a dialectic influenced also by the history, social and physical circumstances of the society in question (Figure 2.1). This, of course, opens endless possibilities, but the point being made is that the religious system cannot be understood without reference to the basic role of the natures of the individuals involved, as well as other aspects, synchronic and diachronic, of the socio-cultural structure.

## Magic in western societies

We have already noted the incidence of magical practices even in our supposedly sophisticated western societies. Many people believe in improbable events, like the landing of aliens from spaceships; many consult astrologers; many carry a St. Christopher or avoid walking under ladders. The Anglican church is still willing to exorcise evil spirits, though perhaps with some ambivalence about the practice. And we have seen how, in many other societies, ritual practices are interlaced with practical ones: Malinowski (1935) has described the manner in which technical pursuits and ritual acts run in parallel or are interwoven. Sometimes superstitious behaviour results from previous performance being linked to an auspicious outcome: A led to B then, perhaps it will do so again. More often it is a consequence of tradition: an undefined 'they' say that touching wood will avert evil consequences. But in the western world many more people perform such actions than really believe in their efficacy. Although few really think that the topping out ceremony when a building is completed has any consequences, the practice still continues in many places. Is it performed because it always has been, or is there still an uncomfortable feeling that, if it is not performed, all will not be quite so well as it might be?

Some forms of religious ritual bear close resemblances to these everyday forms of superstitious behaviour, and Rozin and Nemeroff (1990) have investigated the role of two processes, contagion and similarity. Contagion suggests that things once in contact with each other can continue to influence each other subsequently, or that the effects of contact may persist. The effect may be positive, as in the laying on of hands, the use of religious relics, or the wearing of clothing previously worn by a loved one or by a football star; or the effect may be negative, as in pollution. In either case it can be described as involving the transference of an essence which contains something of the nature of the source: in the negative case it may be held that the contamination can be removed by purification, for instance by ceremonial washing. Furthermore the effect may be forward, the essence passing from source to recipient, as in the two cases just mentioned, or backward, when the recipient acts on the item with the intention of influencing the source. The latter occurs in sorcery, as when burning the clothes of an individual is thought to harm the owner. Swallowing can be seen as a special form of contagion, essence being transferred to the swallower – as in the Christian Mass, or the Hebrew dietary prohibitions.

Experiments in the USA in which individuals' responses to the idea of wearing a sweater, which had previously been worn by a desirable or undesirable person, were assessed showed that negative forward contagion was ubiquitous (i.e. people did not want to wear it if it had been worn by an undesirable person); positive forward contagion (sweater worn by a desirable person) occurred in a sizeable minority; and there was also evidence for backward contagion. If objective evidence for the transference of an essence is totally eliminated, moral or symbolic reasons may be given: thus some people refuse to wear second-hand clothes however well cleaned or sterilised. Since the most frequent type of contagion is negative and forward, it has been suggested that belief in contagion stems from a mechanism evolved to protect against micro-organisms, and thus has a biological basis. However the concept of contagion is not clearly present in children before the age of seven, and Rozin and Nemeroff see its development as being influenced also by culture.

As we have seen, contagion was clearly important in the early development of Christianity, for objects which had been in proximity to the tombs of saints were used as relics. They were treated as if they were part of the saint's body, sharing its sanctity. In the mediaeval era reverence for the bones of saints played an important part in many Christian churches. Supposed to have magical properties, they were usually kept in reliquaries in the church, but sometimes taken out to heal the sick or assist in ritual. In Catholic churches their role was to some extent taken over by images of the Virgin Mary. Why sanctity should be seen as concentrated in parts of dead bodies is far from clear, but the association has been related to the supposed connection between asceticism and miraculous powers. As the saint denied his bodily needs, he acquired miraculous powers, the culmination of the process being death, when the bodily remains were seen as having concentrated spiritual power (Wilson, 1983b). While that may be the explanation, the psychological power of contagion is likely to be an underlying issue. In other cases the treatment of relics as having holy properties – even pieces of cotton wool said to have been soaked in tears from an image of the Virgin Mary – clearly exemplify the principle of contagion.

Perhaps related to such phenomena is the manner in which even a word can acquire some of the properties of that which it signifies. Present day scholars owe the priceless Genizah collection of fragments of documents from around 900 AD to the fact that Jews were forbidden to destroy any document which contained the ineffable name of God (Macintosh and Shiftiel, 1997), a fact of even more interest when one considers the attitude of Jahweh to 'graven images'. Perhaps, also, part of the power of tradition stems from a similar phenomenon: the repetition of gestures, verbal formulae, or mantras which are believed to have been potent in the past may be perceived to have retained that potency in the present.

The law of similarity holds that things that have a superficial resemblance also have a deep resemblance. This also may operate positively or negatively, forwards or backwards. It often makes good sense, for it is better to treat something that looks dangerous as if it were dangerous: there is no difficulty in supposing the tendency to have been a product of natural selection.

A common manifestation involves the use of icons. Such objects have often been (and sometimes still are) treated as having miraculous powers: for instance touching such an object may be seen as having therapeutic potential. An example of forward similarity is given by attempts to harm someone by sticking pins into his photograph or image. Clearly the use of images in ritual depends on the principle of similarity, and the supposed beneficial effects of touching a statue depends on both similarity and contagion. Unlike contagion, the law of similarity seems to appear quite early in young children, and to decrease with age. It would seem to be a similar phenomenon to the tendency to believe that beings that are categorised together must have a common basic essence (see pp. 87–8).

Icons play an important role in some Christian religious groups: while some regard the portrayal of deities as blasphemous, others see them as giving a visual presence for focusing religious acts. Many other cultures use images of deities which are seen as having a spiritual quality or as serving to assist the worshipper to focus on the deity: here the law of similarity clearly applies. The importance of similarity to the holy figure is exemplified by the way in which icons in the form of statues or paintings of Confucius in China (Murray, 1997) or of the Virgin Mary in the Eastern Orthodox church, served as a focus for worship as though they were the individual portrayed. In ordinary life we manipulate mental images of objects as though they were the objects themselves, and the use of idols and icons can be seen as riding on this capacity.

However in the Christian Church practices involving the ascription of mystical properties to material objects tend to give rise to controversy. For instance, Christians celebrate the Resurrection of Christ from the dead by a re-enactment of the Last Supper in which bread and wine represent the body and blood of Christ. Roman Catholics have understood the ceremony to involve the actual transformation of bread and wine into the substance of the body and blood of Christ. This belief depends on the Aristotelian distinction between the properties of an object that are available to the senses and its underlying 'substance' or essence, a presumption similar to that which we have seen to be present in children's responses to living beings (pp. 87–8). It is thus supposed that the 'substance' of the bread and wine have been changed although the external appearance remains. This belief is not accepted by Protestants, who regard the bread and wine as merely symbolic. At the Reformation the Church of England rejected both the use of relics and the doctrine of Transubstantiation, the Articles of Religion proclaiming 'The Body of Christ is given, taken, and eaten, in the Supper, only after an heavenly and spiritual manner' (see also p. 117).

Firth (1996) has discussed the intellectual compromise between commemoration and re-enactment implied in the theory of transubstantiation. Simple commemoration of the Last Supper and the death of Christ might tend to impoverish churches which follow a plain symbolic interpretation, whereas the belief that bread and wine are really converted to the body and blood of Christ engages the emotional attention of the faithful. But if conversion actually occurs it would imply that Christ has actually died again and the sacrifice at the Crucifixion would no longer be unique (see also Goody, 1997).

## Summary

Ritual performance tends to differ from everyday behaviour in being attention-getting and memorable, and in creating an atmosphere suitable to the occasion. The forms that religious rituals take, the actions and artefacts used, their symbolism, and the sequence of the actions involved, have many parallels in secular life, and are such as to appeal to human sensitivities.

The maintenance of a ritual must depend on mutual influences between pan-cultural psychological characteristics and the religious system in the context of the history of the society and its current social and physical circumstances. There is likely to be ambivalence in the use of ritual, artefacts, and imagery, some holding that they augment religious devotion, others that they detract from it.

Two forms of magic, involving the principles of contagion and similarity, occur in religious rituals and in everyday life.

# 11 Ritual
## Motivation and consequences

Those present on a ritual occasion may see it as anything from a boring obligation to a life-preserving necessity. In this chapter we ask about individuals' motivation in participating in ritual activities. Does their involvement result from any of the propensities which we have suggested to be important for religious belief? Are there other issues involved? How is the motivation to participate linked to the consequences of performance?

## The motivation of the participants

Given the great variety of reasons for participating in religious ritual, it is convenient to distinguish between the religious specialists, the central figures (if any), and other participants or spectators.

### Religious specialists

Considering the first of these, in many ritual performances with some degree of formality it is usually the task of the religious specialist to conduct the affair and often also to clarify what is going on to the other participants: the specialist may see a goal in the ritual which is less accessible to the laity. In some such cases the former's attempts to tie down the purpose of a ritual may mitigate against the value to the participants of being able to form their own interpretations.

Most ritual specialists no doubt 'believe' (see Chapter 3) in the authenticity of the performance. They see it as a necessary element in the religious system, or simply regard it as proper that the deity should be worshipped. They may be motivated to perform the ritual because they believe it has important consequences, usually of a spiritual nature, for those who take part. In any case, where they are officiating at a *rite de passage* their words and actions are performative in the sense of Austin (1975): 'I baptise thee in the name of the Father, and of the Son, and of the Holy Ghost', and the words are the act. The ritual is effective simply because it is performed, provided it is performed correctly.

There may also be a (perhaps unconscious) desire to maintain a belief system, perhaps because it maintains their own position.[1] Of course there may be some ritual specialists who are involved in the hope of preferment, or merely out of habit, but they need not concern us.

## *Others*

If there are central figures among the other participants, the ritual may be a *rite de passage* marking transformation to a new life stage or entry into a new relationship. Again, their participation may be in part performative: 'With this ring I thee wed'. Other aspects of their participation need no further comment.

For other participants, each may have a different reason for being present. A primary issue in nearly all cases must be a desire for some sort of religious experience: this may take the form of believing that participation in the ritual is a duty appropriate to the religious system, whether this is expressed as worship, thanksgiving, repentance, or in some other way. In such cases the ritual can be seen as a way of affirming their attitude and allegiance to the religious system as a whole. Participation may also satisfy one of the personal needs discussed in Chapter 5, though each participant may have a different reason for being present, and for many the reasons may be partially or wholly unconscious. Some may seek a sense of individual reassurance, a confirmation of the self, a sense of efficacy, a belief that the vicissitudes of the world can be coped with. They may seek a sense of belonging to a community. Indeed, the subjective experiences expected may be the primary goal for attending or performing the ritual. This is especially the case with rituals which bring ecstatic experiences, satisfy a desire for dramatic participation, or perform a cathartic function, and also for those that are meditational in nature. Where the ritual involves a *rite de passage*, participants may attend to witness the couple being married or the adolescent initiated – and at another level they may be motivated by anticipation that the ritual will bring recollections of, reflections about, or hopes for, comparable ceremonies involving themselves or those close to them.

A thoughtfully analysed example of a ritual with primarily idiosyncratic subjective consequences is provided by the *puja* ritual of the Jains (Humphrey and Laidlaw, 1994). In this the celebrant usually acts alone: although the *puja* can be communal, there is no congregational aspect. It involves a series of loosely prescribed acts which have been transmitted ostensively, with minimal explanation. Humphrey and Laidlaw argue that in this ritual (and indeed in most others) the celebrant adopts a 'ritual stance' in that he or she has an agent's awareness of his or her actions, but this is preceded or accompanied by a conception of the action as seen from outside, so that the actor both is and is not an author of his acts. While what the actor does is not linked to his or her intentions in doing it, what he does is structured by prescription not just in the sense that rules are followed, but in that only following the rules counts as performing the action. Though some participants see the *puja* as leading to personal gain, consisting perhaps of the acquisition of good *karma*, it is essentially a meditational performance, without expectation of any help from a supernatural being, and its consequences are essentially unknowable to the outsider. The ritual act can be seen, like a 'natural kind', as having an underlying essence, but there is no official theory of the *puja*: the interpretation placed on it, its meaning to the participant, though usually having reference to some aspect of Jain doctrine, may differ markedly between individuals. This is facilitated by the very fact that the actions of the ritual are simple and standardised, allowing the mind to wander (see also Morris, 1992).

While the experiences that the *puja* provides are in part intellectual, the ritual actions induce also emotional experience, and in other rituals this is the primary issue. Although participants in such rituals are mostly willing to give propositional meanings associated with the actions, it sometimes seems that the celebrant becomes lost in the action, and that the emotional experience is primary, as though a particular kind of consciousness is allowed to emerge through the ritual. Episodes of this type are more conspicuous in 'ecstatic' religions, where the achievement of a particular emotional state appears to be the important goal of the ritual: such rituals usually involve repeated actions. Humphrey and Laidlaw (1994: 232), describing a ritual performance for the removal of spirits, suggest that there is a continuum of such states of consciousness:

> There is the exaltation of the rhythmic act, then the sudden inspiration which makes people oblivious to everything around them, then a kind of sympathetic 'possession' (seen by falling to the floor and making circular movements), which is not regarded as serious unless it is also manifest outside the temple and prevents normal functioning, and finally there is spirit possession, in which the subject's normal personality is replaced by some manifestation of the spirit or spirits.

The Jewish Passover Seder provides in many ways a marked contrast to the *puja*. While the *puja* is essentially individualistic, celebration of the Passover can be a social, family occasion, in which all those present participate actively. It is celebrated even by many secularised individuals, and can be seen as a response to the dispersal of Jews, adapted to reaffirm their essential unity. Providing a vision of an essential part of the history of the Jews appropriate to their current experience, it supplies a sense of community to take the participants through the coming year. The order of Seder has been set out in many versions, but these retain an essential similarity, the details of setting and actions contributing to a dense network of meanings which are apparent to the orthodox. While all participants may not be so fully informed, the historical and socially binding significance of the ceremony is available to all (Fredman, 1981).

Since individuals may attend rituals for many reasons, and ascribe many meanings to the occasion, it thus makes little sense to seek for a single meaning of a ritual for the participants, except in so far as it has one assigned to it by those in charge. 'The complexity and uncertainty about a ritual's meaning is not to be seen just as a defect.... It can also be a source of that strength, evocative power, resilience and mutability which may sometimes sustain and preserve ritual performance' (Lewis, 1980: 8–9). But there seems no reason to suppose that the motivations of those participating, while depending on their involvement in the religious system, differs from those that lie behind actions in the secular sphere.

## Consequences of ritual

It will be apparent that many of the desired or expected consequences of ritual performance follow directly from the motivation of those involved. This is the case both for rituals with a consciously recognised external goal, such as requesting a deity to heal the sick or make the harvest succeed, and those in which the subjective experience is primary. The latter, however, is important in both. Requests to the deity involving the mere mouthing of words are seen as less likely to be effective, and worship must involve loyalty and awe: without feeling it becomes mechanical and empty.

But there are also further consequences which are perhaps less clearly involved in the motivation of the participants. For instance, rituals in themselves create a distinction between the everyday and the special, between how things are and how they should be (Smith, 1987). This may be accompanied by a sense of purification and of closeness to the deity. Desire for these feelings may be part of the motivation for taking part.

There may also be further consequences which, not consciously formulated, are less likely to have played a part in the motivation of the participants. For instance, participation demonstrates commitment to the religious system, and in doing so may augment that commitment, for the participant would lose face if he or she now reneged. Rituals performed for sickness may serve to identify its supposed cause, replacing an aetiology of blind fate with that of an evil spirit or human error. Thereby certainty replaces anxiety, therapeutic procedures may be indicated, or divine intercession requested. Rituals of mourning may distance the individual from his emotions, or allow him to express them, and thus ameliorate the grief itself (Hood *et al.*, 1996). Funeral rites force mourners to behave publicly in ways that acknowledge their loss, and may serve to elicit social support from others (Pargament, 1997).

Other consequences, even if not consciously perceived, may be even more important in some rituals. For example, in the case of *rites de passage*, the ritual creates a new self-image and a new social identity. Initiation ceremonies that involve suffering result in a temporary diminution in personal identity and enhance identification with a new category of persons: such consequences may be important both for society and individual. The principal participants, the emerging adults or the marrying couple, will be better able to see themselves in their new social roles after the ceremony. So also will the onlookers, for they must change their relationships with the participants, requiring a re-adjustment also of their own self-systems. This is even more important in the case of a funeral, where the ceremony symbolises the cessation of the relationship with the deceased, or that the deceased has acquired the status of an ancestor. Even the more meditative types of ritual enhance or explore the nature of the self, and perhaps discover new interpretations of what the self can be (Humphrey and Laidlaw, 1994). Such consequences on the self-systems of those involved will be the more marked, the more salient the performance. How far they contribute to the motivation to participate is an open issue[2].

In general, then, consideration of both the causes and the consequences of ritual involvement are in harmony with the view that it reflects a number of human propensities and needs. However, no one cause or consequence is likely to be ubiquitously relevant or important.

## Ritual and social structure

Many ritual performances are closely related to the social structure, and express social relations, hierarchy, equality, and so on (Lewis, 1980). While we saw earlier (pp. 50–7) that the precise nature of the causal relations underlying parallels between religious systems and social structure are controversial, shared ritual performance is likely to enhance the cohesiveness of a group. However diverse the motivations of individual participants, and however diverse their experiences while participating, the very fact that they are sharing a particular ritual practice, a particular objective, will be an element in the diverse mental associations of the participants, and thus the ritual in itself can enhance integration. In so far as participation strengthens belief in, and adherence to, the religious system, and acknowledges commitment to that system, it strengthens the feeling of community with other like-minded individuals. This role of ritual in integration holds not only among peers: the constancy of ritual in the major world religions can provide a link between the generations. How far such integration may be part of the intentions of participating individuals is an open issue.

As mentioned earlier, many anthropologists have seen the significance of religious rituals in their consequences upon group structure or integration. Thus Durkheim (1964) regarded ritual as a primary mechanism for reinforcing the sentiments and solidarity of the group. Likewise Radcliffe-Brown (1952: 157) argued that 'rites can therefore be shown to have a specific function when, and to the extent that, they have for their effect to regulate, maintain and transmit from one generation to another sentiments on which the constitution of the society depends' (see also Leach, 1954). The Jewish Seder, for example, re-enacts a crucial episode in the course of Jewish history, and marks the uniqueness of the Jewish people.[3]

As evidence for this integrative function, it has been argued that the centrality of ritual has been responsible for the endurance of Freemasonry over several hundred years: the rituals were contrived by a group of nobles and tradesmen who were forming lodges for fellowship, and were designed specifically to maintain the solidarity of the organisation (Piatigorsky, 1997). As an exception that helps to prove the rule, in some hunter-gatherer societies which have little hierarchical structure and in which property inheritance is of minimal importance, funerals tend to be matter-of-fact and involve little ritual (Woodburn, 1982).[4] Thus if individuals desire to feel part of a community, this may be partly due to the existence of norms of social cohesion, and ritual participation by individuals will augment both social cohesion and those norms.

Death poses a threat not only to individuals but also to the social structure that individuals have come to value. Many rituals connected with death tend to emphasise social stability, or the continuation of the social order, on a 'The king is dead, long live the king!' principle (Bloch and Parry, 1982). Such rituals can also give a stamp of legitimacy to social positions. In the Tang dynasty in China the funeral and memorial ceremonies, showing filial respect for dead ancestors, probably had the consequence of connecting the Emperor with the ancestral founders of the dynasty and thus confirming his position as the Son of Heaven (Welter, 1996). How far such consequences on social integration provide part of the motivation for participation is an issue concerning which generalisations would be extremely hazardous.

A fiesta associated with the Virgin of Guadalupe provides an interesting example of the relevance of ritual to divisions between sub-groups within the society. This was studied in a Mexican village which had been economically developed. Modernisation had produced a cultural continuum from what had been two ethnic communities, the village being half Mayo Indian and half Mestizos. Although the people gave straightforward answers when asked about their ethnicity, most interaction was ethnically neutral. The Guadalupe fiesta provided a forum for people to express their family's position on the continuum. By the way in which they participated in the ritual dramas families illustrated the cleavage, and then overcame it by avowing the Virgin's protection for all Mexicans without regard to ethnicity. Those who participated in the clearly recognised Mayo aspects of the fiesta were predominantly the poorest, while those who emphasised the more orthodox religious behaviours tended to be the wealthiest (O'Connor, 1989). Thus ritual can not only prop up the social order, but also contribute to social change. It can present alternatives to the existing social order, and can contribute to feelings of equality in the face of status divisions in society as well as confirming inequality.

The nature of the ritual may be related to that of the society in a variety of ways. It has been suggested that in non-industrial societies the nature of ritual occasions bears some relation to the density of the society. Societies with low density and little social differentiation tend to have *ad hoc* rituals, while high density, differentiated societies tend to have universally standard-ised occasions where people from different walks of life can meaningfully participate, and which provide a basis for recognising anonymous others as co-members of the group (Reeves and Bylund, 1992).

Douglas (1970a and b) has suggested that religions could be arranged along a continuum of increasingly ordered ritual. At one extreme lie soci-eties which show extreme ritualism and control: this is associated with a tightly knit social life. At the other lie societies which go in for bodily expres-sions of abandonment involving ecstatic and trance experiences: these are unstructured societies, valuing informality. Douglas thus postulates a corre-spondence between the social order and the symbolism of ritual. While this relation between societal structure and religious practice seems to have some generality, the mechanism is controversial. Others (e.g. Lewis, 1971) have argued that some ecstatic cults are the result of physical or social pressures. Distinguishing 'peripheral' possession cults, such as Pentecostalism and spirit possession cults which co-exist with a more dominant religion like Christianity, from 'central' ones in which the main religious focus is on spirit possession, like shamanism, Lewis sees the former as a form of social protest enabling those with little political influence to advance their interests. The flexibility in Pentecostal ritual may support efforts to bring about polit-ical and social change (Alexander, 1991). This is in harmony with the views that, in the ecstatic cults of less privileged classes, women tend to have a status more equal to that of men, and that women are more open to mystical experience than men (Weber, 1965). In 'central' possession cults, where the religious system is focused on rites related to spirit possession, the pressure comes not from sources internal to the society, but from external social and physical circumstances.

In most of the instances discussed in this section, the data indicate rela-tions between ritual and aspects of social structure, but the ascription of a causal link is, to varying degrees, conjectural, and it is at least possible that the structure of the ritual and that of the society are independent products of properties of the human mind. Where a causal link does exist, it is by no means clear that the societal consequence contributed to the motivation of the participants. Where a ritual has been initiated by religious specialists or other authorities, it may be aimed at maintaining a social order or religious system, as seems to have been the case with the Freemasons. In such cases maintenance by ritual specialists may have the unconscious intention of maintaining the religious system, a goal which may also be in their own interests. And in some cases far-sighted and altruistic individuals may attend as participants in religious rituals out of a sense of duty to the community and with a view to increasing the group's social cohesiveness or to reaffirm the social hierarchy. However, it is not necessarily the case that the social consequences of an individual's participation coincide with the goal(s) he or she had in going: rituals can become part of social practice, continuing through force of tradition with no clear perception of their function in the society among the participants.

Nor need there be any relation between participation and acceptance of the beliefs of the religious system. Of course there may be individuals who accept the beliefs because they want to contribute to the coherence of the community for their own good or that of others, but that raises again crucial questions of exactly what belief means (see Chapter 3).

## Prayer

Prayer can be treated as a form of ritual behaviour, even when it takes place in private. Often it can be seen as a form of ritual affirmation of belief in a supernatural being, but it takes many forms. It can involve supplication, or reflection on accepted religious truth. It may involve conversation with the deity, or contemplation in which no words are used and thoughts are not dwelt upon, when it may be associated with religious experience (see Chapter 15). It may take a predetermined form, or be idiosyncratic (e.g. Hood *et al.*, 1996; Poloma and Pendleton, 1991).[5]

Usually, prayer has the form of a linguistic interaction. The believer may imagine himself to be addressing a personified god who listens to and (hopefully) will answer the prayers. Such prayers imply an assumed relationship with one or more supreme beings. Prayer is perhaps most obviously seen as dialogue when it is addressed to ancestors, but the implication of a responding other is always there (Goody, 1995). If I reach to pick up my pen from the desk, I am not concerned with any possible response by the pen; but if I speak to another person I do so with at least some consideration of their possible response. 'To speak is to assume the possibility of a response' (Zeitlyn, 1995: 189), and in addressing a supernatural entity it is difficult not to believe that a response will be forthcoming: faith in the god's responsiveness is built into the very act of praying. If the believer does have any doubt, he may cover himself with reasons why an answer might not be given – insincerity, sins not repented, or inadequate faith, for instance.

While the content of such prayer varies widely, it often involves requests that the deity should intervene to improve the supplicant's spiritual or material well-being. The believer feels that action has been taken to obtain what seemed to be unattainable, and gains indirectly a sense of self-efficacy. A study of the praying practices of Dutch youth indicated that nearly all prayers were related to trouble or need. 'There was no need common or childish enough to be excluded' (Janssen *et al.*, 1990: 105). But while the needs consisted of concrete issues and unhappinesses, the effects were formulated abstractly and in general terms (help, support, favour, trust, blessing, and so on). The prayer thus seemed more like a way of coping with inevitable, incurable unhappiness than an attempt to obtain a specific outcome. Such prayer brings comfort because the supplicant believes that he can manipulate the deity – or at least that the deity will listen sympathetically given certain conditions.

But not all prayer involves intercession. Often it can be seen as worship of a higher being. It has been suggested that humans have a need to venerate something greater than themselves, but that view seems to rest solely on the observation that some individuals do venerate others. In any case, in everyday life it is often a good tactic for those not at the top of a hierarchy. But other explanations for worship are also possible, not necessarily as alternatives but as applying to different individuals or at different times. For instance, a consequence of worship can be a subjective state which is felt as religious experience. Here worship takes on the properties of meditation. According to its nature, it may involve a feeling of awe at the overwhelming nature of the deity, or, with a more contemplative attitude, a merging of the 'I' and the 'Me', and of the self with the Other. Worshipful prayer may also be seen as cementing the relationship with the deity by praise, thanksgiving, affirmation, resignation, penitence, or by promise of future dedication. Such worship may be 'pure' in the sense that it is given solely because it is appropriate to the relationship with the deity, or involves homage to one who should receive homage; but it may also involve hope of reward, or confession of sin in the hope of forgiveness, or the expectation of the transfer of some degree of power from an all-powerful being. Prayer, just like long-term human relationships (see Chapter 13), involves reciprocity, though the hoped for reward may lie in the distant future.

Prayer is also a way of constructing reality, of making sense of the world – or of maintaining a reality previously constructed. In Islam, where prayer five times a day is obligatory to the strict believer, requests are generally not involved. Much prayer can be seen as an internal dialogue within the self-system in which problems are talked through, anxieties allayed, and responsibility for action placed elsewhere.

Because of the combination of supernatural and everyday characteristics in a deity, prayer is almost inevitably paradoxical. The deity is seen as omniscient, yet the supplicant's needs must be formulated. And the deity is seen as all-powerful and able to intervene, and yet at the same time with human characteristics in that he can withhold his help, or behave with grace or compassion. And in prayer the supplicant is trying to decrease the distance between himself and the deity, yet it would be presumptuous (and perhaps blasphemous) to claim too much proximity.

Prayer may involve a second, indirect, stage – as when a priest says prayers for a supplicant. Here the implication is that the priest is especially empowered to intercede with the Almighty, in the same way that many Catholics believe in the intercessionary powers of the saints. If the priest says the prayers, and especially if the supplicant rewards him for doing so, the priest may have little emotional or intellectual involvement. If the prayers are said communally, they may also have socially integrating consequences, binding the congregation together as a social unit.

## Sacrifice

Sacrifice involves a personal offering to the deity of something of value to the giver, who incurs costs as a consequence of the action. Like prayer, sacrifice implies a relationship between the sacrificer and the deity. That relationship is a hierarchical one – the sacrificer sees himself or herself as inferior to the deity, and may be uncertain as to the acceptability of the offering.

Sacrifice was a major ritual element in early Hebrew religion, and has played a role in the religions of nearly all preliterate societies. Much of the literature refers to such contexts, where the sacrifice usually involves a victim or an item of potential food value to the sacrificer, and the sacrifice is seen as more or less obligatory.

For Christians the paradigmatic example is provided by the image of Christ on the Cross. Christ's death can properly be seen as a judicial murder. However, by metaphorical extension it came to be referred to as a sacrifice: through extension of the range of situations covered by the term 'sacrifice', Christ's death was seen as a unique sacrifice bringing to an end any need for further sacrifice. In the early centuries after Christ's death, a time of persecution for the sect, the concept of sacrifice was extended to cover Christian martyrs. Subsequently it became even more extended to cover any example of giving up something of value or putting oneself to inconvenience for the sake of the deity (Sykes, 1991). Thus pilgrimages can be seen as a form of sacrifice, tithes have carried some of the same psychological concomitants as sacrifice, and more generally the giving up of the delights of the flesh, and even trivial acts of self-denial or just giving time to religious activities, can be seen in a similar light. Thus if study is seen as a form of worship by members of holy orders, and study is a form of prayer, the distinction between prayer and sacrifice fades. In this way, even trivial acts of self-denial are seen as comparable to, but in no way equivalent to, Christ's self-sacrifice on the Cross.

In spite of this extension in the use of the concept, research on sacrifice in preliterate societies can throw some light on religious practice today. Innumerable theories have been advanced to account for its incidence, and these are not necessarily rivals: no doubt more than one may be applicable in any one case (Evans-Pritchard, 1954). Some emphasise immediate psychological effects on the sacrificer (catharsis, abnegation, etc.), involving an effect on the relationship with the deity and/or a change in the self-system. The sacrifice may enable the sacrificer to see himself or herself as a worthy servant of the deity. Or, just as when feeling we have wronged another, we attempt retribution, so sacrifice may allay feelings of guilt for past misdeeds. Or the sacrifice can be seen as a recognition of relative status, comparable to paying homage. Yet again the giving up of something valuable may be regarded as a symbol of devotion or love. Or, as in long-term personal relationships, costs may be incurred in the hope of long-term gain or the avoidance of disaster: the costs are a sign of commitment to the relationship and hope comes from belief (trust, faith) in the good-will of the Other.

No doubt there may also be social elements, intentions both to display the participant's own religious orientation and to demonstrate to others how much he can afford to give to the gods. Evolutionary theory indicates that some extravagant ornaments, like the peacock's tail, have been selected for in evolution because they indicated that the bearer could afford to sustain the handicap that they entailed (Zahavi, 1977; Cronin, 1991). Expenditure on cars, clothes and jewellery is an analogous human device for demonstrating wealth and power: the magnitude of a sacrifice may similarly be used to demonstrate simultaneously devotion to the deity and material wealth to peers. The practice of cutting off a finger to propitiate the deity, found in a number of societies (Burkert, 1996), may also have had an element of showing off, for an individual would not mutilate himself if he did not feel confident of his ability to cope in the mutilated state.

Potentially, sacrificial practice could seriously deplete the resources available to the individual, family, or group: in this context Firth (1996) has reviewed evidence that, although sacrifice may be an act of great symbolic significance, yet economic considerations usually influence its timing, nature, or amount. In some circumstances the Nuer may even substitute a wild cucumber for the ox, which is the proper object of sacrifice (Evans-Pritchard, 1956): analogously, Abraham substituted a ram for his son.

Sacrifice may involve the wastage of the sacrificial offering, though in many societies it is not destroyed but is used as food by the priests or by the group as a whole. This, of course, gets over the economic problem, but it raises a question about how the gods are perceived to see the situation. Where it is burned, there may be a feeling that the offering is being conveyed up to the gods in the smoke. Or perhaps the gods are seen to be satisfied by the mere killing, or as consuming an intangible essence of the sacrificial animal. The last hypothesis would be in keeping with the finding, discussed in Chapter 7, that animate objects are seen to have an essential essence: killing an ox eliminates its oxishness, which is perhaps what the gods like, and conveniently makes its flesh available to mortals. The Tikopia actually refer to an immaterial counterpart of the sacrificial animal, which is taken away and presumably eaten by the gods. On the basis of such facts Firth suggests that, while sacrifice is basically a symbolic act of grave significance, it may also involve notions of rationality and prudent calculation.[6]

Although regarding Christ's death as ending the need for further ritual involving animal sacrifice, the early Christian church instigated another ritual, Mass or Holy Communion, which was seen as perpetuating into the present the sacrifice of Christ (see p. 107). The central importance of Christ's sacrifice led to the use of the Cross as a symbol, and that has made possible subversion of that symbol for political ends (Hinde, 1997b). In coming to terms with the apparent wastefulness of the evolutionary process, some Christian theologians used the analogy of the Crucifixion to suggest that there could be no progress without suffering. This facilitated the use of the imagery of sacrifice to justify death in war. A picture much publicised in World War I showed a soldier lying at the foot of the Cross with a small, neatly sanitised, bullet hole in his forehead, and the inscription 'Greater love hath no man than this'. Many war memorials involved a sword superimposed on a Cross, again equating the soldiers' death with Christ's sacrifice (Sykes, 1991). Similar imagery was prevalent on both sides in World War II, and Hitler used the vocabulary of sacrifice to persuade the German people to accept losses and deprivations of ever-increasing magnitude (Stern, 1975).

## Summary

The motivations leading to ritual performance are diverse, differing between the ritual specialists, the central figures (if any), and other participants, and also according to the nature of the ritual. The Jain *puja* ritual, in which the celebrant usually acts alone, is contrasted with the Jewish Passover Seder, which is essentially social.

The consequences on individuals are similarly diverse: those on the self-systems of the participants are often of special importance.

Ritual involvement may depend on some of the same propensities as were discussed in Chapter 5.

Ritual performance can also have important social consequences. It may aid social integration and facilitate the continuity of the social system.

Prayer and sacrifice are considered as special forms of ritual. Prayer may take the form of a request, linguistic discourse, worship, supplication, a search for comfort, or a means for the construction of reality. It can appear to be paradoxical – for instance in the spelling out of needs to a supposedly omniscient being.

Sacrifice occurs in some form in very many religions. In Christianity the sacrifice on the Cross is seen as removing the necessity for further sacrifice. Sacrifice may involve the consumption of valuable resources, but devices to avoid this are often used.

# 12 Moral codes
## Background considerations

People have propensities to behave both prosocially and antisocially. If most individuals are generally prosocial and cooperate with each other, an aberrant individual who behaves selfishly will be able to exploit the others and is likely to prosper at their expense. If group life is to be possible, prosocial tendencies must be encouraged and antisocial ones discouraged. Successful group life thus depends on a reduction in the proportion of selfish individuals and/or on means whereby individuals who do behave selfishly can be detected and their activities inhibited. Or, to put it more generally, a balance must be set between the natural tendency of every individual to assert himself or herself on the one hand, and actions conducive to the public good on the other. Individuals make judgements as to what is right and what is wrong, and these judgements contribute to a moral code. Transgressions elicit social disapproval. While this can act as an adequate deterrent, a moral code is usually enforced by sanctions, and a very effective (because unfalsifiable) source of sanctions lies in the expectation of a less satisfactory existence after death. It is thus not surprising that moral codes tend to be associated with religious systems.

Because a moral code necessarily has an abstract structure, we expect that structure to have a foundation, and are accustomed to find it in the religious system. But does that necessarily mean that the moral code originates with the religious system? It may be legitimated, purveyed, and stabilised by the religious system, but how far does it derive from and depend on religion? These are critical questions today, and will be considered in this and the next two chapters, and again in Chapter 18. First, this chapter considers briefly the relations between moral codes and world religions, and proposes that a scientific approach can contribute to understanding their nature. This prepares the way for a consideration of the relation between moral codes and basic human propensities.

### Religious systems, moral behaviour, and moral codes

The relations between religious involvement and moral behaviour by individuals are far from clear-cut. Reviewing the (mostly North American) literature, Hood et al. (1996; Wulff, 1997) conclude that more religious people report that they are less likely to indulge in substance abuse, non-marital sexual behaviour, and crime than do less religious individuals, though the relations are weak. There is, however, little evidence that the more religious individuals are in fact more honest or helpful in their behaviour, although they claim that they are. As we have seen (pp. 40–1), there is some evidence that when those scoring highly on intrinsic religiosity do help, their behaviour stems from the helper's own needs, while those high on quest tend to help according to the needs of the person receiving the help. Furthermore religious individuals tend to be high on prejudice. Although research in this area relies heavily on self-reports and is difficult to interpret, it seems to suggest that the difference between the moral behaviour of more and less religious individuals is much less than one might expect (see further discussion in Chapter 17).

That, however, is an entirely different question from the effects on society as a whole of the moral code purveyed by its religious system. Since no societies lack a code of conduct, hard data on this issue are not available, but it is reasonable to suppose that such a code is essential for societal integrity. While for many Christians belief is the crucial aspect of religion, for most the moral code comes at least a close second, and for many it is the primary issue. Thus Braithwaite wrote:

> A man is not, I think, a professing Christian unless he proposes to live according to Christian moral principles and associates his intention with thinking of Christian stories; but he need not believe that the empirical propositions presented by the stories correspond to empirical fact.
>
> (cited Vidler, 1963)

Other philosophers have argued that governments should promote beliefs if, whether true or false, they promote good conduct in the citizens (Broad, 1925).

In other world-religions the holding of a particular set of beliefs seems, at least to an outsider, to be less essential than in Christianity, with more emphasis being placed on the code of conduct. For instance Confucianism (which, though linked with ancestor worship, can be seen from a Western perspective in many respects as a primarily social system), emphasised an ideology and a system of values and correct behaviour maintained by ritual. The diverse traditions within Buddhism are united by the search for enlightenment rather than any particular set of beliefs. For many, the path leading to the cessation of suffering has three constituents: morality, involving a disciplined way of life causing harm neither to oneself nor to others; meditation, leading to the creation of wholesome states of mind; and wisdom, seeing the world as it is but with the ability to stand aloof from it (Carrithers, 1983). Hindus pride themselves in their freedom from dogmatic assertions. In the Bhagavad-Gita three paths to the Absolute were indicated. The path of knowledge included not only book-learning but also the direct apprehension of reality and the interconnection of all things. The path of action involved, alongside contemplation, pursuing the activities appropriate to the caste to which one belonged – for Brahmans sacred ministration, for the Kshatriya warfare, for the Vaisya agriculture or business, and for the Sudra menial service. Some later Hindu thinkers laid the emphasis on good works, for self-forgetfulness could lead to self-realisation: the Christian preoccupation with sin was seen as itself sinful. The third path of loving devotion involved concentrating on the idea of God and being led by him (Zaehner, 1962).

Of course this point must not be overstated, for all religions involve a large element of belief, and beliefs affect the moral code. In China some of the central beliefs have involved ancestors, and the respect that should be shown to them: spirits and ancestors were tied into a set of beliefs that matched the social system. Hindus regard the transmigration of souls as self-evident and assume that time is cyclic: with belief in reincarnation, ethical conduct becomes a means of generating personal merit which can augment the chances of a better life next time. For the conventional Christian who had only one life for which he or she would be judged and saved or damned forever, the difference between good and bad behaviour has been an even more serious issue (Bruce, 1996). The point being made is that, while belief in dogma is more central for most Christians than for adherents to many other religious systems, in all world religions moral codes are underpinned by beliefs.

## Can a scientific approach help?

Since the Enlightenment many thinkers have sought to find a basis for a universal moral code that did not depend on revelation but was logically consistent and autonomous. On one issue there has been a fair degree of agreement, namely that science is concerned with how the world works, and not with how it should work: it has been assumed that science could have nothing to say about values. Even some of those who are unable to accept any form of religious belief find a scientific approach to morality unsatisfying: thus Ruse (1994: 23) argues that, for the evolutionist, morality rests on the contingencies of human nature so that there are no ultimate foundations, 'just a biological illusion of objectivity', and expresses the feeling that morality should be something more than this, though the precise nature of that 'more' would be seen differently by different people. In this and the next two chapters I shall argue that such a conclusion must not be accepted too readily, and that science in fact has a great deal to say not only about our capacity to make moral judgements, but about which actions we see as right and which as wrong (though some will argue that that is not necessarily the same as what *is* right or wrong). Moral codes and moral judgements must come from somewhere: if they are not the product of divine revelation, they must be the product of human minds. Since the issues are complex, it may help to set out first a view of the essential bases of moral codes. For the sake of simplicity, we may assume for the present that social behaviour is of two kinds, prosocial and antisocial.

## Social living carries or has carried biological value

Earlier in human evolution (and today), belonging to a group or community could augment the ability of an individual to survive and reproduce. Natural selection acted to enhance behaviours conducive to group integration: these are summarised in Chapter 16.

At a crude level of generality, all individuals have the capacity (or may develop the capacity) to behave self-assertively and antisocially, and all have the capacity to behave prosocially and selflessly. If a community or society was to survive and to benefit the individuals composing it, it was necessary that assertiveness and self-centred behaviour should be curbed and prosocial and cooperative behaviour encouraged, at least in so far as behaviour affecting fellow group members was concerned. Natural selection therefore acted to enhance prosocial behaviour and a tendency to behave with reciprocity to in-group members. However, the potential for conflict between self-seeking and prosocial behaviour is always present.

## Individuals make value judgements

The members of every society make value judgements about the actions and character traits of their peers. It is reasonable to suppose that the capacity to make such judgements has been selected for, since success in a group depends on the ability to understand and predict the behaviour of other group members (Humphrey, 1976). Furthermore, such value judgements can contribute to group integrity if antisocial behaviour is condemned (see pp. 169–72). Not only actions – murder, stealing, incest, self-sacrifice, and so on – but also the dispositions that are seen as leading to actions – selfishness, courage, honesty, chastity, greed – are seen as more or less good, more or less bad. The capacity to make such judgements is acquired as a consequence of growing up in a group situation, but which actions are judged as good and which bad will depend on the nature of that situation (see pp. 183–4): most individuals brought up in a harmonious group will see prosocial behaviour as good.

## Development of a moral code

Each individual tends to have views about how others should behave which differ from his views about how he should behave. While he may feel that it is important that he should behave prosocially, that will be diluted by his need to achieve his own goals; but his feeling that others should behave prosocially will be enhanced by his need to achieve his own goals. Although the judgement made by one individual about how another should behave will differ from the way in which that individual thinks he should behave, there will tend to be general agreement about how *others* should behave. The collective views about how others should behave become incorporated into a moral code, which places high value on behaviour conducive to in-group harmony.

The term 'moral code' implies that the code has the approval of the individual who holds it, and usually of at least most members of the group in question. It is incorporated into the self-systems of individuals, and thus reduces the discrepancy between how individuals think they should behave and how they think others should behave. In addition, individuals tend to adhere to the moral code because of fear of the disapproval of others (see pp. 154 and 170–2). However, an individual may continue to see certain types of self-serving behaviour as being 'right for him', and may use cognitive devices to justify this as congruent with the moral code (see below).

### Other influences on the moral code

While the moral code is concerned in the first instance with behaviour conducive to group harmony, such as prosocial behaviour, cooperativeness and reciprocity, as it becomes codified it is susceptible to manipulation by those in a position to do so. Thus principles concerned with the maintenance of a social hierarchy may be incorporated. For that and other reasons, individuals' value judgements (of themselves and others) and the moral code, although closely related, are unlikely to be identical.

The moral code is usually endorsed and purveyed by the religious system of the society. Religious specialists are then likely to incorporate precepts concerned with religious practice, which may be such as to reinforce their own status. Influences from religion usually tend to conserve the moral code. But to say that a religious system purveys a moral code does not imply that the religious system has created it. Nor does it imply that individual piety is necessarily correlated with unselfish behaviour: the data on this point are far from clear, in part because of the diversity of measures used and the frequent occurrence of a curvilinear relation between religiosity and unselfishness or prejudice (see also Chapter 17) (Wulff, 1997). As discussed later, norms concerning sexual and other aspects of behaviour may also be incorporated.

In the longer term moral codes change as a consequence of a two-way interchange between (a) what people actually do, which depends both on their prosocial tendencies (see above) and on antisocial ones (self-assertiveness, antisocial behaviour, etc.) and (b) what the moral code says they should do (see pp. 147–9). Thus moral codes are not immutable: they also differ between societies according to the society's history, environment, and so on (see pp. 146–7).[1]

### Religious moral code and societal ideology

The moral code forms part of the ideology ( used in the sense of a system of ideas about phenomena, especially those of social life)[2] but it is possible for a society's ideology to clash with a religiously purveyed moral code: for instance, the two may differ about the appropriate way to behave to an enemy in time of war. Tension arises if ideology and moral code are too discrepant.

### Moral code and individual moral judgements

As noted above, the value judgements of individuals and the moral code may be discrepant. There are three principal reasons for this. First, circumstances may have changed, so that what was conducive to harmonious group living is so no longer. Second, there may be a question of the lesser of two evils. To steal infringes the moral code, yet it may be seen as morally right to steal to save life. It may even be seen by some as morally correct to take a life, if that act saves many others. In wartime, killing of out-group members may be seen as right if it protects in-group members or their way of life. Third, as noted already, individuals may use defence mechanisms to convince themselves that certain self-serving actions are justified. Although the moral code is generally accepted by the society, it is thus possible for an individual to disagree with judgements based on it in particular contexts. But in all such cases, the individual's judgement, if not stemming from divine guidance, must come ultimately from basic human psychological characteristics shaped by experience in society.

Furthermore, the judgements of individuals are influenced by the moral code of their society and codes differ between societies. So, for instance, amputation might be seen as just punishment for stealing by members of some societies but not others.

### Role of pan-cultural propensities

Summarising the above, it follows that both what individuals see as right and wrong, and the nature of the societal moral code, are influenced by the pan-cultural psychological propensities of individuals. In both cases these are also influenced by, and influence, each other, the society's history and circumstances, and manipulations by others – but each of these depends also on pan-cultural psychological characteristics through the two-way influences illustrated in Figure 2.1 (p. 20). While some will feel that this is just a way of saying that the issues are complicated, it at least indicates that there is no need to postulate a supernatural law-giver, and that the route to understanding lies in teasing apart these two-way relations.

There is, however, the further problem of whether there are 'ultimate' criteria for right and wrong. To that question, it is by no means clear that there is an answer. From what has been said so far, it might seem that we could go a long way on the assumption that actions are 'right' if they are conducive to harmony in the in-group, but in practice this simplicity is distorted by (a) The tendency of individuals to make moral judgements about how others should behave that differ from the judgements they make about their own behaviour, because their self-seeking propensities distort moral judgements to their own advantage; (b) The problems of weighing dissimilar consequences against each other (the autonomy of the individual versus the integrity of the group; the right to privacy versus the public good; the rights of the foetus versus those of the mother, etc.); (c) The proper limits of the in-group; and (d) The fact that every action has diverse and ramifying consequences which may affect many beside the individuals immediately involved. For these and other reasons, most moral judgements involve right versus wrong only in the sense that a decision must be taken, and the matter is more usually one of more right versus less right, or more wrong versus less wrong. I shall not attempt here to enter the jungle of moral philosophy, nor do I have the competence to do so, but a bottom line assumption is necessary. I shall proceed on the certainly over-simple assumption that actions are the more right, the more they are conducive to consequences for others comparable to those the actor would expect them to benefit from. This assumption has the merit that it emerges directly from the principle of reciprocity, discussed more fully in the next chapter, and can thus (according to arguments to be set out there) probably be seen as an evolved moral disposition.[3] However it carries obvious dangers. Such a formulation puts the actor in a Big Brother position: he may be mistaken about what is best for others, he may deceive himself about what is best for others to his own advantage, or he may simply not know. And the conclusion he comes to will depend on the culture in which he is living. However, given that or some related assumption(s), an appreciation of the dialectical relations between individual's moral judgements and the moral code will facilitate auspicious decisions in the face of moral dilemmas. The enforcement of those decisions is, of course, another matter (see pp. 239–41).

## Development of the moral code in the individual

Not only do all human beings have the potential for developing an ability to discriminate between the right and wrong actions of others, they tend also to evaluate their own actions, feeling guilt if an action fails to meet internalised moral standards and shame if their actions in general are seen to fail to meet such standards (Lewis, 1992). While humans differ from most other animals in this respect, that does not mean that a moral sense or conscience is 'inborn' in humans, but only that humans have the potential to develop a capacity to make such evaluations. It has been suggested that conscience arises primarily as a consequence of the internalisation of parental standards, but that this process is influenced by the manner in which the child experiences the parents and their requirements for his or her behaviour: for instance, if the child experiences the parents as rejecting, he or she will adopt a dismissive attitude towards parental values. Internalisation implies that the moral standards gradually become independent of their source in parental values, but they may of course be influenced by subsequent experience (Voland and Voland, 1995).

It is important to note that, while parental example no doubt plays an important role, the standards incorporated from the parents will be in part those which the parents think should apply to the child, not those that they think should apply to themselves. In biological terms, this is because, as the child develops, its demand for resources increases and is likely to exceed the costs that the parents would incur in providing them, costs and benefits being assessed in terms of their effects on probable subsequent breeding success (Trivers, 1974). Conflict between parent and child is therefore likely to increase, and the parents will show some tendency to persuade the child that 'right' behaviour is that which fosters their own interests.

A 'moral sense' is not a unitary entity, and in a mature form it must require a 'theory of mind' (that is, an ability to interpret the behaviour of others in terms of intentions, etc.), the ability to empathise, and the ability to evaluate one's intended actions. All of these can be seen as basic human characteristics, involving complex developmental processes and developed to a different extent in different individuals.[4] Evaluating one's future actions involves comparing present intentions with their probable consequences, and it is probably for that reason that children's behaviour does not indicate the full emergence of a moral sense until they are several years old (Eisenberg and Strayer, 1987).

Of course, the view that a theory of mind depends on pan-cultural characteristics is not incompatible with the clear cultural differences in the salience and content of the moral code. Since virtually all children are brought up in circumstances in which they receive evaluations from parents or other caregivers, the development of a moral sense is virtually ubiquitous. But the evaluations that caregivers make of children's behaviour are in large measure determined by the cultural norms, values and practices of the society, so that both what is considered to be right and what wrong, and the route to the development of prosocial behaviour, may differ between cultures (Goody, 1991). However, in general, the children who are most likely to show prosocial behaviour are those who acquire good socio-cognitive skills (e.g. are able to take another's perspective), have a sophisticated understanding of moral problems, and can empathise with others: such development is facilitated by a caregiver who is sensitive to the child's needs, and shows prosocial behaviour himself or herself (Bowlby, 1969/82; IJzendoorn, 1997; Miller *et al.*, 1991).

What is seen as good or bad is thus determined in large measure by what the caregiver responds to with approval or disapproval, and that differs to some extent between cultures, over time, and between individuals in any one culture. Often those values are (or have been) purveyed by the religious system: most religions involve precepts about how one should or should not behave. These precepts, whether or not they are perceived as dictates of the religious system, are internalised and incorporated into the self-system. They thus come to feel 'natural', individuals strive to live up to the 'ideal self' that they have incorporated, and the moral systems of other cultures become difficult to accept. The critical questions, then, concern the content of moral codes. While it would certainly be rash to claim that moral codes can be deduced from basic scientific principles, science has a good deal to say about their nature and genesis.

## The dynamic nature of moral codes

Moral codes do not appear suddenly out of nowhere, nor are they necessarily cast in stone. They have been constructed by individuals, and can be seen in the first instance as incorporating individuals' views about how others should behave. The bases of those views are discussed in the next chapter: first it is important to stress the dynamic nature of moral codes.

Although moral codes may have considerable stability, they are better seen as a dynamic product of long-term bi-directional influences between how people behave and how the current moral code stipulates that it is appropriate for people to behave (see Figure 2.1). They evolve slowly over time. Change is often a consequence of a continuing dialectic between those in a position to change the *status quo* (or who think they are in a position to do so), and those who wish to maintain things as they are. Both may be acting according to what they see as 'right'; both may be acting according to what they see as their own best interests.

In Christian countries, the relations between churches, state and people have been complex: while the churches have often appeared to be the source of standards of behaviour, in fact they have often followed society in deciding what is acceptable. For instance, slavery was accepted in the New Testament, and the Anglican Church only ceased to take St. Paul literally after slavery had become institutionally unacceptable in society. The same is true of the subordinate social, moral, and intellectual position of women: at the time of writing the Church of England is still not unanimous about their ordination. In the longer term in Britain, the Church has rarely prevented society from doing what it wanted: the Protestant nature of the Anglican Church is the result of Tudor politics. Sometimes society looks for guidance to the Church; sometimes it looks for a rubber stamp; sometimes it ignores the Church and gets on with its own thing. The moral code thus has a limited degree of flexibility, with new values continually emerging and being superseded as the result of the dialectic between what people do and what people are supposed to do. As noted in Chapter 2, as divorce became more permissible, marriages became less stable, and as marriages became less stable, divorce became more acceptable. Again, as women became more independent, the norms for women changed, and as those norms changed, it became more possible (though not necessarily easy) for women to lead more independent lives. But the flexibility is not infinite: where moral codes appear to remain stable for long periods, it is nearer the truth to say that they fluctuate between limits, with stability maintained by dynamic forces, rather than that they are absolute. As we shall see later, the sources of that stability can be sought in human nature. At the same time, the role that religion has played in the past is not to be underestimated: it has acted as a sounding board for this dynamic, playing an important role in setting limits to fluctuations and change. In this, it has been armed with powerful tools – supernatural authority and the threat of eternal damnation.

The balance between stability and change depends in part also on the relations between the moral code, individual moral judgements, and other aspects of the socio-cultural structure. We have already seen (Chapter 3) how everyday attitudes to women are related to the religious belief system, women being esteemed more highly in societies with a female deity. As another example, Bruce has argued that fundamentalist and Pentecostal Protestants held puritanical views in part because of their poor economic situation. Their view that television was evil because it transmitted satanic messages was influenced by the fact that they could not afford it. When their financial position improved, their attitude to television changed. '...asceticism is easier when one is poor. Increased prosperity means that the required sacrifice gets relatively bigger and bigger' (1996: 149).

To look at the issue from a slightly different perspective, any code must have been selected over time from a range of possible ones as the result of two-way influences over time between the code and the behaviour of individuals. The question becomes, therefore, can a scientific approach, even if only qualitative, provide understanding of how choices are made? Are there any basic principles that determine or set limits to what people see as appropriate behaviour? As noted above, it is often claimed that these are issues beyond the reach of science, because science cannot provide a value system for human behaviour. In what follows I shall argue that moral codes are constructed by human minds, and are in principle accessible to scientific analysis. This does not imply that what is natural is always right, but rather that an understanding of the human mind can indicate the source of the moral judgements that we make. Nor does it in any way underestimate the role that religious systems have played in maintaining moral codes. I shall be concerned primarily with codified precepts, though I shall suggest that other aspects of a culture's moral outlook have similar bases.

## Categories of precepts within moral codes

While in any society the precepts may seem to be aspects of a single moral code, it is helpful to see them as involving three overlapping categories. The first refers to the belief system, the narratives, and/or the religious specialists directly. I include here the first two theological virtues of Christianity, faith and hope; rules about behaviour and attitudes towards supernatural entities, including the first four Hebraic Commandments;[5] and admonitions concerning the status of the priests or other specialists. Such precepts may be critical in integrating the whole social order: thus, in keeping with earlier Chinese religions, Buddhism in China first promoted itself as the best religion for the protection of the state, legitimating hierarchy by appeal to a cosmic vision and the leader's place in it (Orzech, 1996). Similarly, some of the laws of the Chinese Han period were directed towards maintaining the cosmic balance of the universe by regulating seasonal activities and so on, and by the maintenance of social stability and political cohesion (Loewe, 1994). A Taoist cleric born in China in 406 CE created a set of reformist rules for the organisation of the Taoist church which aimed to achieve harmony and order by categorisation and hierarchy. They included, for instance, stipulations for record-keeping, and directions for the maintenance of a Quiet Room in each house, where the priest could communicate with the celestial authorities (Nickerson, 1996). In the shorter term responsibility for seeing that such rules are upheld rests mainly with the religious specialists, whose position depends on their success: for example the Brahmans have been the principal upholders of the Hindu caste system.

The second category, which may overlap extensively with the others, concerns the maintenance of the religious and/or social group. This may overlap with the first group (e.g. 'Thou shalt have none other gods but me'), or with the third (e.g. 'Thou shalt not kill' with the implication that this refers to in-group members and not to out-groups, as discussed on pp. 159–60). While neighbouring groups may assimilate each other's customs, there are nearly always differences (Reif, 1993), and all major groups – tribes, clans, cities, nations – emphasise the importance of duty to the in-group, which must include demarcating the in-group from outsiders. Directives about ritual performance and dietary prohibitions may also be included here, for they may contribute in important ways to group integrity (cf. Douglas, 1970a). In Islam and Judaism such divinely given laws are central to religious observance and experience. In many non-literate societies the secular and religious systems are virtually indistinguishable, and in more complex societies they are often mutually supportive, rulers holding their position by 'divine right'.

The third category of precepts, and the one of most interest in the present context, concerns aspects of the behaviour of individuals or dealings between individuals. Although prescriptions about social behaviour differ between cultures, it is they that make group life possible, and it is not surprising that there are basic similarities, as well as differences, among cultures. To mention three examples from very different cultures, the God-given Hebraic Commandments 5–10 require individuals to honour their parents and forbid murder, adultery, stealing, bearing false witness, and coveting neighbours' possessions. The Chinese Han 'Scripture in forty-two sections' (c.65 CE) records Buddha as listing ten 'evil things' – killing, stealing, adultery, duplicity, slander, lying, lewd speech, envy, hatred, and delusion: others, such as desire, sloth, doubt, passion, and desire, are referred to in other sections (Sharf, 1996a). And the Nuer regard adultery, homicide and incest as sins against the spiritual order (Evans-Pritchard, 1956).

It is with this third category that we are primarily concerned, though the others must also be considered. The precepts are part of the socio-cultural structure, and must be compatible with other aspects of that structure. For example, most societies are at least in some degree hierarchical, and there are rules, often implicit, about whom one should respect. But these vary with the structure of the society, and differ in nature between individualistic and collectivistic societies; and rules about adultery differ according to the marriage system. Among Hindus, the behaviour seen as appropriate for an individual has depended on his or her caste. Among the Navajo and many other groups appropriate behaviour is prescribed for different categories of kinship relation (Porterfield, 1998).

One further distinction which has been made should be mentioned, namely that between moral and conventional transgressions. The former are defined in terms of their consequences on the rights and welfare of others, while conventional transgressions involve transgressions against the rules and norms that structure social interactions within social systems. Considerable experimental evidence indicates that in western societies the former are regarded as both more serious and less modifiable than the latter (reviewed Blair, 1997), and it has been argued that they depend on the formation of two distinct conceptual domains (Turiel, 1983). We shall return to this issue in the next chapter.

There has long been a debate as to whether there are universal standards of what is right and what is wrong, or whether ethical questions should be judged solely against cultural norms. The approach adopted here involves neither of these two extremes. Rather it is suggested that all ethical systems are ultimately based on certain basic human propensities, but that cultures differ in the balance between those propensities, and in the addition of precepts relating to local conditions. The values that people hold are thus neither completely relative, nor universal, but limitations to their diversity are set by properties of the human mind. These properties include tendencies to behave prosocially and antisocially, to recognise a norm of reciprocity, to seek status, to behave sexually, to maintain group distinctiveness, and perhaps a concept of 'common good'.

## Summary

Moral codes have almost invariably been part of, or closely related to, religious systems, and are central to some. A scientific approach can provide considerable insight into their natures.

Individuals have propensities to make moral judgements: in the first instance, actions considered good are those that contribute to intra-group harmony. The views of individuals as to how others should behave to them contribute to a moral code, which is influenced also from other sources. What is considered good and what bad differs to some extent between cultures.

The development of a moral sense in the individual requires a 'theory of mind' and occurs over the early years of life.

Moral codes are not carved in stone, though they have considerable stability: they can be seen as the result of a dynamic interchange within society between what people do and what they are supposed to do. They are usually purveyed by the religious system, which contributes to their stability.

It is convenient to distinguish between precepts concerned with the maintenance of the religious system, those maintaining group distinctiveness, and those concerned with inter-personal relationships.

# 13  Moral codes

## Prosocial behaviour and reciprocity

Moral codes make social life possible in the face of the socially disruptive, selfish and assertive propensities of individuals. Much such antisocial behaviour stems from over-expression of behaviour that is normally quite acceptable. For instance, all humans need to feel that their behaviour is in some degree autonomous, but group-living demands that autonomy be curbed in some respects. That everybody has the capacity to behave in a self-assertive and socially disruptive fashion needs no elaboration, for it is antisocial behaviour that catches the headlines. But it is equally true that everybody has the capacity to behave prosocially, and prosocial behaviour is usually coupled with the expectation of reciprocity. This chapter is concerned with the ubiquity of the principle of 'Do as you would be done by', and argues that it stems from our biological nature.

## Prosocial behaviour and group formation: introduction

Because most people desire and expect a peaceful society, disruptions are salient. Much is written about the human capacities for aggression, self-assertiveness, and selfishness, but less attention is paid to the fact that all individuals have the potential for developing a prosocial disposition. In fact, a great deal is now known about the circumstances and early relationships which minimise tendencies to show self-seeking behaviour and maximise positive tendencies in the course of development (see p. 164). Our present concern is with the evolutionary processes which ensured that individuals have this potential to develop prosocial behaviours.

Most obviously, parents are usually prepared, within limits, to make sacrifices for the sake of their children (Trivers, 1974). This, of course, is not a specifically human trait. Natural selection necessarily operates to ensure that individuals tend to act in a way that maximises their reproductive success: a species whose individuals did not reproduce effectively would soon become extinct. We can be sure that the tendency of human parents to ensure the successful development of their children is part of our biological heritage.

Parents, of course, share a high proportion of their genes with their children: by looking after their children they are ensuring the survival of individuals who have genes similar to their own, including especially those that give rise to the tendency to look after their close relatives. While children inherit half of their (rare) genes from each parent, they are similarly related to their full siblings, and also have some of their genes (though a smaller proportion) in common with more distant relatives, nephews and nieces, cousins and so on. Thus an individual who helps a relative may in doing so be helping an individual who is likely to behave in a similar way to his own relatives: this will lead to the selection of a propensity to help relatives provided that such actions do not diminish the reproductive success of the helper by an amount determined by the degree of his relatedness to the recipient – that is, by the probability that the relative will in fact share that propensity. Thus it is in the biological interests of parents to look after their offspring, where the probability is one-half, if the biological benefit to the offspring is more than twice the cost to the parent, cost and benefit being measured in terms of their probable effects on long-term reproductive success. With more distantly related individuals, the benefit would have to be greater or the cost to the donor less. A given act will be to an individual's reproductive advantage if its cost to the actor is less than half its benefit to a sibling, one-quarter to a niece, nephew, or grandchild, or one-eighth to a cousin and so on (assuming no inbreeding) (Hamilton, 1964; Trivers, 1974, 1985). To help relatives is part of our biological heritage.

A number of predictions from this approach fit what we know about human behaviour. Thus individuals do tend to help kin more than non-kin (e.g. Betzig *et al.*, 1988; Borgerhof Mulder, 1991; Chagnon and Irons, 1979; Essock-Vitale and McGuire, 1980, 1985; Eisenberg and Mussen, 1989; Irons, 1991), and individuals are more attached to blood-relatives than to step-relatives (Daly and Wilson, 1988). The Israeli kibbutz system minimised family bonds by the group-rearing of children, but this encountered strong resistance, and the practice became diluted.

In the early stages of human evolution, when many of our current psychological propensities were being determined, humans probably lived in small groups of mostly related individuals. Thus natural selection for behaviour conducive to the welfare of kin could operate to promote prosocial behaviour to in-group members. However, an increase in group size, and a tendency to mate with out-group members (see pp. 178–80), would require prosocial behaviour to be extended to relatively distantly related individuals. Two mutually supportive processes seem to have been involved. First, if groups were to be viable and to maintain their integrity, in-group members must be treated differently from outsiders. The tendencies for individuals to seek to become members of groups, to see themselves as members of groups, to differentiate between in-group members and outsiders, and to regard the former more favourably, are so ubiquitous that they must be regarded as pan-cultural human characteristics.

Second, humans have the potential to behave in a self-seeking way, so that to give help to others if it is continually to one's own disadvantage is not a sustainable strategy in the long run. Not, that is, unless one also receives comparable help or compensation, or expects to receive it, in return. It is thus hardly surprising that human relationships largely depend on individuals 'doing as they would be done by', or that the moral codes of human groups include precepts requiring individuals to behave to others in ways that they would like others to behave to them. I shall refer to such precepts as involving 'reciprocity'. We shall return to the characteristics of groups in Chapter 16: here we focus on prosocial behaviour and reciprocity.

None of this should be taken as suggesting that prosocial behaviour or reciprocity are hard-wired and independent of experience. While all humans have the potential to develop in such a way that their behaviour will be predominantly prosocial, the extent to which they do show such behaviour is strongly influenced by experiences during development and by the current situation: as we shall see later, the nature of such influences may themselves have been adapted by natural selection.

## Reciprocity and prosocial behaviour in human interaction

### Reciprocity in world religions

Their view of an immanent God helped the Jews to see humanity as sacred: since man had been created in God's image, transgressions against a fellow human being were seen as a denial of God himself. Prosocial behaviour and reciprocity are central for Jewish and Christian teaching. While the view that Christianity replaced the earlier 'Eye for an eye and a tooth for a tooth' version of morality with an emphasis on mercy and love does scant justice to the Old Testament, Christianity does emphasise the *initiation* of prosocial behaviour as well as reciprocity, as in the precept 'Whatsoever ye would that men should do unto you, do ye even so to them' (St. Matthew, 7, 12); and 'Love your neighbour as yourself'.[1] Although Christ put a further gloss on this by indicating that fairness should be based on a principle of social justice ('Each according to his need') rather than on equality or equity (see below), much of his teaching can be interpreted as involving injunctions to behave to others as you would like them to behave to you – even requiting evil with good, and behaving with humility. And the principle applies not only to behaviour, but also to character traits: thus we admire the generous person who is alive to the problems of others and tries to help them, but despise the coward and the selfish man because they are concerned only with their own affairs. Such precepts can also be understood as conducive to group solidarity, an issue which may have been of special importance to the early Christians.[2]

Similarly, the four great virtues in Buddhism are friendship or benevolence, compassion, joy in others' joy, and equanimity – the latter being related to self-restraint (Smart, 1996). In a similar vein, the classic work on Confucian precepts, the 'Book of rites', contains the following passage:

> In the highest antiquity they prized (simply conferring) good; in the time next to this, giving and repaying was the thing attended to. And what the rules of propriety value is that reciprocity. If I give a gift and nothing comes in return, that is contrary to propriety; if the thing comes to me, and I give nothing in return, that also is contrary to propriety.
>
> (Yang, 1957: 291)

According to Fung Yu-lan (1952), Confucius is said to have distinguished between *chung* (doing to others what one likes oneself) and *shu* (not doing to others what one does not like oneself). Although altruism was also valued in some circumstances, the principle of reciprocal response was applied to social relations of all kinds, and in fact the network of reciprocity was seen as embracing the whole universe.

As another example, in the 'Declaration of the Parliament of the World's Religions', based on a gathering in Chicago at which all the major world religions and many minor ones were represented, the 'Golden Rule' of 'Do as you would be done to' was accepted as basic as a matter of course (Küng and Kuschel, 1993).

### Reciprocity in personal relationships

In these cases religions present reciprocity as a precept which should guide behaviour: we must also ask how far it actually does so. We shall see that much recent work on human relationships does in fact use reciprocity as an explanatory principle for how people behave in their relationships.

Specifically, the family of 'exchange theories' is based on the supposition that both formal and personal relationships can be seen as involving processes of reciprocal exchange. To take one example, 'equity theory', adopting a formal approach, advances a number of propositions. The first states that (1) individuals tend to try to maximise what they can get. However, if everyone did this, society would be chaotic. Therefore (proposition 2), groups work out systems for ensuring that rewards and costs are equitably distributed among individuals, and usually achieve this by rewarding those who treat others equitably and punishing those who do not. Proposition 3 states that individuals who find themselves to be inequitably treated will become distressed and (proposition 4) attempt to restore perceived equity if they believe their arousal to be due to the inequity. Equity can be restored by manipulating either one's own rewards or costs, or those of the other party, for instance by compensating someone whom one has injured or taken advantage of. Alternatively 'psychological equity' can be achieved by processes akin to the 'cognitive restructuring' or 'selective evaluation' used to maintain the congruency of the self-system (see Chapter 2) – in other words by distorting one's perceptions of the other individual's outcomes. For instance, instead of compensating a victim a harmdoer may convince himself that it was an accident, or that the victim did not really suffer, or that he got what he deserved (Walster *et al.*, 1978).

Interestingly, a number of recent studies of married couples and other dyads have shown that, under some circumstances, the partners may feel uncomfortable not only if they see themselves as under-benefited but also if they feel over-benefited (e.g. Prins *et al.*, 1993). This implies that they are guided by a 'social contract' requiring reciprocity. If an individual feels that he has been over-benefited in a relationship, he may feel uncomfortable, or he may show gratitude, thereby acknowledging his debt and implying that he will make the matter good in the future. Gratitude tends to be greater, the greater the cost incurred by the other party (Trivers, 1985).[3]

Crucial to the restoration of equity are judgements about what is fair, and here the moral code may interact with the societal ideology. Within any one society, at least three principles may operate – equality for all parties; each should receive in proportion to the costs they have incurred; and social justice, each should receive according to his need (Lerner, 1981). In addition, what an individual feels he deserves varies with his 'investments', in the sense of that with which he is invested. Status, wealth, class, beauty, sex, personal characteristics and so on may each, in different societies, contribute to an individual's investments, so that high status or beauty may be associated with expectations of greater rewards. Some would argue that an interaction is 'fair' if each participant gains in proportion to his or her 'worthiness'. Reification of such value differences in a moral code may make it easier (or be designed to make it easier) for the less privileged to accept their lot. Clearly, on all these issues immense cultural variation is present. Culture-specific rules indicate whom one should help, when one can ask for help, how much help should be given to others, and so on. Furthermore, individuals differ in what they value: some (especially masculine individuals) may emphasise justice, others (the more feminine ones) affection and relationships (e.g. Gilligan, 1982). And individuals seek for different rewards in different relationships. Thus complete agreement on a moral code is unlikely to be achieved within any society: there will always be some differences of opinion about what is 'fair' or 'just'.

As an aside, we may note another complication. While exchange theories were originally concerned with tangible resources, in personal relationships these are not the only, or even the principal, issue. Love, respect, information and so on are likely to be even more important than concrete goods. Foa and Foa (1974) have pointed out that such resources have properties quite different from material goods. While if I give you some food, I have less, if I give you love I may have more – or at least feel that I have more. But at the same time I should feel slighted if my love were not returned, so reciprocity still operates. Interestingly, the Buddha's doctrine for laymen involved a similar principle – in doing good for others, one also creates a good frame of mind in oneself (Carrithers, 1983). Similar sentiments have been expressed by Christians, Jews, and no doubt adherents to many other religions.

### Trust and commitment

In real-life situations, reciprocity is rarely immediate: in close relationships we incur current costs in the hope of future gains, and it is thus essential to be committed to the relationship, to have trust in the partner, and to believe that the partner is committed. The ability to trust is influenced by early experience: Bowlby (1969/82) argued that it is derived from the feeling of security provided to an infant by a caregiver who is sensitive and responsive to its needs. This is incorporated into the 'internal working model' of relationships which influences subsequent social behaviour (see p. 90).

While the tendency to trust others is to some extent characteristic of the individual, its other determinants depend on the situation. Trust between strangers is most likely to be present if they have common short-term goals, and if each sees the potential benefits of cooperation as greater than the costs. As they become acquainted it is facilitated if they perceive each other positively and as unlikely to exploit them. Honesty may therefore pay, because the behaviour one shows indicates the sort of person one is, and whether one can be trusted in future. And it is important to display good intentions from the start: prosocial behaviour should not wait on the perception that it will be reciprocated, it is necessary to take the initiative, or at least to display in initial negotiations a readiness to behave positively, so that trust can be established. As we have seen, Christian teaching emphasises strongly that it is initiating good behaviour that will bring later reward (though the reward may come much later):

> There is no man that hath left house, or brethren, or sisters, or father, or mother, or wife, or children, or lands, for my sake and the gospel's. But he shall receive an hundredfold now in this time, houses, and brethren, and sisters, and mothers, and children, and lands, with persecutions; and in the world to come eternal life.
>
> (Mark, 10, 29–30)

And 'Give and it shall be given unto you; good measure, pressed down, and shaken together, and running over, shall men give into your bosom. For with the same measure that ye mete withal it shall be measured to you again'. This is made into a moral precept: 'For if ye love them which love you, what thank have ye? for sinners also love those that love them'; and coupled with the promise of reward in Heaven: 'But love ye your enemies, and do good, and lend, hoping for nothing again; and your reward shall be great, and ye shall be the children of the Highest' (Luke, Chapter 6). Again, 'It is more blessed to give than to receive' (Acts, 20, 35).

Once a relationship is established, trust depends on belief in the partner's commitment, and the determinants of commitment differ according to the type of relationship. In a personal relationship, commitment may be determined by external factors, as in an arranged marriage, or it may be endogenous, arising gradually as the relationship develops. It is influenced by a number of factors, including satisfaction with the relationship, the availability of alternatives, and belief in the partner's commitment. It may involve fine-tuned knowledge about situations in which trust is and is not appropriate. In a formal (as opposed to a personal) relationship, commitment may be ensured by power differentials or economic forces intrinsic to the social structure (Hinde, 1997a).

In a group situation, where any two individuals are likely to meet only seldom so that individual commitment cannot be an issue, observation of the prosocial behaviour of others may help (see below), but a norm of reciprocity or 'social contract' is probably essential. The perception that other in-group members are more like oneself than out-group members, and are preferable to out-group members (see p. 199), will clearly facilitate this. But in any situation in which reciprocity operates, a reputation for trustworthiness will benefit the individual, because he is more likely to receive help from others if they believe that he will reciprocate. In practice, most people tend to believe optimistically that the world is just and that rewards for good deeds will come along, in spite of evidence to the contrary (Lerner, 1981).

Since, even in this world, reciprocation for costs incurred is seldom immediate, it is hardly surprising that both trust and trustworthiness are valued qualities in most societies. This does not mean that it will pay individuals to be trusting and trustworthy in all circumstances: we shall see later that in harsh conditions or in a highly competitive society they might do better to be self-assertive (p. 164).

### Reciprocity with the deity

Although we are concerned here with moral principles guiding social behaviour, exchange theory is also revealing about some aspects of religion. We have seen that, for many, an important support for belief comes from the feeling of relationship with the deity: this relationship resembles in some ways a secular relationship, and also requires reciprocity. Rewards, in this life or in another, require good behaviour. The god is more likely to answer requests if offered a quid pro quo – perhaps a promise to build a chapel or to undertake a pilgrimage (see p. 158). If the god is saddened by bad behaviour, reparations in the form of good behaviour or sacrifice are necessary. Since the goals are often long term, trust in the partner is essential: here it is seen as faith. And, just as in personal relationships the expression of gratitude is an important cultural tool for the maintenance of reciprocity as it involves acknowledgement of indebtedness for services received and the implication of repayment, so also in relationships with the deity – though here it is called worship.

This issue is to be seen most clearly in the relationships of mediaeval Christians with their saints. The saints were venerated because of their miraculous powers or for their ability to intercede on the supplicant's behalf with higher authority. When illness came or disaster threatened, the supplicant often made a vow to do something thought to be pleasing to the saint, such as visiting the saint's shrine. The more costs that were incurred in carrying out the vow, the more likely would the saint be to provide help – hence pilgrimages to distant places, perhaps made barefoot and without financial support other than that which could be obtained from alms received along the way or, in the case of collective vows, the building of a chapel or shrine. The gift, service, or pilgrimage was an essential part of the vow, a quid pro quo for the favour requested. (This, of course has a clear parallel in close human relationships – people see the sacrifices that their partners make for the sake of the relationship as indications of their love, and are likely to reward them accordingly.) Often, of course, monasteries acting as guardians to a saint's shrine were the beneficiaries of the donations made. Oaths made to saints were seen as absolutely binding, but the saint was expected to carry out his or her side of the deal. If the saint proved ineffective, the supplicant could try another – there seem always to have been plenty to choose from – or move up the hierarchy by appealing to the Virgin Mary. Indeed saints have sometimes been punished if they did not provide the required favours, and it has not been unknown for supplicants to threaten a saint if their requests were not met (Wilson, 1983b).

Describing the Portuguese *romarias*, village festivals organised around the memory of a saint, Sanchis (1983: 267) writes that the vows made:

> constitute routine investments and are a part of normal life and of the way that the universe functions. Between the two societies, the human and the 'divine', that of vulnerability to the destructive forces of the cosmos and of the passions and that represented by 'sanctity', a solidarity is established and maintained through these repeated exchanges. On the one side are offered homage in the form of suffering, long journeys on foot.... In return one obtains an increased sense of security, certainty that one is protected and a contact with the sacred...'

And 'This sense of obligation inherent in the structure of the universe and in the nature of things' is sometimes hidden behind psychological reactions attributed to the saint, some saints being seen as more obliging than others.

The supplicant may see an act of devotion in terms different from those of the ecclesiastical authorities. The purchase and burning of a candle may be seen by the ecclesiastical authorities to symbolise the consumption of pride and egotism in the individual and the re-kindling of the love of God, but a study in Parisian chapels indicated that supplicants saw it as a private act of devotion, or as a gift made to obtain the granting of a wish or to render thanks (Wilson, 1983a).

### Limitations in the extension of reciprocity beyond the dyad

The Hebraic commandments concerned with social behaviour dealt in prohibitions rather than with positive behaviour, but at least two of them contain limitations on their applicability. The Israelites were not permitted to bear false witness or to covet the possessions of their 'neighbours'. The meaning of the term 'neighbour' is controversial but it is usually taken to signify 'fellow Israelite' or those whom one lives near or with whom one comes into frequent contact. The first interpretation is implied, for instance, by 'Thou shalt not avenge, nor bear any grudge against the children of thy people, but thou shalt love thy neighbour as thyself...' (Leviticus, 19, 18). The second is illustrated by: 'if a stranger sojourn with you in your land, ye shall not vex him' (Leviticus, 19, 33). Again, Exodus 22, 21 reads 'Thou shalt neither vex a stranger, nor oppress him: for ye were strangers in the land of Egypt': the word 'stranger' here is identical in the original to that used in Leviticus, and again means 'resident alien' (Emerton, pers. comm.).

It is accepted that the Hebraic commandments were translated from scrolls which had no punctuation. While usually understood as involving a series of separate commandments (Exodus, 20, 13–17) – 'Thou shalt not kill. Thou shalt not commit adultery' and so on, it has been suggested that all, like those concerned with bearing false witness and covetousness, were seen as applying to neighbours. Thus Deuteronomy (5, 17–21) gives 'Thou shalt not kill. Neither shalt thou commit adultery. Neither shalt thou steal, neither shalt thou bear false witness against thy neighbour. Neither shalt thou desire thy neighbour's wife...'. Such an interpretation is apparent in several verses in Leviticus, 19, and it is claimed that it was the interpretation given by the rabbis of the Talmud, who determined that an Israelite was not liable for murder unless it were a fellow Israelite that he had killed (Hartung, 1995; but see critique by Chait, 1996), a limitation also found in Islamic law.

Thus for the Israelites, neighbour usually meant other Israelites or local residents, and the Hebraic commandments applied at least primarily to behaviour to other members of the group. The divine instructions in Deuteronomy (20, 10–18) leave no doubt that the Israelites were to subjugate or kill all males in the cities that they encountered, and indeed in all the cities within reach of the land they occupied. The Bible records how hundreds of cities were destroyed and thousands of men and women slaughtered. The Israelites saw themselves as God's Chosen People. 'Righteousness' consisted largely in following rules that were conducive to in-group cohesiveness. This, of course, is not to say that the Hebrews were always hostile to representatives of other groups.

Jesus often showed a similar in-group bias: for instance he was not eager to heal the daughter of the Canaanite woman (St. Matthew, 15, 21–28); and he instructed his disciples 'Go not into the way of the Gentiles, and into any city of the Samaritans enter ye not: But go rather to the lost sheep of the house of Israel' (St. Matthew, 10, 5–6). Although the story of the good Samaritan indicates that Christ's vision was broader than that, for early Christians 'agape' probably had reference primarily to those who shared the same beliefs. It was not until after Jesus's death that the Apostles took the Gospel farther afield. Since then, the view that all humans are appropriate recipients of one's good will has had a chequered history over the centuries. We shall return to this issue later.[4]

## Extension of prosocial behaviour and reciprocity within the in-group

### *The evolution of prosocial behaviour and reciprocity*

So far we have seen that principles conducive to prosocial behaviour and reciprocity seem to contribute in important ways to the moral codes of most religions, and that such principles do in fact play an important part in everyday relationships. Now the question arises, where do these principles come from? Equity theory assumes that 'society' or the 'group' works out a system for rewarding those who treat others equitably and punishing those who do not. That, however, is not the whole story: the evidence suggests that a propensity to learn to behave prosocially and with reciprocity is part of human nature.

As discussed above, one probable source for prosocial behaviour lies in natural selection favouring individuals who fostered the welfare of their kin, provided the costs are not too great. But as human groups grew larger, their cohesiveness must have depended on prosocial behaviour directed towards, and on cooperation with, individuals who were only very distantly related. We must therefore ask how prosocial behaviour could become extended to a wider group, and how the principles of behaving prosocially to in-group members, and of reciprocity, could have become a usual part of human behaviour.

Significant here is the finding that reciprocity is not solely a human characteristic. Studies of some animal species have shown that individuals are more likely to behave unselfishly to others who have behaved or are likely to behave unselfishly to them. For instance, vampire bats forage at night, and on any one night not all individuals are likely to be successful. On returning to the communal roost, successful foragers feed unsuccessful ones. They thus seem to be behaving unselfishly, giving up their own food, though thereby they may be saving the lives of others. However, it has been shown that individuals are most likely to feed other bats from whom they have previously received food: thus the unselfish donor is repaid when it is itself unsuccessful. Such data suggest that the bats keep a tally of help given and received (Wilkinson, 1988). This is described by biologists as 'reciprocal altruism' (Trivers, 1985). In apes, individuals take the costs of unselfish behaviour into account, being more likely to help if the costs to themselves are not too great (Harcourt, 1991). How widespread reciprocity is among animals is controversial, and in any case it cannot be presumed that a principle that operates in one animal species also operates in others, let alone in humans: superficial human/animal comparisons are dangerous (Hinde, 1987). But this and other examples can be taken as suggesting that natural selection may have operated in a similar way in humans to produce a predisposition to develop prosocial behaviour and reciprocity. And, as we have seen, it is reasonable to suppose that the principle of reciprocity in some form is common to all societies. Of course there are cultural variations – for instance in what counts as an investment, what counts as fair exchange, and in which relationships reciprocity is expected. But there is, so far as I am aware, no evidence to suggest that the basic principle of reciprocity is not applicable in at least the great majority of societies in just the way that equity theory (see above) suggests.

The relations between selection for behaving prosocially to kin and behaving prosocially to other individuals are likely to be complex. On the one hand, in groups of only moderate size, they are likely to be positively related: A's readiness to incur costs for the sake of B will depend both on A's perception of the genetic relation between A and B and on his/her assessment of the likelihood that B will reciprocate, and B's readiness to reciprocate will depend in part on B's perception of their relatedness.[5] Related individuals will be seen as more likely to reciprocate. (This does not deny that many cases of kin-selected prosocial behaviour do not depend on expected reciprocation: maternal suckling obviously does not.) This is exploited in the use of kin relationship terms to refer to non-related individuals in the same national (e.g. 'brothers-in-arms') or religious (e.g. 'children of the Lord') group. On the other hand, it is also the case that incurring costs to benefit unrelated individuals can come into conflict with behaviour conducive to the welfare of kin. Thus parents may be unwilling to let their sons go to war, their valuation of the common good conflicting with their concern for their offspring; and family members may be divided by civil strife (Richerson and Boyd, 1998).

## Conditions for prosocial behaviour and reciprocity

Now when two individuals interact, the outcome for each usually depends not only on what he does, but also on what the other does. This produces a number of complications, which can best be illustrated by a well-known model usually referred to as the Prisoners' Dilemma. It is so-called because it is usually described as concerning two criminals who cooperated in a crime and are to be questioned by the police separately. If they both agree to insist on their innocence, and stick to the agreement, they will both get off. But if one turns state's evidence on the other, and the other does not confess, the former will get a light sentence and the latter a heavy one. If both turn state's evidence, they will both get an intermediate sentence. A similar argument can be applied to cases where the outcomes are not punishments but positive rewards for cooperating or defecting, as in Figure 13.1a. If each is uncertain what the other will do, the best strategy will be to defect, when he will gain either 12 or 4, depending on what the other participant does. If he were to cooperate, he would get only 8 or 0.

However, the participants may not be entirely self-seeking. It may be that one is willing to sacrifice his own interests for the other, as might be the case with parent and child, or that each wishes to maximise their joint benefits. The latter, which might be the case for a couple in love, is illustrated in the 'transformed matrix' shown in Figure 13.1b. Clearly, the outcomes that each partner will receive will depend on the sizes and relative sizes of the rewards and on the attitudes of each participant to the other (Kelley, 1979). In the present case, in which each wishes to maximise the joint outcome, they will clearly do best if each cooperates. The important point here is that the choice that brings the best personal benefit is not the same as that which brings the best joint outcome. We shall see the importance of that later.

Now suppose that we have a population made up of two sorts of individual, some behaving selfishly and some unselfishly. It is unlikely that unselfish behaviour could be maintained in such a population, because an individual who behaved selfishly to others in a group of individuals who behaved unselfishly to him would clearly have better access to resources and reproduce more effectively: if children tended to resemble their parents in their selfishness/unselfishness, such selfish individuals would become more frequent in the population.

But there are circumstances in which that would not be the case. This has been shown in a computer simulation of the Prisoner's Dilemma game. Given a reward matrix of the type shown in Figure 13.1a, each player will be tempted to defect, for defection brings a higher reward whether the partner chooses to cooperate or to defect. However, if the game is played a number of times, or if there is some other method by which each can predict the other's behaviour, this will affect their choices. If each believes the other will cooperate, and cooperates herself, each will get 8 units. If A believes B will cooperate, A may be tempted to defect and score 12. But on the next round B would then not trust A, and each would be likely to score 4. In the long run, if each trusts the other, it will usually pay to cooperate. It has in fact been demonstrated that the best strategy is one of 'tit-for-tat', where each cooperates on the first encounter and subsequently reciprocates what the other did on the previous one. Ideally this tit-for-tat strategy, or cooperation given reciprocity, involves the individual never being first to defect, retaliating only after the partner has defected, and in general forgiving single acts of selfishness (Axelrod and Hamilton, 1984): this, of course, parallels the Christian teaching that individuals should initiate prosocial behaviour, as noted above. If the reward obtained is an index of successful reproduction,

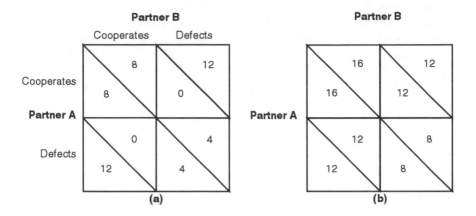

*Figure 13.1* The Prisoners' dilemma: (a) Given matrix; (b) Matrix transformed to
maximise joint outcomes. The outcomes for each participant depend on
the choices made by both. The outcomes for A are shown in the lower
left triangles, those for B in the upper right ones.
*Source*: Redrawn from Kelley, 1979.

and if a number of individuals play in a group, cooperative interactions
among those who reciprocate towards each other will continue, but interactions between those who cooperate and non-cooperaters will become rare.
When a variety of strategies were tested against each other, tit for tat turned
out to be the best in small groups. In certain circumstances (see below),
selection can make it impossible for non-cooperating individuals to invade a
population of individuals who are using the tit-for-tat strategy (see also
Hauert and Schuster, 1997).

Further propensities contributing to the maintenance of reciprocity are
related to the dynamics of groups. We tend to like people who play fair with
us, and to play fair with those we like. These tendencies augment in-group or
intra-dyad reciprocity. Furthermore, we watch each other behaving, and
assess each other's characteristics from what we see. Thus it may pay A to be
generous to B because C, observing A's generosity, will subsequently trust
him or be more likely to be generous to him; but if C observes A refusing to
give help when requested by B, he may categorise A as unhelpful and decline
to help him. Those who are seen to be generous to others, and reliably to
reciprocate assistance received from others, will be more likely to receive
help if they need it in the future. For such reasons we value our reputations.
This is referred to as 'indirect reciprocity' and could facilitate cooperation
among relatively diffuse networks of individuals (Alexander, 1987; Nowak
and Sigmund, 1998). It could provide an additional benefit for initiating
cooperative behaviour in interactions with a stranger: not only would any
relationship with the stranger that develops be more likely to be profitable,
but the prosocial behaviour might enhance one's status among third-party

witnesses (see Boone, 1998). However, the effectiveness of this strategy could easily be undermined by individuals who create deceptive reputations for themselves in order to vicitimise the credulous (Richerson, pers. comm.).

Of course, in the real world the situation is more complicated, for rewards for the same combination of choices may change over time, each individual encounters many others, and so on. The success of the tit-for-tat strategy is limited to a range of circumstances. But that such a strategy can be successful in the admittedly artificial situations of experimental games suggests that 'Do as you would be done by' so long as the partner reciprocates could be a wise choice in personal interactions.

But taking the initiative in prosocial behaviour could be a viable strategy only if the group contained a reasonably high proportion of individuals who would reciprocate. An individual in a group of self-assertive individuals would do better to be self-assertive himself, and not risk being exploited. The evidence indicates that natural selection has operated to ensure that individuals are disposed to behave in a manner appropriate to the circumstances in which they find themselves, on the supposition that the social environment of development will be generally similar to the adult environment.[6] While it is not possible adequately to summarise the vast literature on this issue here, it is broadly true to say that children are more prone to show prosocial behaviour if they are brought up in a warm, caring environment, where parental control is sufficiently firm yet sufficiently sensitive and subtle for the child to internalise the criteria of good and bad behaviour, forming a conscience, and not come to believe that behaviour should be determined solely by external rewards and punishments. By contrast, children brought up with strict unquestioning discipline and without warmth tend to be more self-assertive and aggressive (e.g. Baumrind, 1971; Hinde *et al.*, 1993; Miller *et al.*, 1991). It is reasonable to suppose that the latter kind of upbringing would prevail when conditions were harsh and competitive. Data from experimental games indicate that individuals who are cooperatively oriented tend to adjust their behaviour to match that of their opponent, while competitively oriented individuals tend to behave competitively whatever the behaviour of the opponent (Kelley, 1979). There is also some admittedly slender evidence that a particular temperament may have different consequences according to the conditions: 'difficult' temperament in children is associated with psychiatric risk in western countries, but in famine conditions in East Africa it was associated with survival, probably because infants with such a temperament were more assertive (De Vries, 1984; see also Belsky, 1997).

*Maintenance of reciprocity*

But we must ask how 'cooperation given reciprocity' or 'Do as you would be done by' could be maintained in the long term. How does it come about that individuals continue to use cooperation as a long-term strategy, cooperating not only with particular others but also with previously unknown group members? Here there are two views. One takes the usual approach, supposing that natural selection acts at the individual level: the genes of individuals who are most successful in surviving and leaving offspring will be best represented in the next generation. The other supposes that natural selection operates through competition not only between individuals but also through competition between groups.[7]

In the former case it is postulated that selection has operated so that individuals have the capacity to develop values about what is right and wrong, and to enunciate rules of conduct, such as those suggested by equity theory (see above), which will be conducive to their survival and reproduction. The institution of 'rules of conduct' represents an important but too little discussed stage in human evolution – a transition in some ways equivalent to the distinction between Kant's acting in accordance with a rule and acting on a rule (Cronin, 1991). As argued above, the moral code reflects how *others* should behave, not how individuals wish to behave themselves. Individuals who abide by the moral code, which has been elaborated over time to suit the circumstances of that society, will be better able to flourish there, in part because they will have better relationships with other group members. While the maintenance of such a moral code could depend on appropriate approval/disapproval from others, it would clearly be greatly facilitated if individuals acquired a conscience which could be triggered by the moral code of the society. That moral code would be basically conducive to the reproductive interests of the individuals in the society though, as we have noted, moral codes are open to manipulation by individuals in positions of power acting in their own interests. On this view, 'the evolution of the human capacity and propensity to absorb a culture was accompanied by the evolution of psychological mechanisms that tended, at least in the environments of evolution, to keep culturally influenced behavior directed towards reproductive goals'. Thus 'culture is something individuals use and manipulate in pursuit of the proximate goals that, in the environments of human evolution, were reproductively advantageous' (Irons, 1991: 60; see also Alexander, 1987; Symons, 1979). In most circumstances, individuals who abide by a code of reciprocity are better able to survive and reproduce because others are likely to behave prosocially to them and because those who do not follow the code are likely to be punished for their 'antisocial' behaviour.[8]

We may note here that, while codes conducive to prosocial behaviour towards in-group members are often discussed, the emphasis can be on antisocial behaviour to out-group members. Gang loyalty, and all which that can entail, can be an extreme example: the case of the Ku Klux Klan was mentioned earlier. Military codes can be such as to encourage forms of behaviour that would not be acceptable in other contexts. All-male clubs can involve values to the disadvantage of women. As the term is used here, however, moral codes are usually conducive to cooperative behaviour within a whole society.

The second and less generally held view, depending on cultural group selection, requires more explication. Computer modelling indicates that a tit-for-tat strategy would be likely to be effective in maintaining cooperative behaviour only in small groups. In larger groups, where each individual meets particular others only rarely, the important issue may be, not that individuals expect to receive rewards commensurate with the costs that they have incurred, but rather that individuals will incur costs for the benefit of others if doing so effectively increases the frequency of individuals who behave in that way, independently of payback to the individual. The question therefore arises, could such a strategy be maintained by competition between groups, groups consisting of cooperators winning out over groups of individuals who did not cooperate with each other?

There is an obvious immediate problem. Natural selection between groups could operate only in the absence of much gene flow between them. In practice inter-marriage between human groups seems to have been sufficiently frequent to support a considerable exchange of genes between groups, leading to the diminution of any genetic differences between them. Furthermore, that selection at the group level could be important in the evolution of unselfish behaviour is improbable, because selfish individuals within any group would be more successful, and all groups would tend to come to consist of similarly selfish individuals. However the efficacy of group selection is a controversial issue, and there are signs that opinion is changing towards the view that it can operate in some circumstances (Wilson and Sober, 1994). The following paragraphs summarise an argument put forward by Boyd and Richerson (1985, 1988, 1991, Richerson and Boyd, 1998) which invokes competition at the group level and depends in large measure on computer modelling of possible scenarios.

Suppose that societies in which individuals behave unselfishly for the sake of other group members will win out, either economically or militarily, over societies composed of selfish individuals. For this to be the case it would be necessary for groups to differ consistently in selfishness, and there are a number of processes which act against this and tend to erode group differences: cultural practices may be copied from one group by another, and inter-marriage may occur. Furthermore, as noted above, if selfish individuals are more successful, they will come to predominate in each group. Computer simulation indicates that, other things being equal, processes promoting cooperation, which depend on the extinction of selfish groups, will be overcome by the tendencies towards non-cooperation, all groups will come to consist mainly of non-cooperators, and group differences will disappear (even if the groups remain intact).

However, things are not equal, for mechanisms collectively labelled as 'tradition' tend to maintain cultural consistency. For instance, children learn from others in the society. This involves not only being taught rules of behaviour by parents and others, but also a more intangible soaking up of a feeling of what is right and what is wrong. They observe others' actions and the responses of others to those actions, as well as the consequences of the action for the actor. However the influences that they receive are diverse, and those of the peer group may counteract those of the parents, so that individuals may switch from being unselfish, as a result of parental influence, to being selfish, in conformity with a peer group (or possibly vice versa). They might, for instance, perceive that selfish individuals do better, and try to emulate them. In such circumstances computer modelling indicates that, within local populations, selfish behaviour will come to predominate unless populations are very small, seldom mix with each other, and it is difficult for individuals to discriminate between the outcomes of behavioural options. Thus any tendency for inter-group competition to favour the predominance of unselfish behaviour will be ineffective.

Suppose, however, that individuals, instead of learning from the observed consequences of others' behaviour, have a strong tendency to acquire the behavioural traits that are most common among possible role models. Often the consequences of others' behaviour are hard to see, and doing as most people do is likely usually to be a good policy. This would cause any behaviour that was common in the population to increase: if unselfishness were common, it would become even more so. If authority promoted conformity, and if there were penalties for not conforming with what others do or believe, as there are with religious beliefs, the precept would spread even further. Thus differences between groups would be maintained, and selection between groups could operate to favour unselfish behaviour.

Such a tendency to imitate the majority might well evolve under natural selection if the environment were heterogeneous, so that groups from time to time moved into unfamiliar environments where old practices were less effective. Natural selection and individual learning would together ensure that those types of individuals who did best in the new environment became most common, and it would then pay naive individuals to copy those who had come to predominate in the population. Conformist behaviour would be favoured because it would lead to the acquisition of behaviours that were locally successful. Behaviour concerned with traits whose consequences were hard to discern would be especially likely to spread.

Now in complex societies individuals belong to many groups. An individual may belong to a number of groups relevant to different traits; and some behaviours may be acquired from one or both parents, others from religious leaders, others from work mates. This model of cultural evolution indicates that selection between groups could favour cooperators if cultural transmission is frequency dependent, as indicated above, and if cultural influences from outside the group are small (i.e. the group is 'culturally endogenous').

As we shall see (p. 200), individuals are prone to like others with attitudes similar to their own, especially if those attitudes concern unverifiable beliefs.

In addition, conformism, involving the learning of traits from the majority, is more likely to predominate over learning from observation of the consequences of others' behaviour if the latter are difficult to discern. Religious beliefs as well as values come into this category. But this in itself will not necessarily ensure the spread of religious beliefs or values because, while some individuals will interpret the consequences of religious practice as confirming the beliefs, others may do the opposite. However, we have seen that some religious beliefs may be readily assimilable because they are related to existing predispositions (Chapter 5). In other cases, religious beliefs may be assimilable because they can be linked to symbols which can be readily apprehended, such as plant or animal totems (pp. 95–6). And if religious beliefs and values lead to greater coherence in the group, they may make the group more effective in cooperative projects (e.g. hunting) and/or in competition or conflict with other groups, and then the values and beliefs could spread by group selection. This could well currently be the case with rival religious beliefs, where in-group cohesion and socialisation are powerful forces in recruiting new members (see pp. 208–10). Prosocial values are especially likely to spread because individuals prefer to be with others whom they like, and are more prone to accept their ideas (Blackmore, 1997; Eagly and Chaiken, 1984). Furthermore, since conformism involves individuals acquiring the most frequent in-group traits, it is no surprise that religious leaders and their followers denigrate out-group practices.

### Some complexities

Of course human societies involve relationships much more complex than these simple models suggest. Each individual has relationships with many others, and in each relationship a diversity of issues are involved. A person may obtain some rewards from one relationship, some from others. And individuals are neither consistently single-minded nor consistently selfish or unselfish. More importantly, opportunities for cheating are always present. A society could never be successful if these tendencies to cheat were not regulated. As proposed by equity theory (see above), members of societies develop rules, and in view of the foregoing it is not unreasonable to suppose that societies with rules that lead to social cohesion are more likely, other things being equal, to be successful. But a system of rules or a social contract is not enough for the feeling of community necessary for a prosocial code to flourish. The formation and integrity of a community depends on a sense of continuity with the past, a narrative of experiences shared by individuals, which provides a framework within which the moral code operates (Burnside, 1994).

The view that these properties of societies are underpinned by propensities to behave prosocially and to abide by the principles of reciprocity, which are the products of natural selection, is now well supported by evidence. Views about how those propensities are maintained are based on models which necessarily omit many of the complexities of real life situations. The preceding discussion thus leaves open the question of how far predispositions to develop prosocial behaviour and to show reciprocity, and to value them in others, are maintained by individual or cultural group selection, though it would seem that some involvement of the latter is probable. While religions have played an important part in nurturing these propensities, the evidence indicates that they depend ultimately on basic psychological predispositions.

### The development of reciprocity

It is not being claimed that a propensity to behave prosocially and with reciprocity to in-group members is independent of experience. Rather it is suggested only that such a propensity is a pan-cultural characteristic, present in at least the majority of individuals, though to varying degrees. Its pan-cultural occurrence may depend on common features in the ways in which children are reared in different societies, though that in turn might depend on pan-cultural characteristics in parental behaviour and the social environment. But there are always likely to be some individuals who, by virtue of nature or nurture (Mealey, 1997), adopt strategies that do not involve reciprocity. What is clear is that humans have the potential to develop and to display both prosocial or antisocial behaviour, and that moral codes strengthen the former. The conditions of development under which prosocial tendencies come to predominate are thus crucial: some research on that issue was mentioned on p. 164.[9]

### Further support for reciprocity

In modern societies some rules may be imposed by force: police and other law enforcement agencies seem to be an inevitable accompaniment of societal complexity. But of more interest here is the fact that in personal relationships a series of psychological mechanisms operate to promote and maintain reciprocity, mechanisms which again seem to be a direct or indirect result of natural selection.

It has been shown experimentally that individuals are adept at detecting infringements of a social contract. In these experiments subjects were presented with a logical rule of the type 'If P, then Q', and shown a series of cards each of which showed the P condition on one side and the Q on the other, though only one side was visible. For instance in one experiment subjects were told that students' papers had been processed according to the rule 'If a person has a "D" rating, his documents must be marked with a "3"', and asked which cards must be turned over to see if the rule had been infringed. The four cards shown were D, F, 3, and 7. The correct response is to turn over only the first and last cards. In such tasks considerably less than half the subjects gave the correct response. However, if the problem referred to a social contract, the success rate was much higher. For instance, subjects were asked to imagine they worked in a bar with the rule 'If a person is drinking beer, he must be over 20 years old', and shown cards marked 'drinking beer', 'drinking coke', '25 years old', and '16 years old'. Again the correct answer is to turn over only the first and last cards, but here three-quarters of the subjects were successful. Ingenious controlled experiments by Cosmides and Tooby (1992) rule out explanations for the difference other than that people have a special ability for detecting infringements of social contracts. For instance, if the reward gained is not illicit, or if the task is to detect altruism, subjects do much less well. Cosmides and Tooby therefore ascribe this ability to an 'adapted module' for the detection of cheating on social contracts. Although the ability to detect cheating is present in children only 3 years old or even younger, it is not necessarily the case that it is independent of experience (Cummins, 1996): it is quite possible that individual learning plays a considerable role, since socialisation involves the frequent invocation of comparable contracts by the mother or other caregiver or teacher ('If you do X, I will do Y'). Most probably this ability is something that everyone is predisposed to acquire in the course of socialisation: in any case its importance cannot be doubted.

If detection of a cheater is valuable, it will be even more so if the individual is recognised as a cheater on the next encounter. An experimental study in which students were asked to report which of a series of photographs they had seen on a previous occasion indicated that photos of individuals which had previously been labelled as cheaters were remembered preferentially to those whose photographs had been initially accompanied by irrelevant information or labelled as trustworthy. The difference was not present for photos of persons labelled as of high status (Mealey *et al.*, 1996).

As we have seen, the emotions are also important in regulating exchange, and in many cases it is reasonable to suppose that they have been selected to do so in evolution. We have seen that when an individual feels that he has been unfairly treated, he feels angry and tries to rectify the situation (see also Frank, 1988). Reciprocally, if an individual feels that he has behaved unfairly, he feels guilt and may try to make reparation. Guilt leads to a focus either on how the deed can be undone or the damage repaired, or on psychological self-justification ('It was his fault, really'). It is elicited when an individual feels that he has infringed, or is about to infringe, the moral code incorporated in his self-system. Since people do not like to feel guilty, the possibility of experiencing guilt helps to maintain a culture of prosocial behaviour and reciprocity: people guide their behaviour in order to maintain a self-image of which they will subsequently be able to approve. The abilities to empathise with others, and to feel sympathy, are also important here – and these also must surely be pan-cultural psychological characteristics.

Shame is similar, but the focus is not so much on a specific action as on a global evaluation of the self, perhaps as a consequence of a specific action. Shame is a highly negative state and, in an extreme form, may lead to confusion, inability to speak, a desire to disappear or hide, and in the longer term to depression and a variety of psychopathologies. An individual experiencing shame is not necessarily aware of the fact: although blushing and experiencing the physical state associated with shame, he may laugh it off, or label his state as embarrassment rather than shame, or feel sadness or anger. Even if aware of his state, he may evade it in a number of ways, for instance by dismissing the issue from active consideration. Shame can also be removed by confession. This seems to involve looking at oneself from the perspective of the confessor, and thus disengaging oneself from the self which is the source of the shame. Confession is most likely to be effective if it involves the person who has been injured and if that person gives understanding and love. Religious confession involves a priest who, by virtue of his ordination, is seen as able to deliver God's forgiveness and love (Lewis, 1992). But the important issue here is that the negative qualities of shame act as a powerful deterrent to entering situations in which one will feel shame – namely those in which one transgresses one's internalised standards (see also Kagan, 1984).[10]

It is not only within dyads that emotions play a role. There is also a sense of collective responsibility: one individual who perceives another to be behaving unfairly to a third party feels morally outraged, and this may lead him or her to intervene. The probability of intervention is related to the perceived relationship of the transgressor to the third party and the seriousness of the infringement. Computer modelling has shown that such moralistic punishment is a potent mechanism for the maintenance of social norms: a small number of punishers can be effective in maintaining cooperative behaviour in a largish group (Boyd and Richerson, 1991, 1992). The tendency to intervention is likely to be a product of cultural selection: it can become associated with an excessive reification of moral principles unsuitable to changing circumstances.

Sticks are seldom effective without carrots, and the denigration of those who offend is usually coupled with the giving of rewards to those whose upholding of the moral code is especially conspicuous. Most societies have institutionalised methods for rewarding those whose altruism can serve as an example to others (Alexander, 1987; Darwin, 1871).

As an extension of equity theory (p. 154), not only should individuals who fail to behave in a particular way be punished, but so also should individuals who fail to punish others who do not live up to the required standards. People do in fact find it rewarding not only to uphold the moral code but also to see that it is upheld: the perception of reciprocity, both in our own actions and those of others, is important to us (Clayton and Lerner, 1991). However, whether such a sense of moral outrage is a human characteristic adapted through natural selection in order to enhance group coherence and solidarity; whether it is something we are simply socialised into; whether we have a disposition to acquire it; whether it is something we acquire because it pays us to be seen as upholders of the social order; or whether all of these are the case, does not matter for present purposes: recognising reciprocity seems to be pan-cultural. What is clear is that, as well as an inherent tendency to advance our self-interest, we also develop a tendency to uphold a moral code of prosocial reciprocity – or at least to see that others do so. Indeed, it has been convincingly argued that the basis of altruistic acts lies in an identification with collectivist concepts, in terms of which the individual conceives his goals and structures his life (Heal, 1991) – and a society's moral code could constitute just such an ideal. However, if the code is outmoded, such moralistic behaviour can have adverse consequences (Richerson, pers. comm.)

Thus both emotions and cognitive mechanisms help to oil the wheels of reciprocity. In general the distinction, made both in common speech and by psychologists, between thinking and feeling is far less clear-cut than has previously been assumed. There is now neurological evidence that brain-injured patients who lack emotion are often also poor decision-makers (Damasio, 1994). In so far as emotions can be seen as preceding action, anticipation of possible feelings of guilt prompt us to behave fairly, while anger or resentment prompt us to stick up for our rights. In addition, the expression of emotions affects the other party. The possibility of eliciting anger makes him less likely to cheat in an interaction: gratitude makes him willing to accept indebtedness, at least for a while, or may itself be rewarding to him in enhancing his self-image. Of course all this must be interpreted against a background of the earlier discussion of close relationships, where the goal of each partner may be to please the other rather than himself, and the expression of love signifies commitment, and thus enhances the trust of the partner.

Of course people can dissemble. Most emotions can be at least partially concealed or exaggerated. One individual may deceive another to increase his own outcomes, and the ability to deceive is also a basic human characteristic. So is the ability to detect deception, but individuals are more successful at deceiving others if they also deceive themselves. A person who is conscious of lying may give himself away by not meeting the eyes of his partner, or fiddling with his clothes, but a person who conceals the real nature of his action from himself and convinces himself that he has been fair or generous will act as if he really were so – just as an actor is more convincing if he feels himself into his part. Here defence processes may come into play, for instance an individual may reflect on his prosocial actions and forget or devalue antisocial ones (see p. 30).

However, the extent to which reciprocity is expected or even acceptable is a cultural matter. Individuals who are indiscriminately prosocial are likely to be seen as unreliable partners: if they are prosocial to non-members of the group they may be seen as disloyal or as traitors.

To summarise these issues, the pan-cultural occurrence of prosocial behaviour and reciprocity depends on basic human psychological propensities, but is not solely a behavioural matter, for it depends also on a range of pan-cultural cognitive and emotional mechanisms. Perhaps it is as well here to emphasise yet again that to regard human moral values as based in pan-cultural propensities does not for one moment suggest that what is natural is necessarily good: humans have self-assertive and antisocial propensities as well as prosocial ones. The moral code reflects how individuals believe that others should behave, not necessarily how they wish to behave themselves.

## Relative values

However, in real life we are often faced with the necessity of making judgements about relative 'goods' – for instance is A's need greater than B's? In a series of experiments designed to explore these issues, Petrinovich (1995) posed subjects with dilemmas requiring a decision to save the lives of some individuals but not others. For instance, they might be asked to consider a situation in which six people wanted to board a lifeboat in which there was room for only five. The data showed that subjects decided to save human rather than non-human individuals, not to save members of the Nazi party, to save individuals related or friendly to the respondent rather than strangers, to save a number of individuals rather than one, and to save preferentially individuals who were endangered through no fault of their own. There was also a small tendency to save individuals of public value (an eminent violinist or scientist). At least some cultural universality was indicated in that there were few differences between United States and Taiwanese subjects, but there were some sex differences: for instance women tended to agree with questions concerned with whom they would save (as opposed to whom they would allow to die) than did men. All this, of course, does not take one very far, and it seems reasonable to suppose that both individual and cultural differences could be found in, for instance, which individuals were of public value.

## The role of religion

In conclusion, one may ask 'What is the role of religions (speaking generally) in all this?' To summarise the suggestion being made here, human beings, given certain environmental circumstances, readily develop tendencies to behave prosocially, and to behave in accordance with a principle of reciprocity. They also, given certain environmental circumstances, readily develop tendencies to behave antisocially. In practice, most individuals have the potential to behave either prosocially or antisocially. These tendencies are the product of Darwinian forces. Whereas individuals may wish to behave in ways that differ from the ways in which others believe they should behave, there is more general agreement about how *others* should behave. The latter becomes reified into a moral code which is incorporated into the self-systems of individuals. This moral code tips the balance in favour of prosocial behaviour by predisposing individuals to behave predominately in a prosocial fashion and to discourage others from behaving antisocially. The moral precepts do not stem from religion but from the nature of human beings. Nevertheless moral precepts require an ideological basis: this can take various forms, social, legal, political, or religious, but the most effective in the past has been religion. Religious precepts encourage both prosocial behaviour and the punishment of transgressors. In this religion has been aided both by claiming that the precepts come from a superior authority and therefore cannot be questioned, and by the unverifiable view that rewards or punishments will come in an after-life. While we can now sometimes see the values in a society's ideology as having little to do with religion, in most societies the two have been inseparable, and the religious system underpinned the moral code. We shall return to this issue in the final chapter.

## Summary

It is suggested that moral codes derive from certain basic human propensities, of which the most important are those to show prosocial behaviour to kin and to display reciprocity. These seem to be basic to the moral codes of the major world religions.

Reciprocity plays a basic role in interpersonal relationships, and has been studied in detail by social psychologists in the context of exchange theories. In dyadic relationships it requires trust in the partner and commitment to the relationship. In groups in which individuals seldom encounter each other, it is facilitated by a moral code. Reciprocity is normally restricted to in-group members.

There is evidence that a tendency to act prosocially and to reciprocate behaviour received are products of natural selection: tendencies to behave prosocially towards kin and to show reciprocity are well known in other species. There is incomplete agreement as to whether the selective processes which gave rise to these principles in humans operated only at the individual level, or whether cultural group selection was also involved.

Individuals' views about how other group members should behave become reified into a moral code, which becomes incorporated into the self-systems of individuals, and influences their behaviour. In the past, religious systems have been the principal purveyors of this moral code.

Some mechanisms acting to maintain a principle of reciprocity in the face of the self-assertiveness of individuals are discussed. These include the ability to detect cheating on social contracts and various emotions conducive to the maintenance of reciprocity.

# 14 Moral codes

## Other principles

Although prosocial behaviour and reciprocity have been discussed at some length, these are by no means the only principles on which moral codes depend. In this chapter we consider some other issues that are clearly important, though with no implication that the list is complete. In each case the moral precepts are in line with pan-cultural psychological propensities.

## Status seeking

Self-assertiveness and status-seeking can be seen as the principal forces with which moral codes must cope. Assertiveness by others endangers one's own position, may diminish one's own access to scarce resources, and may be destructive of the social order. Indeed, it may not have escaped the reader's notice that this is implicit in equity theory (see p. 154, proposition 1). As a result of individuals' assertiveness (which may be not unrelated to the need to feel in control of one's life, pp. 56–8), some degree of hierarchy is virtually ubiquitous in human societies – though the importance of, and criteria for, status differ between societies and between the sexes. And this affects moral codes in another way, for assertive individuals or groups, if in a position to do so, may use the moral code to impose their will, or their view of what is right, on others. In many societies, power often utilises the postulation of supernatural support (Boyd and Richerson, 1992).

Moral codes often seem to perform a balancing act between maintenance of the status of some and ameliorating the lot of others. Even churches that maintain that all men are equal recognise degrees of authority and even of sanctity. Indeed the Anglican church has accepted social inequality, as in the Victorian hymn:

> The rich man in his castle
> The poor man at his gate
> God made them high or lowly...

In fact it could be said that Christianity does not do very well in this matter, even though there are no implications of class distinctions in

Heaven.[1] In Buddhism the differences are at least clearly temporary, for all sentient beings will attain Nirvana eventually, and in Hinduism all beings contain the essence of life. But there are two sides to this issue: a moral code that condemns some to lowly status is incompatible with an emphasis on prosocial behaviour and reciprocity, while too much emphasis on equality can lead to a form of individualism that is destructive of personal relationships and of society. Too much emphasis on 'Why should I not have everything that he has?' can have negative consequences. In practice, in personal relationships a balance must be found: successful personal relationships depend on each partner being able to satisfy needs for autonomy as well as connectedness (Baxter, 1990), and connectedness depends on a desire to satisfy the needs of someone whose needs are not the same as one's own (Hinde, 1997a). In society, however, the recognition that individuals have different needs is too often used to justify the manipulation of some to serve the needs of those more powerful.

Most moral codes contain precepts concerned with behaviour appropriate to the individual's position in society. For example, the Anglican Catechism requires the confirmand to recite his duties, and these include:

> To honour and obey the King (or Queen), and all that are put in authority under him (her): To submit myself to all my governours, teachers, spiritual pastors and masters: To order myself lowly and reverently to all my betters...and to do my duty in that state of life, unto which it shall please God to call me.

Most such precepts seem to be directed towards safeguarding the positions of those of higher status, and were probably originally imposed from above. Their existence points to the need of those in controlling positions to avoid conflict. Attempts to exert status virtually always encounter resistance: that, of course, is a truism, but we can see it as part of the pan-cultural propensities to feel in control of one's life (pp. 56–8) and to seek reciprocity in personal relationships (Chapter 13). For that reason, those in positions of power do best if they avoid the use of force and use power, guile, or persuasion to convince the rest that the rules are in their own interests. These may include the suggestion that divine support is enjoyed by those in positions of power, and designation of humility as a virtue leading to ultimate reward for those lower in the hierarchy. The rules may also be affirmed by those lower down because humility seems like a good strategy in their current circumstances: resignation to the present state of affairs may have been a wise policy in the conditions of persecution in which the Christian code first developed. Or those lower down may prefer their current status to the chaos that might ensue were the *status quo* to be upset.

Not all status differences are to be seen in such negative terms. The parent–child relationship involves a difference in status, but involves (mainly) positive behaviour on both sides. Many other valued aspects of relationships in other contexts, such as protectiveness and loyalty, may have arisen by co-option from the parent–child pattern. However, even in that case precepts requiring respect for parents and ancestors are usually present, and can be seen as a reflection of the tendency of parents to teach children to behave in ways that are conducive to the welfare of the parents (see p. 145).

It is reasonable to suppose that assertiveness, contextually appropriate, is conducive to survival and reproductive success, and the claim that status-seeking is a pan-cultural characteristic seems straightforward. The criteria by which status is assessed are, of course, diverse, but it seems reasonable to suppose that nearly all individuals are assertive in some degree in some sphere and that, in the few who are not, defence mechanisms operate to protect them from the need to be so. Social status has been shown to be associated with longevity and reproductive success at least in a number of pre-literate societies (Betzig *et al.*, 1988).[2]

## Regulation of sexual relations

Another issue concerns the regulation of marital and sexual relations. With respect to marriage, much of the evidence from the West suggests that religiosity is associated with marital happiness. However, one must be careful about generalising. Religion may have promoted *perceived* happiness by making divorce unacceptable and thus emphasising the need to make the best of the current situation, but with increasing acceptance of divorce and the recognition of sexual equality, marriages held together by religion can become far from happy (Hood *et al.*, 1996). We shall see later that differences in religious orientation between wife and husband may be deleterious.

Every culture has rules specifying when and where sexual relations are or are not permitted, but there is great cultural variation. Thus, the view that sex is intrinsically sinful, even within marriage, seems to be peculiar to some Christians: by contrast, in the Hindu tradition it is seen as a model for mystical union (Smart, 1996). Again, sexual relations during the period termed in the West adolescence are permitted or encouraged in some societies, prohibited in others; some cultures are monogamous, some polygamous, and a few polyandrous; and the extent to which sexual relations and even reproduction is limited to married partners differs dramatically between societies.

Some precepts affect reproduction directly. That humans have an ability to adjust their behaviour to augment their reproductive success has been well documented in a number of societies (Betzig *et al.*, 1988). Differences in sexual practices can be seen as resulting from the translation into social precepts of practices which have been seen to be reproductively successful in the conditions prevailing, though other issues concerned with the social structure, property inheritance, and so on are also involved. The processes by which this translation occurs have been little investigated, but simple copying of practices seen to be successful could be basic, followed by codification of the practices most common in the society.

Most of these precepts are such as to increase the number of children reared:[3] this is hardly surprising since practices that increase reproductive rate are likely, given adequate resources, also to increase the number of adherents to the religious system. Most world religions require sexual intercourse between married partners: while intercourse during menstruation may be forbidden, this is likely to concentrate it during the woman's fertile period. Some world religions prohibit or limit contraception – perhaps most clearly in Islam and Catholic Christianity, with Hindus and Buddhists having some bias in that direction. Where resources are scarce, prolonged breast feeding inhibits further conception, but enhances the chances of the child already born and thus long-term reproductive success.

Another major issue lies in the efforts of men to prevent themselves from being cuckolded. A double standard of morality, with men allowed more sexual licence than females, is virtually ubiquitous: though the extent of the difference between the codes applicable to men and to women differs widely, the direction of the difference is almost certainly always the same. Although unacceptable in modern society, this tendency can be understood in biological terms. Since a woman can always be sure that the child in her womb is her own, whereas a man can never be certain that his partner's child is his, it is in the reproductive interests of any man who contributes resources to a child's development to ensure that his partner has not been inseminated by another male. Hence the emphasis in many cultures on female chastity and modesty, and also more extreme practices which lower female desire or opportunity for intercourse, such as clitoridectomy, claustration and foot-binding. While males thus tend to restrict extra-marital mating by females, the issues for women are different. For one thing, hitherto women have usually had less power than men. More importantly, extra-partner mating by the male does not necessarily decrease the reproductive success of the female, unless he transfers resources elsewhere. In harmony with this, studies of jealousy in western society indicate that male jealousy tends to centre on sexual issues, female on the transfer of resources (Buss, 1994; Buunk, 1995). None of this, of course, should be taken as implying that what is natural is right, but knowledge of the bases of human behaviour may help to create a more just world.

Incest taboos are found in virtually every society. While they have diverse consequences on such issues as the distribution of resources in the group, the fact that mechanisms for the prevention of inbreeding occur also in non-human species strongly suggests a biological origin. The origin of incest taboos has been a matter of considerable controversy, but a scenario currently seen as probable takes us back to the evolution of sexual reproduction itself. This has posed a problem for biologists because reproduction by some method such as budding is obviously much simpler in that it does not involve the need for two individuals to come together. A current view is that sex probably arose because sexual reproduction enables an organism to detect parasites. Many infectious agents can mutate in a manner which enables them to remain undetected by the immune system of the host, but the immune system of genetically distinct offspring, produced by sexual reproduction involving individuals who are not too closely related, is able to spot them. Inbreeding between closely related individuals produces less genetic distinctiveness, and thus less immunological protection in the offspring (e.g. Bittles and Neel, 1994). In addition, and perhaps more importantly, inbreeding can lead to recessive lethal alleles becoming homozygous. A study in an area of Pakistan where first cousin marriages are common showed that child mortality was associated with low educational status in the mother, low age of the mother, and a short birth interval, but when all these were controlled for, consanguinity still accounted for a significant proportion of the variance (Grand and Bittles, 1997). Although the effect was not large, it is reasonable to suppose that consanguinity would have been a relatively more important source of infant mortality earlier in human evolution, when the other factors were more similar between mothers. Thus marriage to a close relative could be biologically disadvantageous.

There are also ways in which marriage to a close relative can be desirable. In a small static community, a related spouse may be the most readily available, and even the only one available. The premarital arrangements are likely to be simplified, compatibility with in-laws is facilitated, there is less need for dowry or bridewealth, and land holdings remain within the extended family (e.g. Bittles, 1994). Furthermore, from a genetic point of view, closely related individuals share more genes, so that an individual mating with a relative would be more likely to be perpetuating his or her own genes than one mating with a non-relative (Read and Harvey, 1988). There are thus both advantages and disadvantages in marriage to a close relative. At the same time, there are circumstances in which mating with a very distantly related individual, less likely to be adapted to local conditions and having a markedly different gene complex, is also likely to be disadvantageous.

Evidence is in fact accumulating that, in a number of species including humans, mating takes place most readily between individuals who are only moderately closely related to each other, so that the adverse biological and social effects of both inbreeding and of breeding with individuals too distantly related are avoided. The point of optimal balance is likely to vary with conditions, both because lethal recessives are more likely to accumulate in large demes, and because the desiderata of marriage to a relative will vary with the social circumstances. Of course the genetic relatedness of another individual is not immediately apparent, but in small communities this would not be an issue as family histories would be known. In addition, there is evidence for a mechanism by which inbreeding is avoided: this involves a reluctance to mate with an individual who became familiar in early life. That such a principle still operates is supported by data showing that individuals brought up together under the Israeli kibbutz system rarely married

(Shepher, 1983), and by the poor reproductive success of the Taiwanese 'minor marriages', where husbands and wives had been raised together as children (Wolf, 1970, 1995).[4] Since mating with close kin was unattractive to most individuals, it is reasonable to hypothesise that those who failed to conform to the usual practice would have met with social disapproval, and that this became reified into a taboo in most or all societies (Bateson, 1995).

It must be said that there is controversy as to the extent to which inhibitions against mating with close kin has a genetic or solely cultural basis (Borgerhoff Mulder and Mitchell, 1994; Durham, 1991), and that this scenario does not explain the wide differences between cultures in the precise nature of the incest taboo, or all the strange prohibitions against marrying relatives to be found in the Anglican prayer book. Presumably the cultural differences arose in relation to other differences between socio-cultural structures, such as differences in the way in which property is inherited (see Goody, 1962).

Sexual activities are also influenced by status-seeking. In societies where polygamy is permitted, the immediate incentive to taking another wife is often the enhanced status that having a number of wives and/or offspring brings. However the ultimate issue is not perceived status, but reproductive success. If resources are limited or unpredictable, and the successful rearing of children depends on what the husband can supply, the birth of too many children could result in lower viability or reproductive potential in those children. Thus most polygamous societies have rules or customs limiting the number of wives a man can take according to his resources.

Status-seeking may also affect sexual behaviour in a quite different way. We have seen that religious specialists are seen as having special qualities, arising from a supposedly closer contact with the deity or because they are seen to make sacrifices for the good of others. We shall see later that certain kinds of religious experience are associated with an ascetic life-style. Thus joining a religious community may be a means of enhancing one's own perceived status, even though it results in a reduction in reproductive success. There may also be positive consequences for the individual or his or her relatives in terms of access to scarce resources (Crook and Osmaston, 1994).

## Maintenance of group distinctiveness

Early in human evolution group membership was probably advantageous to the individual in a number of ways: it may have facilitated hunting, involved the sharing of experience, or been important in competition with other groups. Certain characteristics of group behaviour appear to be ubiquitous, and it is likely that they (or the predisposition to acquire them) are the product of natural selection. To be specific, people find group membership rewarding, behave in ways that will augment the integrity of the group to which they belong, see their own group as favourably distinct from other groups, and elaborate group-specific norms and rules. Such tendencies could arise through individual selection. Given that it is better to be a member of a group, groups will be better integrated, and more effective in competition with other groups, if members hold the group in high regard. If it were advantageous to an individual to advertise his loyalty to his group, his behaviour would be likely to augment group distinctiveness. And group leaders would seek to promote such attitudes in their own interests.

The extent to which the propensities to exhibit these several aspects of social behaviour are *separate* products of natural selection is an open issue: we have seen (p. 29) that the self-system of individuals involves a social self, individuals identifying with groups of which they approve and approving of groups to which they belong: their social behaviour may be related to this. However, the ubiquity of these characteristics of group behaviour strongly suggests that natural selection has been involved – though the means by which group distinctiveness is maintained are, of course, almost infinitely diverse.

The maintenance of group distinctiveness has had an important influence on moral codes. The dietary prohibitions in Leviticus have been given diverse interpretations (e.g. Douglas, 1970a), but it seems that effects on health are unlikely to have been primary, and that their main function was the maintenance of group distinctiveness. Smart (1996: 102) comments that the Jewish ban on pork, whether or not it has hygienic consequences, has 'a certain positive, non-rational facticity which by its very non-rational character imposes a separate shape of life on the pious Jew, who is constantly reminded in the nitty gritty of day-to-day existence of the demands made on her by God'. The same probably applies to male circumcision, seen as essential by Jews and Muslims. Although there is evidence that it is associated with reduced levels of penile and cervical cancer, such an effect has not been found in all studies. Circumcision is regarded as having profound religious significance: carrying out the operation on Jewish babies on the eighth day represents part of Abraham's covenant with God, and is a sign of group membership.[5]

We have seen that, in the context of national, ethnic and religious groups, neighbour usually means a fellow group member. Groups and societies often use symbols (flags, national anthems), rituals (national parades), and metaphors (brothers-in-arms; sharing a motherland or fatherland; brethren in Christ) to encourage their members to see each other as interrelated and as interdependent, while the out-group members are seen (especially in nationalistic propaganda) as different, dangerous, evil, and even sub-human. The Koran puts a higher value on those who go out and fight for their faith than on those who passively accept it. The killing of another believer is a sin, requiring atonement if accidental but involving eternal hell if deliberate: such strictures do not apply to the killing of a non-believer.

This is not just a matter of other societies or earlier times. Several times in this century western nations have encouraged their members to kill members of other nations; and the closer-to-home slaughter in the former Jugo-Slavia elicited much more public concern than that in the more remote Rwanda. But perhaps things are improving. In Britain at the beginning of the nineteenth century a beggar could obtain relief only in his own parish. Later in the century centralised voluntary institutions took over, and gradually the central government accepted some responsibility. Now we know that the criteria of race and colour by which out-groups have often been distinguished are superficial and misleading in that they do not represent fundamental differences, and we see that religious differences are not differences in basic humanity. Both government and individual citizens feel some responsibility for the suffering of individuals who live thousands of miles away, and aid to third world countries (though insufficient) is seen as a normal part of western budgets. From a biological point of view, this can be seen as an extension of the boundaries of the in-group. Westerners can note that many centuries ago Buddha taught that the traditional injunctions against killing, stealing, lying, and so forth should apply widely, to embrace not only other peoples but all living creatures. Perhaps there is hope that the propriety of extending the principle of reciprocity to all humans can become generally accepted, though it seems likely that some preferential treatment of those seen as related will remain.

Divisions within society may also be reflected in the moral code. Some of the rules that societies develop are applicable to all members, some concern the incumbents of particular roles, some are applicable to particular relationships. For instance lay followers of Buddha were expected to abstain from taking life, stealing, lying, drinking intoxicating liquor and engaging in sexual relations outside marriage. But householders were required to observe a more exacting life-style, and lives of monks and nuns were regulated in even greater detail (Teiser, 1996). Again, some rules may apply in some contexts but not in others – among some Hindus there are exceptions to all the obvious rules so that, for instance, lies have been permitted or even encouraged where women were concerned, or when the well-being of a cow was at stake (Zachner, 1962).

Finally, in the west animals have traditionally been seen as differing from humans in not possessing souls. Moral precepts concerned with behaviour to others did not, therefore, apply to animals. The issue is, of course, quite different in those eastern religions which involve a belief in reincarnation. And, for very different reasons, the distinction is becoming much less clear-cut in the west.

## The 'common good'

We have seen that it may be in the interests of individuals that the group to which they belong should run smoothly. Many of the 'duties' listed in the Anglican Catechism could equally, and perhaps more charitably, be interpreted as designed for the 'common good'. This, however, raises the difficult question of what determines the 'common good'. Clearly, the views of the more privileged members of society are likely to differ from those less well-off, and may be concerned with protecting their own privileges. Also there may be matters in which individual interests are seen to take precedence over the common good – for instance in issues involving privacy and freedom from torture.

## The dialectic

We may now return to the point made earlier – namely the continuous dynamic between the behaviour of individuals, the current code of conduct, and other aspects of the socio-cultural system. Considering the first two of these, any tendency for the behaviour of individuals to be guided by the principle of reciprocity will push the code towards behaviour conducive to the common good, but this will always be in conflict with the self-assertiveness of individuals. The distinction between in-group and out-group, incorporated in social norms, influences the behaviour of individuals, but the norms may be affected if some in-group members treat out-group members as if they belonged to the in-group. The vigour of such debates fluctuates with time, but whether they concern the propriety of throwing Christians to the lions or the rights of immigrants, differences of opinion are likely always to be present. But the bases for evaluation will be of the same nature as those through which the code evolved in the first place – reciprocity and status-seeking, the control of sexual relations, and in-group/out-group relations – influenced by tradition and local conditions.

### Interactions with other aspects of the socio-cultural structure and with current conditions

It is just because social and environmental conditions change, and because of the inevitable conflict between individuals seeking their own good and that of the group as a whole, that codes change and differ between societies. Religious specialists can provide a stabilising influence on current values, but we have seen (pp. 79–80) that their teachings may be influenced by public opinion. And inevitably, the course of the dialectical relations between the behaviour of individuals and the current moral code will be influenced by other aspects of the socio-cultural structure. In a violent society, an individual may ensure his own personal safety by establishing a reputation as one who seeks immediate revenge for slights or insults at all costs, and vengeance will be seen as a virtue, but in societies where violence is controlled by police and the law, personal vengeance is likely to be frowned upon. Again, in a situation where competition within and between groups is usual, the propensity of young men to engage in aggressive behaviour is likely to be encouraged, but in a modern society it is not. If the society is one in which individuals rely on reciprocity with many others, it will pay individuals to cultivate a reputation for prosocial behaviour and for returning favours received. If, however, kin-groups are emphasised, all-round beneficence may result in the individual acquiring a reputation as a poor kinsman (Irons, 1996b).

We have already mentioned the tendency for some degree of compatibility between the different aspects of the socio-cultural structure. This comes up most obviously over boundary issues – who is and who is not to be treated as an out-group member with respect to which issues. The Buddhist prohibition on killing extends even to animals, whereas in Islam the ban on killing applies primarily only to fellow believers. In wartime in many societies, in-group members may be encouraged to kill members of particular out-groups, unless particular conditions are met – for instance if they have surrendered.

As another example, beliefs about the precise nature of the dead are related to the respect that is felt to be due to ancestors. In Christian countries this is largely limited to looking after graves and some obligation to carry out wishes they may have made in life, practices that can be seen as based on the principle of reciprocity, the doer hoping that his wishes will similarly be honoured after he has gone. But if the dead are considered to be living in another world, and especially if they are seen as able to influence events in this one, far more elaborate duties may be called for. Often reciprocity still prevails: the dead need to be helped on their way, and if they do not get the help which they need, they may return to upset their descendents. By contrast, among hunter-gatherers who live from day to day and whose hierarchical distinctions are minimal, the rules for mourners or other survivors are also minimal, and little danger is associated with contact with the body or the site of death (Woodburn, 1982).

As a very different type of case, an emphasis on contemplative religious experience (see Chapter 15) is often associated with asceticism and even celibacy: this can lead to tensions with aspects of the moral code concerned with family life. However, a contemplative attitude fits well with vegetarianism, both involving a gentle and harmless attitude towards other living beings (Bruce, 1996).

## Summary

In addition to prosocial behaviour and reciprocity, among other propensities that contribute to moral codes are self-assertiveness and status-seeking, regulation of sexual relations, in-group/out-group relations, and perhaps recognition of a principle of 'common good'.

The maintenance of, and changes in, a moral code depend on diachronic, dialectic relations between the code existing at any one time and the behaviour of individuals in the society. The code also affects, and is affected by, other aspects of the socio-cultural structure.

# 15 Religious experience

Prosocial actions may be 'put on' or may 'come from the heart'. In the same way, religious observance may involve an unfeeling performance of ritual actions or feelings of extra-sensory reality and even experience of the presence of a deity. For some, the essence of religion lies less in the belief, the ritual, or the values, and more in experiences involving a special awareness which may be interpreted as transcendental, as a mystical experience of unity (e.g. Otto, 1917; see Tambiah, 1990). Indeed many deeply religious people see such experience as fundamental.

There is, of course, a continuum between mechanical observance and intense religious experience, so that it is difficult to define religious experience precisely except to say that it must involve a sense of reality beyond that available to the senses. As such, it seems remote from basic human propensities evolved under the influence of natural selection. However it is heuristically useful to distinguish between the eliciting circumstances, the experience itself, and its interpretation, and on that basis this chapter argues that the distinction between religious experience and some types of secular experience is not so clear as might appear.

## Incidence

While most discussion of religious experience focuses on its more extreme forms, many would claim that some everyday experiences have a religious flavour. William James (1892) wrote of religion as 'the feelings, acts and experiences of individual men in their solitude, so far as they apprehend themselves to stand in relation to whatever they may consider the divine'. While we shall consider the diversity of religious experiences later, to attempt a precise definition to delimit the phenomena is hardly a profitable undertaking.

That experiences interpreted as religious are widespread cannot be doubted: according to one study over a third of the adults in England said that they had been influenced by a presence or power different from their everyday selves, though not all referred to this presence as God (Brown, 1987). Sir Alister Hardy, Professor of Zoology at Oxford, set up a unit to gather first-hand reports of such experiences. Defining religious experience in terms of communion with a superhuman force or being, he requested personal accounts of such experiences through notices in newspapers and other media in 1969/70. Several thousand replies were received. While such responses to open-ended questions are notoriously difficult to evaluate (Hood *et al.*, 1996), around one-third were positive, many going beyond the definition given and indicating that 'religious experience is really something quite ordinary, commonplace if you like' (Robinson, 1977a: 15), though it must be noted that some of the experiences reported might not be generally described as religious. In any case, such experiences are impossible to describe adequately in words, in part because the words just do not exist and in part because of the paradoxical nature of the experience itself (Hardy, 1979; Robinson, 1977b). In an analysis of some of the material, Beardsworth (1977) emphasised that, apart from a few cases involving changes in illumination, most of the accounts had a 'dependent, personal (I-You) basis'. In so far as they could be called hallucinations they were not primarily of sensations, but of *meetings*, and they were accompanied by strong emotion which coloured not only the experience itself, but also the situation leading up to it. Beardsworth suggests that it is the affect and need for the other that creates the image of the Other, and not the other way round. On this view the experience can be related to the 'search image' which is postulated to explain the fact that, when looking for something, we are able readily to pick out not only that object from others but also something resembling it.

Evidence for the prevalence of religious and mystical experience comes also from survey studies using the replies to one or a few specific questions. In an extensive review of these issues, Hood *et al.* (1996) concluded that over one-third of American adults claim some intense religious experience, that such experiences are more frequent in women than in men and in older than in younger individuals, that they are characteristic of the educated and affluent, and that they are associated with psychological health and well-being rather than pathology or social dysfunction.

A different type of evidence for the importance of such experiences comes from the rise during recent decades of movements which claim to 'expand' or 'deepen' or induce 'higher states of' consciousness. In many alternative religious traditions, it is the personal religious experience that is emphasised. Mysticism can be of more use in times of change or trouble than religion founded solely on belief in dogma. How much significance should be attached to the precise words used to describe these religious or pseudo-religious experiences is difficult to assess, as it is not always easy for the outsider to see in what sense they are 'higher' or 'purer'. Many of them, like Zen Buddhism and Transcendental Meditation, have eastern origins, and involve a technique for altering experience which is claimed either to have beneficial effects on health and performance in the secular world or to deepen the experience of the present. Although in some cases aiming for communal good,[1] the supernatural is generally of minor importance and the focus is on inducing a form of subjective experience different from the everyday. Thus among the claims made for Transcendental Meditation are that it has provided an impetus for research on 'higher' states of consciousness and brought to light their benefits in practical life: in addition validation is claimed through links with modern science (Chalmers, 1990).

In this chapter we shall see that religious experiences have many characteristics in common with experiences of a more secular nature. Specification of the similarities and differences is, however, made difficult by the inadequacies of language. In what follows we shall discuss in turn the circumstances in which, or technique by which, such experiences are induced; the nature of the experiences; and the interpretations given to them. Paranormal experiences, such as telepathy and psychokinesis, can, however, safely be omitted: they lack the ineffable nature of religious experiences and can readily be described in everyday language. They are not generally regarded as religious, though when associated with spiritualist sessions they necessarily have implications of an after-life. Their bases have been discussed in depth by Humphrey (1995). Near-death experiences were mentioned earlier (Chapter 5).

## Situations and techniques

Some experiences interpreted as religious come during the course of everyday life. In a study carried out on a national sample in the USA, 1467 subjects who said that they had been close to a 'powerful spiritual force' were asked what had triggered their religious experiences. The responses were categorised, and the percentage of subjects reporting each type of trigger calculated. Fourteen categories of trigger were reported by at least 15 per cent of the subjects who reported at least one religious experience, and of these 8 per cent had no overt religious connection. Of the latter group, the highest was listening to music (49 per cent), and others were beauties of nature, watching children, reading a poem or novel, childbirth, sexual activity, creative work and looking at a painting. The five with religious associations were prayer (48 per cent), attending services, listening to a sermon, reading the Bible and being alone in church. (The category 'moments of quiet reflection' (42 per cent) has not been included in either of these categories.) These data must, of course, be seen as specific to the particular society in which they were obtained (Greeley, 1975).

Mystical experiences are often triggered by natural beauty: these may or may not have a religious flavour. Significant here is evidence that the appeal of some natural landscapes is a rather basic matter, and is due to mechanisms developed early in the evolution of our species. Thus it is well established that people prefer natural to artificial landscapes, and that natural landscapes can reduce stress for dental and surgical patients and for prisoners (Ulrich, 1993; Heerwagen and Orians, 1993). A New York study showed that landscapes, and especially peaceful landscapes, are also commonly preferred as pictures in houses (Halle 1993). Among landscapes, savannah is particularly attractive, especially for children. Savannah was almost certainly the environment of early human evolution, and certain characteristic features of savannah would have provided conditions conducive to survival, such as vantage points and hiding places (Appleton, 1975; Balling and Falk, 1982; Orians and Heerwagen, 1992). There is also evidence that the relative attractiveness of landscapes rich in 'prospect' (i.e. vast expanses and overviews) as compared with those rich in 'refuge' depends on the mood of the viewer (Mealey and Theis, 1995). Another feature of many landscapes that has been shown to be attractive is 'mystery', or the promise of more information if only one could enter the scene, and it has been suggested that this is related to the human need to understand and explore (Kaplan, 1992): mystery can also contribute to religious experience. Of course, none of this denies that fashions in landscape preferences have changed with time, or that other influences operate (Thomas, 1983): the issue of importance in the present context is the apparently basic appeal of experiences which are conducive both to religious and to secular experience.

Others have found religious paintings conducive to religious visions. In such cases it seems that a sort of mystical illusion is created, with uncertainty as to whether it is a painting or reality that is being perceived (Stoichita, 1995).

Prayer and meditation, two forms of religious practice which are not always clearly separable, are everyday activities for some, and form a link with the special techniques used to induce religious experience. Meditation may be solitary or communal, silent or accompanied by chanting; and may focus on real entities, a part of the body, an activity, or an abstract notion. In some cultures prayer and meditation are of major importance. For orthodox Jews, Moslems, and some Christians the regular practice of religious observances provides a form of religious experience. For Brahmans, the whole of life is supposedly directed towards achieving a state in which the self is conquered, desire is banished, and the intellect is cleansed so that the individual can live in absolute moderation, at peace with himself and with the world. Even this is not the ultimate step, for detachment is seen as only the first step on the path that leads towards union with the infinite.

Special techniques used to induce religious experience can be divided into (1) Those involving temporary deprivation of a natural resource, such as food, sleep, or oxygen (by breathing control). These are often carried out in solitude, and can lead to ecstatic or hallucinatory states; and (2) those that involve heightened bodily movement and sensation, are usually communal, and can lead to a non-hallucinatory trance or even physical collapse (Wulff, 1997). We shall be concerned primarily with some examples of the former.

Techniques of Yoga and Buddhist or Yogic/Upanishadic meditation are performed to bring about 'liberation' involving isolation of the soul from the world and from all other souls. This is achieved by mastery of the mind, the senses, and the body, by concentration on particular tasks, such as calligraphy or manual labour, or special techniques, such as concentrating on a particular word or object, or even on 'nothingness'. Buddhist meditational techniques are based on simple and observable phenomena, such as breathing, concentrating on a single object, and subjugating the body. For example, a Westerner describes one approach as follows:

> There is a range of methods available: counting the breath; watching the breath; observing thoughts on an inhalation, letting them go on the exhalation and observing what is there when they have gone; repeating the Buddha's name; repeating a name of the Buddha, suddenly stopping it and looking into the gap so caused, searching the heart....

In a related technique the practitioner may try to discover what 'just sitting' is by examining all thoughts that arise and letting them go until the mind quietens down and a trance state is achieved (Crook, 1990: 159). The success of such techniques may be affected by the cultural background of the subject. It is well established that they are accompanied by physiological changes, feelings of comfort, pleasure, and detachment, and by changes in perception (Wulff, 1997). Transcendental meditation, a method originating in the East but now much used in the West, is said to have both immediate and long-term effects (see Orme-Johnson *et al.*, 1988).

The physiological changes accompanying yoga and meditation differ. The differences are consistent with the view that yogis try to disengage themselves from the phenomenological world, while disciples of Zen seek not to withdraw from objects but to see them more clearly (Wulff, 1997).

The techniques used to induce religious experience by Christian mystics seem less physical, though they may involve fasting and isolation. Specific techniques are taught much less than is the case with the eastern religions, and generalisations are hard to make. While Eastern techniques are mostly aimed at isolation or loss of self, Christians more often emphasise the possibility of experiencing proximity to God, though to claim actual union would be seen as blasphemous.

Some mystics have found solitude conducive to religious experience, and there may be parallels here to the effects of sensory deprivation, which is known to induce intense subjective experiences. One experimental study has shown that isolation of individuals high in intrinsic religiosity, coupled with religious suggestion, can produce religious experience (Hood, 1995).

The religious experiences induced by heightened bodily movement and sensation may be of a different nature. In some church services, such as those held in the Pentecostal church, loud music and the sense of communal participation in singing and chanting can produce high arousal which may lead to speaking in tongues and even to physical collapse. Being part of a crowd can induce strong emotions also in secular contexts. However, comparable states may be induced in single individuals (see p. 128).

Finally, prolonged stress and fear, such as that induced in the trenches in

World War I, can provide a context for visions and experiences, some of which are seen as religious (Winter, 1995).

Whether these various techniques and situations have a common basis has been a matter of considerable controversy. One suggestion is that they have the common consequence of stopping the flow of thought and bringing the mind to 'one-pointedness' (Batson and Ventis, 1982). Others have attempted a physiological approach. Fischer (1986) has suggested that either a decrease in sub-cortical arousal, as in meditation, or an increase, as in ecstatic states, can lead to a state in which a transformation of the objective and familiar time/space world occurs so that the self experiences oneness with the universe and sees beyond the limits of physical space/time. On this view differences between forms of meditation would be due to different cortical interpretations of sub-cortical processes (see Wulff, 1997). Of course, not only the technique or circumstances, but also the personality of the individual in question, can affect the nature of religious experience.

The point being made here is that most of the contexts mentioned in the preceding paragraphs, music, solitude, group experiences, natural beauty, sexual activity, and so on, can also produce subjective experiences which seem to resemble religious experiences but are not interpreted as having religious connotations. The same is true of drugs and hypnosis, which are more often used in secular contexts, but may induce religious experience, especially in those with a religious background.

## The nature of religious experience

As we have seen, experiences labelled as religious are diverse, and a number of attempts have been made to identify their essential elements. One authority lists six types (numinous experience of the holy; mystical experience of unity; wonder and gratitude; personal transformation; moral obligation; and courage in facing suffering and death), and points out that the first three are often associated with 'nature', whereas in the last three nature plays a smaller role (Barbour, 1994).

More usually, two main types are claimed, one involving approach to God or to some transcendental presence, inducing awe and dependence, and the other a feeling of profound peace, perhaps involving union with God but at the same time coupled with the experience of being part of a living, exciting, and essentially unitary world. Smart (1960: 27; see also 1996), in creating an imaginary discourse between representatives of world religions, allows the Christian to distinguish between the '*numinous experience* – the experience which grows out of worship and the submission of oneself to God', and which conveys a contrast between the 'unholy, unclean, puny sinner and the terrible, pure, majestic Godhead...' on the one hand, and the mystical experience which gives a sense of inner oneness or 'of merging with God or the Absolute' on the other. The former tends to involve a personal god, the latter often an impersonal essence. Numinous experience tends to go with religions where the god is seen as other, and the purity and perfection of the deity contrasts with the sinfulness and weakness of the worshipper – though sometimes it is evil spirits that are experienced. By contrast mystical experience, arising from a contemplative approach, involves a new state of mind, often with disappearance of the subject/object distinction and a degree of union with the ultimate, and is associated particularly with non-theistic religions. It tends to be achieved through a contemplative life steered towards 'a sort of pure consciousness in which recognisable attributes are absent' (Smart, 1996: 43). Descriptions of mystical experiences often include a sense of timelessness or of going beyond time, an absence of self-consciousness, standing outside oneself, a heightened sense of awareness, a consciousness of beauty, bliss, love and so on, and a feeling of either community or isolation. In the highest states of consciousness achieved by Yogic practitioners all traces of duality are said to vanish and the conscious and thinking ego to disappear. Some individuals who claim mystical experiences emphasise the need to 'renounce the world'. Thorpe (1962: 98) defined mysticism as 'the awareness of values, in part at least, above and beyond the scope of current symbolism to express'. Transcendental meditation has been described by a Christian as enabling 'the mind to transcend thinking and enter into a deeper state of consciousness in which we can experience...the presence of the Divine at the very centre of our being' (Smith, 1993: 17). Although such experiences are usually positive in nature, they may afterwards leave the subject with a sense of loss.

According to Smart, numinous experience generates fear, respect, or humility, and leads to devotion, love, and spontaneity; while contemplative or mystical experience produces serenity and happiness, and creates self-awareness, a sense of wisdom, and equanimity. Contemplative experience is often associated with asceticism. Some authorities differentiate a third type, involving a sense of being at one with the world or the cosmos. But in any case such categories may blend or overlap with each other, and many aspects of experience are shared. Smart (1996: 173) therefore suggests that 'the differing experiences might apply to the same entity'.

Smart's discussion tends to refer to the more intense experiences rather than the day-to-day feelings of communion with the deity claimed by the ordinary believer, and the distinctions he makes are not ubiquitously recognised in less precise discussions of the issues: perhaps that is inevitable because of the essential ambiguities of the words used in reports of such experiences and in discussions of the topic. Mystics may not be bothered by their inability to describe their experience to others: they feel that they have lived in their vision, and its incomprehensibility to others is unfortunate, but cannot be helped. Even the distinction between 'ecstasy' and 'mystical' experience is far from clear – though perhaps in the former it is the state of excitement that predominates while the latter has a more transcendental quality. Some authors claim that there is a common source for, or common elements in, all religious experiences; others claim distinctive characteristics for their own particular brand, perhaps thereby helping to authenticate their own belief system (see also Hood, 1995).

Although religious experiences are not infrequently described as involving proximity to a deity or as providing a new light on reality, there is some difference of opinion as to how 'real' the experience is – though here words become even more treacherous. Stoichita, citing a vision of St. Teresa of Avila, reports that she describes her vision as 'different from the *real* presence of the divine as manifested in the Holy Sacraments.... It is...*unreal*, imaginary and therefore personal, private and, consequently, uncontrollable'. On this view, the 'ecstatic vision takes place in the soul of the chosen one' (1995: 27). Elsewhere this author quotes St. Teresa as saying 'Though imaginary, I never saw this vision with the eyes of my body or any other, only with the eyes of my soul' (1995: 45).

Such experiences are not favoured by all religious traditions, and especially not by the more intellectual ones. Not surprisingly the Confucian Chinese literati, but also over the centuries many sections of the Christian church, have been hostile to displays of religious emotion, which they have seen as incompatible with their own views – perhaps in the Christian case because a mystical union with God was seen as blasphemous, or as infringing the Church's role as mediator with the Almighty (Stoichita, 1995).

Nevertheless the Christian Church has a heritage of influential mystics, though to be acceptable the claimed experience had to maintain the sacredness of the Almighty, with the distinction between God and the soul intact. Most mystics have been found in religious orders, and for the experience to be recognised by the authorities the mystic had to continue to obey his ecclesiastical superiors in preference to his vision, must not pretend to a special source of wisdom, and must continue to lead a virtuous life (Kolakowski, 1982). Other criteria often used for assessing whether an experience was genuinely religious have included the requirements that its consequences should be in harmony with the virtues prescribed by the belief system, that it is compatible with orthodox doctrine, that it enhances the integrity of the community, and so on. On all such issues the judgement of the religious authorities was to be taken into account (Wainwright, cited Donovan, 1979). Sometimes that judgement seems to have been related to current church concerns: thus acceptance of visions of the Virgin Mary has often been linked with an official preoccupation with sexual suppression (Warner, 1976). Such criteria seem to be merely parochial (in that they assess the compatibility of the experience with a particular belief system), and circular (for believing oneself to have had experience of the supernatural both depends on previous, though perhaps second-hand, knowledge of the supernatural, and is taken as evidence for it).

Some other types of religious experience must be mentioned briefly. While reports of those discussed so far mostly come from the subjects themselves, those involving spirit mediums in trance states speaking in an incomprehensible language, foretelling the future, healing, and so on, come predominantly from bystanders. Firth (1996), writing about spirit mediums in Malaysia, treats such states as a category of mental disorder which has been put to social use in a system of therapeutic aid. It appears that the mediums can either put themselves into a trance, or allow a trance to be induced by music or other means. Of special interest is the fact that the state involves dissociation between two selves, or displaying an aspect of the self-system other than that presented in everyday life (see pp. 28–9). The medium is freed from normal social inhibitions: as a vehicle of communication for the spirits he can express issues about the patient or the community in a way that would normally be impossible. The trance thus serves as a sort of safety valve for individual and collective views.

'Regenerative experiences' are those which lead to or facilitate a change in orientation, such as being 'born again' or 'renewed'. Such experiences are usually characterised by feelings of wonder and awe. Less dramatic experiences may maintain a previously acquired religious orientation. Thus this category can cover a wide range of phenomena ranging from St. Paul's experience on the road to Damascus to mere everyday experiences of spiritual well-being.

Also sometimes recognised as a distinct category (Donovan, 1979), 'charismatic experiences' refer to the reported experiences of particular individuals who are seen as 'Holy People' – apostles, prophets, gurus, or shamans. The importance of such individuals lies in their influence on others, either through the power which comes to be invested in them, or through the example, be it of saintliness, peace of mind, or wild abandon, that they provide.

Since it is hardly possible to have, or at least to convey, a complex experience without putting it into words which are not the experience itself, and since the words used will depend on the individual in question, it is nearly impossible to compare the religious experiences of two individuals: we can only compare their interpretations (but see Smart, 1996: 169). And in so far as the words may be inadequate for some aspects of the experience, it is always possible for a believer to describe an experience as a religious one, or to claim a sensitivity to the numinous denied to his peers. It is reasonable to infer from the available descriptions that religious experiences have much in common with some rather special secular experiences: whether, without the interpretations put upon them, they would be the same cannot be proven or disproven.

## Interpretation

The nature of an experience depends in large measure on the attributions made about it. This is true in the everyday world, and equally true of religious experience. Our response to hearing the doorbell ring depends on the interpretation we give, which depends in turn on our expectations. In the same way, those who are religiously inclined may interpret the beauties of nature as evidence of God's handiwork. In general, the nature of religious experience depends on the belief system of the individual: Christians are more likely to have an experience of Jesus than are Buddhists, Moslems to sense the guiding hand of Allah than that of Christ. Thus the nature of the experience cannot be taken as evidence for the veracity of the belief system (Donovan, 1979). Even its incomprehensibility and indescribable nature cannot be taken as evidence for its other-worldly nature, for some clearly secular experiences, such as love and sexual activity, have similar properties.

That both the experience and interpretation of visions are subject to outside influences is suggested by St. Teresa's first complete vision. This took place on the feast of St. Paul, and it is noteworthy that St. Paul was the first to have a similar experience, and that he, like her, regarded it as the 'soul's perception' (see above) rather than a physical perception. In addition St. Augustine, in speaking of visionary experience, had commented on St. Paul's vision. St. Teresa also said that the Christ who appeared to her resembled (though also differed from) the Christ depicted in paintings of the Resurrection. On another occasion she described seeing the Mother of God descending and placing herself 'just where the picture of Our Lady is situated. It then seemed to me that I could no longer see the painting, but Our Lady herself looking, I think, a little like the picture the Countess had given me as a present' (Stoichita, 1995: 48). How far the words she used in describing her visions are to be seen as descriptive devices, and how far the circumstances of the vision and the resemblances to which she referred are to be seen as causal to the visions, as Stoichita suggests, must be regarded as open issues. However it must be noted that the most striking effect of a painting regarded as 'well-painted' at that time was that it could lead to an ecstatic visionary state.

But it must be emphasised that none of this detracts in any way from the reality of the experience itself, nor does it necessarily disprove that of the believer's interpretation. And that experience seen as religious may have religious consequences is not to be doubted: it may both confirm the subject's beliefs and impel the subject to actions compatible with those beliefs or with the associated moral code. Self-reports indicate that religious experiences can lead to happiness and existential well-being as well as to more religious involvement (Poloma and Pendleton, 1991). Experience interpreted as religious may make the subject more prone to interpret experience as religious in the future.

## Religious experience and comparable secular experience

It is difficult to draw a line between experience that is clearly religious and experiences of a more secular nature. The emotions aroused in many secular gatherings are not clearly different from those involved in religious ones, and aesthetic experience would seem to have much in common with religious experience. The view tentatively suggested here, though with an important reservation, is that the experiences are essentially the same, and it is primarily the interpretations put upon them that differ. Thus a given event may be given a secular interpretation by one observer ('His lucky day') and a (pseudo-) religious one by another ('Providence intervened'). The same technique or situation, leading to the same experience, may have different interpretations put upon it. The reservation is this: it must be remembered that the distinction between experience and interpretation is not so clear-cut as this model would imply, because the interpretation affects the experience. A given experience, say of intense beauty, might activate a stored belief that beauty is divinely given, which would then change the nature of the experience (see also Lederose, 1981).

Parallels between religious and secular experience are of two types, one putting the emphasis primarily on cognition and the other primarily on subjective and aesthetic issues, though inevitably both must be involved (see p. 172). Most of the former depend on a picture of religious experience as a resolution of previously experienced uneasiness: thus Hood *et al.* (1996: 189) refer to religious experience as 'the understanding in a religious vocabulary of the process of discontent and its resolution...'. The psychoanalyst D.W. Winnicott (1953) identified the realm of religious experience as one that bridges inner and outer realities, as that area between reality and fantasy ('transitional space') where human creativity emerges. This view of religious experience is compatible with a cognitive model advanced by Batson and Ventis (1982). They suggest that religious experience resembles that of creatively solving an intellectual problem in that both involve four stages: preparation, including a baffled struggle to solve a problem; incubation, during which the attempt is given up; illumination, in which a solution appears; and verification, in which the solution is elaborated and verified. In the same way, it is suggested, intense religious experience involves stages of existential personal conflict or crisis; self-surrender involving confusion and exhaustion; a stage in which the subject perceives a new self-image which provides a foundation for building a new reality more in keeping with experience; and a stage in which the new self-image is expressed in improved social functioning. Three factors that facilitate religious experience, drugs, meditation, and religious language, are each held to affect some of these stages, a combination of one of the first two with the third affecting all four. Batson and Ventis cite accounts of religious experience which fit this model, and suggest that religious traditions develop a pattern of facilitators for the four stages. However, the parallel with creative thinking requires further verification.

The second type of parallel is with aesthetic experience. This, like religion, has no clear defining characteristic. Its nature depends on the observer as well as on the object or scene experienced, and involves meanings which may depend on the culture and on associations peculiar to the experiencing individual. Dancing is often thought to be the earliest human art form, and

Langer has emphasised the close relation between dance in its earlier forms and religion. She (1953: 175) described dance as 'appearances of influence and agency created by virtual gesture'. (By virtual she meant that the dance may be governed not by real emotion but by imagined feeling.)

> What is created (*by dance*) is the image of a world of vital forces, embodied or disembodied; in the early stages of human thought when symbol and import are apprehended as one reality, this image is the realm of holiness; in later stages it is recognised as the work of art, the expressive form which it really is.
>
> (1953: 193)

Apparently many Hindus consider dance without prayer to be vulgar, and Hindu critics of the theatre distinguish from the feelings experienced by the actors, spectators and characters, the feeling that shines through the play itself.

> This last they call *rasa*; it is a state of emotional knowledge, which comes only to those who have long studied and contemplated poetry. It is supposed to be of supernatural origin, because it is not like mundane feeling and emotion, but is detached, more of the spirit than of the viscera, pure and uplifting.
>
> (Langer, 1953: 323)

Turning to accounts of aesthetic and religious experience in the West, the problem of language is paramount. While at least some aesthetic experiences depend on basic human characteristics, on the perception of symmetry,[2] unity, balance, and so on, or on responsiveness to particular sorts of landscapes (see above), they are just as difficult to describe in words as religious experiences, and perhaps for that reason those who write about them do not all share a common view. What we see as beautiful is in part a cultural issue: we have all been instructed *ad nauseam* to appreciate the beauty of the daffodils. But many of the words used to describe aesthetic experience are similar to those used to describe religious experience. In a recent review Collinson (1992) notes that, for instance, aesthetic experience is described as 'arresting', 'intense', 'utterly engrossing', involving active contemplation with sustained focus of attention. It involves a recognition of the self-contained meaning of the object, and a loss of awareness of self. It involves considering the object not in relation to what might accrue from it to ourselves: 'all things appear the more beautiful, the more we are conscious merely of them, and the less we are conscious of ourselves' (Schopenhauer, 1969). Collinson (1992: 133) describes a 'will-less receiving in which a person is entranced, as if experiencing a revelation, as well as searching attentiveness'.

There is a slight problem here in that both religious and secular experiences are usually spoken of as positive, but some aesthetic experiences arouse negative feelings. Collinson instances some of the paintings of Francis Bacon, but argues that it is necessary to distinguish the direct appeal, which is usually but may not be positive, from the ultimate delight in a new clarity which the object induces.

Of special interest is Collinson's insistence on the impact of aesthetic experience on the self. The self is first lost in that it becomes absorbed in what it contemplates and explores. But it is then regained, and what has been experienced becomes part of the self: the experience is described as involving clarity and a sense of acquaintance with reality or truth. There are clear parallels here with religious experience. Contemplative meditation in prayer seems to have much in common with contemplation of beauty in nature or art: aesthetic experience tends to be a solitary issue, describable by such phrases as 'communing with nature' or 'closeness to reality', and thus comparable to the mystical experiences of individuals. It may be suggested that the similarities are at least compatible with the view that they are not inspired or guided by a supernatural being, but are simply the product of human minds in particular circumstances.

Some studies have indicated a common physiological basis to a variety of fantasy and reality-altering experiences in everyday life and (pseudo-) religious experiences. For instance, in a group of female students such experiences were found to be correlated with absorption and hypnotisability, and both were also correlated with mysticism and diabolical experiences (i.e. feelings about the presence of evil spirits). Out-of-body experiences were correlated with hypnotisability. This suggests that a propensity to be involved in imaginative or counter-factual experiences is common to all of these, and that subjects label their experiences according to their expectations and the context (Spanos and Moretti, 1988). It has indeed been suggested that a neurophysiological approach can provide a key to the understanding of religious and mystical states (d'Aquili and Newberg, 1993), and there seems to be no evidence for differences between the concomitants of religious and similar secular experiences: of course, the physiological concomitants can tell us nothing about the nature of the experience (Hood *et al.*, 1996).

A study in Xi'an, in the People's Republic of China, found that the frequency of experiences of *déjà vu*, night paralysis, extra-sensory perception, out-of-body experiences and faith in a sixth sense were equal to or higher than those in Western populations. The author argues that since the Chinese engage in no formal religious practices this cannot be the result of religious faith, but must be universal in some sense, anomalous experiences being a source of, rather than caused by, religious faith (McClenon, 1988).

It thus seems that religious and aesthetic experience have much in common. It may be suggested that religious experience lies on the extreme of a continuum together with intense aesthetic experiences and with the experiences of unreality that are not so uncommon in everyday life. Of course the possibility that there are differences cannot be totally ruled out. For instance it has been argued that aesthetic experiences demand an object in a way that some religious experiences, or at least some mystical experiences, do not. But religious experiences are often at least facilitated by an object or an imagined object: we have already seen that relics, crucifixes, altars, idols, and paintings may facilitate worship, may be worshipped as though they were themselves divine, and may stimulate religious experience.

If religious experience is not fundamentally different from some forms of secular experience, the potential for such experience is likely to be present in all individuals, at least early in life. It is probable that the two are to be distinguished primarily by the interpretation put on the experience, and this is influenced by the cultural and social experience of the individual in question. Links between religious and secular experience do not necessarily pose a problem for the believer, who can argue that if there is a numinous, it pervades all the world: such links do, however, suggest that religious experience is less special than has sometimes been thought. Although Freud (1930) saw religious experience as derived from the infant's feelings of helplessness, it must be admitted that its ontogenetic and phylogenetic sources at present remain matters for speculation.

## Summary

Religious experience is difficult to describe, largely because the words do not exist, but appears to be widespread. It is helpful to consider separately the facilitating conditions, the experience itself, and the interpretation. It is suggested that the difference between religious experience and certain types of secular experience, such as aesthetic experience, lies primarily not in the experience itself but in the interpretation, in so far as experience and interpretation are separable.

# 16  Social aspects

It is almost impossible to imagine an *entirely* idiosyncratic religious system. Belief is seldom, if ever, solely an individual matter: it depends on interaction within a community. Many behavioural aspects of religious systems tend to be social, including ritual, prayer and in some cases also religious experience. And codes of morals stem from and refer to the conduct of individuals in social situations. Social aspects of religious systems have been referred to in every one of the preceding chapters, and it is necessary here only to draw the threads together. First, however, it is helpful to review briefly some general findings about the dynamics of groups.

## Group dynamics

Individuals see themselves not only as autonomous individuals, but also as partners in relationships and as members of groups. One's 'self' includes both an 'individual identity' and a 'social identity', the latter being derived from emotionally significant relationships, groups or categories to which one sees oneself as belonging (Tajfel and Turner, 1986). Thus an individual may see herself as female, a member of a married couple, mother of a son, a member of the Muslim religion, and so on. Social identity becomes part of the knowledge structures of the self-system.

Members of a psychological group not only see themselves, talk about themselves, and label themselves as a group, but they also see themselves as more similar to each other than to outsiders on issues relevant to the criteria by which they define the group. They are likely also to see themselves as interdependent. And the more they see themselves as similar to each other, and the more they see themselves as interdependent, the more cohesive the group, and vice versa. Members of a group tend to elaborate and adhere to their own norms of behaviour, values, and explanations of events. They tend to denigrate out-groups; and while members of their own group are individually distinct, members of out-groups are seen as undifferentiated entities (Rabbie, 1991; Tajfel and Turner, 1986). Group identification is most pronounced in individuals who score highly on collectivism (vs individualism) and on relational (vs autonomous) orientation (Brown *et al.*, 1992).

It may be that individuals are intrinsically predisposed to value group membership. In any case, it can have profound effects on their outlook on life. Group membership not only provides a sense of security, it can influence an individual's picture of the world. People need to find support for their attitudes and beliefs (Festinger, 1957). Not surprisingly, therefore, they are attracted to others who have attitudes similar to their own, because their own attitudes are thereby confirmed (Byrne, 1971), and they tend to match their attitudes with those whom they like or admire. Especially significant in the present context is the finding that individuals are especially likely to be attracted to others who share their beliefs if they are temporarily confused (Byrne and Clore, 1967), or if those beliefs are otherwise unverifiable (Byrne *et al.*, 1966). And recognition of shared group membership both facilitates the perception of shared attitudes and authenticates the potential of others to provide verification.

Group membership also affects self-esteem. Since people like to think of themselves positively, they tend to associate with groups they evaluate favourably and to evaluate favourably groups with which they identify, even if objective evidence for their high regard is lacking.

## Social aspects of religion

### Individuals and culture

Religious representations are shared by most members of the society, and are thus to be seen as located in the minds of individuals – as well as, in literate cultures, being stored permanently in verbal form. The representations of individuals are affected by influences from others, especially from individuals who are close or salient to them. Internalised in the minds of individuals, they affect their behaviour and relationships, and how individuals behave and conduct their relationships affects the religious system. Thus there is a diachronic dialectical relation between the religious system as represented by each individual and aspects of the socio-cultural structure (Figure 2.1). It is when the effects of the socio-cultural structure on the individuals are more potent than those of differences between or changes in individuals, that we speak of the power of tradition.

The dialectical relations can be seen, for example, in Papal pronouncements. By declaring the Immaculate Conception in 1854, the Pope was both responding to eighteenth-century scepticism on such matters and simultaneously asserting his own and the Church's authority. When, in 1950, the Pope announced from St. Peter's that Mary was taken up body and soul into Heaven, he was confirming what had long been a popular belief. The crowd of nearly a million responded with thunderous clapping and tears of joy (Warner, 1976).

### Social aspects of acquisition

Leaving aside cases of adult conversion, religious systems are usually acquired gradually in the process of socialisation. While teaching may play some role, it is seldom the whole issue. The religious system, like social knowledge and the scripts relating to behaviour in social situations, becomes part of the self-system of each individual. Acquisition depends in part on pre-existing properties of the human mind, but it is facilitated by social factors in a number of ways. Most importantly, as noted above, people are attracted to others who resemble themselves in attitudes and other characteristics, and they are attracted especially to others who share their unverifiable beliefs, such as those inherent in religious systems, probably because they provide consensual validation of those beliefs – validation that can be obtained in no other way (Chapter 7).

The contribution of religion to the individual's social identity can have widespread repercussions. Sharing a religious system makes the individual part of a community, with consequences for his/her self-esteem and sense of self-efficacy. Where interpenetration between social and religious systems is considerable, the sharing of the religious beliefs and attitudes augments societal identity: this can be facilitated by religion-associated rules of behaviour, and by ceremonies associated with *rites de passage*, including methods of dealing with death. Religion can help the individual cope with problems of group life, such as status hierarchies: it can both justify the position of those at the top and ameliorate the lot of those less fortunate by ascribing merit to humility or offering hope for better things to come in this life or the next.

### Social aspects of observance

While religious observance can be an entirely individual matter, participation as a member of a congregation may add greatly to the intensity of the experience. Reciprocally, the experience of worshipping together contributes to the resilience of religious communities.

### Religion and the social system

Sociologists and anthropologists have often suggested that religious symbolic systems are related to the structure of the social system, which they re-represent (e.g., Durkheim, 1964). For instance, in many religions it is apparent that beliefs about the after-world must be modelled on this world. We have seen that in ancient Egypt and in ancient China the deceased were seen as inhabiting a realm closely resembling the everyday world, and the divine hierarchy in Hinduism has been said to parallel the caste system (Moffat, 1979). The Christian Heaven has parallels with a mediaeval court (p. 104). As mentioned in Chapters 4 and 12, there must also be some coherence between the religious moral code and other aspects of the society's ideology.

Particular ritual practices focusing on religious symbols may have a powerful influence on social integration. Thus religious images may be used to confirm or augment secular power. Mentioned previously in Chapter 10, Our Lady of Guadalupe, derived from the vision of an Indian in 1531, became the patroness of Mexico and the badge of the Independents in the Mexican revolution. And, as we saw earlier, her image has helped to integrate ethnic communities.

Such influences are likely to be two-way, the religion enhancing social integration and social integration augmenting the influence of religion. Indeed Guerin has argued that anxieties about death, control, and so on are 'utilised or created by groups' (1998: 53) in order to induce individuals to engage in religious practices so that the benefits of forming cooperative and reciprocating groups becomes possible. The word 'created' here seems too strong: we have to do with diachronic dialectical influences between the individual and the socio-cultural structure.

An association between religion and group cohesion is seen especially in immigrant groups. Migrants inevitably lose many aspects of their social identity, but are united to their co-national immigrants by language and religion. The common religion tends then to be fiercely maintained and provides a powerful integrating force, enabling individuals to come to terms with social change (e.g. Bruce, 1996). Of special interest here is the role that religion has played in maintaining the integrity of the Jews in the absence of a common homeland. Male circumcision is a public declaration that the boy has been entered into the Covenant and can become a full member of Jewish society. Where Jewish communities have retained their integrity, knowledge of the Law and daily routines, with public and private ritual, reaffirms their group identity. The dietary prohibitions serve as a constant reminder of their distinctiveness. Such rules, and the laws of endogamy, tend to minimise social intercourse with gentiles. Conversely, dilution of the community tends to be associated with a decrease in religiosity.

Another important issue here is the sense of identity with ancestors or, to a lesser extent, descendants. In Judaism this mainly takes the form of a transference of pain across time. Jews remember and identify with the sufferings experienced in Egypt. Even among the non-orthodox and the secularised, celebration of the Passover serves as a reminder of Jewish identity (see p. 128) (Fredman, 1981). In Christianity it is more a transference of blessing across time: the presence of Christ on earth two thousand years ago is taken as an indication of his presence today.

While some religious ritual practices are isolated from the everyday world, religious groupings can exert an important influence on the secular world through philanthropy or other forms of social action. Though this is becoming less evident in the modern world within states, many of the most active relief agencies have a religious basis.

In many societies secular rituals and other public occasions often have a religious component, and social transitions (e.g., marriage) may be authenticated by religious ritual. Religious ritual may be taken over for secular purposes. Thus civil ceremonies in the secular Soviet state had many similarities with the religious ones which preceded them (Lane, 1981), and Shinto has been used for ceremonial purposes in Japan (Smart, 1996).

Influences between religious and social systems are not all one-way, for secular considerations may affect the religious system. Thus the Chinese Zhou emperors saw their authority as derived from Heaven, and called themselves Sons of Heaven. However, when the Zhou empire broke up, independent rulers seized power in separate states, arrogating to themselves the titles and functions of kings. But, having acquired their status by force of arms, they could not claim the power of heaven and so worshipped lesser gods with more circumscribed powers. Centuries later, when the states were again unified, the worship of Heaven returned (Loewe, 1994).

### Religious and secular power

Religious rituals and images have often been used to authenticate secular power. Thus the Pope's proclamation of Mary as the queen of Heaven not only expressed her triumph, through her virginity and Assumption, over evil, and emphasised her ability to intercede with Christ, but at the same time her association with the allegorical figure of the Church made her regal authority an assertion of the Church's power. Over the centuries images of the Virgin have been believed to deter enemies and to bring victories on numerous occasions (Warner, 1976).

Religion may also be important in the internal dynamics of nation-states. For instance, religious ritual can result in stabilisation of the system of authority. The Babylonian ritual of *akitu* originated as a harvest festival, but came to emphasise not only the supremacy of Marduk over other gods, but also the distinctions between classes in the city and the king's position with respect to the more privileged citizens: in the latter case it both legitimised the rule and indicated the limits of his power (Kuhrt, 1987). In the Chinese Tang dynasty, the court ritual, inherited from antiquity, was justified on both cosmological grounds, the ritual being an integral component of the universe, and on social grounds, the ritual imposing restraint on the social hierarchy and the unruly appetites of man. The rite could be adjusted to support the current dynasty, enabling the emperor to affirm the benevolence of the cosmic order and his place in it. The scholars made changes in the ritual because they stood to gain by pleasing the emperor (McMullen, 1987).

Religion can also contribute to national identity. The states of western Europe have nearly all had their own national saints (Soboul, 1983). God has been seen as an ally by both sides in the two world wars. In a recent survey of the ethnographic and political histories of Poland and Turkey, Hann (1997) focused on the relations between religion and nationalism. In

Poland the Roman Catholic Church, in alliance with the Solidarity political movement, played a prominent part in the revival and maintenance of nationalism during the Cold War era. After the end of that period, it extended its influence into practically every aspect of the citizens' lives (thereby arousing the resentment of some). In Turkey, Islam, operating behind a facade of secularism, never lost its hold on the majority of the population, and has produced a generation of Islamic intellectuals. In both countries the religion, together with other factors such as opposition to an alien power, and a common language, has made a significant contribution to national identity and has come to have a complex relation with state power.

Religion can play a key role in the long-term stabilisation of the social/religious structure, 'right-thinking' providing a degree of power. An interesting example is provided by the cyclic relation between High and Folk Islam, as described by Gellner (1992). The former referred to the religion of the scholars, the latter to that of the people. The boundary roughly corresponded to the territory governed from the centre and that of self-administering tribes. The theology of High Islam provided the town dwellers, and to some extent the whole population, with its charter and constitution, which could be used in protests against undue taxation and other excesses by the state. However, the saint cults (the saints often being living individuals) and mystical exercises of Low Islam provided better consolation for deprivation than did scholastic theology, though the more privileged urban dwellers looked down on its hysteria, dancing, snake-charming and saint cults. The rural Muslims were seen as inadequate Muslims by the scholars, but their reverence for local saints supposedly linked to the Prophet by genealogy, and to urban religion through supposed scholarship by the saint's ancestors, allowed them to identify with the central tradition. The danger for the central authorities came when a respected scholar allied with the aggressive peripheral tribes. The preacher could rebuke the tribes for their lax observance of the traditions of Islam, and unite them in his support in cleaning up the corruption in the city by action likely to bring them booty. While not all such movements were successful, from time to time a purified order was thereby established, until such time as the former situation re-asserted itself.

### Divisiveness

Religious differences have also been the source of or justification for much conflict and suffering within societies. In some cases, they are central: thus both Arabs and Jews believe they have a religious claim to Jerusalem (e.g. Firestone, 1996). When communities of differing religion are in conflict over such an issue, religious loyalties become central to the self-systems of those involved. Each community is integrated the more strongly by the perception of the common beliefs, and the other community is seen as more alien, with actions against it justified. More often, religious differences reflect sectarian issues. Thus the conflict in Northern Ireland has roots in both economic (Murray, 1995) and religious (Bruce, 1996) issues. The latter have been exacerbated by the Catholic nature of the South, which the Protestants in the North have seen as an absolute impediment to the union with the South desired by the Catholics. Although religious faith may be unimportant to many individuals on both sides, the two communities are defined by their religions. In general, religious differences are unlikely to be a cause of conflict unless they have negative effects on one of the parties concerned: more usually they are used to justify conflict concerned with more material issues.

Problems may also arise if the authorities of a central religion see their positions threatened by local religions or cults. Christian communities have sometimes seen their relationship with the divine through their saints to be more direct than that mediated by the priests, and this has led to resentment on both sides (Sanchis, 1983), the ecclesiastical authorities sometimes trying to suppress local saints (Wilson, 1983a and b). The role of the Spanish Inquisition needs no comment. However, it must be emphasised that the extent to which religious differences are liable to give rise to conflict differs markedly between religions. The Hindu Gita implied that faith in any god is faith in the true God, and Hinduism has nearly always been tolerant of a diversity of beliefs and practices. Christians, however, have at times been encouraged to fight non-believers, and for Muslims it has been a duty. In the tenth and eleventh centuries Islam was more tolerant of Jews and Zoroastrians than they were of Hindus, who were regarded as idol worshippers.

## Summary

Individuals incorporate their personal and social relationships into their self-concepts, and their behaviour to in-group members differs from that to out-group members.

Socialisation is critical in the acquisition of a religious system. Counter-intuitive beliefs depend in large measure on consensual validation. Involvement in the religious system may bring a sense of community.

Within any society, there is a continuing dialectic between the accepted system of beliefs, values and religion and the behaviour of individuals. The religious system may affect and be affected by society. It has facilitated integration within societies, it has been used to authenticate the power of rulers, and it has had a divisive influence.

# 17 Persistence

The preceding chapters have focused on particular aspects of religious systems, the primary aim being to show how each could be understood in terms of basic human propensities. Here we summarise some of those issues in an attempt to find an explanation for the persistence of religious systems in the face of evidence contrary to a literal interpretation of the beliefs. The term 'persistence' is used here in an overall descriptive sense, but it will be apparent from the preceding chapters that, when one starts to look at the processes involved, 'persistence' can be a misleading term. We have to do with a continuing dialectic between individuals and their social environments, constrained by pan-cultural human propensities in such a way that religious systems have been reconstructed more or less the same in the minds of successive generations. The persistence of moral systems has already been addressed in Chapters 12 to 14, and the persistence of religious experience follows from the relation between its interpretation and the belief system, and from its intrinsically rewarding character. The focus here will be on why beliefs and rituals persist.

## The adaptedness of tradition

Perhaps the first thing to be said is that it has nearly always been a good plan to follow in the steps of the preceding generation. Indeed, we may well be adapted to do so: after all, they did sufficiently well to reproduce, otherwise we should not be here. The religious practices which have served a community in the past may therefore reasonably be expected to do so in the future. However, as we have seen, there have been, and will always be, discordant voices. Not all religions place great emphasis on dogma, but for those that do, academic research has provided plenty of material for dissidents. The problem is why religion persists when the truth-value of its dogma has been undermined, when its rituals are abandoned by many, when its moral precepts are frequently disregarded.

## Stability and change in belief systems

At first sight, religious systems provide beliefs that are clear-cut and static. Yet in practice change can and does occur. Dramatic change may accompany socio-political change, as in the formative days of the Soviet Union. Or change may be stimulated by the gradual recognition that another system brings better rewards, secular or spiritual, as in colonisation. Firth (1996) has described how the traditional religion of the Tikopia, in which the chiefs were the intermediaries between the gods and the people, as well as the ultimate source of economic and political authority, has been replaced by Christianity, which now provides the validation for the supposed mystic powers of the chiefs. As a result of this change, the traditional gods were regarded as becoming quiescent, though not as ceasing to exist. Or yet again, the emphasis in existing beliefs may be manipulated by those in power, or shifted as a consequence of demand from the laity, as has been the case with the Virgin Mary (see pp. 79–80).

Another source of change lies in the relations between religion and the social system. As noted in Chapter 1, in western countries religion is now losing many of the secular functions that were formerly allied with it. While it is still the case that many charitable enterprises have a religious affiliation or basis, the greater involvement of the state in welfare, education, and health has removed some of the activities that maintained religion as central in people's lives. In addition the break-up of small-scale communities, and the diversification of religious systems, has inevitably reduced the impact that any one religious system can have.

But in any case, people form their own views of life and the world, and though these may be shaped by the religious system, they may also induce change in it. Codification may provide a conservative force, but it also provides a concrete system against which the individual can contrast his or her own views, so that it can also provide a stimulus for change.

And there are always countering forces that emphasise the implausibility of the deities that have been postulated. Most obvious is the growth of science: natural events formerly explained by divine action are now understood, or at least given a generally acceptable scientific explanation. Important also are the contradictions inherent in most systems of religious belief. How can a benevolent creator have permitted a world with so much suffering and evil? How can a religious system, carrying its own moral code, apparently condone the slaughter, cruelty and exploitation portrayed in, for instance, the Old Testament? How can religions which value brotherly love have been so antagonistic to each other? How can there be so many diverse and incompatible systems of religious beliefs, with the adherents of each believing their own to be the Truth? If this religious system represents the only Truth, how can it be that adherents of other systems sometimes behave in such an exemplary fashion?

Of course all these questions have answers, satisfying to the adherents of each system, even when to the outsider the answers seem contrived and circular. The point being made is that religious systems are best seen as processes, subject to opposing forces for stasis and for change. What, we must therefore ask, are the forces that promote the maintenance of the systems? We shall see that it is important to distinguish between the persistence of the system, and the maintenance of religious adherence in individuals.

## Relative vulnerability of religious systems and organisations

Are religious systems more likely to persist if they are authoritarian and dogmatic, or flexible and liberal? Christianity has taken both courses, responding to the growth of science in two ways. For some it has become more categorical, insisting more rigidly on its basic beliefs: for others it has adapted, relinquishing some of its beliefs and re-interpreting others. Both courses have been taken within post-Reformation Christianity. Thus while fundamentalists may affirm that the Bible is divinely inspired and is to be interpreted literally, more liberal theologians see it as offering moral precepts and wisdom, prepared and selected by humans to suit the needs of their time, but providing a view of a transcendental order.

It is thus of interest to consider the persistence of different organisations within Christianity. We may distinguish between four types of religious organisation: churches (e.g. the Roman Catholic Church, the Protestant Church), denominations (e.g. Methodists), sects (groups usually seceding from a church and making considerable demands on their members), and cults (small, loosely knit groups with common interests but usually without a sharply defined belief system). Wallis (1976) has suggested that these can be seen as differing along two dimensions. First, is the institution seen as respectable or deviant? In general, churches and denominations are seen as respectable, cults and sects as deviant. Second, does it consider that it is the sole bearer of the Truth, or does it recognise the legitimacy of others? Churches and sects tend to see themselves in the former category, denominations and cults in the latter. Of course there are problems in any classificatory system: for instance, Mormons are seen by many as deviant, but see themselves as the Church of Jesus Christ of Latter-Day Saints; the Church of England did qualify as a church, but is now best seen as a denomination; and sects may become denominations if they survive.

These distinctions are related to differences in the factors which lead to persistence. Bruce (1996) argues that churches which insist on the unique veracity of their own view tend, in the modern world, to become less demanding denominations or to fragment – though, perhaps for the reasons discussed below, the Roman Catholic Church is an exception here. The rigidity of sects similarly makes them demanding on their members and liable to come into conflict with the longer established belief systems in the society. While most church members are simply born into the society, to join a sect requires new beliefs and loyalties. Furthermore, in that sects usually differ markedly from mainstream religions, they have difficulty in recruiting new members. However, sects can prosper in a society tolerant of sub-cultures, like the USA. Denominations and cults are vulnerable in a different way – namely because their beliefs and practices are not sufficiently distinct from those of other organisations, their members may drift elsewhere, or initially distinct denominations may unite, as with the Congregationalists and Presbyterians. Though cults have proliferated in recent decades, they lack not only distinctiveness but also the respectability and stability provided by an historical tradition: they therefore tend to have difficulty in main-taining the commitment of their members, who are selective in what they accept.

Within this scheme Bruce (1996), refining an earlier suggestion by Kelley (1972), has summarised data showing that memberships of the more liberal Protestant denominations have declined in numbers in recent years much more than have the more conservative ones. Since the nineteenth century the Anglican Church has emphasised intellectual subtlety and flexibility in training clergy, and Anglican theologians (unlike most of their Catholic counterparts) have been open about religious problems and uncertainties. During this period the Church of England and the principal nonconformist churches have declined, while the evangelical and charismatic groups have grown in strength. The declining congregations of the former may indicate that they have been victims of their own honesty: perhaps most people prefer cut and dried instructions about what to believe, and are alienated by uncertainty and open debate.

The Roman Catholic Church's relative stability has been achieved in another way. It has claimed to have unique access to the ultimate truth, any deviation being heretical, because the Apostles as a group, or Saint Peter in particular, supposedly inherited Christ's authority, which has then been passed on to successive incumbents of the office of Pope. The Church thus has the authority to settle all theological disputes and to regulate behaviour. As we have seen (Chapter 6), its decisions may be such as to accommodate popular demand, but the guiding hand of authority is always present to ensure the continuation of the system. Thereby it can make limited conces-sions to its congregations, but yet maintain its own integrity. The Mormon Church similarly claims unique legitimacy. But the success of some of the eastern religions, with their tolerance of considerable flexibility in belief and practice, shows that the maintenance of dogma is not a *sine qua non* for the persistence of a religious system: while the greater importance of extended families and of kinship networks may be important here, it seems that the structural beliefs and narratives, though often seen as central in Christianity, are not essential for the persistence of a religious system.

Another major factor favouring the more conservative churches lies in their ability to recruit children, who grow up in their parents' faith. The gradual acquisition of the religious system, and the slow realisation of its significance, may contribute in an important way to its maintenance. By contrast, the enthusiasm of liberals for embracing diversity leads to less control over the religious adherence of their children, and to low motivation to proselytise and recruit. Furthermore the more liberal groups often have difficulty in uniting around a common plan of action, and lose members to narrower organisations with more clearly defined goals (Bruce, 1996; see also Stark and Bainbridge, 1985).

Yet another issue may be the demands made by the religious system. In the 1960s and 1970s those communes that were more demanding on their members were more successful in keeping them. If the more conservative denominations are more demanding, and that seems to be the case, that may contribute to their stability. At least two mechanisms may be involved. One is the irrational feeling that if one has put effort into a project, one does not wish to see that effort wasted by abandoning it: having taken the risk of declaring one's faith, one does not want to go back on it. Another is that the perception that if others are incurring costs on behalf of the religious system, this must indicate their commitment to it, and thus its stability and value.

These are, of course, all generalisations to which exceptions can be found, but they are applicable sufficiently widely to indicate clear relations between the organisational aspect of a religious system and processes affecting its persistence. While it is at first sight surprising that the more liberal organisations should be more vulnerable than those who insist on narrowly formulated beliefs and practices, it is in harmony with the view that people need the security which a feeling of self-efficacy can bring (p. 56), and that this is fostered by unquestionable belief.

## Flexibility and the persistence of individual belief

The factors influencing the persistence of religious systems are not necessarily the same as those making for the persistence of belief by individuals, and it is to the latter that we now turn. While we have seen that flexibility in Christian religious systems seems to be associated with vulnerability, this is not the case with the eastern religions, and flexibility can be conducive to the maintenance of belief by individuals. Not only can the beliefs or their interpretation change over time, but individuals can make their own interpretations according to their needs. Thus many Christians now hold that the narratives in the Bible were never really intended as truth, but are myths used to convey a lesson, the descriptions being stories, perhaps based in fact, but embellished in the course of verbal repetition. On this view God is not literally as depicted in the narratives, and we must search behind them for the reality, treating them as attempts to portray the inexpressible. The material world, the world of science, is seen as only part of reality: science cannot know the 'real' transcendental world, indeed no one can more than partially understand it, but one day all will be revealed. On this view, both science and scriptures provide merely a temporary and partial understanding. Clearly, there is a contradiction between the desire for certainty, and the facilitation of persistence of belief associated with the idea of 'partial revelation'. Perhaps certainty is more effective in the maintenance of religious *systems*, while in the rapidly changing modern world flexibility, even if less satisfying, facilitates the maintenance of *individual belief*.

There is also the question of relative 'truth': how can there be so many religious systems, each maintaining its own 'truth'? Here again, a liberal approach can help with the recognition that there is a sacred power, common to all religions, each religion acknowledging that power in its own way. Yet others see their religion as a personal matter, between the worshipper and the deity: just as an individual's relationships with different others have differing properties, so also do God's relationships with diverse others inevitably differ.

Another sort of liberalism puts the emphasis on the consequences of religion. It does not matter all that much what you believe, so long as it makes you feel better or the beliefs have beneficial consequences for society. The distinction between good and bad religion lies not in whether you subscribe to the 'truth', but in whether the system to which you subscribe makes you feel good and behave well. That raises the question of the consequences of religious involvement, to which we shall return shortly.

## Coping with problems

In considering the improbability of religious beliefs, we have seen that, outside the religious sphere, we use fantastical thinking which is not aimed towards literal truth. We use pretence, we day-dream, we read novels and enjoy paintings, literature and drama which do not portray the world exactly as it is, and on the whole we do not misinterpret them (Harris, 1997; Johnson, 1997). This, of course, does not deny that fantastical thinking can be dangerous.

We may also note that deeply held beliefs are hard to relinquish, and contrary evidence may cause them to be held even more firmly. This is the more likely to occur the more strongly the belief is held, the more public the believer's commitment, and the more support received from fellow believers (Festinger *et al.*, 1956).

With these points in mind, let us take an outsider's view of how believers deal with problems which seem insuperable to a rationalist, by bringing them into line with their belief system.

The problem of evil, recognised by Christians as the most potent single difficulty, is met by believers in a variety of ways. Perhaps God has limited His own powers in order to give humans scope to exercise the free will they see themselves as having. Perhaps calamities are due to human lapses. Perhaps the evil is really good, sent to put us on our mettle. Perhaps our imperfection prevents the execution of God's plan for the world. Perhaps we just do not understand.

In addition, knowledge of the deity can be seen as accumulating gradually over the centuries, and thus as inevitably incomplete at any one time. The praise bestowed on some of the more unpleasant acts perpetrated by the Israelites according to the Old Testament can then be ascribed to their relatively unsophisticated ideas and to their worship of a tribal god with great potential for anger: the concept of the deity has now changed to a loving God who can bestow beneficence on all humanity. With the growth of science, He has become a transcendent Being who pervades the universe but has limited His powers for His own purposes, permitting evolution rather than one-off creation. All attacks on doctrine, and also the diversity of creeds, are explained on the view that what is now believed can be at most a partial revelation. Christianity sees itself as a later and more complete revelation than Judaism, and Islam sees itself as more complete than either.

The ultimate incomprehensibility of final truths can then be given as evidence for the importance of faith. Perhaps all faiths can be seen as gropings after Truth which no religious system (or only one) comes near to grasping. And the good deeds of those who worship gods other than one's own can be ascribed to God's willingness to accept whatever furthers his purpose. Comparable views are shared by some scientists. For instance Campbell (1991: 93) argues that since many scientists,

> no longer believe in what they suppose to be the literal referents of religious words, they lose sight of the possibility of great truths for which there is no literal language, which must be metaphorically or figuratively expressed if to be communicated at all.

However, this seems to be a straw man, since lack of belief in literal referents is surely compatible with belief in truths expressed metaphorically (see also Richardson and Wildman, 1997).[1]

Such arguments are often coupled with an emphasis on the 'mystery of holiness'. This serves a dual function: it not only 'explains' our inability to understand the contradictions within the belief system, but also has an attractive quality. As we have seen (p. 188), there is evidence of a quite different sort that 'mystery' has an evocative quality, calling on human needs to understand and explore. In an extensive series of experiments comparing the attractiveness of paintings, 'mystery', the promise of more information if one could enter further into the scene, was the strongest predictor of preference (Kaplan, 1992). The properties of the deity are just such as to preserve mystery and tantalise inquiry. And since God is presented as unknowable, incomprehensible, any proposition can be self-validating. Since He is omnipotent and omniscient, yet man has free will and is subject to error, inconsistencies in religious systems are acceptable. Of course, it is argued, you cannot prove His existence, and anyway there would be no virtue in faith if you could, but that does not mean that He does not exist: His existence can never be disproved.[2]

In subtle ways, the moral teaching of the church may also reinforce its influence. For instance, 'if desire, as natural as breath or sleep itself, is sinful, then the Christian, like a man in the grip of a usurer, must always run back to the Church, the only source of that grace which can give him reprieve' (Warner, 1976: 51).

The believer's arguments also often contain an element of circularity, of the type 'The priest says it is God's will, and that must be so because the priest is guided by God'. The view that religious specialists pass on truths which come from a higher authority not only provides an unassailable base for their pronouncements and practices, but also gives them considerable power. 'God will only answer your prayers if you have faith' – and if you cannot be absolutely certain, it is only your fault if He does not answer. An even more effective procedure is to leave the background conditions necessary for a proper request undefined, so that when ritual directed to a particular end does not work, a scapegoat can always be found (p. 113).

Such arguments are, of course, irrefutable, but they are also unconfirmable, and unsatisfying to the modern mind both because there is nothing that cannot be explained along these lines and because they are incompatible with the current *Weltanschauung*. They can, however, be seen as products of the human mind attempting to maintain congruence in the self-system (see pp. 26–32): humans can not only invent gods in their own image, they can protect their creations from practically every form of contradictory evidence.

In partial summary of these issues, it will be apparent that defence mechanisms, identical with those used to protect secular aspects of the self-system (see pp. 30–1), are used to protect religious beliefs in a number of ways:

1  Cognitive restructuring. In the everyday world one can deal with evidence that contradicts one's beliefs or expectations in a number of ways. One can misperceive one's own or the other's behaviour or the situation, attend selectively to confirmatory evidence, interpret evidence as though it were confirmatory, or discredit new information that seems to diminish congruency. In the case of the maintenance of religious beliefs, selective attention, selective interpretation, and discrediting contradictory information are particularly conspicuous. Individuals attend to reports that confirm their beliefs, interpret the stoicism of martyrs as proof of Christianity, interpret chance events as 'God's will', and disregard (or re-interpret) the evidence from human suffering that God is not benevolent.

2  Selective evaluation. Individuals see congruent events as more important than incongruent ones. For a believer the occasional report of a miraculous cure can never be out-weighed by reports of innumerable failed ones.

3   Selective interaction. Individuals are attracted to others who provide congruency, preferring to make friends with others who see them as they see themselves. In the same way believers prefer to associate with those who share their beliefs.

4   Response evocation. Individuals present themselves in a way that elicits a response from others that will confirm their self-image. We have seen that this is the case with individuals high on intrinsic religiosity, but may also play a part in the maintenance of beliefs: individuals behave as though their beliefs were true and thereby see their beliefs as confirmed by their own behaviour and by the acceptance by others of that behaviour. The believer's religion is so central to his self-system that it is more than impolite to question his beliefs.

The maintenance of individual belief is fostered also by the diversity of forms taken by belief. Only for a minority of individuals does it permeate every aspect of the self-system: for most people religious beliefs are incorporated into only part of the self-system, or into only one of a number of selves. The religious self can be brought out when it serves the occasion, when the needs that it serves become pressing. But at other times, when other rewards beckon or the inadequacies of beliefs become salient, it can be quietly put away.

Thus the religious believer protects his or her belief system as part of the integrity of the self. To relinquish cherished beliefs inevitably involves decreased self-esteem and a decreased sense of self-efficacy. Of course scientists protect their own theories in the same way, but the necessity for peer acceptance of scientific conclusions makes it a less viable strategy.

## Social forces

There are also powerful social forces conducive to the maintenance of both religious systems and individual belief. For one thing, every society contains individuals who have strong reasons for maintaining the belief system. In the past British monarchs would have lost their divine right if the belief system had collapsed. Political leaders may exploit religion for their own ends: for instance patriotic sacrifice in war has been justified by comparing it with Christ's sacrifice on the Cross (Sykes, 1991). Religious leaders have often had considerable secular power, and it has therefore been in their interests to maintain the system. The parish priest acquires a certain charisma by virtue of his office, so it is in his interest to maintain belief by the promise of rewards in Heaven, or by insistence that there is positive value in faith – though of course he may not be consciously motivated in that way.

The priest's ability to transmit his message is facilitated by his authority: individuals are more prone to accept statements or commands from individuals whom they presume to be of high status – especially if the situation provides a 'truth-frame', as does a church or other house of worship. Many of the Christian saints came from the more privileged sections of society: though they may have achieved their status by rejecting worldly things, their origins may have added to their authority. Ample experimental evidence shows that people are very ready to accept authority, even when they are ordered to do things that they would otherwise see as unacceptable (Milgram, 1974).

Furthermore, religious occasions serve to maintain both the system as a whole and the involvement of individuals. This is perhaps especially the case with religious festivals, which can combine secular enjoyment with worship. Festivals celebrated in the name of a saint can maintain the honour of his or her name and the renown of his or her shrine, as well as providing spiritual comfort and secular enjoyment to the laity (Hertz, 1983). The use of relics and artefacts helps to perpetuate the beliefs and the system. And it is not only grand public occasions that contribute to maintenance: in the long run such occasions as domestic family prayers may have an even greater effect.

Finally, the strong social psychological influences on the maintenance of belief by individuals must be mentioned. A feeling of social isolation is aversive, so to feel part of a group is its own reward, and to feel part of a group whose members think as you do is even better. At least one study has shown that members of a church tend to have more extensive social networks than comparable individuals not affiliated to a church (Kennell, cited Pargament, 1997). This social aspect of religion appeals especially to the lonely and the underprivileged.

## Religious beliefs and individual well-being

### *Basic propensities*

While the argument that the continuation of the Christian Church for so long implies that its beliefs are true and validly interpreted cannot be upheld, its persistence does suggest that it has depended on basic aspects of the human psyche. The case for this was argued in Chapter 5: individuals hold religious beliefs in part because they have certain psychological propensities – in particular a need to attribute events to causes, a need to feel that one understands the world and has some measure of control over events, a need to share experience in personal relationships, and a need to feel that there is continuity after death. It is comforting to believe in a powerful entity who is on one's side, and who will intervene if appealed to. Even adverse events are more bearable if they can be attributed to a specific causal agent. If such an entity is personified, becoming someone whom one can blame or worship, in whom one can confide, with whom one can discuss the day's events, whose affection one can feel, he or she becomes even more appealing.

It was further suggested that such propensities are pan-cultural, found (though with differing strengths) in virtually all individuals, and thus likely to have been due to the action of natural selection. On this view, natural selection has acted not merely to enhance (for instance) understanding of the world, but also to enhance monitoring of that understanding. Individuals need to *feel* that they understand, and it is the perception of inability to understand that leads to distress, and distress then leads to further efforts to understand. Belief in a deity brings perception that one can understand. The same principle applies to the other needs satisfied by religious belief: perception of one's inability to control one's life, perception that one is friendless, lack of certainty about mortality, lead to distress.

Perhaps such issues can be encapsulated in the proposition that religious systems provide 'peace of mind', a coherent view of the world, giving a semblance of order to a wide range of human experiences which might otherwise appear chaotic. This, of course, is a difficult issue to document, but seems to be true for many religious people. A coherent view of the world implies that an individual sees himself and his relationships according to his circumstances without major discrepancies – in other words, he has an integrated self-system. We shall return to this tentative suggestion later.

## Does religious adherence make people feel better?

It is often claimed that religiousness has beneficial consequences in ways additional to those that have already been mentioned. Religious individuals certainly believe that their faith brings happiness, and better health. And intercessory prayers to avert disasters, to mitigate stress, or for successful outcomes would scarcely be offered unless they had some positive outcomes, though those might be solely subjective. The evidence that religiosity has beneficial consequences comes mostly from studies comparing aspects of religiosity with aspects of well-being, and has recently been summarised by Hood *et al.*, (1996), Pargament (1997), and Beit-Hallahmi and Argyle (1997). There are, however, a number of difficulties in its interpretation and it is as well to consider them first. We can then turn to some representative studies, before considering the means by which religion could produce effects on health and well-being.

### *Methodological problems*

First, problems inevitably arise from the diverse nature of religiousness, for individuals may believe and not practice or practice and not believe, and from the diversity of religious beliefs and denominations. It is thus highly desirable that studies should specify precisely the nature of the religiosity and the population studied. For instance a meta-analysis, that is an analysis of the studies previously reported, indicated that internal religiosity was much more likely to be associated with good rather than bad mental health, but external religiosity showed an even greater tendency to be associated with bad mental health, and for quest the data were indeterminate (Batson *et al.*, 1993). Again, while the relations between religiosity and mental health tend to be positive, institutional faith can contain the seeds of psychopathology if misinterpreted or misapplied (e.g. Hood *et al.*, 1996).

In any case, 'being religious' does not have the same meaning for different individuals. Within any one society religious observance may be related to diverse factors including personal characteristics, life experiences, and social influences. As a result, the satisfactions it brings are not the same from one individual to another. For example, one study (using a factor analysis of Q-sort items) found that members of a theologically conservative church tended to fall into one of three categories – authority-seekers, comfort-seekers, and social participants (Monaghan, 1967). Another identified seven types – humble servants of God, self-improvers, family guidance seekers, moralists, God-seekers, socially-oriented servants of God, and 'religious egg-heads' (Gorlow and Schroeder, 1968).

Second, religiousness has been measured in a number of ways including the assessment of specific issues, such as church membership, church attendance, the saying of private prayers, and religious experiences; questionnaires assessing attitudes to religion; and multi-dimensional questionnaires concerning a number of aspects of religiousness. Some of the latter have exploited psychological techniques validated in other contexts. Most involve some form of questionnaire, and although the methods now available for enhancing the validity of questionnaires are sophisticated, problems still arise in their construction, administration, and interpretation (see Brown, 1987, for a critical review).

One issue is of special significance in the present context. While it is possible to guard against dissimulation in responses to a questionnaire, it is less easy to detect self-deception. Defence mechanisms operate, and some individuals see the world through rosy spectacles, whereas others do the opposite. To take an example from another field, it is possible, using an observational technique in the laboratory, to divide children into four groups on the basis of their mother/child relationships. Mothers of 'avoidantly attached' children appeared in a significantly better light than other mothers on self-report dimensions, but *not* when their interactions were recorded by an impartial observer. Mothers of such children tend to have a 'Dismissive/idealising' style when interviewed about their recollections of their own childhood (Stevenson-Hinde and Shouldice, 1995). There is a possible parallel here with studies of the beneficial effects of religiosity, many of which have also been based on self-reports. The beneficial correlates are found especially in individuals high on intrinsic religiosity, but we have seen that the self-reports of those high on intrinsic religiosity do not correlate well with the way that they behave (pp. 40–2): there is thus a possibility that there is something in common between intrinsic religiosity and the idealising style reported in studies of mother/child relationships.

Third, religious involvement may be associated positively with some aspects of well-being, and negatively with others. In their survey of the literature, Batson and Ventis (1982) found that absence of mental illness and neurotic symptoms was positively correlated with measures of religious involvement, but personal competence and self-control, self-acceptance and self-actualisation, open-mindedness and flexibility were negatively correlated. While the positive effect with mental health could be interpreted as an effect of religion on mental health, the negative correlations may suggest that people low on self-acceptance, personal competence, and so on, understandably seek religion because it fulfils some of their needs. But the nature of the religious involvement is also an issue: as we have seen, extrinsic religiosity tends to be negatively related to mental health, intrinsic positively.

More recently, Gartner (1996) found that religiosity correlated positively with beneficial differences in physical health, mortality, suicide, drug use, alcohol abuse, delinquency and criminality, divorce and marital satisfaction, well-being, and depression, but negatively with authoritarianism, dogmatism, suggestibility and dependence. The relations between religious involvement and anxiety, psychosis, self-esteem, sexual disorders, intelligence, and prejudice were ambiguous, with some studies showing positive and some negative correlations.[3]

Fourth, most of the detailed data come from western societies, and thus their generality is in question. Consider, for instance, Marx's view that religion provides a fantasy world, with hope of later rewards, for the oppressed in societies in which individuals are alienated from the products of their labours. This might be applicable to many individuals in the industrialised world, but much less so in pre-literate societies.

Fifth, there are issues concerning the nature of the relation between religious observance and its supposed outcome. Some problems here are statistical in nature: most of the data are correlational, so one cannot tell, for instance whether well-being is conducive to religiousness or religiousness is conducive to well-being. Thus Idler (1995) points out that in longer epidemiological studies religion seems to have a protective effect on health, but cross-sectional studies often show higher levels of religiousness to be associated with poorer health, because people in crisis turn to religion for support.

Furthermore, absence of a significant correlation may conceal a curvilinear relation, high and low but not intermediate religiousness being associated with well-being. For example, one study found that both people with strong religious beliefs and those with no religion tended to have low scores on a measure of psychological distress. The highest distress levels were found among those who had not made a religious commitment, belonging to a religion not out of choice but out of indifference: the author describes them as 'self-estranged'. The low distress levels of those who rejected all religious belief was ascribed to commitments to other, non-religious, beliefs (Ross 1990). Such data strongly suggest that low distress is associated with coherence in the self-system (see below).

Finally, where the statistical relation seems straightforward, the nature of the psychological mechanism may be far from clear. In a study of students at the University of Western Ontario, those having an affiliation with a religious group on campus were found to have better health and to handle stress better (Frankel and Hewitt, 1994). The authors cited four theoretical mechanisms that could be involved, namely (1) Religiousness might be associated with constraints on high-risk behaviour, drinking and smoking. (Other studies showing a relation between religiousness and health indicate that the relation is due to an association between religiousness and inhibitions on risk-taking and impulsiveness in a variety of spheres. Religious people tend to consume less alcohol and to smoke less); (2) Religious involvement may increase the availability of social support from fellow church members; (3) It may be associated with a greater ability to make sense of and cope with experiences; and (4) Religion may be associated with an ability to accept that suffering exists and thus to cope with it. The authors felt that their data indicated the importance of social support and possibly of a belief in a just God which helped them to experience less stress than those without such belief.

### Some empirical studies

Given such problems, it is not surprising that some studies show a positive relation between religion and health or well-being, some show a negative relation, and others are indeterminate. Comprehensive summaries of studies on the relations between religiosity and stressful life events have been given elsewhere (see above); Pargament (1997) emphasises that the effects are often small and depend on the type of religiosity, the individual and the situation. Here we consider a few representative studies.

We have already seen that religion may help people to cope with their mortality (Chapter 5). A number of studies have provided evidence for a relation between religiousness and better health. For instance, priests tend to live longer and to have better health than most lay people, and relations have been found between religiosity and the incidence of many diseases, including cancer, heart disease, and stroke (Levin, 1994). Other studies indicate that conversion experiences can reduce symptoms of illness (e.g. Bergin, 1983; Wills, 1984). The effects appear to depend on active participation in religion rather than passive allegiance (Hannay, 1980).[4]

Another study, involving a cross-sectional study of all English-speaking, non-institutionalised adults in the USA, confirmed that high levels of religious practice, involving prayer and active participation in religion, were associated with better health. However, of the measures of religiousness used, only those related to religious practice were positively related to health: feeling close to God, or the nature of the beliefs held, were not. Furthermore, those with a conservative religious affiliation showed poorer health than those with a more liberal one. The authors of this careful study suggest several explanations for the latter finding: the conservatives might have been more fatalistic, have resisted medical intervention, and understood medical instructions less well, but have been more likely to over-eat and be sedentary. In addition, indirect effects of social class may not have been identified (Ferraro and Albrecht-Jensen, 1991).

A study of students at Protestant colleges, which attempted to come to terms with the psychological mechanisms involved in the relations between religiousness and psychological adjustment, used scales to assess religious motivation, religious beliefs, and religious problem-solving style: the last involved three dimensions (collaborative, deferring, and self-directing) and the person's relationship with God, and was seen as intervening between the first two and psychological adjustment. All three were found to be associated with adjustment. In addition, while those who believed in a benevolent, guiding, stable and powerful God tended to show little anxiety, belief in a wrathful God was not related to anxiety level. The authors suggest that anxiety is related to belief in an unpredictable God (Schaefer and Gorsuch, 1991).

One study indicating that intrinsic religiosity was associated with mental health was cited above. Another, using scales to assess depression and self-esteem, found that intrinsic religiousness was associated with greater 'psycho-spiritual health', but individuals high on quest reported personal distress and low spiritual well-being (Genia, 1996). But, as emphasised already, such associations are difficult to interpret because, while religion may have beneficial consequences, those who need it may be the ones who go for it.

Religion often seems to help individuals to cope with severe handicaps or traumatic life events. Paraplegics may refer their handicap to God's will; trauma victims have been found to turn first to the clergy for help; and a number of studies have shown that religion can ameliorate distress in cancer patients, in bereavement, and so on (cited Thompson and Vardaman, 1997).

Religion may help in the severe stress of battle. In a survey in the United States army in World War II, about 75 per cent of soldiers who had been in combat said that they were helped by prayer when the going was tough. This was especially the case for those highly stressed in battle, and for those with less adequate resources for dealing with stress (Stouffer *et al.*, 1949). On the whole, battle experience seemed to weaken traditional church religion, but to increase concern with basic religious ideas (Allport *et al.*, 1948).

Religious involvement can help or hinder marriage. Studies in the USA have found that people with strong religious convictions and who attend church regularly are more satisfied with their marriages than non-religious individuals, but the greater the denominational difference between husband and wife, the greater the chance of unhappiness (Ortega *et al.*, 1988). In a study which assessed denominational homogamy, church attendance, and belief in the Bible, only the first was strongly associated with marital happiness, with church attendance weakly so (Heaton and Pratt, 1990). A strict religious up-bringing is associated with sexual problems in marriage (Masters and Johnson, 1970; Argyle and Beit-Hallahmi, 1975).

Loneliness can also be ameliorated by religious involvement, though the nature of the involvement preferred differs between individuals. On the whole more privileged people prefer organisational religion, while the more deprived prefer traditional beliefs and a devotional orientation (Campbell and Fukuyama, 1970). Another study found that the amelioration of loneliness among believers depended on the concept of God held by the individual: a wrathful God was related to greater loneliness, the mere existence of God was unrelated, and a helpful God was related to less loneliness (Schwab and Petersen, 1990).

Not surprisingly, religion has also been found to be associated with aspects of social behaviour – for instance with less delinquency among Mormon adolescents (Chadwick and Top, 1993). College students studied in the United Kingdom and the USA in 1978–79 and 1988–90 showed greater humanitarianism and less prejudice if they had strong religious commitment, but greater racism if they showed only moderate religiousness than if they claimed no religious affiliation. It is suggested that modest identification with a dominant faith may go with conventionality: students who seek strong guidance, or identify with a less pervasive religion, may be less conforming and less racist (Perkins, 1992).

### Mechanisms

The data thus suggest that religiousness can have positive consequences of several kinds. Given that, one must ask what it is about religiousness that produces such effects, though it is unlikely to be the same aspect of religiousness in all cases.

In some cases the mechanism seems fairly straightforward. Thus it is hardly surprising that the expectation of a wonderful after-life should reduce the fear of death. Another issue important in some cases is the reduced level of risk-taking associated with religious involvement: those denominations whose members have greater longevity tend to be those that proscribe drinking, smoking and sex (Levin, 1994). And the influence of religiosity in ameliorating loneliness can be seen as involving an (imaginary) relationship with a beneficent and empathetic deity whose help would always be appropriate.

Another very important factor must be the social support obtained. As an example, correlational evidence obtained in the south-eastern USA indicated a positive association between church attendance and the availability of social resources: those who attended tended to have larger social networks, more contacts with other network members, received more types of social support, and saw their relationships as more supportive, than non-church goers. This is in harmony with the view that religion leads to social contacts, and social contacts are conducive to better health – though, as so often in this area, there is always the possibility that the causal relation is in the other direction, people with larger networks being more likely to be recruited into the congregation (Ellison and George, 1994; see also Bradley,

1995; Idler and Kasl, 1997). Again, a study of over-sixties indicated that the better adjustment of church members was most marked for those in homes, fully retired, or in poor health, and there was no significant difference for those still fully employed: this again suggests that religion often operates through the provision either of social support or something to do (Moberg and Taves, 1965).

Another study pointing in the same direction involved research on the families of homicide victims. Although a high proportion used religious coping, this was negatively related to well-being. Of the six religious coping variables studied, only perceived support from the clergy and church members was related to less distress: passive dependence on God, pleading, feelings of anger towards God, and attempts to lead a better life, were all related to greater distress (Thompson and Vardaman, 1997).

Again, seeking help from clergy, or from fellow church members, was associated with less distress among student relatives of those involved in the Gulf War just before the start of active hostilities. Discontent with God, pleading for a miracle, and efforts to be good were all associated with more concurrent negative mood. Pleading was associated with some improvement between the initial assessment and a second one a week after the UN victory, perhaps because it gave some emotional release or because, with victory, it gave a sense of mastery and control (Pargament et al., 1994).

In general, social support is not always efficacious. For instance, when one individual gives help to another, it is important that the recipient's self-esteem should not be impaired, that the help given should be appropriate and not excessive, and that the relationship between donor and recipient should not be conflictual (Dunkel-Schetter and Skokan, 1990; Sarason et al., 1990). It is possible that such conditions are especially readily met in a network based on common religious belief.

Any effect of religion on health must operate through physiological intermediaries (Comstock and Partridge, 1972). We may note here that an increasing body of evidence indicates that not only external events but also private thoughts and beliefs can affect the neurochemical and hormonal balance, which in turn affects subjective states. Transcendental meditation (which claims to be a non-religious technique) has been shown to reduce systolic and diastolic blood pressure in African-Americans in a three-month trial (review, Alexander et al., 1996). Meditation and religious observances are also likely to induce the release of endorphins which promote feelings of well-being. It is thus possible that religious observance can promote a favourable physiological state (see McGuire, 1988; McGuire and Essock-Vitale, 1981).

This suggests that something which might be called 'peace of mind' may often be basic to the relations between religiosity and well-being or health. 'Peace of mind' is, of course, a loose concept, but it could refer to a lack of dissonance between views of, or attitudes towards, the self in a wide variety of situations – in other words to a well-integrated self-system, involving a sense of self-efficacy. While proof of this hypothesis is necessarily lacking, a number of aspects of the data are in harmony with it.

First, two studies of very different natures indicating a relation between state of mind and health or well-being may be mentioned. One showed that evaluations of their own health status by elderly individuals were predictors of their own mortality and functional ability, contributing significant further information to other health status indicators obtained from self-reported health histories or medical examinations. While poor self-ratings of health predict a trajectory of decline, the data did not yet show that they accelerated it (Idler and Kasl, 1995). The second example involves a cross-cultural comparison between different religious groups. Tibetan refugees living among Hindus, in what was to them an alien culture, had fewer financial and material resources, but nevertheless reported greater life satisfaction than the Hindus. The authors of the study ascribe this to a difference in outlook. Both groups believed that a person's actions determine his destiny in the next life, but while the Buddhists were looking forward, busy accumulating a positive legacy, the Hindus were straining to pay off debts incurred by past misdeeds. The high quality of life reported by the Tibetans seemed to be related to their religious beliefs which stress self-contentment and the pleasure of living in the presence of the living god, the Dalai Lama: these Tibetans had modest demands for a good life – enough to wear and eat without having to worry, good health, and the opportunity to sit with friends, eating and talking together (Fazel and Young, 1988).

Given a relation between state of mind and health or well-being, are there effects associated specifically with the nature of religiosity? A number of studies indicate that, where religiousness is associated with better health or well-being, the relation depends on firm belief rather than religious practice (though active participation may be a sign of, or contribute to, firm belief). For instance, a detailed study of a sample taken from the General Social Survey (a national cross-sectional sample in the USA) in 1988 showed that firm religious beliefs were related to perceptions of life quality, even when public and private religious involvement was controlled for statistically. The data indicated that the contributions of church attendance and private devotions to well-being were primarily indirect, involving the strengthening of religious beliefs and world views. Whereas religious faith appeared to buffer the negative effects of trauma, divine interaction (i.e. how close the respondent felt to God and how often she or he prayed) did not. The author concludes that 'religious symbols and beliefs provide an interpretative framework through which individuals can make sense of everyday reality' (Ellison, 1991: 89).

Again, active religious participation by Glasgow residents was found to correlate with distance from the cultural base of the religious denomination (i.e. increasing Church of Scotland, other Protestant denominations, Roman Catholics, and non-Christian religions): Hannay (1980) suggests that the assurances provided by active religion protect against the instabilities of urban living. And, as another example, we have seen that religious systems that leave no room for debate tend to be more stable, and are therefore presumably more satisfying to the participants (pp. 208–10).

However, the firm belief system does not necessarily have to be a religious one. For instance, an analysis of 2500 replies to a questionnaire by American women showed that certainty of belief, whether it involved strong religiousness or a confident non-religious outlook, was associated with better mental and physical health (Shaver *et al.*, 1980). Some other studies showing this were cited above (Perkins, 1992; Ross, 1990). The suggestion here is that firm and active religious belief can facilitate the integration of the self-system, but it is not the only route to that end. On this view, luke-warm believers, and those whose religious belief is conventional only, tend to have less well-integrated self-systems than those whose religiosity is firm and active, or than those who have achieved a coherent world view in other ways (though the latter is only an hypothesis). The tendency of the luke-warm believers towards conventionality can be interpreted as a seeking for certainty by individuals whose self-systems lacked integration.

A similar conclusion is indicated by a comparison between the self-reports of those who claimed to have helped Jews in Nazi-occupied countries in World War II and those who did not. This showed only a weak effect of religiosity, but a higher proportion of rescuers described themselves as 'very religious' or 'not at all religious' than did non-rescuers: the latter described themselves in intermediate terms as 'not very' or 'somewhat' religious more often than the rescuers (Oliner and Oliner, 1988). Prejudice, also, has been found to be higher in those who attend church occasionally than in those who attend frequently or not at all (Adorno *et al.*, 1950).

Three other lines of evidence are in harmony with the view that integration of the self-system is a critical issue. First, the divided loyalties of those in religiously heterogamous marriages is associated with less marital happiness (see also Burleston and Denton, 1992; Tzeng, 1992). Second, we have seen that a number of studies indicate that the social support afforded by the religious community is an important issue. However the deleterious effects of intrusive support, support that infringed self-esteem, or support given in a conflictual relationship are in harmony with the view that the social support should be such as to support the self-system. Third, it may be tentatively suggested that the reduced level of risk-taking associated with religious involvement is due to a reduced need to seek other forms of sensation, resulting from a more integrated self-system.

Thus, as a preliminary conclusion from this selection of studies, it is suggested that many of the positive effects or correlates of religion can be seen as primarily concerned with the integrity of the self-system. The nature of religion's contribution is considered further by Pargament (1997).

This leaves open the question of whether the nature of the deity believed in makes a difference to any beneficial consequences of religion. Some things seem clear. It seems likely that an impersonal God would be unlikely to contribute to the comfort derived from religion by the lonely and by those in high stress situations, and it is not surprising that, in such cases, the concept of a helpful God is more effective than a wrathful one. And a deity who did not provide an after-life could not ameliorate fear of death. In general the comparative evidence is not very helpful: most studies have involved Christian or Jewish subjects, and the inter-denominational differences found could be confounded by class differences. However, there is evidence that adherents to groups with rather rigid systems (e.g. Mormons, Seventh Day Adventists, Orthodox Jews) tend to enjoy good health (Levin, 1994): they may have more integrated personalities.

In any case, the primary issue with which we are concerned is not whether religious adherence is good for the individual, but the reasons for its persistence in the face of evidence that is contrary to its beliefs. And we have seen that religious beliefs are resilient, so that even doubters may turn to religion if other methods of coping seem unavailable: after all, if a prayer might bring relief, the only argument against praying for a non-believer is the infringement of personal integrity involved. And an individual's beliefs are maintained not so much by the good that they do him, but by the good that he believes them to do. So if he sees himself to be healthier, or a better person, that is what matters. Many religious sects try deliberately to foster such beliefs: evangelical Christians organising beach services for children had a chorus in which the word 'Happy' was repeatedly spelled out – 'I'm H.A.P.P.Y., I'm H.A.P.P.Y., I know I am, I'm sure I am, I'm H.A.P.P.Y.'.

## Gender and personality

Two matters which affect religious involvement must be mentioned briefly.

### Gender differences

Although men are more likely to be religious specialists than women, this is probably due to cultural restrictions on women, and a number of studies have shown that women are more likely to be involved in religious activities than men (Beit-Hallahmi and Argyle, 1997). As one example, in a sample of 2276 students in their last year or two at school, the girls tended to be more severe in their moral judgements than the boys, and severity was positively associated with indices of religious belief and practice (Wright and Cox, 1967).

Since women generally have had lower status and power than men, this difference could be seen as due to the appeal of religion to the oppressed. However, it seems to be a matter of gender rather than sex. It is now recognised that masculinity and femininity cannot be represented as the opposite ends of a linear continuum, but are better seen as dimensions orthogonal to each other, sometimes crudely referred to as instrumentality and expressivity. An individual's masculinity/femininity can be represented as a point on a graph with two axes, masculinity and femininity. It is thus important to distinguish biological sex from masculinity/femininity as dimensions of gender: while on average men are more masculine than women, men may have some feminine characteristics, and women masculine ones. Not only do women tend to be more religious than men, but high scores on femininity tend to be associated with religious activities in both men and women (Thompson, 1991).

There are reasons why religion might appeal more strongly to those high on femininity. First, femininity tends to be associated with a greater role in and need for relationships, and with greater dependency. In general, in part because of a biological bias and in part as a result of differential socialisation, women in western society define themselves in the context of their relationships and evaluate themselves in terms of their ability to care for others, whereas men place more value on power and authority (Gilligan, 1982). Women place more emphasis on commitment in relationships, and have a stronger aversion to risk-taking, a characteristic negatively associated with religiosity (Hinde, 1997a; Miller and Hoffman, 1995). Second, women, at any rate in recently industrialised societies, are more prone to suffer from anxiety and to have low self-esteem than are men: they may therefore have greater need for religious faith.

In harmony with this, men and women have tended to experience God differently, with girls and women tending to see God as Love and emphasising relationships with God and with the community, while boys and men tend to see God as authoritarian and emphasise God's power and judgement and their own spiritual discipline (e.g. Hertel and Donahue, 1995). In addition, women tend to entertain an image of God as more like their father, men as more like their mother. If the deity is seen as male, he is likely to be more attractive to women than to men. Such an hypothesis is in harmony with data showing that women preponderate much more in Protestant churches than in Roman Catholic ones, where the Virgin Mary is a prominent figure. A study of Roman Catholic children found that boys' images of God were related more to the Virgin Mary than to Jesus, those of girls more to Jesus (Deconchy, 1968).

In so far as the greater religiosity of women is related to their lower status, one must ask why, now that times are changing and women's right to equal status is more generally recognised than was formerly the case, do not women abandon religion more than they do? A study of sixty-one middle-class women, college students or adults recruited through churches of diverse faith, indicated that some simply did not perceive the unequal treatment of women in the church and, of those who did, nearly a fifth accepted it. Among the remainder, a few tried to change the situation, and some left their religious affiliation. But the great majority of those who perceived the injustice used a cognitive defence, for instance comparing their church favourably with other churches or with the secular world, or accepting it as part of traditions that are being changed, or by interpreting it in their own way – perhaps substituting 'Our Being' for 'Our Father'. Such women emphasised their relationship to God and to others as positive aspects of their religion, and said that they experienced God's power not just in God's goodness to them but also in the work that they felt that God empowered them to do for others (Ozorak, 1996).

### Personality

We saw earlier that parental and family influences play a major part in the religiosity of young children, but that their influence may decrease as the child grows up. In harmony with this, genetic studies comparing monozygotic with dizygotic twins, reared apart or together, have yielded no evidence for a genetic influence on religiosity in young children, but with adults the situation appears to be quite different. Waller *et al.* (1990) found that individual differences in religious attitudes, interests, and values arose from both genetic and environmental influences, genetic factors accounting for about 50 per cent of the variance.

However, relations between religiousness and aspects of personality are on the whole weak and difficult to interpret (review, Beit-Hallahmi and Argyle, 1997). In modern societies there is a (weak) relation between the psychological characteristic of authoritarianism and religious belief, the relation being especially strong for Catholics and Fundamentalists: authoritarian personalities tend to be incapable or unwilling to question their beliefs and to be racist (Adorno *et al*, 1950). A similar relation holds for the related dimension of dogmatism. Suggestibility is also higher in religious than in non-religious people, but this may be because suggestible people seek guidance. A number of studies show that conversion or heightened commitment is especially likely to occur during adolescence, an intellectually tempestuous time accompanied by doubts about identity and a desire for rational explanations for everything (Elkind, 1971; review Hood *et al.*, 1996).

There is some evidence that people highly prone to fantasy also report vivid imagery, are susceptible to hypnosis, report telepathic and psychic experiences, and differ from non-fantasy prone individuals on measures of imagination, creativity, and suggestibility (Lynn and Rhue, 1988). Such individuals might well be prone to religious involvement.

## Method of acquisition

The means by which religious beliefs are acquired may also contribute to making them especially resilient. As we have seen (Chapter 7), they build on domain-specific principles and are usually acquired during early socialisation when the child is especially susceptible to the beliefs and outlook of respected adults. The internalisation of beliefs in childhood may underlie all future development. Of course the childhood beliefs may invite adolescent rebellion, but their influence may persist in a semi-conscious fashion or in opposition to a new found perspective.

## Ritual and ritual specialists

The roles of ritual and of ritual specialists in the maintenance of religious systems and especially religious rituals deserves special comment. Of course, it is not only religious rituals that persist: many secular rituals have a similar resilience. A degree of ceremonial ritual is found valuable in registry offices and in other civic ceremonies. National ceremonies, Remembrance Days, and so on tend to have their own ceremonial rituals. Academic and military institutions preserve their rituals. In the secularisation of the Soviet Union, aspects of the religious rituals used for *rites de passage* were incorporated into the new ceremonies (Lane, 1981). In all these cases, officials of some sort have a responsibility for the maintenance of the ritual.

Several issues seem to be involved here. One is that ritual is seen as enhancing the feeling of community within a family, an institution, or a nation. But important also is the matter of tradition: actions are seen as good if 'things have always been like that'. Just why institutions, practices, and objects should be revered because of their age is an interesting issue. Of course a shopkeeper likes to write 'Established 1824' above his door because it testifies to the viability of his business. But why should we venerate old buildings, old artefacts, and especially old customs? Has it anything to do with the desire for continuity after death? Perhaps evidence that the past survives to the present facilitates belief that the present will survive into the future. Evidence for such a view would be hard to get. In any case, as now to be discussed, with religious ritual other factors may operate.

One of these is the supposition that the ritual is in some way divinely ordered. Procedures that are divinely inspired must be inviolable. Second, rituals are usually conducted by elders, chiefs, or religious specialists, whose status depends on the maintenance of the religious system. Since one of their functions is to conduct rituals, it is in their interests to maintain the rituals as part of the system. It was suggested earlier that this may provide an explanation for the relative conservativism of religious buildings: churches, synagogues, and temples tend to retain a consistency of form when secular buildings change in many ways. Is this in part because their form facilitates the form of rituals which help to sustain the beliefs which sustain the system?

In practice, 'official' religious systems sustained by religious specialists are often accompanied by 'local' cults. Sometimes the relation has been a smooth one: thus in China local religions have continued alongside the major imported ones, and probably played as important a role in the life of the laity. Sometimes, as we have seen, there is conflict, and then it is in the interests of the religious specialists to maintain their own system. Thus in sixteenth-century Spain saints played a major role in the life of the laity, many of whom might make confession to a priest only once a year. But from time to time reforms were made to regularise local customs and ensure that they did not conflict with Rome, to prevent the profaning of sacred places, and so on (Christian, 1981). In addition, at times in Christendom the church has had great secular power, and has both used this power to maintain the religious system and used the religious system to maintain its power. In a variety of such ways the religious specialist has played a major role in ensuring the persistence of beliefs.

Special problems are raised by those rituals, of which prayers can be regarded as a special case, that have a specific goal. The ritual may be thought to ensure good weather for the harvest, or prayers may be offered in the expectation of benefits to be received. Sometimes, of course, they are successful. This may be a matter of chance, but it may also be a direct result of the commitment of the supplicant: prayer for recovery from illness may be associated with a strong desire for, and belief in, recovery (James, 1892). But often they are not successful, and then some explanation is called for.

In the first place, adults are especially prone to magical thinking when they lack information, in conditions of uncertainty, and in the face of inexplicable phenomena (Woolley, 1997). Thus prayer may be resorted to even when, at another level, there is little faith in its efficacy. And, as we have seen, some children believe that wishes can come true. Second, faith in a ritual's efficacy may be based merely on hearsay: in western societies most people who believe in paranormal phenomena have not experienced them, but have merely heard of others who claim to have done so (Humphrey, 1995). Hope for success may thus only be partial.

But when failure is undeniable, many evasions are possible – for instance the gods may be assumed to be angry or, as noted above, failure can be ascribed to inadequacy of the ritual or prayer. Faith in success may be seen as a necessary condition for the ritual's efficacy, and doubt or suspension of judgement must almost always be lurking below the surface to take the blame. Often prayer is seen as an adjunct to, rather than a substitute for, personal action, so failure can be ascribed to lack of effort.

Turning to religions in non-literate societies, Evans-Pritchard (1937) listed twenty-two reasons why the Zande do not perceive the futility of their magic. Among those of special relevance to the western world are: magic is employed against mystical powers, and its action cannot be easily contradicted by experience; a particular procedure may be seen as unsuccessful, but this is not generalised to related types of magic; contradictions between beliefs are not noticed because the beliefs are not present at the same time and function in different situations; the culture has ready-made patterns of belief with the force of tradition behind them; the experience of an individual counts for little against accepted opinion, contradiction showing only that the experience is peculiar; magic is used only to produce events which are likely to happen anyway (for instance rain is produced in the rainy season; magic is seldom asked to produce a result by itself but is associated with empirical action effective in its own right); the efficacy of procedures is not tested (for instance a man who uses a particular medicine always does so and so cannot perceive that things would be the same if he did not); and beliefs are so vaguely formulated that they cannot be disproved. It will be apparent that similar issues operate today not only for religious procedures like prayer, but also for many aspects of superstitious behaviour (the rabbit's foot, St. Christopher medal) and the taking of medicines. A further one, not mentioned by Evans-Pritchard, is the feeling 'Well, it cannot do any harm' or 'It might work'.

Turning to acceptance of divinatory procedures, this involves two stages – first acceptance of the procedure in general as valid, and second, acceptance of the result of a particular divinatory session. With regard to the first, divination may involve recognition of a relationship between a spirit and the diviner, the spirit possessing the medium and speaking through him or her. Of course, the claimed relationship may be fraudulent but, if that possibility is disregarded by the supplicant, the medium must necessarily be seen as speaking the truth.

In any particular session, divination may involve a technique or device which requires interpretation by the diviner. Acceptance of that interpretation by the client will depend on his perception of the authenticity of the diviner. The latter may seek to establish validity by repeating procedures to see if the answers are consistent. In any particular session, the answers to questions may appear to be irrelevant, inconsistent, or contradictory, but most questions can be taken to have more than one meaning, so the diviner can re-define the meaning of the question, understand a divinatory response to be made to an earlier question, see the question to have been inappropriately framed, see a contradiction as re-framing a question, and so on (Zeitlyn, 1995).

## The religious system

The term 'religious system' has been used throughout this book to emphasise that the different aspects of religion influence each other. This is, of course, by no means a necessary consequence: they could be independent. Thus people perform rituals which are quite independent of their religious beliefs, and have experiences that resemble religious experiences but are without a religious interpretation. To summarise briefly how these different aspects of the system affect and support each other:

- Structural beliefs form the bases of the narratives.
- Narratives expound and extend the structural beliefs, may present the moral principles in an assimilable form, and influence the form of religious experience. Since they become familiar to all, they contribute to social integration.

- Rituals reinforce the structural beliefs, often re-enact the narratives, may refer to the moral principles, and provide a background for religious experience. They may also contribute to social integration.
- The moral code may include reference to the importance of acceptance of the structural beliefs and the narratives, is related to the rituals, and regulates social behaviour inside as well as outside the religious system.
- Religious experience draws its images from and reinforces the structural beliefs and the narratives and related mythology, and may be part of the ritual. It may be communal.
- Social aspects, involving the religious specialists and secular authorities as well as peers and in some cases the ancestors, pervade all the above.

Now in previous chapters we have seen that each of these aspects of religious systems depends on pan-cultural psychological characteristics and can, at least to a large extent, be understood on that basis. But one must also ask whether the integration of these several aspects into religious systems is merely a chance consequence of their nature, or whether that integration itself results from the nature of the human psyche. We have seen that the different aspects are emphasised to a different extent in different religious systems, but are they ever entirely independent of each other? So far as I am aware, the data necessary to answer this question are not available, but the fact is that integrated religious systems are ubiquitous. Confucianism may be primarily concerned with how people should behave, but it is coupled to a belief system, even though it is one that does not involve a deity. Hermits may live alone, but is not their way of life justified by contrast with the social world?

And a possible mechanism is available. We have seen that individuals seek a coherent view of the world. We like to feel that we have a continuing self, even though we do behave differently according to the situation. It is at least possible that the integration of religious systems is a consequence of people's need for congruence between the various facets of their lives. One could go further than that, and ask whether in some cases it is not just because religious systems provide a way of integrating not only the different facets of individuals' lives, but also the social, ideological, political and ethical systems of societies, that they are so resilient. That brings us back to the further question of whether an integrated religious system as a whole could be a product of natural selection: as we saw in Chapter 2, the evidence for that is equivocal.

A final point here is that the several components of a religious system do not merely influence each other, they are mutually supportive. That raises the crucial question of whether some of the components of a particular system can survive without the others. To be specific, how can a religiously purveyed moral code continue if the beliefs central to the system are not acceptable? We shall return to this in the next chapter.

## Summary

Religious systems are not immutable: their stability must be seen as the dynamic resultant of forces for stability and change. A number of factors influence the stability of any particular religious system: on the whole, within Christian churches, conservativism is associated with stability, but in the Catholic Church this is assisted by the presumption of the divine authority of the Pope and Bishops.

The factors making for the persistence of a religious system are not necessarily the same as those that make for continuing adherence by the individual. Individuals use a variety of defence mechanisms to maintain congruence between their religious beliefs and their self-systems, their expectations and experiences.

A variety of social and political forces are also conducive to the persistence of religious systems and to the continuing involvement of individuals.

Evidence that pan-cultural psychological propensities are important for involvement in a religious system is reasonably convincing. Evidence that involvement improves aspects of life-quality is beset by methodological problems, but suggestive. The provision of 'peace of mind', contributing to the maintenance of the integrity of the self-system, is suggested as an important correlate or effect of religious involvement. The social support received from religious involvement seems also often to be relevant but, within limits, there is no evidence that the precise nature of the beliefs held is important. Not surprisingly, gender and personality factors are related to religious involvement.

The factors conducive to the persistence of ritual and the role of religious specialists are discussed briefly.

Perhaps most important for persistence, the different aspects of a religious system are interdependent, and mutually support each other.

# 18 Conclusion

In the first chapter I argued that, although the basic beliefs of religious systems are unacceptable, a purely destructive approach to religion is at present inappropriate. Although based on the incompatibility between modern knowledge and a literal interpretation of religious beliefs, it would involve taking away what appears to be a source of comfort to many people without an adequate substitute. Such an approach assumes that belief in dogma is all there is to religion, and neglects the fact that moral principles have been purveyed by religious systems, within which they were part of a whole way of life. It also involves the neglect of a fascinating scientific question – what is the basis of the ubiquity and persistence of religious systems? And that poses a question of critical importance for the next millennium: how can those products of a religious outlook that are valuable be preserved when the basic beliefs are rejected as literal portrayals of reality? This chapter brings together some of the relevant discussion from previous chapters, but may carry a greater slice of personal bias than is, I hope, apparent in the earlier ones.

The approach may seem to boil down to an evaluation of religion, an enterprise which would seem both arrogant and absurd to the traditionally-minded, who see no problem in the ubiquity of religious systems, except perhaps in their diversity. But, for those who regard a transcendental explanation as inadequate, or feel that an appeal to supernatural explanations involves a sacrifice of intellectual integrity, the phenomena of religious observance must be aligned with what is known of other aspects of human psychological functioning. For adherents to religious systems, understanding their psychological concomitants need not diminish their appeal or their efficacy.

## The down side

A basic issue is that religious belief is incompatible with what non-believers see as establishing 'truth'. To many of those brought up in a tradition which values truth, even though not understanding its ephemeral character, it is morally repellent to accept a system based on revelation, a system which involves an obligation not to treat all evidence impartially. A unique and final truth, exempt from rational inquiry, is simply not on. In any case, even if a religious system does bring social benefits, it may still not convey the most adequate picture of the world.

I acknowledge that beliefs of one sort or another play an essential part in every aspect of our lives, but modern western science is conducted according to conventions which make the nature of the inherent beliefs, and of such 'truth' as it presents, apparent. The fruits of scientific research are (or should be) universal public knowledge, subjected to scrutiny by other scientists and all others interested. The efforts of scientists to be disinterested and unbiased, and the scepticism involved in the systematic testing of research findings, contribute to distinguishing scientific from religious 'truth' (Ziman, 1996). Scientists know only too well that beliefs and theories are fallible. Science may not always lead towards truth, though we would like to believe that it does, but the very nature of the practice of science involves the capacity to adjust its beliefs in the light of new knowledge to a greater extent than that of most religious systems.

Second, the individual needs for which religion provides are not always socially desirable. Not only may religion cause conflict or be used to justify it, but its use by some individuals may involve manipulation of others, to the detriment of the latter. Those seeking prestige and advancement may strive for advancement in a religious hierarchy. Dogmatic assertion and conviction of righteousness may produce an imagined superiority over others that is socially divisive. Religious practice has involved assumptions about the inferiority of whole classes of individuals. Even those aspects of religion conducive to maintenance of the social order, to stability, may have negative consequences, as with the church's role in the maintenance of the institution of slavery. It may entail a conservative attitude emphasising respect for authority rather than freedom, imagination, and originality. Such conservatism has acted to delay the ordination of women and to denigrate homosexuality.

Extrinsic religiousness, especially, is associated with prejudice, and some studies indicate that religious people, apart perhaps from some of the most devout, tend to be more prejudiced than non-believers. This is often related to claims of exclusive access to divine truth, which can readily accentuate in-group/out-group prejudice, especially in the case of small sects. Indeed, a church may favour or condone racial prejudice: this has been the case both with the Mormons in the USA and the Dutch Reformed Church in South Africa. The horrors of the Inquisition, and of the Spanish Conquistadores, are well-known. Wars, persecutions and much suffering have been based on, or ascribed to, differences in religious beliefs. With the exception of Quakers and certain other groups, religious believers have tended to be less opposed to war than non-believers.

Of course the advance of science has also led to suffering as well as benefits, and out-group intolerance is not the prerogative of religious groups. In recent history the supporters of Communism have been the victims of comparable intolerance in the USA, as have its opponents in the Soviet Union. Racism is not the prerogative of Nazism. Furthermore many aspects of modern secular culture have consequences far less desirable than those of religion, such as the self-centred competitiveness which sometimes accompanies capitalist enterprise. And certain individual characteristics are common to both religiousness and to behaviour in secular contexts – for instance uncritical acceptance of conventions and unconstructive thinking in in-group/out-group terms.

Nothing that has been said indicates that religion is '*wrong*'. It is always open to the believer to argue that the approach adopted here is dealing with externalities and misses the central core of religious experience – though many would find such a line of argument unsatisfying. And there is no claim that a solely rational approach can (yet?) offer all the other benefits enjoyed by religious adherents. Science does not easily offer emotional comfort: many find it less help, when facing an operation, to know that there is a fifty-fifty chance that all will be well than to be told that God is looking after them. Science cannot easily cope with the problem of mortality. Most people do not perceive science as able to explain chance events. So far secular knowledge has failed to provide either an adequate moral code or the conviction that one should abide by it. Of course, such judgements must never be final: it may be that the mentalistic revisions advocated by some scientists, which take account of mental states, will go much farther in these respects than traditional science has done so far (Sperry, 1988).

## Consequences of belief promoting persistence

Virtually every society involves a social hierarchy, and religion provides ways of legitimising it for some and coping with it for others. For those at the top, it can be used to justify their position, and it can make more acceptable the lot of those at the bottom. Religion can provide a means for stabilising the *status quo* and reducing conflict.

At the individual level, we have seen that religious observance can be seen as resulting from pan-cultural psychological propensities. Religious experiences are important to many. Some have even suggested that humans will always have needs and desires which cannot be satisfied in a secular world, so that religions will always be necessary (Stark and Bainbridge, 1985): that, of course, remains an open issue, and in any case much depends on what is included as 'religion'. It may also be that some of the comfort and reassurance that religion can bring are required only by those who lack other sources of support, but, in a society where it seems there will always be losers, it is hardly seemly for others to say that this source should be removed before there is something to replace it. While it would be wrong, because condescending, to see religion as a panacea for underdogs, so long as there are underdogs there may be need for a panacea.

Considerable research has been devoted to assessing the relations between religiousness and physical and mental well-being, but many conceptual and statistical problems are involved. Correlational studies cannot demonstrate cause–effect relations, and much depends on the particular religious orientation of the subjects. We have seen, however, evidence that some sorts of physical ailment and psychological distress are less prevalent among religious participants. A main effect seems to operate through the provision of 'peace of mind' and enhancement of the integration of the self-system: the social support received from fellow believers and the resulting feeling of community may contribute to this. The less self-indulgent life-style and reduced risk-taking of religious participants may also be important. Believing in itself seems to relieve distress only in the case of loneliness and for older individuals (Chapter 17).

## Similarities between world religions

If a particular religious system can bring benefits to some individuals, we must ask whether some other system would not have done just as well. While every religious system must be to some degree compatible with other aspects of the socio-cultural system, so that there are limits in the extent to which religions can be successfully transplanted, we have seen that there are many points of contact between the major religious systems. Another religious system may therefore be equally effective in providing for human needs in its own cultural setting (see pp. 65–6).

## Religions and moral codes

Perhaps the most urgent issue today concerns the moral codes. While in many ways the social consciences of individuals are now applied more widely than formerly, dealings between non-related individuals fall far short of the 'do-as-you-would-be-done-by' maxim. No doubt the causal bases for this are multiple, and include the growth of individualistic capitalism and the increasing gap between rich and poor, as well as the increase in the scale of society, with the dispersal of kin, 'neighbours' becoming more diffuse, and personal relationships down-played. The disruptive forces in society, and the results of human egoism multiplied by the powers of technological, commercial and governmental domination, seem to be becoming too powerful for community impulses to cope with. The values that operated in small-scale communities were by no means always beneficent, but on the whole they worked: it seems very difficult for large-scale societies to re-establish anything comparable. Moral systems face special challenges today from the growth of technology. Sometimes, as with genetic engineering, the moral implications are not immediately apparent. Sometimes, as with environmental issues and global warming, the moral implications are clear but run counter to the individual interests of many of those involved in controlling the technologies in question. In such cases the 'common good' has a new, less provincial, meaning.

In previous chapters it has been suggested that moral codes are based in human nature, and must promote those aspects of human behaviour conducive to group living while not eliminating individuality. Moral aims must be to some degree congruent with the society, and society with the moral aims. A moral code must have limited flexibility, enabling it to strike a proper balance between controlling and accommodating to changes in society. It must also be coupled with a degree of tolerance for the views of those of other societies, and tolerance tends to be incompatible with strongly held beliefs.

Moral codes inevitably differ in some respects between societies in relation to their histories and other aspects of their socio-cultural structures. Societies differ in both ecology and history, and must be expected to have somewhat different value systems. It may not (yet?) be possible for all fully to adopt some of the desiderata which Westerners see as self-evident – equality, democracy, adequate privacy, openness. However, this does not justify a complete cultural relativism which, if taken to extremes, could be taken to mean that people could subscribe to any values, or even to no values. This is a critically important issue, for a society could develop a code by which the oppression of some groups was legitimated, or a code which insisted on the rectitude of its own beliefs so rigidly that individuals were encouraged to propagate them by force. From the perspective of most outsiders, such codes could not be condoned. More importantly, just because moral codes are rooted in the nature of humankind, there are limits to the cultural variation that will be tolerated in the long run.

The suggestion that what we value is in part due to our nature may be greeted as naive by those who are concerned with cultural differences. But, just in case there is any misunderstanding, this is not the same as saying that values are in our genes. As discussed in Chapter 2, the basic propensities are products of interaction between genes and organism with aspects of the environment that are more or less common to all humans – but there will be differences in both genetic constitution and experience, so that no two individuals are quite the same. Furthermore values are shaped in development, and no two individuals develop in precisely the same environment. Cultures differ, and any one culture changes with time: what is good in one place or at one time may not be so at another. Of course these considerations also emphasise the complexity of the issues. I have argued that a rational approach is relevant to the issue of moral values and can help both in the analysis of how value systems come to be and in the acceptable limitations of their values and precepts. However, it must be admitted that we do not yet understand sufficiently well the immensely complex interplay between the biological, ecological, cultural and historical forces operating, to be able to prescribe for a particular situation. The discussion in this book has been concerned only with the general principles underlying moral codes, but an approach which draws on the natural and social sciences and on the humanities, and which indicates that moral systems must be based both in human nature (its 'good' aspects but taking into account also its 'bad' ones) and in the society's history and current situation, and must change to meet new situations, does at least provide a starting point, and perhaps the only possible starting point.

New problems are constantly arising, but it may help to see that the judgements we make are rooted in the existing code, which is rooted in turn in our nature. Ultimately, we deplore the use of nuclear weapons because we would not want them used on us, or because we identify with those on whom they would be used, or because it would be detrimental to what we see as the 'common good'. We deplore environmental pollution for similar reasons: it may affect us or our descendants, and the polluters are receiving benefits which outstrip their own costs, while imposing costs on others. Many, perhaps most, problems involve conflicting issues: for instance the ethics of abortion involves conflict between the life of the foetus and the well-being of the mother. But in all such cases our judgements stem from moral codes which are based on shared principles.

We shall always need a code that is culturally acceptable, fitting our circumstances, but at the same time we must remember that our culture is shaped by the moral code that we have. We must not reject the code handed down by the religious system which has been its guardian, but we must be prepared to amend it for our current circumstances in the light of our knowledge of how people behave and have behaved. The suggestion that a moral code depends on value judgements whose bases can never be available for study, so that a rational approach is irrelevant, is a superficial view. It is also a council of despair.

If this approach is correct, and there seems to be no other reasonable possibility, four caveats follow. First, some conflict between individual autonomy and the social order is inevitable. If it were not so, the moral code would be superfluous. Individuals tend to assert their own interests, but a world in which individualism was allowed full rein would be socially impossible. The law can be seen as an attempt to underwrite rationally the precepts and prohibitions of the moral code.

Second, the moral code, and indeed the law, that emerges at any one time is not necessarily the best for all people: it may be engineered by one subgroup in order to bind others to its will, or it may be a botched-up code compromising what is believed to be best for several different sub-groups. In such circumstances, tension and change is both inevitable and proper.

And third, it seems that although, almost by definition, a successful moral code must be conducive to social cohesion, and so can vary only within limits, nevertheless there can be no absolute moral code, valid for all people at all places in all times. The moral codes espoused by religious systems, especially those of revealed religions, tend to be seen as immutable, as handed down by the deity, and are insensitive to a changing world. We can see the beliefs and ethical aspects of a religious system coming apart as modern Catholics try to keep their key beliefs while using contraception and allowing priests to marry. No precept can be pushed to its extreme, even if this seems to lead to wishy-washy indecisiveness. Codes based on (supposedly) Christian principles led to the cruelty and inhumanity of the Inquisition; a code based solely on personal freedom leads inevitably to social disharmony and over-population; and too much emphasis on social cooperation could lead to the demise of individuality. But that is not an argument for complete relativism: since they are based on pan-cultural characteristics, moral codes can vary only between limits if societies are to be viable.

Fourth, and related to the preceding points, many of the problems that societies face will be new problems, arising from scientific advances and cultural changes. Old rules cannot always be trusted. In the modern world, giving preference to one's kin, leaving many descendants, or pushing the interests of one's kin group, are no longer seen as desirable as they used to be. However the *principles* that moral codes are derived from shared views about how others should behave in the interests of social harmony, that they are based in human propensities which are conducive to that end (with no implication that all that is natural is good), and that current codes are likely to have been based on aspirations that served well in the past, may serve as a starting point for the future.

All religions have extremists, but Christianity and Islam have set their moral codes in more absolute terms than have some eastern religions. The problem of aligning what has been valuable in the past with the requirements of the present requires both tolerance and wisdom. In this context, the western world can perhaps learn from the example of Gandhi, though the details of what he advocated are appropriate only for his own culture. Hinduism has absorbed many moral codes, and Gandhi rejected much that he disliked but recognised Hinduism's importance as a social force. He saw Hinduism as the timeless nature of India, and regarded it as the duty of the enlightened Hindu to preserve what should be preserved according to his conscience. Gandhi defended temple worship, domestic rites, and the veneration of the cow. While wholeheartedly condemning the treatment of the Untouchables, he recognised that the division of society into castes temporarily made a more ordered whole. 'Gandhi accepted religions as they are: they were organisations of finite human beings the purpose of which was, through rites, ceremonies, and symbols, to lift man out of his purely temporal dimension into a state of being that transcends time' (Zaehner, 1962: 184).

## Moral authority?

The view of the nature of moral codes suggested here says nothing about how moral codes are purveyed or enforced. At present, it would seem, people may adhere to the moral code of their culture through their acceptance of the religious system (perhaps backed up by carrot and stick in the form of Heaven and Hell), or because the society's ideological system has become part of their self-systems, or because of a civil legal system. These, however, are not independent: because religions have played a major part in influencing the ideology of every society, and in guiding socialisation and the legal system, they are still important in the maintenance of everyday values. But in the West, at least, changes in society have been correlated with a decrease in the effectiveness of religion as a way of life, and there is no accepted authority in moral matters. In the absence of religion, many could (and indeed do) maintain their moral code on rational grounds. Many more do so by operating standards assimilated in the course of socialisation. But might not there always be selfish individuals who evaded the code and exploited others? Might not they be the thin end of a wedge? Might not their selfish behaviour spread among others who witnessed its success? Would not this lead to social anarchy? The law could perhaps cope with the more major problems, but not with the everyday issues of selfish and self-centred behaviour. If we were to dispense with religion, would we not still need, as well as a secular code of values, a secular means for inducing individuals to incorporate those values? Even if clear-cut solutions for our intractable moral problems could be formulated, it might be one thing to specify a code of conduct, but quite another to persuade people to abide by it.

If the moral code is not seen as having supernatural authority, whence can its influence and authority be derived? So far it has helped to have an unquestionable divine authority: to replace it may not be easy. Merely espousing moral standards is likely to be ineffective: they cannot just float on society, but must be anchored in a new orientation – some would say, a more feminine orientation – acceptable to at least the great majority of individuals. Surely they cannot be imposed by governments – one would not want politicians dictating one's morals. Indeed any form of elected body would be seen as unreliable because of the unreliability of the electoral process. From academics? Do they know enough about life outside the ivory tower? And adherence to a moral code is unlikely to follow merely from the supposition that it is compatible with cultural and scientific analysis. In any case, while social scientists know a great deal about how to manipulate people's beliefs and behaviour, that brings one to another set of moral problems concerned with the propriety of manipulating individuals to conform with 'Big Brother's' views. The line between persuasion and coercion is often a difficult one to draw.

From parents? Here perhaps is the best hope, but parents will be less likely to socialise their children to show socially constructive behaviour if they have not experienced the beneficial effects of such behaviour themselves – and that would be facilitated by a world more equitable than most people experience at the moment. Movement towards such a world would certainly be helped greatly by a more general appreciation of the dependence of all individuals on relationships with others, and of the mutual relationships between individuals and the socio-cultural structure – but these are ideas not easy to put across. Certainly it seems to be very difficult for a state, with its bureaucratic structure, to promote the face to face interactions in small-scale communities in which moral systems have functioned in the past. And individuals find it easy to provide reasons for pursuing their own interests.

And even in an equitable world new problems would still arise, problems perhaps beyond the individual parent. Perhaps the only hope in such cases lies in the use of expert (not solely scientific) views about the probable consequences of alternative courses of action – not to formulate a moral code, but as a component of the continuing dialectic between the current code and the collective view. It would be essential to remember that consequences are always diverse, so that the expert views would have to embrace many perspectives, and not only those obviously pertinent to the issue in question. Each of the currently pressing ethical problems – the use of biological, chemical and nuclear weapons, the range of permissible uses of genetic engineering, human cloning – have diverse consequences, physical, environmental, social, aesthetic, medical. The expert views must therefore be drawn from the humanities and the arts as well as from the social and natural sciences.

## Peace of mind: integration of the self-system

A final issue is that of the individual's world view. We have seen that some of the beneficial consequences of religious involvement seem to come from the peace of mind that it can provide. 'Peace of mind' implies compatibility between and acceptance of the diverse aspects of the self-system – attributions, attitudes, relationships, behaviour, in the many life-situations that one encounters. But the peace of mind that religion offers is not necessarily acceptable nowadays: we are sceptical of all-embracing 'truth', and we are more aware of the diversity of natural causation, and of the variations in attitudes and relationships that complex society requires. 'God wills' is not an adequate explanation for all the vicissitudes in our lives. Many non-religious people appear to have peace of mind, but whether that stems from a rational outlook is an open issue. Science can, we have seen, provide an understanding of moral codes. But science deals with causes – we can find functional, evolutionary, developmental, and immediate causes for what we do. At the same time we have the impression that we have free-will, that we make decisions and choose what we do. That may or may not be only an impression, but it is what we think or feel that matters. It is by no means clear that the impression that we have free-will, that our behaviour is not determined, is compatible with the causal explanations that science provides. Would accepting an entirely deterministic view of the world mean abandoning the impression that we are in control of our actions? What would be the consequences of that on moral behaviour? But if we do not accept the scientific view, what are the alternatives? Must we accept the transcendental? Or humanistic values without enquiring about their source? I suspect that at this point both scientists and religious believers have to accept the view that 'One day, it will all become plain', though with very different expectations about the route by which that will come about.

# Notes

## 2 Some background issues

1 An almost identical list has been used by Smart (1996), but includes in addition a 'material or artistic dimension', involving issues, some of which are included here under 'experience'.

2 *Darwinism and human behaviour*. At present at least two groups of behavioural scientists are interested in how far human behaviour can be seen as a product of natural selection acting in the evolutionary past to favour survival and reproductive success. One group, the 'evolutionary psychologists', attempts to demonstrate that the 'evolutionary design' of aspects of behaviour provided efficiency, economy, and precision in operation (Barkow *et al.*, 1992). For example, the aspects of the opposite sex that humans find attractive appear to be such as would have maximised their reproductive success (Buss, 1994). And, as another example, human pregnancy sickness seems to be a device for protecting the foetus from toxins (Profet, 1992). Evolutionary psychologists tend to postulate an 'adapted module' for each characteristic found to meet their criteria of adaptedness.

The second group, the 'human behavioural ecologists', are concerned with how ecological and social factors affect behavioural variability within and between populations: this involves attempts to demonstrate that the behaviour shown tends to maximise the reproductive success of the individual concerned (or that of close relatives) as the result of 'evolved behavioral tendencies'. For instance, among the Kenyan Kipsigis the size of parental land holding is related to the son's reproductive success because land is handed down to sons rather than to daughters, and also to the reproductive success of the daughters because girls brought up on large farms reach menarche earlier (Borgerhoff Mulder, 1991).

There is also a variety of models concerned with the probability that cultural traits will be passed on to succeeding generations. Such theories depend on specifying items of information (beliefs, values, rules, etc.), often referred to as 'memes' (Dawkins, 1976), and assessing the extent to which, and the mechanisms by which, they are transmitted. There is disagreement as to how far individuals adopt or ignore 'memes' because of their effects on genetic fitness, or how far this involves 'cultural selection', that is, the success of the 'memes' in invading new minds (Borgerhoff Mulder and Mitchell, 1994). In the latter case, that success depends on the choices people make in deciding between alternative memes, and that in turn *ultimately* on pan-cultural psychological characteristics. However, the acceptance of one meme can affect the probability that others will be accepted: examples of this are found in the ways in which defence mechanisms are used to protect religious beliefs. Cultural evolution can involve patterns of behaviour that are deleterious to reproductive success. Much of the discussion in the present book concerns the extent to which individuals accept 'memes' because they satisfy basic needs, and are thus of a type which facilitates or did facilitate survival or reproduction, or because of the influence of authority (Irons, 1996b). Co-evolutionary theories – for instance 'gene-culture co-evolution' (Lumsden and Wilson, 1981) and 'co-evolution' (Durham, 1991) – assume that cultural evolution, though independent of biological evolution, interacts with it.

3   This term is used because the cultural norms, values, beliefs, etc., are related to the social structure, and because they affect each other. The mechanisms that underlie the acquisition of culture are presumed to be products of human evolutionary history. It must also be presumed that, in the past, they have generally produced behaviour that is biologically adaptive, though that is certainly not always the case today (Flinn, 1997).

4   One can speculate that some of the secondary uses may stem from the primary one, the red robes of high officials signifying the danger of crossing them, while others have different derivations – perhaps red for warmth from fire.

5   More recently McAdams (1996) has preferred to regard the 'I' as a *process* of knowing and the 'Me' as a *product*, but since, to take the metaphor perhaps too literally, the knower must be changed by what is known, and what is known is changing continuously with experience, it would be better to see both as interacting processes. Perhaps even more stimulating is Blackmore's (1989, 1997) suggestion that the 'I' *is* the self-image, a model of the 'self in the world': on this view there would be no distinction between the 'I' and the 'Me'. Words are peculiarly treacherous here, but such an approach would seem to have links with some Upanishad texts where these two aspects of the self are not differentiated, and with yogic vision where the knower is the same as the known (Carrithers, 1983; Fontana, 1990). For present purposes, however we can neglect these speculative issues and focus on how we use the concept of 'self' in everyday life.

6   Bowlby suggested that the infant elaborates an 'Internal Working Model' of itself, significant others, and its relationships with them: this model, though modifiable, forms the basis of subsequent social interactions. The effects of rearing by multiple caregivers may stem in part from the greater sensitivity of the natural parents, but it is also likely that the inconsistent treatment received from multiple caregivers leaves the child without a coherent 'Internal Working Model' of self and others and thus lacking a consistent sense of self. In harmony with this view is the finding that maternal sensitivity promotes infant security (Cassidy and Berlin, 1994).

## 3   Structural beliefs: the nature of religious belief

1   As we shall see later, beliefs in counter-intuitive entities are also found not only in the religious sphere. Surveys cited by Woolley (1997) indicate that about a quarter of the adolescents and adults in the USA believe in ghosts, and beliefs in UFOs are widespread.

2   Others distinguish between 'belief' and 'faith', seen as an attitude of openness to God, or seek God inside the self (Armstrong, 1993).

3   Some writers have suggested that preliterate people live in a mystical world, and that their thinking is based on premises that differ from those accepted in our society. They link this to a tendency to relate to, rather than to control, the natural world (e.g. Lévy-Bruhl, 1923). This, however, is surely an idealised view, for members of all societies must live in the real world, and religious and empirical ways of thinking, if they are indeed distinct, must co-exist (Evans-Pritchard, 1965). In both literate and preliterate societies this may be achieved by the adop-

tion of religious attitudes sporadically to suit the occasion or the instant. For example, Malinowski (1935) pointed out the extent to which religious and secular activities may be inter-digitated. In their horticultural activities, the Trobrianders may bless the soil for fertility, then clear it in a rational way, then perform a magico-religious ceremony to prevent diseases, and then plant the seeds in a skilful manner. Later further magic for the success of the crops follows. And in the industrialised West, just as we have seen that different aspects of the self-system are revealed in different social contexts, so people's religious selves may be prominent at some times and in some contexts and not others.

4 Interestingly, the growth of scientific knowledge has eroded the literal acceptance of what was once Christian dogma, but has had little effect on Islam (Gellner, 1992).

5 Just how far-reaching or how strong such influences between different aspects of the self-system are is a matter of considerable interest, as yet far from resolved. While there is clearly some tendency to acquire knowledge systems that are at least not contradictory across domains of the (internalised) socio-cultural structure, some bodies of knowledge are more autonomous than others. It is relevant that colour classifications are affected by social change only to a limited extent, while other bodies of cultural knowledge may depend for their transmission and hence for their very existence on specific institutions. Thus,

> culture should not be viewed as an integrated whole, relying for its transmission on undifferentiated cognitive abilities. Rather it seems that human cognitive resources are involved in different ways in the many more-or-less autonomous psychological sub-systems that go into the making of culture.
>
> (Atran, 1993: 60)

## 4 Structural beliefs: dynamics, codification, and relation to the social system

1 Among the more colourful of these was Bishop Colenso, a former mathematician, who became the first Bishop of Natal. Before he became Bishop he had already acquired some doubts about the literal truth of the Bible – in part from Sir Charles Lyell's *Principles of Geology*, published between 1830 and 1833, which threw doubt on the possibility that there had ever been a universal flood. Colenso's doubts were exacerbated by an early Zulu convert who expressed disbelief that all the animals, from hot countries and cold, could have been accommodated in the Ark. He went on to write a scholarly analysis of the first five books of the Old Testament, but his heretical views led to attempts to depose him and to actions in both ecclesiastical and civil courts (Guy, 1983).

2 In Buddhist thought the distinction between sacred and profane is marginal (Orru and Wang, 1992), and many public rituals in the more traditional western societies combine the two.

## 5 Structural beliefs: why do individuals hold religious beliefs?

1 We shall see later that the properties of thought processes differ between the physical and social domains: in harmony with this, this cultural difference appeared in attributions about behavioural but not about physical events.

2 Kolakowski seems to argue both ways. On the one hand he states that belief in God and belief in immortality are intimately linked, because there seems no point to a god if humans are not immortal. If the human species dies out and if the world burns up until there is nothing left except God, what is the point of God? On the other hand he does not accept that the fear of death is a sufficient

cause for the concept of immortality. If it were, 'why have sharks – who avoid death as much as we do – failed to create their own images of hell and heaven?' (1982: 152). While I am not suggesting that fear of death is the *only* cause, this argument seems to be born of prejudice.

3 It has been suggested (Guerin, 1998) that religions typically act to increase anxiety over death and other vicissitudes in order to involve people in the religious system, which then has beneficial consequences on the integration of society. No doubt the effects have been two-way, religious involvement decreasing anxieties in some contexts and increasing them in others (See Figure 2.1 and Chapter 17).

## 6 Structural beliefs: religious representations

1 It is suggested that Epicurus was really an atheist, downplaying this aspect of his beliefs out of concern over persecution (Long and Sedley, 1987).

2 This discussion must be qualified in two respects. Often, household gods are recognised alongside an official religion: this was the case for much of Chinese history. Second, I have referred to the representations of deities in different cultures, but within cultures the representations of deities may be far from uniform: each individual forms his or her own representations, based on assumptions that are to some extent idiosyncratic.

3 It is perhaps worth reflecting that, in ordinary life, we tend to ascribe two sets of characteristics to holders of roles in society – those pertaining to any incumbent of the role, and the person's individual characteristics.

4 This was foreshadowed in Velasquez's painting of the *Coronation of the Virgin*, which shows her being crowned by the Trinity (Wulff, 1997).

## 7 Structural beliefs: the development of beliefs

1 Whether separate biological and psychological domains are present for children growing up in cultures which see animals in anthropomorphic terms is unclear.

2 This is an area of intense experimentation and controversy, though consensus about basic principles has emerged. One model postulates that early knowledge is acquired selectively and then re-represented at a succession of cognitive levels, thereby becoming available to consciousness, manipulable, and accessible to other cognitive domains. According to this model, during development the child focuses first on external data and forms new representations within cognitive domains: this can lead to elementary behavioural mastery based on a sequence of independently formed representations. Later, the child pays less attention to the external data, the internal representations becoming the focus of change. The partial disregard of the environment can lead to errors, and perhaps to a temporary decrease in performance. In a third phase, the internal representations are brought into line with external data. During these phases knowledge is re-represented with less detail at successive levels, as abstractions in, as it were, higher level languages, and becomes available to consciousness and to verbal report (Karmiloff-Smith, 1992). The details of this model are not important for present purposes: the important issues are that knowledge is acquired selectively at each stage, the child responding and making assumptions appropriate to the task in hand.

3 However, there are difficulties, and some objects seem to fall between categories. To defend the thesis of domain-specificity, Atran (1987) found it necessary to argue that living kinds that enter the domain of human function and use (eating, farming, entertainment, etc.) become ambiguous. Fruit and vegetable, for

instance, indicate concepts concerned with artefacts rather than natural kinds. It seems likely that bridges between domains become easier to cross as development proceeds, and knowledge becomes more integrated (Bloch, 1993; see also Boyer, 1993a, 1993b).

4 A brief summary of the manner in which information about sequences of behaviour appears to be stored is given in Chapter 8.

5 Parents in societies with aggressive supernaturals tended to reward children for self-reliance and independence, and depended more on punishment than on rewards. Lambert *et al.* (1959) favour the view that hurt and pain in infancy causes anxiety through conflicting anticipations of hurt and nurture: conflict is reduced by conceiving the deity as aggressive and thus compatible with human anticipations of hurt. The resulting tension in the child's ambivalence is accompanied by vicarious anxiety on the part of the parent, which leads to practices that reinforce the self-reliance.

6 Atran (1990) earlier distinguished between schematised and non-schematised representations.

7 The role of authority figures differs between cultures: in those with a revealed religion and an hierarchy of religious specialists their role clearly differs from that in small-scale societies where the religious system is closely interwoven with the social system.

## 8 Narratives

1 Here, as everywhere in the study of religious phenomena, generalisations must be treated with caution. Goody (1997) has argued that in many African societies the cosmologies are largely non-narrative.

## 9 Ritual: background considerations

1 Humphrey and Laidlaw (1994) regard the category of ritual as too inclusive and vague to be useful, and prefer instead the category of 'ritual action'. Its characteristics are: (1) Ritual action is non-intentional in the sense that the identity of the action does not depend on the agent's intention in acting. (2) The action is stipulated by constitutive rules which establish an ontology of ritual acts. Thus the person performing the ritual aims at the realisation of a pre-existing ritual act or sequence. (3) Ritual actions are archetypal in that they are seen as discrete entities with their own histories. (4) They are available for further assimilation to the actor's intentions, attitudes and beliefs. The present discussion, while continuing to use the term ritual for the sake of brevity, draws to a considerable extent on their ideas.

2 The curious position of religious specialists was recently demonstrated in the British Court of Appeal. A sacked priest was debarred from taking his appeal to an industrial tribunal because 'A minister of religion serves God and his congregation but does not have an employer. There is not a contract that he will serve a terrestrial employer in the performance of his duties'. When it was suggested that God was his employer, the Judge replied 'I don't think you have an address for him so you will not be able to serve any documents' (*Independent*, 12 July 1997).

3 'Instruction on certain questions regarding the collaboration of the non-ordained faithful in the sacred ministry of the priest', 13 November 1997. See *Tablet*, 22 November 1997: 1491 and 1514.

## 10  Ritual: form and sequence; magic

1 In the distantly related squirrel monkey, fear of snakes can be primed by contact with live insects (Masataka, 1993).
2 The use of other animate cultural symbols, such as eagles or lions, probably depends on properties that humans have learned to associate with them or legends connecting them with religious figures.
3 Lawson and McCauley (1990) propose that the complexity of a religious system is proportional to the extent to which the conceptual scheme is committed to the existence of personally active superhuman agents and their number. The more such agents, the greater the number of figures who can entitle rituals and the greater the number who can alter the arrangements of other superhuman agents. A wide range of rituals addressed to different deities for the benefit of the participants is then possible. Larson and McCauley comment that it is no coincidence that Unitarians have little ritual. These authors, it must be noted, are little interested in the religious system and its associated beliefs, but claim that their approach may offer guidelines for anthropological field-workers.

## 11  Ritual: motivation and consequences

1 Perhaps related to this is the striking conservatism of buildings where religious rituals are performed. Churches, synagogues, temples are more conservative in design than contemporary secular official buildings, perhaps because the unverifiable beliefs involved require constancy in the ritual.
2 Perhaps it is not too far-fetched to draw a parallel with Rosenblatt's (1997) analysis of the practices of tattooing, scarification, and body-piercing among the 'modern primitives' of San Francisco and elsewhere. These practices are no longer seen as disreputable, but have undergone a renaissance with often a spiritual significance. They are used to represent and objectify a 'primitive', intuitive, and affective self which is seen as opposed to the public, rational self, just as, for many, religious observance strengthens a self which is seen as opposed to the everyday self. The practices themselves may involve pain, and may be ritualised. Like ritual, they involve both public and private acts, and help to make an inner personal self part of the social self. As with ritual, the antiquity of these practices, as well as their supposed associations with earlier stages in human history, gives them added significance.
3 As always, there are exceptions. In their emphasis on the unending cycle of nature, in which the whole of humanity is but one element, much Hindu and Buddhist belief and ritual portrays the essential unity of all life.
4 Further discussion of the symbolism involved in such rituals is given by Bloch and Parry (1982).
5 Reif (1993) gives a detailed discussion of prayer in Judaism.
6 Given the view that it is the sacrifice of an intangible essence that matters, it is only a small step to the notion that it is the act of giving rather than the gift that is important. On this view, it is not difficult to see how the Christian emphasis on the intention behind the act arose.

## 12  Moral codes: background considerations

1 Though norms of behaviour differ between societies, it has been suggested that the observance of even quite trivial culture-specific norms could be adaptive. Thus, in a Californian study individuals were shown videotapes of actors who were or were not showing minor deviations from social norms that were quite trivial in nature (e.g. an actor posing as a junior executive scratched his foot

while speaking). Actors showing deviations were rated less positively than those who did not, and the authors suggest that such behaviour could affect the reproductive success of individuals in a real-life situation (Wenegrat *et al.*, 1996). Of course, while such evidence is compatible with the view that norm-observance is an adapted human characteristic, it is a long way short of proof.

2 *Shorter Oxford English Dictionary*.

3 To repeat what I have said elsewhere, this is not saying that what is natural to the individual is right, but is placing emphasis on the judgements we make about how others should behave in order to promote group harmony, judgements which have probably been influenced by natural selection (see Chapter 13).

4 *Development of moral judgements in the individual.* Premack and Premack (1994) have provided a stimulating though perhaps somewhat speculative outline of the manner in which moral judgements could develop in childhood. Experiments in which young children's reactions to the movement of images on computer screens have been used to assess the criteria by which infants differentiate positive and negative acts. In the first place three-year-olds (and probably younger children) interpret an object that starts and stops without outside influence as having intentionality. Rightness or wrongness is interpreted initially by intensity of movement: soft or weak motions are coded as positive, strong ones as negative. Older infants can interpret the motion of intentional objects as goal-directed, and thus categorise the movement of one object which appears to help another to attain a goal as positive, and a movement which obstructs the other as negative. Later still, characterological judgements (c.g. beauty is good) are added. Children also recognise 'possession' (objects move together) and group membership (intentional objects of equal size and strength that move together), and these provide further material for positive and negative judgements. These primitives often take the form of an expectancy ('If A, then B follows'), and some the form of a moral judgement ('If A, then B should follow'). The further content of moral judgements must involve culture-specific learning.

5 To recognise only one God, not to make graven images, not to take the Lord's name in vain, and to keep holy the Sabbath.

## 13 Moral codes: prosocial behaviour and reciprocity

1 Interestingly, the latter can be taken to mean 'Love your neighbour to the extent and in the same way as you love yourself', or 'Love your neighbour as if he were part of yourself' (A. Macintosh, pers. comm.), and is thus reminiscent of the picture of close personal relationships as involving the merging of two selves (see p. 29)

2 A thoughtful if somewhat despairing article by a former Catholic is of interest in this context. Rejecting the inevitable guilt associated with the doctrine of original sin on which she was raised, and rebelling against the concept of unattainable moral ideals, she points to the moral vacuum that has been left by the pseudo-ideology of the free market. To her, fundamentalist religion offers security but is liable to be stifling, and she rejects a retreat either into self-interest or into communitarianism: the latter, she argues, puts 'belonging' before 'being', and is likely to suffocate as much as to nurture. But she slips in the sentence 'That we treat each other with honesty, respect and consideration is important in all human relations'. Thereby, it would seem, she is suggesting that the principle of reciprocity must be basic (Baird, 1997: 9).

3 The matter is, however, a delicate one: we sometimes interpret the generosity of another as an attempt at manipulation, as though the other party were trying to use the principle of reciprocity to make us do something that we would not

otherwise want to do. We then feel resentment or anger, comparable to that which we feel when unfairly done by.

4 *Another approach to moral values.* Some may wonder whether this emphasis on reciprocity does not involve over-stating its importance as a principle guiding human behaviour. However in so far as moral issues involve our behaviour towards others, precepts must involve putting oneself in the other person's shoes. Given this necessary awareness of other individuals, the selfish individual must be seeing his own view as more important than that of others. Consider, for example, the nature of moral principles from the entirely different perspective of a moral philosopher.

Taylor (1989) has postulated three axes of moral thinking and values. One is based on respect for human life, and includes avoidance of suffering, an emphasis on freedom and self-control, and the view that productive activity and family life is central. The second concerns life-goals – what sort of life is worth living, how can I best make use of my talents, how can I avoid a life of trivia, and other issues which Taylor summarises as 'affirmation of ordinary life' and contrasts with the warrior and Platonic ethics of earlier times. The third of Taylor's axes involves what he calls 'dignity', and is approximately equivalent to what psychologists would call 'self-esteem': the characteristics we see in ourselves as commanding the respect of others.

It will be noted that these axes are not postulated as a result of any objective analysis, and Taylor himself emphasises that they not only overlap, but also differ dramatically over time within societies and between societies at any one time. Thus in the modern West the first axis, involving respect for human life, is paramount: the emphasis on avoiding suffering has become stronger over the centuries, and we see it as receiving less emphasis in some less fortunate countries. And even within the West, the emphasis on freedom and autonomy is stronger in some societies than in others, where the focus is shifted towards the common good. The second axis, involving the sort of life that is worth living, is seen differently in different societies, as well as by individuals within a society: courageous deeds would win respect in a warrior society, the acquisition of resources does so in many modern ones, and what counts as trivia might have little general acceptance. Preoccupation with the meaning of life may be a relatively recent phenomenon. And the characteristics likely to command the respect of others certainly vary not only between but also within societies. So it is clear that societal mores must be understood in the context of the society. Thus Taylor's axes must be seen as at most an heuristic device.

However, it can also reasonably be claimed that reciprocity plays a role in all three of them. With respect to the first, we are social beings and both biologically adapted and socialised to live with others in a society. It is almost impossible to avoid thinking of one's life in terms of one's interactions and relationships with others. As we have seen, the very development of our self-concept depends on how we perceive others to see us. Underlying our respect for the lives of others is the hope and expectation that they will respect ours, that they will not cause us suffering, that we shall have freedom to act autonomously. With respect to the second, underlying the feeling that life is not worth living if one is concerned only with trivia and with one's own ends is the feeling of terror of what it would be like if no one cared for you. And, with the third axis, one would not respect oneself if one lived purely selfishly, nor would one respect others who lived solely for themselves.

5 Humphrey (1997) puts this point more precisely. Every time a kin-selected altruist helps a relative, he is helping someone also likely to carry a predisposition for altruism, and is therefore likely to help his own relatives, which includes

the original altruist. Thus the latter is increasing the pool of individuals from whom he may himself one day benefit. Similarly, every time a reciprocal altruist helps another individual whom he trusts will reciprocate, he is helping another individual predisposed to show reciprocal altruism and who is in that respect a relative. Thus Humphrey suggests that kin selection and reciprocal altruism are both rooted in a trait for behaving altruistically to others who share the trait and who are in that respect related (see also Dawkins, 1976).

6 Though the relevant phases of human evolution took place in a period when the environment fluctuated on a geological time-scale, this supposition of relative stability between generations would still have been more true than in the modern world.

7 Much of this discussion depends on the work of Alexander, 1987; Boyd and Richerson, 1985, 1991; Campbell, 1991; and Irons, 1996a, 1996b.

8 It has been argued that, while natural selection could produce a propensity to reciprocate positive behaviour, it could never lead to the Christian virtues of 'turning the other cheek', returning good for evil, or helping strangers at a distance (Ruse, 1994). However, with regard to the first two issues, there is no suggestion that behaviour resulting from the operation of natural selection is independent of current circumstances. The biological approach accepts that humans have the possibility of accepting abuse or of resisting it, and have been adapted to choose whichever is likely to be the better course in the circumstances. When Christian principles were formulated, fighting back may frequently not have been a wise policy, and it was proper to put the emphasis on the other alternative. With respect to the third issue, of giving help to strangers at a distance, it is intrinsic to both the individual selection and to the cultural group selection hypothesis that the reciprocity principle becomes part of the moral code. The boundaries on the in-group, on those who should be helped, must be learned by the individual, and are subject to extension to strangers at a distance.

9 There is also evidence from studies of both animals and humans that individuals tend to withdraw from situations in which another individual emits signals of distress. It is suggested that comparisons of the individual's experiences with the observed experience of the victim will generate a proscription against the action which caused the victim's distress, and lead to the construction of 'judgements of moral necessity' (Turiel, 1983). Blair (1997) has further proposed that all humans may possess a 'Violence inhibiting mechanism' (VIM) which is activated by signals of distress: on this view the activation of the VIM results in the inhibition of violent action. Developmentally representations of moral transgressions become stimuli for the VIM, and the withdrawal response following the activation of the VIM is experienced as aversive. This leads to the act being judged as bad. Conventional transgressions do not result in victims, and so do not result in activation of the VIM. The distinction between these two views does not matter for present purposes (see also Mealey, 1997): it will be apparent that either could account for the development of some cases of moral behaviour (defined here as behaviour which avoids infringing the rights or welfare of others, see p. 144), and thus of reciprocity, but not for conventional transgressions, which do not result in distress signals from a victim.

10 The precise emotion felt after wrong-doing presents an interesting example of the dialectical relations between basic propensities and the socio-cultural structure. Lewis emphasises how religions differ in their approach to shame, according to whether sin is seen as a consequence of individual action or as ubiquitous. Where failure is the result of particular actions, and can be undone by action in the world, this is the sign of a guilt-oriented society. This, Lewis (1992) suggests, is the case with Judaism and with main-stream Protestantism. Repentance for

failure is associated with commitment to good deeds. In Catholicism, by contrast, the sin of Adam and Eve is borne by all people. There is thus a global attribution of sin which is independent of specific action, and the focus is on shame. Forgiveness comes primarily through confession and absolution, and rewards or punishments are given not in this life, but in Heaven (or Hell).

## 14  Moral codes: other principles

1 In the 1980s I heard a Fundamentalist preacher in the southern USA arguing that God was too wise to let Communists into Heaven.
2 This is not the case in industrialised societies, where diverse factors operate (Szreter, 1996; Vining, 1986).
3 See also Reynolds and Tanner (1983), cited on p. 15.
4 Some possible historical exceptions in ancient Egypt and Iran have been documented by Scheidel (1996). Possible explanations for these are discussed by Irons (1998).
5 The role of genital modification in male competition and female mate choice has been discussed by Rowanchilde (1996).

## 15  Religious experience

1 Transcendental meditators sometimes meditate in large groups, claiming that the effects can reduce crime, violence etc. in adjacent areas (Orme-Johnson *et al.*, 1988).
2 Individuals who are asymmetrical are more prone to health problems. Bodily (especially breast) asymmetry as an indicator of fitness could thus play a part in sexual selection, and it has been shown empirically that breast symmetry is related to fecundity. In addition, in a study of student couples asymmetry in males was negatively correlated with the number of extra-partner copulations (Gangestad and Thornhill, 1997). It has therefore been suggested that the human aesthetic preference for symmetry may be based in the consequences of natural selection (Møller *et al.*, 1995), a suggestion in need of further verification.

## 17  Persistence

1 Another problem with such a view is that it leaves the question 'metaphorical for what?' unanswered.
2 The dilemma of religious 'truth' is epitomised in a Portuguese play about a young woman who claimed to have become pregnant through an act of God. Her doctor (representing science) could offer no proof of the falsity of her claim and (perhaps for reasons of delicacy) was unwilling to confirm her virginity. The priest was not willing to concede a second immaculate conception, but could not deny its possibility without also denying the Virgin birth of Christ (Régio, 1947; see also Lisboa, 1997).
3 In view of such differences, it is recommended that health professionals should take differences in the extent and nature of religiosity into account when deciding on treatment (Shafranske and Maloney, 1996).
4 In a study of religious participation on functioning in a large sample of elderly persons over a twelve year follow-up period, Idler and Kasl (1997) found attendances at services to be a strong predictor of better functioning, even when intermediate changes in functioning were included.

# Bibliography

Acitelli, L.K. and Young, A.M. (1996) 'Gender and thought in relationships'. In G.J.O. Fletcher and J. Fitness (eds), *Knowledge structures in close relationships*, pp.147–68. Hillsdale, NJ: Erlbaum.

Adorno, T.W., Frenkel-Brunswik, E., Levinson, D.J. and Sanford, R.N. (1950) *The authoritarian personality*. New York: Harper.

Alexander, B.C. (1991) 'Correcting misinterpretations of Turner's theory: an African-American Pentecostal illustration'. *Journal of the Scientific Study of Religion*, 30: 26–44.

Alexander, C.N. *et al.* (1996) 'Trial of stress reduction for hypertension in older African Americans, II. Sex and risk subgroup analysis'. *Hypertension*, 28: 228–37.

Alexander, R.D. (1987) *The biology of moral systems*. Hawthorne, NY: Aldine.

Allport, G.W., Gillespie, J.M. and Young, J. (1948) 'The religion of the post-war college student'. *Journal of Psychology*, 25: 3–33.

Allport, G.W. and Ross, J.M. (1967) 'Personal religious orientation and prejudice'. *Journal of Personality and Social Psychology*, 5: 432–43.

Altemeyer, B. (1988) *Enemies of freedom: understanding right-wing authoritarianism*. San Francisco, CA: Jossey-Bass. (Cited Hood *et al.*, 1996.)

Anderson, D.A. and Worthen, D. (1997) 'Exploring a fourth dimension: spirituality as a resource for the couple therapist'. *Journal of Marital and Family Therapy*, 23: 3–11.

Appleton, J. (1975) *The experience of landscape*. New York: Wiley.

d'Aquili, E.G. and Newberg, A.B. (1993) 'Religious and mystical states: a neuropsychological model'. *Zygon*, 28: 177–200.

Argyle, M. and Beit-Hallahmi, B. (1975) *The social psychology of religion*. London: Routledge and Kegan Paul.

Armstrong, K. (1993) *A history of God*. London: Heinemann.

Aron, E.A. and Aron, A. (1996) 'Love and expansion of the self'. *Personal Relationships*, 3: 45–58.

Atran, S. (1987) 'Constraints on the ordinary semantics of living kinds'. *Mind and Language*, 2: 27–63.

—— (1990) *Cognitive foundations of natural history: towards an anthropology of science*. Cambridge: Cambridge University Press.

—— (1993) 'Whither "ethnoscience"?' In P. Boyer (ed.), *Cognitive aspects of religious symbolism*, pp. 48–70. Cambridge: Cambridge University Press.

Austin, J. (1975) *How to do things with words*. Cambridge, MA: Harvard University Press.

Avis, J. and Harris, P.L. (1991) 'Belief-desire reasoning among Baka children: evidence for a universal conception of mind'. *Child Development*, 62: 460–67.

Axelrod, R. and Hamilton, W.D. (1984) 'The evolution of cooperation'. *Science*, 211: 1390–96.

Backman, C.W. (1988) 'The self: a dialectical approach'. *Advances in Experimental Psychology*, 21: 229–60.

Baillargeon, R., Kotovsky, L. and Needham, A. (1995) 'The acquisition of physical knowledge in infancy'. In D. Sperber, D. Premack and A.J. Premack (eds), *Causal Cognition*, pp.79–116. Oxford: Clarendon.

Baird, V. (1997) 'How are we to live?' *New Internationalist*, 289: 7–10.

Baldwin, M.W. (1995) 'Relational schemas and cognition in close relationships'. *Journal of Social and Personal Relationships*, 12: 547–52.

Balling, J.D. and Falk, J.H. (1982) 'Development of visual preference for natural environments'. *Environment and Behaviour*, 14: 5–28.

Bambrough, R. (1969) *Reason, truth, and God*. London: Methuen.

Bandura, A. (1997) *Self-efficacy: the exercise of control*. New York: Freeman.

Barbour, I.G. (1994) 'Experiencing and interpreting nature in science and religion'. *Zygon*, 29: 457–87.

Barkow, J.H., Cosmides, L. and Tooby, J. (eds) (1992) *The adapted mind*. Oxford: Oxford University Press.

Baron-Cohen, S., Leslie, A.M. and Frith, U. (1985) 'Does the autistic child have a "theory of mind"?' *Cognition*, 21: 37–46.

Barrett, J.L. and Keil, F.C. (1996) 'Conceptualizing a non-natural entity: anthropomorphism in God concepts'. *Cognitive Psychology*, 31: 219–47.

Bateson, P. (1995) 'What about incest?' In J. Brockman and K. Marson (eds), *How things are*. New York: Morrow.

Batson, C.D. and Flory, J.D. (1990) 'Goal-relevant cognitions associated with helping by individuals high on intrinsic, end religion'. *Journal of the Scientific Study of Religion*, 29: 346–60.

Batson, C.D. and Schoenrade, P. (1991) 'Measuring religion as quest, (1) and (2)'. *Journal of the Scientific Study of Religion*, 30: 416–29 and 430–47.

Batson, C.D., Schoenrade, P. and Ventis, W.L. (1993) *Religion and the individual*. New York: Oxford University Press.

Batson, C.D. and Ventis, W.L. (1982) *The religious experience: a social-psychological perspective*. New York: Oxford University Press.

Baumeister, R.F. and Wilson, B. (1996) 'Life stories and the four needs for meaning'. *Psychological Inquiry*, 7: 322–77.

Baumrind, D. (1971) 'Current patterns of parental authority'. *Developmental Psychology Monograph*, 4 (1 and 2).

Baxter, L. (1990) 'Dialectical contradictions in relationship development'. *Journal of Social and Personal Relationships*, 7: 69–88.

Beardsworth, T. (1977) *A sense of presence: the phenomenology of certain kinds of visionary and ecstatic experience based on a thousand contemporary first-hand accounts*. Oxford: Religious Experience Research Unit, Manchester College.

Beit-Hallahmi, B. (1989) *Prolegomena to the psychological study of religion*. Lewisburg, PA: Bucknell University Press.

Beit-Hallahmi, B. and Argyle, M. (1997) *Religious behaviour, belief, and experience*. London: Routledge.

Belsky, J. (1997) 'Attachment, mating, and parenting: an evolutionary interpretation'. *Human Nature*, 8: 361–81.

Bergin, A.E. (1983) 'Religiosity and mental health: a critical re-evaluation and meta-analysis'. *Professional Psychology: Research and Practice*, 14: 170–84. (Cited Brown, 1987.)

Berlin, B. and Kay, P. (1969) *Basic color terms*. Berkeley, CA: University of California Press.

Betzig, L., Borgerhoff Mulder, M., and Turke, P. (eds) (1988) *Human reproductive behavior: a Darwinian perspective*. Cambridge: Cambridge University Press.

Bittles, A.H. (1994) 'The role and significance of consanguinity as a demographic variable'. *Population and Development Review*, 20: 561–84.

Bittles, A.H. and Neel, J.V. (1994) 'The costs of human inbreeding and implications for variations at the DNA level'. *Nature Genetics*, 8: 117–21.

Blackmore, S. (1989) 'Consciousness: science tackles the self'. *New Scientist*, April: 38–41.

—— (1997) 'The power of the meme meme'. *Skeptic*, 5: 43–9.

Blair, R.J. (1997) 'A cognitive developmental approach to morality: investigating the psychopath'. In S. Baron-Cohen (ed.), *The maladapted mind*, pp. 85–114. Hove: Psychology Press.

Bloch, M. (1977) 'The past and present in the present'. *Man*, 12: 278–92.

—— (1989) *Ritual, history, and power: selected papers in anthropology*. London: Athlone.

—— (1993) 'Domain-specificity, living kinds and symbolism'. In P. Boyer (ed.), *Cognitive aspects of religious symbolism*, pp. 11–20. Cambridge: Cambridge University Press.

Bloch, M. and Parry, J. (eds) (1982) *Death and the regeneration of life*. Cambridge: Cambridge University Press.

Bokenkamp, S. (1996) 'The purification ritual of the luminous perfected'. In D.S. Lopez (ed.), *Religions of China in practice*, pp. 268–77. Princeton, NJ: Princeton University Press.

Boone, J. (1998) 'The evolution of magnanimity: when is it better to give than to receive?'. *Human Nature*, 9: 1–22.

Borgerhoff Mulder, M. (1991) 'Human behavioral ecology: studies in foraging and reproduction'. In J.R. Krebs and N.B. Davies (eds), *Behavioural ecology*, London: Blackwell, 3rd edn.

Borgerhoff Mulder, M. and Mitchell, S.D. (1994) 'Rough waters between genes and culture: an anthropological and philosophical view on coevolution'. *Biology and Philosophy*, 9: 471–87.

Bowlby, J. (1969/1982) *Attachment and Loss, vol. 1. Attachment*. London: Hogarth.

Boyd, R. and Richerson, P.J. (1985) *Culture and the evolutionary process*. Chicago, IL: Chicago University Press.

—— (1988) 'The evolution of reciprocity in sizable groups'. *Journal of Theoretical Biology*, 132: 337–56.

—— (1991) 'Culture and cooperation'. In R.A. Hinde and J. Groebel (eds), *Cooperation and prosocial behaviour*, pp. 27–48. Cambridge: Cambridge University Press.

—— (1992) 'Punishment allows the evolution of cooperation (or anything else) in sizable groups'. *Ethology and Sociobiology*, 13: 171–95.

Boyer, P. (1993a) *Cognitive aspects of religious symbolism*. Cambridge: Cambridge University Press.

—— (1993b) 'Pseudo-natural kinds'. In P. Boyer (ed.), *Cognitive aspects of religious symbolism*. Cambridge: Cambridge University Press.

—— (1994) *The naturalness of religious ideas*. Berkeley, CA: University of California Press.

—— (1995) 'Causal understandings in cultural representations'. In D. Sperber, D. Premack and A.J. Premack (eds), *Causal Cognition*, pp. 615–44. Oxford: Clarendon.

Bradley, D.E. (1995) 'Religious involvement and social resources: evidence from the data set "American's changing lives"'. *Journal of the Scientific Study of Religion*, 34: 259–67.

Bretherton, I., Ridgeway, D. and Cassidy, J. (1990) 'Assessing internal working models of the attachment relationship'. In M.T. Greenberg, D. Cicchetti and E.M. Cummings (eds), *Attachment in the pre-school years*, pp. 273–308. Chicago, IL: Chicago University Press.

Broad, C.D. (1925) *The mind and its place in nature*. London.

Brooke, J.H. (1991) *Science and religion*. Cambridge: Cambridge University Press.

Brown, L.B. (1962) 'A study of religious belief'. *British Journal of Psychology*, 53: 259–72.

—— (1987) *The psychology of religious belief*. London: Academic Press.

Brown, R., Hinkle, S., Ely, P.G., Fox-Cardamone, L., Maras, P. and Taylor, L.A. (1992) 'Recognizing group diversity: individual-collectivist and autonomous-relational orientations and their implications for group processes'. *British Journal of Social Psychology*, 31: 327–42.

Bruce, S. (1995) 'The truth about religion in Britain'. *Journal of the Scientific Study of Religion*, 34: 417–30.

—— (1996) *Religion in the modern world*. Oxford: Oxford University Press.

Bruner, J. (1977) 'Early social interaction and language acquisition'. In H.R. Schaffer (ed.), *Studies in mother-child interaction*. London: Academic Press.

—— (1986) *Actual minds, possible worlds*. Cambridge, MA: Harvard University Press.

—— (1990) *Acts of meaning*. Cambridge, MA: Harvard University Press.

Buckser, A. (1995) 'Religion and the supernatural on a Danish Island: rewards, compensators, and the meaning of religion'. *Journal of the Scientific Study of Religion*, 34: 1–16.

Burkert, W. (1996) *Creation of the sacred*. Cambridge, MA: Harvard University Press.

Burleston, B.R. and Denton, W.H. (1992) 'A new look at similarity and attraction in marriage: similarities in socio-cognitive and communication skills as predictors of attraction and satisfaction'. *Communication Monographs*, 59: 268–87.

Burnside, J. (1994) 'Tension and tradition in the pursuit of justice'. In J. Burnside and N. Baker (eds), *Relational Justice*, pp.42–52. Winchester: Waterside Press.

Burris, C.T., Batson, C.D., Altstaedten, M. and Stephens, K. (1994) '"What a friend…" Loneliness as a motivator of intrinsic religion'. *Journal of the Scientific Study of Religion*, 33: 326–34.

Buss, D. (1994) *The evolution of desire*. New York: Basic Books.

Buunk, B.P. (1995) 'Sex, self-esteem, dependency and extradyadic sexual experience as related to jealousy responses'. *Journal of Social and Personal Relationships*, 12: 147–53.

Byrne, D. (1971) *The attraction paradigm*. New York: Academic Press.

Byrne, D and Clore, G.L. (1967) 'Effectance, arousal, and attraction'. *Journal of Personality and Social Psychology, Monograph 6*, (whole no. 638).

Byrne, D., Nelson, D., and Reeves, K. (1966) 'Effects of consensual validation and invalidation on attraction as a function of verifiability'. *Journal of Experimental Social Psychology*, 2: 98–107.

Campbell, D.T. (1991) 'A naturalistic theory of archaic moral orders'. *Zygon*, 26: 91–114.

Campbell, T.C. and Fukuyama, Y. (1970) *The fragmented layman*. Philadelphia, PA: Pilgrim Press. (Cited Argyle and Beit-Hallahmi, 1975.)

Cancian, F.M. (1968) 'Varieties of functional analysis'. In D.L. Sills (ed.), *International Encyclopedia of the Social Sciences*, 6: 29–43.

Carey, S. (1995) 'On the origin of causal understanding'. In D. Sperber, D. Premack and A.J. Premack (eds), *Causal Cognition*, pp. 268–308. Oxford: Clarendon.

Carrithers, M. (1983) *The Buddha*. Oxford: Oxford University Press.

—— (1992) *Why humans have cultures*. Oxford: Oxford University Press.

Cassidy, J. and Berlin, L.J. (1994) 'The insecure/ambivalent pattern of attachment: theory and research'. *Child Development*, 65: 971–91.

Chadwick, B.A. and Top, B.L. (1993) 'Religiosity and delinquency among LDS adolescents'. *Journal of the Scientific Study of Religion*, 32: 51–67.

Chagnon, N.A. and Irons, W. (1979) *Evolutionary biology and human social behavior: an anthropological perspective*. North Scituate, MA: Duxbury.

Chait, I. (1996) 'The Torah and the Yanamamo: a Rabbi replies to Hartung'. *Skeptic*, 4: 24–8.

Chalmers, R. (1990) *Scientific research on the transcendental meditation and TM-Sidhi programme. Introduction to Volume 3*, pp. 1429–57. Vlodrop, Netherlands: Maharishi European Research University.

Cheney, D.L. and Seyfarth, R.M. (1990) *How monkeys see the world*. Chicago, IL: Chicago University Press.

Chomsky, N. (1965) *Aspects of the theory of syntax*. Cambridge, MA: MIT Press.

Christian, W.A. (1981) *Local religion in sixteenth-century Spain*. Princeton, NJ: Princeton University Press.

Clayton, S.D. and Lerner, M.J. (1991) 'Complications and complexity in the pursuit of justice'. In R.A. Hinde and J. Groebel (eds), *Cooperation and prosocial behaviour*, pp.173–84. Cambridge: Cambridge University Press.

Collinson, D. (1992) 'Aesthetic experience'. In O. Hanfling (ed.), *Philosophical Aesthetics*, pp.111–78. Oxford: Blackwell.

Comstock, G.W. and Partridge, K.B. (1972) 'Church attendance and health'. *Journal of Chronic Diseases*, 25: 665–72.

Cosmides, L. and Tooby, J. (1992) 'Cognitive adaptations for social exchange'. In J.H. Barkow, L. Cosmides and J. Tooby (eds), *The adapted mind*, pp.163–228. New York: Oxford University Press.

Count, E.W. (1973) *Being and becoming human*. New York: Van Nostrand Reinhold.

Cronin, H. (1991) *The ant and the peacock – altruism and sexual selection from Darwin to to-day*. Cambridge: Cambridge University Press.

Crook, J. (1990) 'Meditation and personal disclosure: the Western Zen retreat'. In J. Crook and D. Fontana (eds), *Space in mind*, pp.156–73. Longmead, Shaftesbury, Dorset: Element.

—— (in press) 'Zen: the challenge to dependency'. In G. Watson, G. Claxton, and S. Batchelor (eds) *The psychology of awakening*. Sturminster Newton, Dorset: Prism.

Crook, J. and Osmaston, H. (1994) *Himalyan Buddhist villages*. Bristol: Bristol University.

Cummins, D.D. (1996) 'Evidence of deontic reasoning in 3- and 4-year-old children'. *Memory and Cognition*, 24: 823–9.

Damasio, A.R. (1994) *Descartes' error*. New York: Putnam.

Daly, M. and Wilson, M. (1988) *Homicide*. New York: Aldine de Gruyter.

Darley, J. and Batson, C.D. (1973) 'From Jerusalem to Jericho: a study of situational and dispositional variables in helping behavior'. *Journal of Personality and Social Psychology*, 27: 100–08.

Darwin, C. (1871) *The descent of man and selection in relation to sex*. London: Murray.

Davies, C. (1994) 'Crime and the rise and decline of a relational society'. In J. Burnside and N. Baker (eds), *Relational Justice*, pp. 31–41. Winchester: Waterside Press.

Dawkins, R. (1976) *The selfish gene*. Oxford: Oxford University Press.

—— (1982) *The extended phenotype*. San Francisco, CA: Freeman.

—— (1993) *Viruses of the mind*. London: British Humanists Association.

—— (1995) 'Good and bad reasons for believing'. In J. Brockman and K. Matson (eds), *How things are*, pp.17–26. London: Weidenfeld and Nicolson.

Deconchy, J.P. (1968) 'God and parental images: the masculine and feminine in religious free association'. In A. Godin (ed.) *From cry to word*. Brussels: Lumen Vitae. (Cited Beit-Hallahmi and Argyle, 1997.)

De Vries, M.W. (1984) 'Temperament and infant mortality among the Masai of East Africa'. *American Journal of Psychiatry*, 141: 1189–94.

Dickie, J.R., Eshleman, A.K., Merasco, D.M., Shepard, A., Wilt, M.V. and Johnson, M. (1997) 'Parent-child relationships and children's images of god'. *Journal of the Scientific Study of Religion*, 36: 25–43.

Donovan, P. (1979) *Interpreting religious experience*. London: Sheldon.

Douglas, M. (1970a) *Natural symbols*. Harmondsworth: Penguin.

—— (1970b) *Purity and danger*. Harmondsworth: Penguin.

—— (1990) 'The pangolin revisited: a new approach to animal symbolism'. In R.G. Willis (ed.), *Signifying animals: human meaning in the natural world*, pp.25–42. London: Unwin Hyman.

DSM IV (1994) *Diagnostic and statistical manual of mental disorders*. Washington, DC: American Psychiatric Association.

Dudbridge, G. (1995) *Religious experience and lay society in T'ang China*. Cambridge: Cambridge University Press.

Dunkel-Schetter, C. and Skokan, L.A. (1990) 'Determinants of social support provision in personal relationships'. *Journal of Social and Personal Relationships*, 7: 437–50.

Durham, W. (1991) *Coevolution: genes, culture, and human diversity*. Stanford, CA: Stanford University Press.

Durkheim, E. (1964) *The elementary forms of the religious life*. London: Allen and Unwin, 1912.

Eagley, A.H. and Chaiken, S. (1984) 'Cognitive theories of persuasion'. In L. Berkowitz (ed.), *Advances in Experimental Social Psychology*, 1: 267–359.

Eibl Eibesfeldt, I. (1975) *Ethology*. New York: Holt, Rinehart and Winston.

Eisenberg, N. and Mussen, P. (1989) *The roots of prosocial behavior*. Cambridge: Cambridge University Press.

Eisenberg, N. and Strayer, J. (eds) (1987) *Empathy and its development*. Cambridge: Cambridge University Press.

Elkind, D. (1971) 'The origins of religion in the child'. *Review of Religious Research*, 12: 35–42. (Cited Argyle and Beit-Hallahmi, 1975.)

Ellison, C.G. (1991) 'Religious involvement and subjective well-being'. *Journal of Health and Social Behavior*, 32: 80–99.

Ellison, C.G. and George, L.K. (1994) 'Religious involvement, social ties, and social support in a southeastern community'. *Journal of the Scientific Study of Religion*, 33: 46–61.

Emde, R. (1984) 'The affective self: continuities and transformations from infancy'. In J.D. Call, E. Galenson, and R.L. Tyson (eds), *Frontiers of infant psychiatry II*, pp. 38–54. New York: Basic Books.

Erickson, J.A. (1992) 'Adolescent religious development and commitment: a structural equation model of the role of family, peer group, and educational influences'. *Journal of the Scientific Study of Religion*, 31: 131–52.

Essock-Vitale, S.M. and McGuire, M.T. (1980) 'Predictions derived from the theories of kin selection and reciprocation assessed by anthropological data'. *Ethology and Sociobiology*, 1: 233–43.

—— (1985) 'Women's lives viewed from an evolutionary perspective. 2. Patterns of helping' *Ethology and Sociobiology*, 6: 155 73.

Evans, D.W., Leckman, J.F., Carter, A., Reznick, J.S., Henshaw, D., King, R.A and Pauls, D. (1997) 'Ritual, habit and perfectionism: the prevalence and development of compulsive-like behavior in normal young children'. *Child Development*, 68: 58–68.

Evans-Pritchard, E.E. (1937) *Witchcraft, oracles, and magic among the Azande*. Oxford: Oxford University Press.

—— (1951) 'Some features of Nuer religion'. *Journal of the Royal Anthropological Institute*, 81: 1–14.

—— (1954) 'The meaning of sacrifice among the Nuer'. *Journal of the Royal Anthropological Institute*, 84: 21–33.

—— (1956) *Nuer religion*. Oxford: Oxford University Press.

—— (1965) *Theories of primitive religion*. London: Oxford University Press.

Evans-Wentz, W.Y. (ed.) (1957) *The Tibetan book of the dead*. New York: Oxford University Press.

Fara, P. (in prep.) *A secular saint: Isaac Newton and representations of scientific genius*.

Fazel, M. and Young, D.M. (1988) 'Life quality of Tibetans and Hindus: a function of religion'. *Journal of the Scientific Study of Religion*, 27: 229–42.

Febvre, L. (1982) *The problem of unbelief in the sixteenth century. The religion of Rabelais*. Cambridge, MA: Harvard University Press. (Cited Tambiah, 1990.)

Ferraro, K.F. and Albrecht-Jensen, C.M. (1991) 'Does religion influence adult health?'. *Journal of the Scientific Study of Religion*, 30: 193–202.

Festinger, L. (1957) *A theory of cognitive dissonance*. Evanston, IL: Row, Peterson.

Festinger, L., Riecken, H.W. and Schachter, S. (1956) *When prophecy fails*. Minneapolis, MN: University of Minnesota Press.

Firestone, R. (1996) 'Conceptions of Holy War in Biblical and Qur'ānic tradition'. *Journal of Religious Ethics*, 24: 99–124.

Firth, R. (1967) *Tikopia ritual and belief*. London: Allen and Unwin.

—— (1996) *Religion: a humanist interpretation*. London: Routledge.

Fischer, R. (1986) 'Toward a neuroscience of self-expression and states of self-awareness and interpreting interpretations'. In B.B. Wolman and M. Ullman (eds), *Handbook of states of consciousness*, pp. 3–30. New York: Van Nostrand. (Cited Wulff, 1997.)

Fiske, A.R., Haslam, N. and Fiske, S.T. (1991) 'Confusing one person with another: what errors reveal about elementary forms of human relations'. *Journal of Personality and Social Psychology*, 60: 656–74.

Fitness, J. (1996) 'Emotion knowledge structures in close relationships'. In G.J.O. Fletcher and J. Fitness (eds), *Knowledge structures in close relationships*, pp. 195–217. Hillsdale, NJ: Erlbaum.

Fletcher, G.J.O. and Fitness, J. (eds) (1996) *Knowledge structures in close relationships*. Hillsdale, NJ: Erlbaum.

Flinn, M.V. (1997) 'Culture and the evolution of social learning'. *Evolution and Human Behavior*, 18: 23–67.

Foa, U.G. and Foa, E.B. (1974) *Societal structures of the mind*. Springfield, IL: Thomas.

Fontana, D. (1990) 'Self-assertion and self-transcendence in Buddhist psychology'. In J. Crook and D. Fontana (eds), *Space in mind*, pp. 42–59. Longmead, Shaftesbury, Dorset: Element.

Forgas, J.P. (1996) 'The role of emotion scripts and transient moods in relationships'. In G.J.O. Fletcher and J. Fitness (eds), *Knowledge structures in close relationships*, pp. 275–97. Hillsdale, NJ: Erlbaum.

Fowler, J.W. (1981) *Stages of faith*. San Francisco, CA: Harper and Row. (Cited Brown, 1987.)

Frank, R.H. (1988) *Passions within reason*. New York: Norton.

Frankel, B.G. and Hewitt, W.E. (1994) 'Religion and well-being among Canadian university students: the role of faith groups on campus'. *Journal of the Scientific Study of Religion*, 33: 62–73.

Frankl, V.E. (1975) *The unconscious god: psychotherapy and theology*. New York: Simon and Schuster.

Fredman, R.G. (1981) *The Passover Seder*. Philadelphia, PA: University of Pennsylvania Press.

Freud, S. (1930) *Civilization and its discontents*. London: Hogarth.

Fung, Yu-lan (1952) *A history of Chinese philosophy*, trans. D. Bodde. Princeton, NJ: Princeton University Press.

Gangestad, S.W. and Thornhill, R. (1997) 'The evolutionary psychology of extra-pair sex: the role of fluctuating asymmetry'. *Evolution and Human Behavior*, 18: 69–88.

Ganshof, F.L. (1961) *Feudalism*. New York: Harper.

Gartner, J. (1996) 'Religious commitment, mental health, and prosocial behavior: a review of the empirical literature'. In E.P. Shafranske (ed.), *Religion and the clinical practice of psychology*, pp. 187–215, Washington, DC: American Psychological Association.

Geertz, C. (1975) *The interpretation of cultures*. London: Hutchinson.

Gellner, E. (1992) *Postmodernism, reason, and religion*. London: Routledge.

Gelman, R., Durgin, F. and Kaufman, L. (1995) 'Distinguishing between animates and inanimates: not by motion alone'. In D. Sperber, D. Premack and A.J. Premack (eds), *Causal Cognition*, pp. 150–84. Oxford: Clarendon.

Genia, V. (1996) 'I, E, Quest and fundamentalism as predictors of psychological and spiritual well-being'. *Journal of the Scientific Study of Religion*, 35: 56–64.

Giddens, A. (1991) *Modernity and self-identity*. Stanford, CA: Stanford University Press.

Gilligan, C. (1982) *In a different voice: psychological theory and women's development*. Cambridge, MA: Harvard University Press.

Gleitman, L. (1990) 'The structural sources of word meanings'. *Language Acquisition*, 1: 3–55.

Good, D. (1995) 'Where does foresight end and hindsight begin?' In E. Goody (ed.), *Social intelligence and interaction*, pp.139–52. Cambridge: Cambridge University Press.

Goody, E. (1991) 'The learning of prosocial behaviour in small-scale egalitarian societies: an anthropological view'. In R.A. Hinde and J. Groebel (eds), *Cooperation and prosocial behaviour*, pp. 106–28. Cambridge: Cambridge University Press.

—— (1995) 'Social intelligence and prayer as dialogue'. In E. Goody (ed.), *Social intelligence and interaction*, pp. 206–20. Cambridge: Cambridge University Press.

Goody, J. (1962) *Death, property and the ancestors*. London: Tavistock.

—— (1968) *Literacy in traditional societies*. Cambridge: Cambridge University Press.

—— (1997) *Representations and contradictions*. Oxford: Blackwell.

Gorlow, L. and Schroeder, H.E. (1968) 'Motives for participating in the religious experience'. *Journal for the Scientific Study of Religion*, 7: 241–51.

Gorsuch, R.L. (1994) 'Toward motivational theories of intrinsic religious commitment'. *Journal of the Scientific Study of Religion*, 33: 315–25.

Grand, J.C. and Bittles, A.H. (1997) 'The comparative role of consanguinity in infant and child mortality in Pakistan'. *Annals of Human Genetics*, 61: 143–9.

Greeley, A.M. (1975) *The sociology of the paranormal*. London: Sage.

Guerin, B. (1998) 'Religious behaviors as strategies for organising groups of people: a social contingency analysis'. *Behavior Analyst*, 21: 53–72.

Guthrie, S. (1993) *Faces in the clouds*. New York: Oxford University Press.

Guy, J. (1983) *The heretic: a study of the life of John William Colenso, 1814–83*. Pietermaritzburg: Natal University Press.

Hall, G.S. (1904) *Adolescence: its psychology and its relations to physiology, anthropology, sociology, sex, crime, religion, and education*. New York: Appleton.

Halle, D. (1993) *Inside culture*. Chicago, IL: Chicago University Press.

Hamilton, W.D. (1964) 'The genetical theory of social behaviour'. *Journal of Theoretical Biology*, 7: 1–52.

Hann, C. (1997) 'The nation-state, religion and uncivil society: two perspectives from the periphery'. *Daedalus*, 126: 27–45.

Hannay, D.R. (1980) 'Religion and health'. *Social Science and Medicine*, 14: 683–85.

Hansen, V. (1996) 'The law of the spirits'. In D.S. Lopez (ed.), *Religions of China in practice*, pp. 284–92. Princeton, NJ: Princeton University Press.

Harcourt, A.H. (1991) 'Help, cooperation and trust in animals'. In R.A. Hinde and J. Groebel (eds), *Cooperation and prosocial behaviour*, pp.15–26. Cambridge: Cambridge University Press.

Hardy, A.C. (1979) *The spiritual nature of man*. Oxford: Clarendon.

Harley, B. and Firebaugh, G. (1993) 'American's belief in an after-life: trends over the last two decades'. *Journal of the Scientific Study of Religion*, 32: 269–78.

Harper, D. (1996) 'Spellbinding'. In D.S. Lopez (ed.), *Religions of China in practice*, pp. 241–50. Princeton, NJ: Princeton University Press.

Harris, P.L. (1994) 'Unexpected, impossible and magical events: children's reactions to causal violations'. *British Journal of Developmental Psychology*, 12: 1–7.

—— (1997) 'The last of the magicians? Children, scientists, and the invocation of hidden causal powers'. *Child Development*, 68: 1018–20.

Hartung, J. (1995) 'Love thy neighbour: the evolution of in-group morality'. *Skeptic*, 3: 86–99.

Harvey, J.H., Agostinelli, G. and Weber, A.L. (1989) 'Account-making and the formation of expectations about close relationships'. In Hendrick, C., *Close relationships*, pp.39–62. Newbury Park, CA: Sage.

Hauert, C.L. and Schuster, H.G. (1997) 'Effects of increasing the number of players and memory size in the iterated Prisoner's Dilemma: a numerical approach'. *Proceedings of the Royal Society of London* B, 264: 513–19.

Heal, J. (1991) 'Altruism'. In R.A. Hinde and J. Groebel (eds), *Cooperation and prosocial behaviour*, pp.159–72. Cambridge: Cambridge University Press.

Heaton, T.B. and Pratt, E.L. (1990) 'The effects of religious homogamy on marital satisfaction and stability'. *Journal of Family Issues*, 11: 191–207.

Heerwagen, J.H. and Orians, G.H. (1993) 'Humans, habitats, and aesthetics'. In S.R. Kellert and E.O. Wilson (eds), *The biophilia hypothesis*, pp.138–72. Washington, DC: Island Press.

Hertel, B.R. and Donahue, M.J. (1995) 'Parental influences on God influences among children: testing Durkheim's metaphoric parallelism'. *Journal of the Scientific Study of Religion*, 34: 186–99.

Hertz, R. (1983) 'St. Besse: a study of an alpine cult'. In S. Wilson (ed.), *Saints and their cults*, pp. 55–100. Cambridge: Cambridge University Press.

Hinde, R.A. (1978) 'Report on replies to a questionnaire concerning the experiences of recent graduates and others abroad'. *Primate Eye*, Supplement No. 11.

—— (1987) *Individuals, relationships, and culture*. Cambridge: Cambridge University Press.

—— (1991) 'A biologist looks at anthropology'. *Man*, 26: 583–608.

—— (1997a) *Relationships: a dialectical perspective*. Hove: Psychology Press.

—— (1997b) 'War: some psychological causes and consequences'. *Interdisciplinary Science Reviews*, 22: 229–45.

Hinde, R.A. and Rawson, J. (1995) 'Ritual: signals and meanings'. In G. Thines and L. de Heusch (eds), *Rites et ritualisation*, pp.21–36. Paris: Vrin.

Hinde, R.A. and Stevenson-Hinde, J. (eds) (1973) *Constraints on learning: limitations and predispositions*. London: Academic Press.

—— (1990) 'Attachment: biological, cultural and individual desiderata'. *Human Development*, 33: 62–72.

Hinde, R.A., Tamplin, A. and Barrett, J. (1993) 'Home correlates of aggression in preschool'. *Aggressive Behavior*, 19: 85–105.

Hoge, D.R., Johnson, B. and Luidens, D.A. (1993) 'Determinants of church involvement of young adults who grew up in Presbyterian churches'. *Journal of the Scientific Study of Religion*, 32: 242–55.

Holmberg, D. and Veroff, J. (1996) 'Rewriting relationship memories: the effects of courtship and wedding scripts'. In G.J.O. Fletcher and J. Fitness (eds), *Knowledge structures in close relationships*, pp.345–68. Hillsdale, NJ: Etlbaum.

Hood, R.W. (1995) 'The facilitation of religious experience'. In R.W. Hood (ed.), *Handbook of religious experience*. Birmingham, AL: Religious Education Press.

Hood, R.W. and Morris, R.J. (1983) 'Toward a theory of death transcendence'. *Journal for the Scientific Study of Religion*, 22: 353–65.

Hood, R.W., Spilka, B., Hunsberger, B. and Gorsuch, R. (1996) *The psychology of religion*. New York: Guilford.

Horton, R. (1960) 'A definition of religion, and its uses'. *Journal of the Royal Anthropological Institute*, 90: 201–26.

Howe, G.W. (1987) 'Attributions of complex cause and perception of marital conflict'. *Journal of Personality and Social Psychology*, 53: 1119–28.

Humphrey, C. and Laidlaw, J. (1994) *The archetypal actions of ritual*. Oxford: Clarendon.

Humphrey, N. (1976) 'The social function of intellect'. In P. Bateson and R.A. Hinde (eds), *Growing points in ethology*, pp.303–18. Cambridge: Cambridge University Press.

—— (1995) *Soul searching*. London: Chatto and Windus.

—— (1997) 'Varieties of altruism – and the common ground between them'. *Social Research*, 64: 199–209.

Humphrey, N.K. and Dennett, D.C. (1989) 'Speaking for ourselves: an assessment of multiple personality disorder'. *Raritan*, 9: 68–98.

Hunsberger, B.E. and Brown, L.B. (1984) 'Religious socialization, apostasy, and the impact of family background'. *Journal for the Scientific Study of Religion*, 23: 239–51.

Idler, E.L. (1995) 'Religion, health, and nonphysical senses of self'. *Social Forces*, 74: 683–704.

Idler, E.L. and Kasl, S.V. (1995) 'Self-ratings of health: do they also predict change in functional ability?' *Journal of Gerontology*, 50B: 344–53.

—— (1997) 'Religion among disabled and nondisabled persons. 2.'. *Journals of Gerontology*, Series B. 52: S306–16.

Ijzendoorn, M. van (1997) 'Attachment, emergent morality, and aggression: toward a developmental socioemotional model of antisocial behaviour'. *International Journal of Behavioral Development*, 21: 703–27.

Ions, V. (1967) *Indian mythology*. London: Hamlyn.

Irons, W. (1991) 'How did morality evolve?' *Zygon*, 26: 49–89.

—— (1996a) 'In our own self image: the evolution of morality, deception, and religion'. *Skeptic*, 4: 50–61.

—— (1996b) 'Morality, religion, and human evolution'. In W. Mark Richardson and W.J. Wildman (eds), *Religion and science: history, methods, dialogue*, pp.375–99. New York: Routledge.

—— (1998) 'Adaptively relevant environments versus the environment of evolutionary adaptedness.' *Evolutionary Anthropology*, 6: 194–204.

James, W. (1890) *Principles of psychology*. London: Macmillan.

—— (1892) *The varieties of religious experience*. New York: Longmans, Green.

Janssen, J., Hart, J. de and Draak, C. den (1990) 'A content analysis of the praying practices of Dutch youth'. *Journal of the Scientific Study of Religion*, 29: 99–107.

Johnson, C.N. (1997) 'Crazy children, fantastical theories, and the many uses of metaphysics'. *Child Development*, 68: 1024–26.

Johnson, C.N. and Harris, P.L. (1994) 'Magic: special but not excluded'. *British Journal of Developmental Psychology*, 12: 35–51.

Johnson-Laird, P. (1980) *Mental models: towards a cognitive science of language, inference, and consciousness*. Cambridge: Cambridge University Press.

Josephs, I.E. (1996) 'Challenging science's holy inquisition: illegitimate psychological phenomena and their study'. *Culture and Psychology*, 2: 211–21.

Kagan, J. (1984) *The nature of the child*. New York: Basic Books.

Kaplan, S. (1992) 'Environmental preference in a knowledge-seeking, knowledge-using organism'. In J. Barkow, L. Cosmides and J. Tooby (eds), *The adapted mind*, pp.581–98. New York: Oxford University Press.

Karmiloff-Smith, A. (1992) *Beyond modularity*. Cambridge, MA: MIT Press.

Keil, F.C. (1986) 'On the structure-dependent nature of stages of cognitive development'. In I. Levin (ed.), *Stage and structure: reopening the debate*. London: Ablex.

—— (1995) 'The growth of understanding of natural kinds'. In D. Sperber, D. Premack and A.J. Premack (eds), *Causal cognition*, pp. 234–67. Oxford: Clarendon.

Kelley, D.M. (1972) *Why conservative churches are growing*. New York: Harper and Row. (Cited Hood *et al.*, 1996.)

Kelley, H.H. (1979) *Personal relationships*. Hillsdale, NJ: Erlbaum.

Kierkegaard, S. (1944) *Kierkegaard's concept of dread*. Trans. W. Lowrie. London: Oxford University Press.

Kirkpatrick, L.A. and Hood, R.W. (1990) 'Intrinsic-extrinsic religious orientation: the boon or bane of contemporary psychology of religion?' *Journal of the Scientific Study of Religion*, 29: 442–62.

Kirkpatrick, L.A. and Shaver, P.R. (1990) 'Attachment theory and religion: childhood attachment, religious beliefs, and conversion'. *Journal of the Scientific Study of Religion*, 29: 315–34.

Kohlberg, L. (1976) 'Moral stages and moralization'. In T. Lickona (ed.), *Moral development and behaviour*, pp. 31–53. New York: Holt, Rinehart and Winston.

Kolakowski, L. (1982) *Religion*. London: Fontana.

Kotre, J. (1971) *The view from the border: a social-psychological study of current Catholicism*. London: Gill and Macmillan.

Kuhn, M.S. and McPartland, T.S. (1954) 'An empirical investigation of self attitudes'. *American Sociological Review*, 19: 68–76.

Kuhrt, A. (1987) 'Usurpation, conquest and ceremonial: from Babylon to Persia'. In D. Cannadine and S. Price (eds), *Rituals of Royalty*, pp. 20–55. Cambridge: Cambridge University Press.

Küng, H. and Kuschel, K.-J. (1993) *A global ethic*. London: SCM Press.

Lambert, W.W. (1992) 'Cultural background to aggression: correlates and consequences of benevolent and malevolent gods and spirits'. In A. Fraczek and H. Zumkley (eds), *Socialization and aggression*, pp. 217–30. Berlin: Springer Verlag.

Lambert, W.W., Triandis, L.M. and Wolf, M. (1959) 'Some correlates of beliefs in the malevolence and benevolence of supernatural beings: a cross-societal study'. *Journal of Abnormal Social Psychology*, 58: 162–9.

Lane, C. (1981) *The rites of rulers. Ritual in industrial society – the Soviet case.* Cambridge: Cambridge University Press.

Langer, S.K. (1953) *Feeling and Form*. London: Routledge and Kegan Paul.

Larson, E.J. and Witham, L. (1997) 'Scientists are still keeping the faith'. *Nature*, 386: 435–6.

Laurentin, R. (1998) 'Look before you sign'. *The Tablet*, 31 January, 153.

Lawrence, D.H. (1964) *The snake*. In V. de S. Pinto and W. Roberts (eds), *The collected poems of D.H. Lawrence*. London: Heinemann.

Lawson, E.T. and McCauley, R.N. (1990) *Rethinking religion*. Cambridge: Cambridge University Press.

Leach, E.R. (1954) *Political systems of highland Burma*. London: Athlone.

—— (1972) 'The influence of cultural context on non-verbal communication in man'. In R.A. Hinde (ed.) *Non-verbal communication*, pp. 315–44. Cambridge: Cambridge University Press.

—— (1976) *Culture and communication*. Cambridge: Cambridge University Press.

Leak, G.K. and Fish, S. (1989) 'Religious orientation, impression management, and self-deception'. *Journal of the Scientific Study of Religion*, 28: 355–9.

Lederose, L. (1981) 'The earthly paradise: religious elements in Chinese landscape art'. In S. Bush and C. Murck (eds), *Theories of the Arts in China*, pp.165–83. Princeton, NJ: Princeton University Press.

Lerner, M.J. (1981) 'The justice motive in human relations'. In M.B. Lerner and S.C. Lerner (eds), *The justice motive in social behavior*. New York: Plenum.

Leslie, A.M. (1987) 'Pretense and representation: the origins of "theory of mind"'. *Psychological Review*, 94: 412–26.

—— (1988) 'The necessity of illusion: perception and thought in infancy'. In L. Weiskrantz (ed.), *Thought without language*. Oxford: Clarendon.

Levi, P. (1989) *The drowned and the saved*. London: Abacus.

Levin, J.S. (1994) 'Religion and health: is there an association, is it valid, and is it causal?', *Social Science and Medicine*, 38, 1475–82.

Lévy-Bruhl, C. (1923) *Primitive mentality*. Oxford: Clarendon.

Lewis, G. (1980) *Day of shining red*. Cambridge: Cambridge University Press.

—— (1987) 'The look of magic'. *Man*, 21: 414–37.

—— (1995) 'The articulation of circumstance and causal understanding'. In D. Sperber, D. Premack and A.J. Premack (eds), *Causal Cognition*, pp. 557–76. Oxford: Clarendon.

Lewis, I. (1971) *Ecstatic religion*. Harmondsworth: Penguin.

Lewis, M. (1992) *Shame: the exposed self*. New York: Free Press.

Lienhardt, G. (1961) *Divinity and experience: the religion of the Dinka*. Oxford: Clarendon Press.

Lifton, R.J. (1979) *The broken connection*. New York: Simon and Schuster.

Lin, Y.-H.W. and Rusbult, C.E. (1995) 'Commitment to dating relationships and cross-sex friendships in America and China'. *Journal of Social and Personal Relationships*, 12: 7–26.

Lisboa, M.M. (1997) 'Benilde ou o Deus-Pai: Dilemas de Deus e do Diabo'. *Boletim do Centro de Estudos Regianos*, 1: 51–7.

Loewe, M. (1994) *Chinese ideas of life and death*. Taipei: SMC Publishing.

Long, A.A. and Sedley, D.N. (1987) *The Hellenistic philosophy, Vol. 1, commentary on section 23*. Cambridge: Cambridge University Press.

Lopez, D.S. (ed.) (1996) *Religions of China in practice*. Princeton, NJ: Princeton University Press.

Lorenz, K. (1935) 'Der Kumpan in der Umwelt des Vogels'. *Journal für Ornithologie*, 83: 137–213 and 289–413.

Lumsden, C.J. and Wilson, E.O. (1981) *Genes, mind, and culture*. Cambridge, MA: Harvard University Press.

Lund, M. (1985) 'The development of investment and commitment scales for predicting continuity of personal relationships'. *Journal of Social and Personal Relationships*, 2: 3–23.

Lupfer, M.B., Tolliver, D. and Jackson, M. (1996) 'Explaining life-altering experiences. A test of the "God-of-the-Gaps" hypothesis'. *Journal of the Scientific Study of Religion*, 35: 379–91.

Lynn, S.J. and Rhue, J.W. (1988) 'Fantasy proneness: hypnosis, developmental antecedents, and psychopathology'. *American Psychologist*, 43: 35–44.

Macintosh, A.A. and Shiftiel, A. (1977) 'St. John's and the centenary of the Cairo Genizah collection'. *Eagle*, 1997, 48–50.

Malinowski, B. (1935) *Coral gardens and their magic*. London: Kegan Paul.

—— (1944) *A scientific theory of culture*. Chapel Hill, NC: University of North Carolina Press.

—— (1954) *Magic, science, religion, and other essays*. New York: Doubleday Anchor.

Markman, E.M. and Wachtel, G.F. (1988) 'Children's use of mutual exclusivity to constrain the meanings of words'. *Cognitive Psychology*, 20: 121–57.

Marks, I.M. (1987) *Fears and phobias*. New York: Oxford University Press.

Markus, H. and Kitiyama, S. (1991) 'Culture and the self: implications for cognition, emotion and motivation'. *Psychological Review*, 98: 224–53.

Markus, H. and Nurius, P. (1986) 'Possible selves'. *American Psychologist*, 41: 951–64.

Marx, K. (1847) *The poverty of philosophy*. Moscow: Progress.

Masataka, N. (1993) 'Effects of experience with live insects on the development of fear of snakes in squirrel monkeys'. *Animal Behaviour*, 46: 741–6.

Masters, W.H. and Johnson, V.E. (1970) *Human sexual inadequacy*. London: Churchill.

McAdams, D.P. (1996) 'Personality, modernity, and the storied self: a contemporary framework for studying persons'. *Psychological Inquiry*, 7: 295–321.

McClenon, J. (1988) 'A survey of Chinese anomalous experiences and comparison with western representative national samples'. *Journal of the Scientific Study of Religion*, 27: 421–26.

McFarland, S.M. (1989) 'Religious orientations and the targets of discrimination'. *Journal of the Scientific Study of Religion*, 28: 324–36.

McGuire, M.T. (1988) 'On the possibility of ethological explanations of psychiatric disorders'. *Acta Psychiatr. Scand.* 341: 7–22.

McGuire, M.T. and Essock-Vitale, S.M. (1981) 'Psychiatric disorders in the context of evolutionary biology. A functional classification of behavior'. *Journal of Nervous and Mental Diseases*, 169: 672–86.

McGuire, W.J. and McGuire, C.V. (1988) 'Content and process in the experience of self'. *Advances in Experimental Social Psychology*, 21: 97–144.

McMullen, D. (1987) 'Bureaucrats and cosmology: the ritual code of T'ang China'. In D. Cannadine and S. Price (eds), *Rituals of Royalty*, pp.181–236. Cambridge: Cambridge University Press.

Mead, G.H. (1934) *Mind, self, and society*. Chicago, IL: Chicago University Press.

Mealey, L. (1997) 'The sociobiology of sociopathy: an integrated evolutionary model'. In S. Baron-Cohen (ed.), *The maladapted mind*, pp.133–88. Hove: Psychology Press.

Mealey, L., Daood, C. and Krage, M. (1996) 'Enhanced memory for faces of cheaters'. *Ethology and Sociobiology*, 17: 119–28.

Mealey, L. and Theis, P. (1995) 'The relationship between mood and preferences among natural landscapes: an evolutionary perspective'. *Ethology and Sociobiology*, 16: 247–56.

Milgram, S. (1974) *Obedience to authority: an experimental view*. New York: Harper and Row.

Miller, A.S. and Hoffman, J.P. (1995) 'Risk and religion: an explanation of gender differences in religiosity'. *Journal of the Scientific Study of Religion*, 34: 63–75.

Miller, G.A., Galanter, E. and Pribram, K.H. (1960) *Plans and the structure of behavior*. New York: Holt, Rinehart and Winston.

Miller, P.A., Bernzweig, J., Eisenberg, N. and Fabes, R.A. (1991) 'The development and socialization of prosocial behaviour'. In R.A. Hinde and J. Groebel (eds), *Cooperation and prosocial behaviour*, pp.54–77. Cambridge: Cambridge University Press.

Mineka, S. (1987) 'A primate model of phobic fears'. In H. Eysenck and I. Martin (eds), *Theoretical foundations of behaviour therapy*. New York: Plenum.

Mithen, S. (1996) *The prehistory of the mind*. London: Thames and Hudson.

Moberg, D.O. and Taves, M.J. (1965) 'Church participation and adjustment in old age'. In A.M. Rose and W.A. Peterson (eds), *Older people and their social world*. Philadelphia, PA: Davis.

Moffat, M. (1979) *An untouchable community in South India: structure and consensus*. Princeton, NJ: Princeton University Press.

Møller, A.P., Soler, M. and Thornhill, R. (1995) 'Breast asymmetry, sexual selection, and human reproductive success'. *Ethology and Sociobiology*, 16: 207–19.

Monaghan, R. (1967) 'The three faces of the true believer: motivation for attending a fundamentalist church'. *Journal of the Scientific Study of Religion*, 6: 236–45.

Morris, B. (1987) *Anthropological studies of religion*. Cambridge: Cambridge University Press.

Morris, I. (1992) *Death ritual and social structure in classical antiquity*. Cambridge: Cambridge University Press.

Morris, M., Nisbett, R. and Peng, K. (1995) 'Causal attributions across domains and cultures'. In D. Sperber, D. Premack, and A.J. Premack (eds), *Causal cognition*, pp.577–612. Oxford: Clarendon.

Morris, M.W. and Peng, K. (1994) 'Culture and cause: American and Chinese attributions for social and physical events'. *Journal of Personality and Social Psychology*, 67: 949–71.

Mulford, M.A. and Salisbury, W.W. (1964) 'Self-conceptions in a general population'. *Sociological Quarterly*, 5: 35–46.

Mundkur, B. (1983) *The cult of the serpent*. Albany, NY: State University of New York Press.

Murray, D. (1995) 'Families in conflict: pervasive violence in Northern Ireland'. In R.A. Hinde and H. Watson (eds), *War: a cruel necessity?*, pp.68–79. London: Tauris.

Murray, J.K. (1997) 'Illustrations of the life of Confucius: their evolution, functions, and significance in late Ming China'. *Artibus Asiae*, 57: 73–134.

Needham, R. (1985) *Exemplars*. Berkeley, CA: University of California Press.

Nickerson, P. (1996) 'Abridged codes of Master Lu for the Daoist community'. In D.S. Lopez (ed.), *Religions of China in practice*, pp. 347–59. Princeton, NJ: Princeton University Press.

Nietzsche, F. (1968) *Twilight of the gods and the Anti-Christ*. Trans. R.J. Hollingdale. Harmondsworth: Penguin, 1889, 1895.

Nowak, M.A. and Sigmund, K. (1998) 'Evolution of indirect reciprocity by image scoring'. *Nature*, 393: 573–7.

O'Connor, M. (1989) 'The Virgin of Guadaloupe and the economics of symbolic behaviour'. *Journal of the Scientific Study of Religion*, 28: 105–19.

Oliner, S.P. and Oliner, P.M. (1988) *The altruistic personality: rescuers of Jews in Nazi Europe*. New York: Free Press. (Cited Wulff, 1997.)

Orians, G.H. and Heerwagen, J.H. (1992) 'Evolved responses to landscapes'. In J.H. Barkow, L. Cosmides and J. Tooby (eds), *The adapted mind*, pp. 555–80. New York: Oxford University Press.

Orme-Johnson, D.W., Alexander, C.N., Davies, J.L., Chandler, H.M. and Larimore, W.E. (1988) 'International peace project in the Middle East: the effects of the Marishi technology of the unified field'. *Journal of Conflict Resolution*, 32: 776–812.

Orru, M. and Wang, A. (1992) 'Durkheim, religion, and Buddhism'. *Journal of the Scientific Study of Religion*, 31: 47–61.

Ortega, S.T., Whitt, H.P., and Williams, J.A. (1988) 'Religious homogamy and marital happiness'. *Journal of Family Issues*, 9: 224–39.

Orzech, C. (1996) 'The scripture on perfect wisdom for humane kings who wish to protect their states'. In D.S. Lopez (ed.), *Religions of China in practice*, pp.372–80. Princeton, NJ; Princeton University Press.

Otto, R. (1917) *The idea of the holy*. Harmondsworth: Penguin.

Ouellette, S.C. (1996) 'Building a useful personality psychology'. *Psychological Inquiry*, 7: 357–60.

Oyama, S. (1985) *The ontogeny of information*. Cambridge: Cambridge University Press.

Ozorak, E.W. (1989) 'Social and cognitive influences on the development of religious beliefs and commitment in adolescence'. *Journal of the Scientific Study of Religion*, 28: 448–63.

—— (1996) 'The power but not the glory: how women empower themselves through religion'. *Journal of the Scientific Study of Religion*, 35: 17–29.

Papadakis, Y. (1995) 'Nationalist imaginings of war in Cyprus'. In R.A. Hinde and H. Watson (eds), *War: a cruel necessity?*, pp. 54–67. London: Tauris.

Pargament, K.I. (1997) *The psychology of religion and coping.* New York: Guilford Press.

Pargament, K.I., Ishler, K., Dubow, E.F., Stanik, P., Rouiller, R., Crowe, P., Cullman, E.P., Albert, M. and Royster, B.J. (1994) 'Methods of religious coping with the Gulf war'. *Journal of the Scientific Study of Religion*, 33: 347–61.

Parkes, C.M. and Weiss, R.S. (1983) *Recovery from bereavement*, London: Harper and Row.

Parkes, C.M., Stevenson-Hinde, J. and Marris, P. (eds) (1991) *Attachment across the life cycle*, London: Routledge.

Perkins, H.W. (1992) 'Student religiosity and social justice concerns in England and the US: are they still related?' *Journal of the Scientific Study of Religion*, 31: 353–60.

Petrinovich, L. (1995) *Human evolution, reproduction, and morality.* New York: Plenum.

Piatigorsky, A. (1997) *Who's afraid of Freemasons? The phenomenon of Freemasonry.* Harvill Press.

Polkinghorne, J. (1994) *Science and Christian belief.* London: SPCK.

Poloma, M.M. and Pendleton, B.F. (1991) *Religiosity and well-being: exploring neglected dimensions of quality of life research.* Lewiston, NY: Mellen. (Cited Beit-Hallahmi and Argyle, 1997.)

Porterfield, A. (1998) *The power of religion.* New York: Oxford University Press.

Premack, D. and Premack, A.J. (1994) 'Moral belief: form versus content'. In L.A. Hirschfeld and S.A. Gelman (eds), *Mapping the mind*, pp.149–68. Cambridge: Cambridge University Press.

Prins, K.S., Buunk, B.P. and Van Yperen, N.W. (1993) 'Equity, normative disapproval and extra marital relationships'. *Journal of Social and Personal Relationships*, 10: 39–53.

Profet, M. (1992) 'Pregnancy sickness as adaptation: a deterrent to maternal ingestion of teratogens'. In J. Barkow, L. Cosmides and J. Tooby (eds), *The adapted mind*, pp. 326–65. New York: Oxford University Press.

Rabbie, J.M. (1991) 'Determinants of instrumental intra-group cooperation'. In R.A. Hinde and J. Groebel (eds), *Cooperation and prosocial behaviour*, pp. 238–62. Cambridge: Cambridge University Press.

Radcliffe-Brown, A.R. (1952) *Structure and function in primitive society.* London: Cohen and West.

Rawson, J. (1995) *Chinese Jade.* London: British Museum Press.

—— (1998a) 'Ancient Chinese ritual as seen in the material record'. In J. McDermott (ed.), *State and court ritual in China.* Cambridge: Cambridge University Press.

—— (1998b) 'Commanding the spirits: control through bronze and jade'. *Orientations*, February: 33–45.

Rayan, S. (1997) 'In defence of Balasuriya'. *The Tablet*, 1st November: 1394–6.

Read, A.F. and Harvey, P. (1988) 'Genetic relatedness and the evolution of animal mating patterns'. In C.G.N. Mascie-Taylor and A.J. Boyce (eds), *Human mating patterns*, pp. 115–31. Cambridge: Cambridge University Press.

Reeves, E.B. and Bylund, R.A. (1992) 'Anonymity and the rise of universal occasions for religious ritual'. *Journal of the Scientific Study of Religion*, 31: 113–30.

Régio, J. (1947) *Benilde ou a Virgem-Mãe*. Lisbon: Brasília Editora.

Reif, S.C. (1993) *Judaism and Hebrew prayer*. Cambridge: Cambridge University Press.

Reynolds, V.E. and Tanner, R. (1983) *The biology of religion*. London: Longman.

Richardson, W.M. and Wildman, W.J. (1997) *Religion and science: history, method, dialogue*. London: Routledge.

Richerson, P.J. and Boyd, R. (1998) 'The evolution of human ultrasociality'. In I. Eibesfeldt and F. Salter (eds), *Ideology, warfare, and indoctrinability*, pp.71–95. London: Berghahn.

Robb, F. (undated) 'The Trinity in Christian thought'. In M.K. Modeen (ed.), *Graces, Fates and Furies*. Aberdeen: Peacock Printmakers.

Robinson, E. (1977a) *The original vision*. Oxford: Religious experience research unit.

—— (1977b) *This time-bound ladder*. Oxford: Religious experience research unit.

Rogers, C.R. (1959) 'A theory of therapy, personality and interpersonal relationships as developed in the client-centered framework'. In S. Koch (ed.), *Psychology: a study of a science*, pp.184–256. New York: McGraw Hill.

Rosch, E. and Lloyd, B.V. (eds) (1978) *Cognition and Categorization*. Hillsdale, NJ: Erlbaum.

Rosenblatt, D. (1997) 'The antisocial skin: structure, resistance, and "modern primitive" adornment in the United States'. *Cultural Anthroplogy*, 12: 287–334.

Rosengren, K.S. and Hickling, A.K. (1994) 'Seeing is believing: children's explorations of commonplace, magical, and extraordinary transformation'. *Child Development*, 65: 1605–26.

Ross, C.E. (1990) 'Religion and psychological distress'. *Journal of the Scientific Study of Religion*, 29: 236–45.

Rowanchilde, R. (1996) 'Male genital modification'. *Human Nature*, 7: 189–215.

Rozin, P. and Nemeroff, C. (1990) 'The laws of sympathetic magic: a psychological analysis of similarity and contagion'. In J.W. Stigler, R.A. Shweder and G. Herdt (eds), *Cultural psychology*, pp. 205–32. Cambridge: Cambridge University Press.

Rubin, M. (1991) *Corpus Christi*. Cambridge: Cambridge University Press.

Rusbult, C.E. and Buunk, B.P. (1993) 'Commitment processes in close relationships: an interdependence analysis'. *Journal of Social and Personal Relationships*, 10: 175–204.

Rusbult, C.E., Yovetich, N.A. and Verette, J. (1996) 'An interdependence analysis of accommodation processes'. In G.J.O. Fletcher and J. Fitness (eds), *Knowledge structures in close relationships*, pp. 63–90. Hillsdale, NJ: Erlbaum.

Ruse, M. (1994) 'Evolutionary theory and Christian ethics: are they in harmony?' *Zygon*, 29: 5–24.

Sanchis, P. (1983) 'The Portugese romarias'. In S. Wilson (ed.), *Saints and their cults*, pp.261–90. Cambridge: Cambridge University Press.

Sangharakshita (1993) *A survey of Buddhism*. Birmingham: Windhorse.

Sarason, I.G., Pierce, G.R. and Sarason, B.R. (1990) 'Social support and interactional processes: a triadic hypothesis'. *Journal of Social and Personal Relationships*, 7: 495–506.

Schaefer, C.A. and Gorsuch, R.L. (1991) 'Psychological adjustment and religiousness: the multivariate belief-motivation theory of religiousness'. *Journal of the Scientific Study of Religion*, 30: 448–61.

Scheidel, W. (1996) 'Brother-sister and parent-child marriage outside royal families in ancient Egypt and Iran: a challenge to the sociobiological view of incest avoidance.' *Ethology and Sociobiology*, 17: 319–40.

Schoenfeld, E. and Mestrovic, S.G. (1991) 'With justice and mercy: instrumental masculine and expressive feminine elements in religion'. *Journal of the Scientific Study of Religion*, 30: 363–80.

Schopenhauer (1969) *The world as will and representation*. London: Dover. (Cited Collinson, 1992.)

Schwab, R. and Petersen, K.U. (1990) 'Religiousness: its relation to loneliness, neuroticism and subjective well-being'. *Journal of the Scientific Study of Religion*, 29: 335–45.

Seligman, M.E.P. (1975) *Helplessness: on depression, development, and death*. San Francisco, CA: Freeman.

Seligman, M.E.P. and Hager, J.L. (eds) (1972) *Biological boundaries of learning*. New York: Appleton Century Crofts.

Shafranske, E.P. and Maloney, H.N. (1996) 'Religion and the clinical practice of psychology: a case for inclusion'. In E.P. Shafranske (ed.), *Religion and the clinical practice of psychology*, pp. 561–86. Washington, DC: American Psychological Association.

Sharf, R.H. (1996a) 'The scripture in 42 sections'. In D.S. Lopez (ed.), *Religions of China in practice*, pp. 360–71. Princeton, NJ: Princeton University Press.

—— (1996b) 'The scripture on the production of Buddha images'. In D.S. Lopez (ed.), *Religions of China in practice*, pp. 261–67. Princeton, NJ: Princeton University Press.

Shaver, P., Lenauer, M. and Sadd, S. (1980) 'Religiousness, conversion, and subjective well-being: the "healthy-minded" religion of modern American women'. *American Journal of Psychiatry*, 137: 1563–68.

Shepher, J. (1983) *Incest, the biosocial view*. New York: Academic Press.

Smart, N. (1960) *World religions: a dialogue*. Harmondsworth: Penguin.

—— (1996) *Dimensions of the sacred*. London: Harper Collins.

Smart, V. (1971) *The religious experience of mankind*. London: Collins.

Smith, A.B. (1993) *Transcendental meditation: an aid to Christian growth*. London: Mayhew McCrimmon.

Smith, H. (1991) *The world's religions*. San Francisco, CA: Harper.

Smith, J.Z. (1987) *To take place: toward theory in ritual*. Chicago, IL: University of Chicago Press.

Smith, W.J. (1977) *The behaviour of communicating*. Cambridge, MA: Harvard University Press.

Soboul, A. (1983) 'Religious feeling and popular cults during the French revolution: "patriot saints" and martyrs for liberty'. In S. Wilson (ed.), *Saints and their cults*, pp. 217–32. Cambridge: Cambridge University Press.

Spanos, S.P. and Moretti, P. (1988) 'Correlates of mystical and diabolical experiences in a sample of female university students'. *Journal of the Scientific Study of Religion*, 27: 105–16.

Spelke, E., Phillips, A. and Woodward, A.L. (1995) 'Infants' knowledge of object motion and human action'. In D. Sperber, D. Premack and A.J.Premack (eds), *Causal Cognition*, pp. 47–78. Oxford: Clarendon.

Spelke, E.S. (1990) 'Principles of object perception'. *Cognitive Science*, 14: 29–56.

Sperber, D. (1985) *On anthropological knowledge*. Cambridge: Cambridge University Press.

—— (1994) 'The modularity of thought and the epidemiology of thought and the epidemiology of representations'. In L.A. Hirschfeld and S.A. Gelman (eds), *Mapping the mind*, pp.39–67. Cambridge: Cambridge University Press.

Sperber, D., Premack, D. and Premack, A.J. (eds) (1995) *Causal Cognition*. Oxford: Clarendon.

Sperry, R.W. (1988) 'Psychology's mentalist paradigm and the religion/science tension'. *American Psychologist*, 43: 607–13.

Spilka, B., Stout, L., Minton, B. and Sizemore, D. (1977) 'Death and personal faith: a psychometric investigation'. *Journal for the Scientific Study of Religion*, 16: 169–78.

Spiro, M.E. and D'Andrade, R.G. (1958) 'A cross-cultural study of some supernatural beliefs'. *American Anthropologist*, 60: 456–66.

Stark, R. and Bainbridge, W.S. (1985) *The future of religion: secularization, revival, and cult formation*. Berkeley, CA: University of California Press.

Stark, R. and Glock, C.Y. (1968) *American piety; the nature of religious commitment*. Berkeley, CA: University of California Press.

Stark, R. and Iannaccone, L.R. (1995) 'Truth? a reply to Bruce'. *Journal of the Scientific Study of Religion*, 34: 516–19. (See also reply by Bruce.)

Steadman, L.B. and Palmer, C.T. (1997) 'Myths as instructions from ancestors: the example of Oedipus'. *Zygon*, 32: 341–50.

Steinberg, M. (1947) *Basic Judaism*. New York: Harcourt, Brace.

Stern, J.P. (1975) *Hitler: the Führer and the people*. London: Fontana.

Stevenson-Hinde, J. (1989) 'Behavioral inhibition: issues of context'. In J.S. Reznick (ed.), *Perspectives on behavioral inhibition*, pp.125–38. Chicago, IL: Chicago University Press.

Stevenson-Hinde, J. and Shouldice, A. (1995) 'Maternal interactions and self-reports related to attachment classifications at 4.5 years'. *Child Development*, 66: 583–96.

Stoichita, V.I. (1995) *Visionary experience in the golden age of Spanish art*. London: Reaktion.

Stouffer, S.A., Suchman, E.A., DeVinney, L.C., Star, S.A. and Williams, R.M. (1949) *The American soldier, II. Combat and its aftermath*. Princeton, NJ: Princeton University Press.

Strickland, B.R. and Weddell, S.C. (1972) 'Religious orientation, racial prejudice and dogmatism: a study of Baptists and Unitarians'. *Journal for the Scientific Study of Religion*, 11: 395–99.

Subbotsky, E. (1994) 'Early rationality and magical thinking in preschoolers: space and time'. *British Journal of Developmental Psychology*, 12: 97–108.

Sugiyama, M.C. (1996) 'On the origins of narrative: storyteller bias as a fitness enhancing strategy'. *Human Nature*, 7: 403–26.

Swann, W.B., Stein-Seroussi, A. and Giesler, R.B. (1992) 'Why people self-verify'. *Journal of Personality and Social Psychology*, 62: 392–401.

Sykes, S. (1991) 'Sacrifice and the ideology of war'. In R.A. Hinde (ed.), *The institution of war*, pp.87–98. London: Macmillan.

Symons, D. (1979) *The evolution of human sexuality*. New York: Oxford University Press.

Szreter, S. (1996) *Fertility, class and gender in Britain, 1860–1940.* Cambridge: Cambridge University Press.

Tajfel, H. and Turner, J. (1986) 'The social identity theory of intergroup behaviour'. In S. Worschel and W.G. Austin (eds), *Psychology of intergroup relationships,* pp.7–24. Chicago, IL: Nelson.

Tambiah, S.J. (1990) *Magic, science, religion, and the scope of rationality.* Cambridge: Cambridge University Press.

Taylor, C. (1989) *Sources of the self.* Cambridge: Cambridge University Press.

Taylor, M. (1997) 'The role of creative control and culture in children's fantasy/reality judgements'. *Child Development,* 68: 1015–17.

Teiser, S.F. (1996) 'The spirits of Chinese religion'. In D.S. Lopez (ed.), *Religions of China in practice,* pp.3–37. Princeton, NJ: Princeton University Press.

Thomas, K. (1983) *Man and the natural world.* London: Allen Lane.

Thompson, E.H. (1991) 'Beneath the status characteristic: gender variations in religiousness'. *Journal for the Scientific Study of Religion,* 30: 381–94.

Thompson, E.P. (1978) *The poverty of theory and other essays.* London: Merlin.

Thompson, M.P. and Vardaman, P.J. (1997) 'The role of religion in coping with the loss of a family member to homicide'. *Journal of the Scientific Study of Religion,* 36: 44–51.

Thorpe, W.H. (1962) *Biology and the nature of man.* London: Oxford University Press.

—— (1963) *Learning and instinct in animals.* London: Methuen.

Thouless, R.H. (1935) 'The tendency towards certainty in religious belief'. *British Journal of Psychology,* 26; 16–31.

Tinbergen, N. (1951) *The study of instinct.* Oxford: Oxford University Press.

—— (1952) 'Derived activities: their causation, biological significance, origin and emancipation during evolution'. *Quarterly Review of Biology,* 27: 1–32.

—— (1963) 'On aims and methods of ethology'. *Zeitschrift für Tierpsychologie,* 20: 410–33.

Toren, C. (1993) 'Sign into symbol, symbol as sign: cognitive aspects of a social process'. In P. Boyer (ed.), *Cognitive aspects of religious symbolism,* pp.147–64. Cambridge: Cambridge University Press.

Towler, R. (1974) *Homo religiosus.* London: Constable.

—— (1985) *The need for certainty: a sociological study of conventional religion.* London: Routledge and Kegan Paul.

Trivers, R.L. (1971) 'The evolution of reciprocal altruism'. *Quarterly Review of Biology,* 46: 35–57.

—— (1974) 'Parent-offspring conflict'. *American Zoologist,* 14: 249–64.

—— (1985) *Social evolution.* Menlo Park, CA: Benjamin/Cummings.

Turiel, E. (1983) *The development of social knowledge: morality and convention.* Cambridge: Cambridge University Press.

Turner, V.W. (1957) *Schism and continuity in an African society.* Manchester: Manchester University Press.

—— (1967) *The forest of symbols: aspects of Ndembu ritual.* Ithaca, NY: Cornell University Press.

Tylor, E.B. (1913) *Primitive culture.* London: Murray, 1871.

Tzeng, M. (1992) 'The effects of socio-heterogamy and changes on marital dissolution for first marriage'. *Journal of Marriage and the Family,* 54: 609–19.

Ulrich, R.F. (1993) 'Biophilia, biophobia, and natural landscapes'. In S.R. Kellert and E.O. Wilson (eds), *The biophilia hypothesis*, pp.31–41. Washington, DC: Island Press.

Van Gennep, A. (1965) *The rites of passage*. London: Routledge and Kegan Paul, 1908.

Vandecreek, L. and Nye, C. (1993) 'Testing the death transcendence scale'. *Journal of the Scientific Study of Religion*, 33: 279–83.

Vidler, A.R. (1963) 'Historical objections'. In D.M. Mackinnon, H.A. Williams, A.R. Vidler and J.S. Bezzant (eds), *Objections to Christian belief*, pp.57–78. London: Constable.

Vining, D.R. (1986) 'Social versus reproductive success'. *Behavioral and Brain Sciences*, 9: 167–216.

Voland, E. and Voland R. (1995) 'Parent–offspring conflict, the extended phenotype, and the evolution of conscience'. *Journal of Social and Evolutionary Systems*, 18: 397–412.

Wadsworth, M.E.J. and Freeman, S.R. (1983) 'Generation differences in beliefs: a cohort study of stability and change in religious beliefs'. *British Journal of Sociology*, 34: 416–37.

Waller, N.G., Kojetin, B.J., Bouchard, T.J., Lykken, D.T. and Tellegen, A. (1990) 'Genetic and environmental influences on religious interests, attitudes, and values'. *Psychological Science*, 1: 138–42.

Wallis, R. (1976) *The road to total freedom: a sociological analysis of scientology*. London: Heinemann.

Walster, E., Walster, G.W. and Berscheid, E. (1978) *Equity theory and research*. Boston, MA: Allyn and Bacon.

Warner, M. (1976) *Alone of all her sex*. London: Weidenfeld and Nicolson.

Webb, N. and Wybrow, R. (1982) *The Gallup report*. London: Sphere Books.

Weber, M. (1965) *The sociology of religion*. London: Methuen.

—— (1976) *The Protestant ethic and the spirit of capitalism*. London: George, Allen and Unwin.

Weinstein, D. and Bell, R.M. (1982) *Saints and society*. Chicago, IL: Chicago University Press.

Welter, A. (1996) 'Buddhist ritual and the state'. In D.S. Lopez (ed.), *Religions of China in practice*, pp. 390–6. Princeton, NJ: Princeton University Press.

Wenegrat, B., Abrams, L., Castillo-Yee, E. and Romine, I.J. (1996) 'Social norm compliance as a signaling system. 1. Studies of fitness-related attributions consequent on everyday norm violations'. *Ethology and Sociobiology*, 17: 403–16.

Wertsch, J.V. (1997) 'Narrative tools of history and identity'. *Culture and Psychology*, 3: 5–20.

White, G.M. (1997) 'Mythic history and national memory: the Pearl Harbour anniversary'. *Culture and Psychology*, 3: 63–88.

Wilkinson, G.S. (1988) 'Reciprocal altruism in bats and other mammals'. *Ethology and Sociobiology*, 9: 85–100.

Wilkinson, R.G. (1996) *Unhealthy societies*. London: Routledge.

Williams J.E. and Best, D.L. (1982) *Measuring sex stereotypes*. Beverley Hills, CA: Sage.

Wills, T.A. (1984) 'Supportive functions of interpersonal relationships'. In S. Cohen and L. Syme (eds), *Social support and health*. New York: Academic Press. (Cited Brown, 1987.)

Wilson, D.S. and Sober, E. (1994) 'Reintroducing group selection to the human behavioral sciences'. *Behavioral and Brain Sciences*, 17: 585–654.

Wilson, E.O. (1975) *Sociobiology: the new synthesis*. Cambridge, MA: Harvard University Press.

Wilson, S. (1983a) 'Cults of saints in the churches of central Paris'. In S. Wilson (ed.), *Saints and their cults*, pp. 233–60. Cambridge: Cambridge University Press.

—— (ed.) (1983b) 'Introduction', *Saints and their cults*. Cambridge: Cambridge University Press.

Winnicott, D.W. (1953) 'Transitional objects and transitional phenomena'. *International Journal of Psychoanalysis*, 34: 89–97.

Winter, I. (1997) *Vision, visuality, and the affective aesthetic experience*, 8th Slade lecture given in Cambridge, March 1997.

Winter, J. (1951) 'Gods'. In A. Flew (ed.), *Logic and language*, pp.190–8. Oxford: Blackwell.

—— (1995) *Sites of memory, sites of mourning*. Cambridge: Cambridge University Press.

Wisdom, J. (1953) *Philosophy and psycho-analysis*. Oxford: Oxford University Press.

Wolf, A.P. (1970) 'Childhood association and sexual attraction: a further test of the Westermarck hypothesis'. *American Anthropologist*, 72: 503–15.

—— (1995) *Sexual attraction and childhood association: a Chinese brief for Edward Westermarck*. Stanford, CA: Stanford University Press.

Woodburn, J. (1982) 'Social dimensions of death in four African hunting and gathering societies'. In M. Bloch and J. Parry (eds), *Death and the regeneration of life*, pp.187–210. Cambridge: Cambridge University Press.

Woolley, J.D. (1997) 'Thinking about fantasy: are children fundamentally different thinkers and believers from adults?' *Child Development*, 68: 991–1011.

Woolley, J.D. and Phelps, K.E. (1994) 'Young children's practical reasoning about imagination'. *British Journal of Developmental Psychology*, 12: 53–67.

Woolley, J.D. and Wellman, H.M. (1990) 'Young children's understanding of realities, non-realities and appearances'. *Child Development*, 61: 946–61.

Wright, D. and Cox, E. (1967) 'A study of the relationship between moral judgements and religious belief in a sample of English adolescents'. *Journal of Social Psychology*, 72: 135–44.

Wulff, D.M. (1997) *The psychology of religion: classic and contemporary*. New York: Wiley.

Yang, Lien-Sheng (1957) 'The concept of *Pao* as a basis for social relations in China'. In J.K. Fairbank (ed.), *Chinese thought and institutions*, pp. 291–309. Chicago, IL: Chicago University Press.

Young, R.L. (1989) 'The Protestant heritage and the spirit of gun ownership'. *Journal of the Scientific Study of Religion*, 28: 300–09.

Yu, A.C. (1987) ' "Rest, rest, perturbed spirit!" Ghosts in traditional Chinese prose fiction'. *Harvard Journal of Asiatic Studies*, 47: 397–434.

Zaehner, R.C. (1962) *Hinduism*. Oxford: Oxford University Press.

Zahavi, A. (1977) 'The testing of a bond'. *Animal Behaviour*, 25: 246–7.

Zeitlyn, D. (1995) 'Divination as dialogue: negotiation of meaning with random responses'. In E. Goody (ed.), *Social intelligence and interaction*, pp.189–205. Cambridge: Cambridge University Press.

Ziman, J. (1996) 'Is science losing its objectivity?' *Nature*, 382: 751–54.

# Name Index

# Subject Index

*Most entries refer to topics ( e.g. development of beliefs; ritual; religious experience) and are not subdivided according to the religious system. Religious systems (with the exception of Christianity and Christian denominations and sects) are indexed, but not subdivided according to topic.*